365 DEVOTIONS TO STRETCH YOUR MIND AND SHAPE YOUR FAITH!

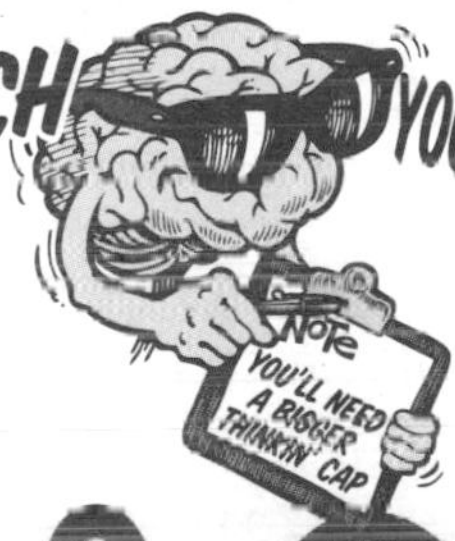

NOTE
YOU'LL NEED A BIGGER THINKIN' CAP

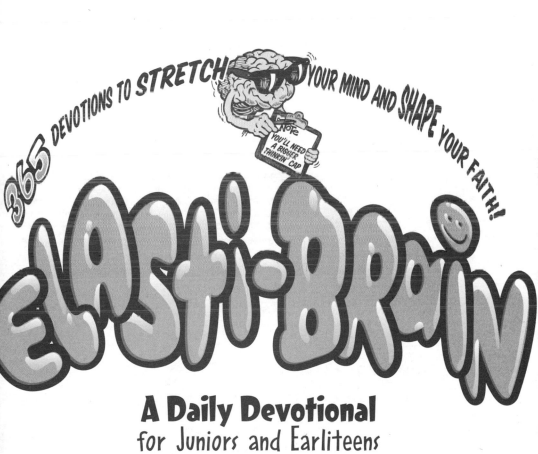

ELASTI-BRAIN

A Daily Devotional
for Juniors and Earliteens

REVIEW AND HERALD® PUBLISHING ASSOCIATION
Since 1861 | www.reviewandherald.com

Published by Review and Herald® Publishing Association, Hagerstown, MD 21741-1119

Review and Herald® titles may be purchased in bulk for educational, business, fund-raising, or sales promotional use. For information, please e-mail SpecialMarkets@reviewandherald.com.

The Review and Herald® Publishing Association publishes biblically based materials for spiritual, physical, and mental growth and Christian discipleship.

The authors assume full responsibility for the accuracy of all facts and quotations as cited in this book.

This book was
Edited by Penny Estes Wheeler
Designed by Ron J. Pride
Cover photos © 2006, Rubberball
Photo on page 5 by Natalie Johnson
Typeset: Officina Sans Book 10.6/12

PRINTED IN U.S.A.
12 11 10 09 08 5 4 3 2 1

Library of Congress Cataloging-in-Publication Data
Elasti-brain : 365 devotions to stretch your mind and shape your faith : a daily devotional for juniors and earliteens / [edited by Penny Estes Wheeler].
p. cm.
1. Children—Prayers and devotions. 2. Devotional calendars. I. Wheeler, Penny Estes.
BV4870.E43 2008
242'.62—dc22
2008019626

ISBN 978-0-8280-2339-9

{Authors}

January: Melanie Bockmann

February: Judy Shull

March: Laura Chen-Davies

April: Ron Reese

May: Colleen Reese

June: Karen Pires, June 1-14;
Crystal Earnhardt, June 15-30

July: Laurie Lyon, July 1-10 and 12-15;
Patti Emanuele, July 16-31;
Rachel Whitaker, July 11

August: Cheryl Porter;
Rachel Whitaker, August 16 and 27

September: Melanie Bockmann

October: Patti Emanuele

November: Emily Eskildsen Graham

December: Trudy Morgan-Cole;
Randy Fishell, December 2

Special thanks to Emily Eskildsen Graham for her editorial contributions.

To order additional copies of
Elasti-Brain, *365 Devotions to Stretch Your Mind and Shape Your Faith,* call **1-800-765-6955.**

Visit us at **www.reviewandherald.com**
for information on other Review and Herald® products.

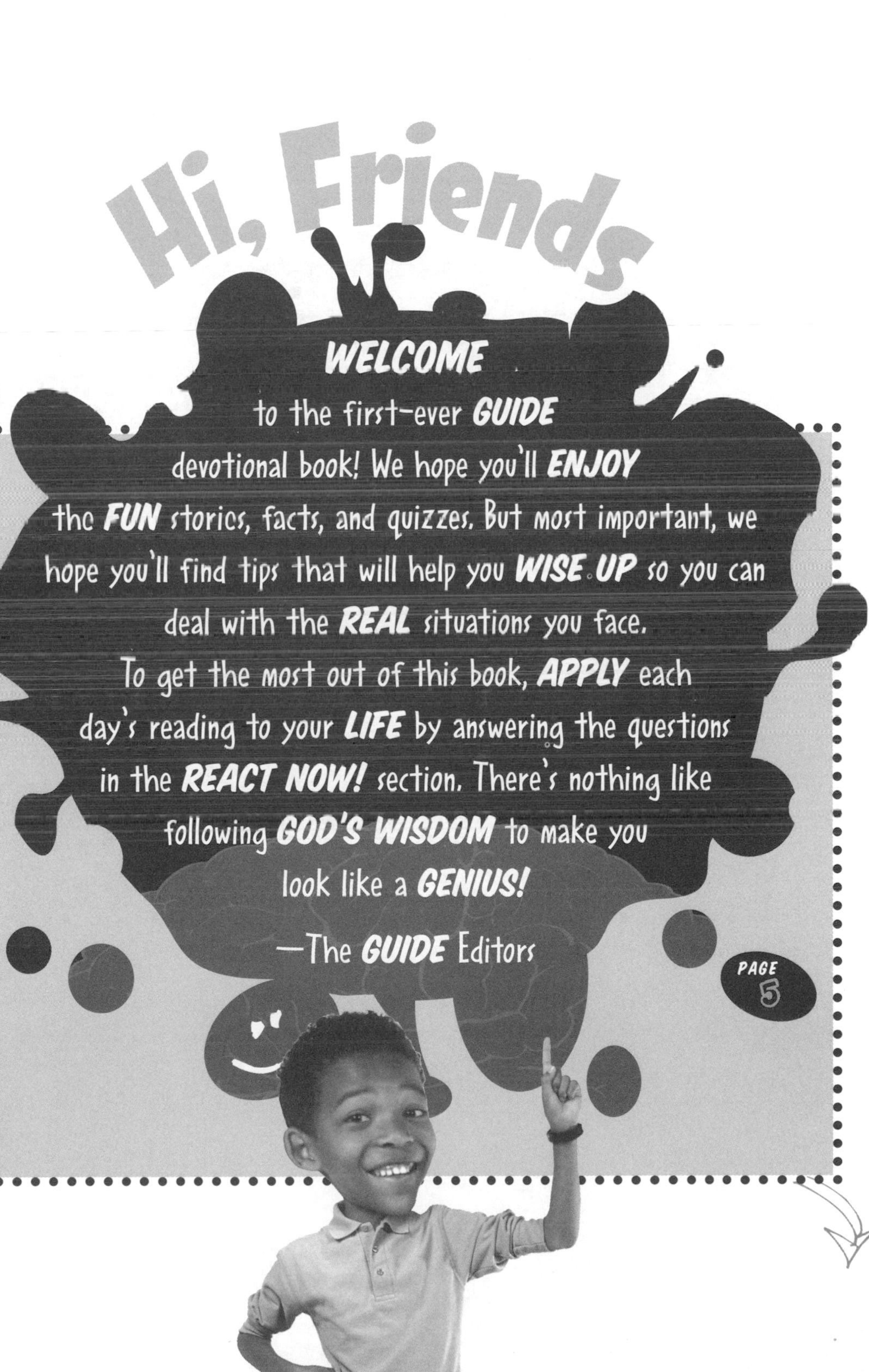

Hi, Friends

WELCOME to the first-ever **GUIDE** devotional book! We hope you'll **ENJOY** the **FUN** stories, facts, and quizzes. But most important, we hope you'll find tips that will help you **WISE UP** so you can deal with the **REAL** situations you face.

To get the most out of this book, **APPLY** each day's reading to your **LIFE** by answering the questions in the **REACT NOW!** section. There's nothing like following **GOD'S WISDOM** to make you look like a **GENIUS!**

—The **GUIDE** Editors

Start stretching!

Find your Prayer Journal on page 378.

Jot down your prayer requests and praises throughout the year.

~ INCREDI-BIBLICAL ~

Being confident of this, that he who began a good work in you will carry it on to completion. Philippians 1:6.

IT'S HARD TO BE PERFECT

Beep! Beep!

Kara turned off her alarm and looked at the calendar on her wall. She took a deep breath as she remembered her New Year's resolution. Starting today, she would never let herself sin again.

The first five minutes went pretty well, but even with her firm resolve, she blew it before breakfast.

She wondered how anyone could ever live up to God's expectations.

Have you ever tried hard to be good—and failed?

HERE'S THE BAD NEWS: *You're not strong enough to be good.* Compared to God, all your self-powered goodness is like the scum on the bottom of your dog's water dish.

HERE'S THE GOOD NEWS: *You're not strong enough to be good.* Yep! It's not your job to perfect yourself. It's God's job to do it—with your permission, and His goodness.

Instead of trying to be perfect:

1. Every morning, ask God for the Holy Spirit.
2. Consciously interrupt your bad thoughts with good ones. (That's called making your thoughts obedient to Christ.)
3. Look at your mistakes as opportunities to allow God to change you.
4. When you feel rebellious, just tell God that He can have all of you, even the rebellious parts. He'll deal with it from there. He can handle it.
5. Remember, being saved is simply accepting Jesus, and then letting God get you ready for heaven.

It's not about the destination. It's about the journey.

Info Splat

The time line for becoming a butterfly is different for each caterpillar, even within a species. It all depends on how long it takes for the caterpillar to acquire enough food for the metamorphosis to occur.

REACT NOW!

If you could change anything about yourself, what would it be, and why? Have you talked to God about changes you'd like to make?

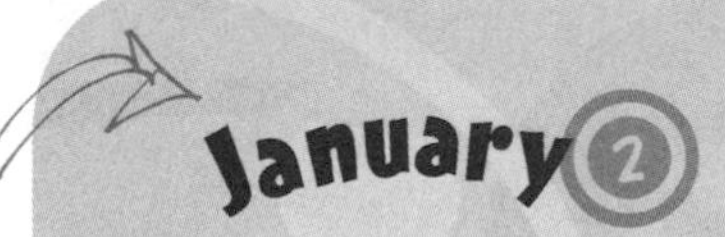

INCREDI-BIBLICAL

I will lie down and sleep in peace, for you alone, O Lord, make me dwell in safety. Psalm 4:8.

YOU'RE GETTING VERY S-L-E-E-E-E-P-Y

Sean read the same paragraph twice and still didn't know what it said. He yawned, trying to force himself to concentrate as he looked down at the page through blurry eyes.

Finally he slammed the book shut. "What's wrong with me? Am I just stupid?"

Sean shook his head and went to the refrigerator for an apple. At this rate, he'd never be ready for the social studies test he faced tomorrow. He felt stressed just thinking about explaining a low test score to his parents.

What Sean doesn't know is that he's actually smart. He just isn't getting enough sleep. According to studies, teenagers need more sleep than both younger kids and adults, but they often get less. Here are some interesting facts.

- Sleep loss interferes with the way teens learn. Teens that get enough sleep also get better grades.
- While you sleep your immune system goes to work to help prevent colds and other sicknesses, and even clear up pimples!
- If you don't get enough sleep, you're more likely to be overweight, because the hormones that tell your body when you've had enough to eat don't work properly when you're sleep-deprived.

Some ways to help yourself sleep better include not drinking caffeine, not watching TV or playing video games just before bed, keeping your room clean and free of distractions, and making sure your room is totally dark while you rest.

Info Splat

According to scientists, dolphins sleep about eight hours a day—but with only half of their brain at a time! This is because they have to be conscious to breathe. If they went into a full sleep, they would suffocate.

REACT NOW!

Are *YOU* getting enough sleep? For a week, try adding one more hour of nighttime sleep and see if you notice a difference in the way you feel.

INCREDI-BIBLICAL

I have learned the secret to being content in any and every situation . . . I can do everything through him who gives me strength. Philippians 4:12, 13.

STRAIGHT FROM THE HEART

Fanny Crosby was a nineteenth-century American songwriter. During her life she wrote more than 8,000 hymns of praise to God—some of which are included in *The Seventh-day Adventist Hymnal*. An amazing love for God burned inside her heart. She was also blind.

When Fanny was only a few weeks old she became sick with an eye infection. The harsh treatment scarred her eyes, leaving her blind. As Fanny grew older, she learned that she was different, that others could do something she could not—they could see. She would never see the faces of her friends, the flowers, the blue skies, or the sparkling stars.

"Soon I learned what other children possessed," she said. "But I made up my mind to store away a little jewel in my heart which I called 'Content.'" One day someone asked, "Fanny, do you ever wish you hadn't been blinded?"

Fanny replied, "Well, the good thing about being blind is that the very first face I'll see will be the face of Jesus."

Today, more than 100 years later, we still sing the beautiful songs that Fanny wrote from her contented heart.

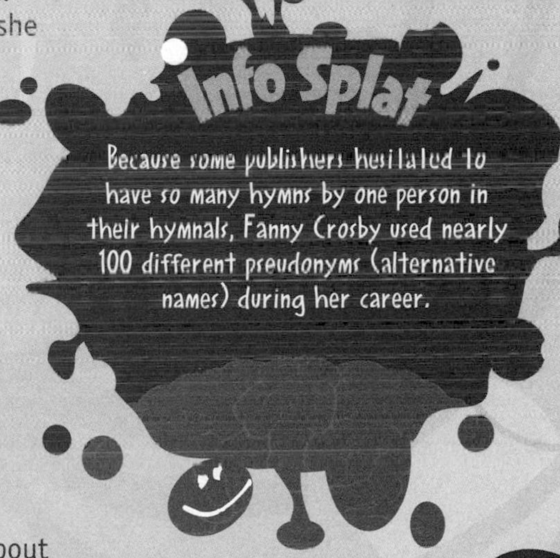

Info Splat
Because some publishers hesitated to have so many hymns by one person in their hymnals, Fanny Crosby used nearly 100 different pseudonyms (alternative names) during her career.

Are you content with your life? What things might you like to change?

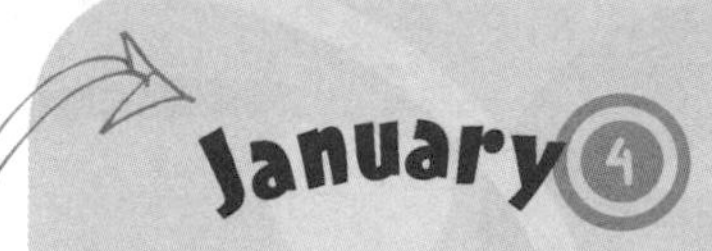

INCREDI-BIBLICAL

Defend the cause of the weak.
Psalm 82:3.

THE MEAN NEIGHBOR

Bones was barking again.

Dakota could hardly concentrate on the book he was reading with his new neighbor's dog making so much noise. With a sigh he closed the book on his thumb to mark his place and walked over to the window.

"What is it this time, Bones?" Dakota wondered out loud as he peeked through the curtains. Though there were no obvious intruders, Bones seemed intent on announcing his ownership of the backyard to the entire neighborhood. Then, as Dakota watched, Bones' owner came outside.

"Bones! Shut up!" the man yelled. Bones kept barking.

"I said 'SHUT UP'!" This time the man strode toward Bones and kicked the small dog in the ribs with his boot. Bones' bark morphed into a pained shriek as he tumbled into the grass and lay there, shaking. Shocked, Dakota watched the man kick the dog again, yelling at him to get into the house. Bones limped slowly through the open door, and the man closed it.

Dakota felt sick. The dog's barking was annoying, but no animal deserved to be treated so cruelly, and Dakota wanted to help the poor thing. He remembered reading in the Bible that in the beginning, God gave humans the responsibility to care for the animals.

What should I do? he wondered. *Should I mind my own business? Should I say something? Should I call the local animal agency and report it?*

Info Splat

There's a link between animal abuse and people abuse. According to a Wisconsin survey, four out of five victims of domestic violence in homes with companion animals said their pets were also abused.

Have you ever been in a situation where you saw an animal or person being abused? What did you do?

INCREDI-BIBLICAL

They will be my people, and I will be their God. Jeremiah 32:38.

LOOK IN THE MIRROR

If you had to describe who you are in only 10 sentences for someone who didn't know you very well, but wanted to be like you, what would those 10 sentences be? It would be hard, wouldn't it?

The Ten Commandments are a summary of God's character. They describe Him as being worthy of our total focus, merciful to people who love Him, and so powerful that even His *name* should be respected. We also find that He values rest, life, loyalty, respect for people and property, honesty, and contentment. Of course, this description just barely scratches the surface of our incomprehensible God!

Info Splat
Just for fun:
Do the math! 111,111,111 x 111,111,111 = 12,345,678,987,654,321.

When Jesus came to earth, He surprised a lot of people by summing up God's character even more. He said that the law could be boiled down to just two commands: love God, and love other people.

The disciple John gave an even shorter summary—God is love.

In heaven, God doesn't need to tell the angels to keep the Ten Commandments, because they know Him and His character personally. That's what God wants for us, too. He even says He's going to write His law—His character—on our hearts and minds.

In the meantime, the Ten Commandments are like a mirror. They help us see how close our characters are to God's. Be patient when you see flaws. God isn't finished with you yet.

Do you think someone who doesn't love God would enjoy heaven? Why or why not?

INCREDI-BIBLICAL

Go to the ant . . .
consider its ways and be wise.
Proverbs 6:6.

NATURE'S CLEANUP CREW

As someone growing up in the new millennium, you've inherited a pretty polluted planet. For example, in order to create a single computer chip it's necessary to purify silicon with high levels of energy and toxic chemicals. This, in turn, creates unwanted by-products like chemical waste. We then try to figure out what to do with these unwanted by-products that keep collecting around us, poisoning the water we drink, the air we breathe, and the earth where we grow our food. We know that we have to do *something* before our planet becomes completely toxic.

Here's the good news: scientists are learning some lessons from nature. Researchers at the University of California have discovered that the marine sponge creates a skeleton for itself made of silica molecules. It does this with exact precision, in normal temperatures using organic chemistry and sunlight. And without producing any hazardous waste! By studying our environment, scientists are figuring out how to use nature's simple processes to create computer chips and other important things while rescuing Planet Earth from more poisonous waste.

Isn't it amazing that answers to some of our biggest questions are found in nature? If we spend time considering the things God has made, we will discover that God has thought of everything. And in discovering God, we discover solutions to our problems.

Info Splat

The shell of an abalone (shellfish) is as strong as steel, but only half as dense. Scientists believe that studying the abalone shell may help engineers build airplanes and vehicles that are lighter, which could save on fuel costs.

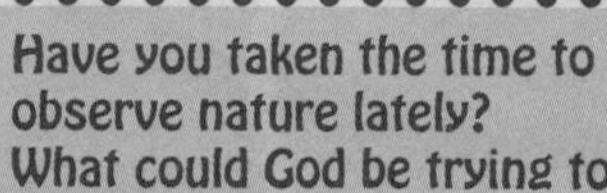

Have you taken the time to
observe nature lately?
What could God be trying to
teach you?

REACT
NOW!

~ INCREDI-BIBLICAL ~

Though I have fallen, I will rise. Then my enemy will see it and will be covered in shame, she who said to me, "Where is the Lord your God?"
Micah 7:8, 10.

HEAVEN'S HEALING POWER

Suhasini screamed and stumbled backwards as sharp pain seized her toe and a burning, tingling sensation radiated up her leg. Thrashing in the dust around her feet was the scorpion she'd just stepped on. Moments before, Suhasini and her mother were preparing to climb onto the back of a large truck that would take them to a Christian meeting. Now she rocked back and forth, crying out in agony.

A crowd gathered, but not everyone was sympathetic. "What kind of god do you serve that would allow this?" some of the Hindu women taunted as they stood over the girl.

"You'd better get her to the clinic before she dies," one of them told Suhasini's mother.

A woman who Suhasini knew was a Christian pushed her way to the front of the crowd. "No," she said boldly. "We're going to pray to our God. He'll take care of it." She knelt by Suhasini and prayed.

Instantly the pain was gone. Surprised, Suhasini stopped screaming and looked up. "I'm fine now. We can go. The pain has stopped," she said, laughing through the tears that still streaked her cheeks. She couldn't wait to tell the missionaries and all her friends how God had healed her.

When Suhasini and her mother climbed into the back of the truck, she saw that some of the Hindu women had decided to come too. "You serve a great God," one of them said quietly.

Info Splat

There you glow again! When scorpions are exposed to ultraviolet light, or black light, they glow in the dark. This is because of a complex mixture of wax and sugars that "waterproof" their exoskeleton.

REACT NOW!

Do you ever wonder why bad things happen in your life? Is it possible that those situations are opportunities for God to be glorified in the outcome?

January 8

Incredi-Biblical

Show proper respect to everyone. 1 Peter 2:17.

"WHAT DID YOU JUST SAY?"

Bye, Shorty!" Angelo waved at the red car pulling out of the church parking lot and then turned to see his dad behind him.

"Excuse me?" Dad asked with a frown. "What did you just say?"

Angelo suddenly felt sheepish standing there in his father's long shadow. "I said, 'Bye, Shorty,'" he mumbled.

Shorty's real name was Bill Stafford, and he was a dwarf. Even though he was an adult, he was shorter than most kids. Angelo didn't know how to react to him when Bill and his family first started attending the same church, but Shorty was outgoing and cool, and soon Angelo realized he wasn't that different. Shorty drove a car (using pedal extenders) and had a regular job and a lot of friends—including the kids from church. Angelo felt comfortable around him.

Now, standing next to his dad, Angelo wondered if he'd become too comfortable.

"Just because he's your size doesn't mean he's not an adult," Dad said. "I expect you to treat him with the same respect as other adults."

"But he doesn't mind," Angelo insisted. "All the kids call him that."

"All the kids but you," Dad said firmly. "You will call him Mr. Stafford." He paused. "You like him, don't you?"

"Yeah, a lot. He's cool."

"Then shouldn't you *want* to treat him with respect, no matter what anyone else is doing?" Dad asked simply.

Angelo nodded. "I guess I didn't think of it that way before."

Info Splat

In Kenya, different handshakes signify different levels of respect. If you respect someone very much, you shake his or her hand with your right hand, while resting your left hand on the inside crook of your right elbow.

REACT NOW!

When you treat other people with respect, they enjoy being around you. Today, look for ways that you can make the people around you feel valued.

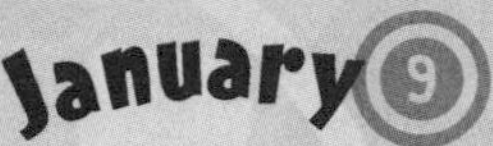

~ INCREDI-BIBLICAL ~

[God is] a father to the fatherless.
Psalm 68:5.
"For I know the plans I have for you,"
declares the Lord.
Jeremiah 29:11.

MISSING DAD

Casey looked at the blank line on his birth certificate and tried to swallow the ache in his throat. The section where his father's name should have been was empty.

Empty, he thought, *like the seat next to Mom at my basketball games*. Empty like the place in his heart at the church's Father's Day picnic. Casey felt angry with his mom for the way her decisions had affected him, and he was sad that he didn't have a dad to be proud of or to talk to about guy stuff.

God, how can I figure out who I am if I don't even know who my father is? Casey wondered, gripping the certificate. *I feel like I'm just a huge mistake. Am I?*

Recently Casey's mom had introduced him to a man she said might be his father. The man was excited to meet Casey and bought him a new skateboard. Casey couldn't stop staring at the man, trying to recognize a piece of himself in him. But the paternity test results proved that he wasn't Casey's dad after all. Casey stood in the hallway of the testing office clutching the skateboard and trying to hold back tears of humiliation and disappointment.

"It's cool. I don't care," Casey said when his mom told him how sorry she was.

"You can keep the skateboard," the man said, trying to be kind.

But Casey didn't want a skateboard. He wanted a dad.

Info Splat

Perez, a boy in the Bible, was born under embarrassing circumstances (Genesis 38), but God had special plans for him. From Perez's descendants came from not only the royal line of David, but also the family of Jesus, the Messiah (Matthew 1:1-16).

REACT NOW!

What circumstance in your life makes you feel bad or seems to hold you back from doing something special? Have you talked to God about it?

~ Incredi-Biblical ~

Though it cost all you have, get understanding. Proverbs 4:7.

DEADLY MISTAKE

In the spring of 1945 Japan was in trouble. World War II was almost over, and Japanese railroads, highways, and bridges had been destroyed by Allied air attacks. Homes were leveled, hundreds of thousands of people were dead, and millions were homeless. The Japanese premier knew that the war had to end—quickly.

The Allies outlined generous terms of surrender in the Potsdam Declaration, which promised the country of Japan that it would remain a nation with its own government, its forces would be allowed to return home, and it would have access to the resources it needed to rebuild industry. Even before Japan received the official document, the media began telling the Japanese people to prepare for surrender.

But the Japanese cabinet knew they couldn't respond to unofficial information, so they confronted the press and told them that the Japanese government planned to keep silent about the new developments—a policy called *mokusatsu*. This turned out to be a fatal error. Besides meaning "to withhold comment," *mokusatsu* can also be translated "to ignore," and this was the meaning that reached the Allies.

Before the translation could be corrected, the Allies responded to what they thought was a rejection of the terms of surrender, and on August 6, 1945, dropped the atomic bomb on Hiroshima.

This costly mistake is a reminder of the terrible consequences that can result when people misunderstand each other.

Info Splat

According to the ***Oxford English Dictionary***, there are more than a quarter-million English words a person can choose from when communicating. These don't include technical words, regional words, or words that haven't yet been added to the dictionary.

Instead of assuming you understand what someone is saying, try this. Put what you think they mean into your own words or ask them to clarify. You might be surprised at what you learn!

~ Incredi-Biblical ~

But grow in the grace and knowledge of our Lord and Savior Jesus Christ. 2 Peter 3:18.

"GIVE MY KID MORE CASH!"

USA Today reported a strange new trend. After companies hire an adult person for a job, their *parents* are the ones who call to negotiate the benefits and salary! Surprised at this shift, the companies say (not surprisingly) that it doesn't make them feel very confident about the person they've hired.

It's natural for our parents to take care of us. But do you often let your parents or other adults in your life do something for you that you should be doing for yourself? As you get older and more capable, you can accept responsibility for taking care of yourself. For example, you're old enough to talk with your teacher if you're having difficulty in school—you don't have to wait for your parents to do it. You're also old enough to have your own relationship with God—not just through your parents.

It's hard for some parents to see their kids growing up, and sometimes they—maybe even your parents—want to do things for you that you can do yourself. They may miss being needed, and they want to be part of your life. But it's healthy to say, "Thanks, Mom and Dad. But this is something I need to learn to do for myself. Can you give me some advice and then let me try it on my own?"

Responsibility means you're growing up into the person God means for you to be. That's something to be proud of.

Info Splat

When a mother eagle decides her young are old enough, she doesn't wait for them to discover it for themselves—she physically pushes them out of the nest. However, Dad is soaring below to catch them if they can't fly on their own.

Are there things in your life you need to take responsibility for? Why not start today?

~ Incredi-Biblical ~

Of what use is money in the hand of a fool, since he has no desire to get wisdom? Proverbs 17:16.

KEN GRIFFEY, JR., WILL HAVE TO WAIT

"Mom, may I borrow some money?" Jordan asked.

"Where's the money you earned mowing the lawn?" Hands on her hips, Mom gave Jordan a puzzled look.

"I spent it on snacks," he admitted. "But I'm online and I've found a great deal on eBay—a whole set of baseball cards that include a Ken Griffey, Jr., rookie card! I really need it for my collection."

Mom sighed. "I'd like for you to be able to add that card to your collection. But you always immediately spend what's in your pocket, then try to borrow more. I'm concerned that you're developing bad money habits."

"Mom, it's a *Ken Griffey, Jr., rookie card!*" Jordan pleaded. "Please have mercy on me. Just this once."

Mom shook her head. "No, Jordan. You need to learn to live within your budget while you're a kid. Otherwise, when you're grown, you'll find yourself with thousands in credit card debt because you hadn't planed ahead and didn't know how to say no." Jordan grimaced, but Mom went on. "If you want, I could help you plan a budget and prioritize your spending so you're not always broke."

Jordan plopped down on the couch. It was frustrating to always have empty pockets when something really important came along. He wondered if he should take Mom up on her offer.

Info Splat

If you borrowed $1,000 on an average credit card and made only minimum monthly payments, it would take almost 22 years to pay it all back. ***And*** you'd pay more than $2,300 in interest—not including the original $1,000!

Are you self-disciplined with your spending habits? If not, ask someone you trust for help with a plan.

January 13

~ INCREDI-BIBLICAL ~

Gray hair is a crown of splendor.
Proverbs 16:31.

HEADS-UP ON HAIR

Have your parents ever told you that you're giving them gray hair? Well, you're off the hook.

It turns out that gray hair happens for another reason. The roots of your parents' hair (and yours!) are surrounded by follicles. In each follicle are color pigment cells that produce melanin, which is what gives hair its color. (It's also what gives our skin its color.) As people grow older, the pigment cells inside the follicle gradually die. That means there is less melanin to color the hair, and—you guessed it—hair grows in shades of gray or white instead of black, brown, blond, or red.

The Bible considers gray hair to be an honor. It's true! Solomon describes gray hair as a crown of splendor. Isn't that a neat way to think of it? If our society valued gray hair as much as Solomon did, then hair salons would probably have a lot less business.

Maybe the next time your mom and dad complain about finding new gray hairs, you can remind them that they're one step closer to wearing that crown of splendor. But now that you know the truth, just don't let them blame that crown of splendor on you.

Info Splat

The first hair dryer was a vacuum cleaner. Around 1900, women used a hose attached to the exhaust of their vacuums to dry their hair. The first real hair dryer was invented in 1920, and a better model arrived in 1951.

What can you do to show the older generations of your family that they are loved and valued?

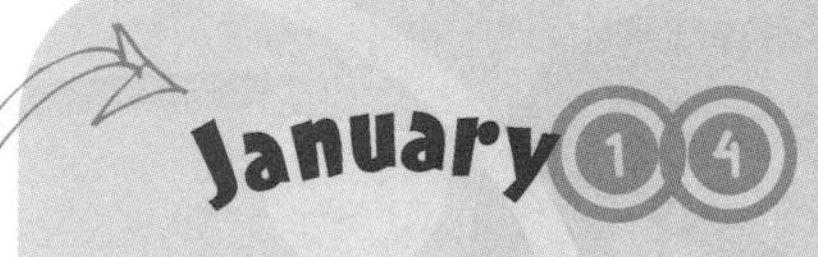

INCREDI-BIBLICAL

If you spend yourselves in behalf of the hungry and satisfy the needs of the oppressed, then your light will rise in the darkness. Isaiah 58:10.

HUNTER TO THE RESCUE

It hurt to watch, but Hunter's eyes were glued to the pictures on the TV news. People whose homes had been wiped out by the hurricane were dirty, hungry, and thirsty. They had no place to go and needed help.

Hunter went to his bedroom and pulled his money jar off the shelf. After counting the bills and loose change, he found he'd saved only $9. *What good is $9 when there's so much need?* he thought. He was going to slide the jar back onto the shelf when he remembered a story about another boy who didn't have much to offer. But Jesus took his five loaves and two fish and used them to feed 5,000 people.

"God," Hunter prayed. "I have only $9. Can You please do with it what You did to the loaves and fish?"

Putting the envelope in the mailbox, Hunter knew that he wouldn't learn what good the $9 did until he got to heaven. But just knowing that he was giving a few thirsty, hungry people some relief made him glad he hadn't spent this few dollars on gum or car magazines.

God doesn't always look for someone who has the most money, the most talent, or the most resources. He just takes whatever we offer and does miracles with it. If you'd like to find out how you can help with world needs, visit www.adra.org.

Info Splat

The World Meteorological Organization gives hurricanes their names. Each name begins with a new letter in order of the alphabet; however, Q, U, X, Y, and Z are never used. To see if you share your name with a hurricane, visit http://kids.earth.nasa.gov/archive/hurricane/names.

REACT NOW!

Money isn't the only way you can help when disaster strikes. What other ways can you be God's hands in a crisis situation?

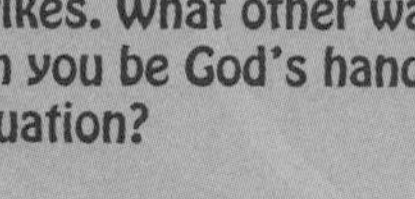

INCREDI-BIBLICAL

Whoever does not love does not know God, because God is love. 1 John 4:8.

WHAT'S YOUR LOVE LANGUAGE?

According to Dr. Gary Chapman, author of *The Five Love Languages*, love can be expressed in five main ways. He calls these expressions love languages, and they include: Words of Affirmation, Quality Time, Receiving Gifts, Acts of Service, and Physical Touch. For each of us there is one expression of love that we find is most meaningful to us. Look at the following statements, and choose the one you think fits you best.

_____ I feel especially loved when people express how grateful they are for me and for the simple, everyday things I do. (Words of Affirmation)

_____ I feel especially loved when a person gives me undivided attention and spends time alone with me. (Quality Time)

_____ I feel especially loved by someone who brings me gifts and other tangible expressions of love. (Receiving Gifts)

_____ I feel especially loved when someone pitches in to help me, perhaps by running errands or taking on my household chores. (Acts of Service)

_____ I feel especially loved when someone expresses feelings for me through physical contact. (Physical Touch)

Which expression of love, or love language, do you "speak"? It's fascinating how God created each of us to experience love in a way that is special to us. For more information on love languages, visit Dr. Chapman's Web site at www.fivelovelanguages.com.

Info Splat

Is it love, or chemicals? The University of Pavia did a study that indicated the mushy feelings of love during infatuation are associated with proteins in the bloodstream called neurotrophins. As romantic love stabilizes, the levels of neurotophins decrease.

REACT NOW!

How can you love the members of your family most effectively? Today, see if you notice love language clues in the people around you.

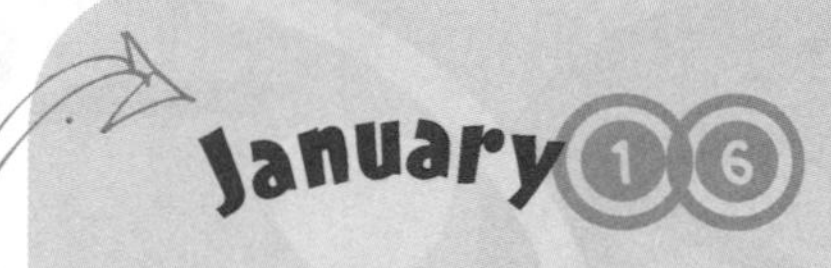

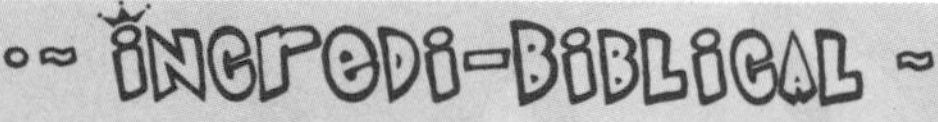

For my house will be called a house of prayer for all nations.
Isaiah 56:7.

SABBATH SCHOOL BLUES

Jake hated Sabbath school. If it weren't for the fact that his parents dragged him there every week, he would never go. It wasn't that he didn't care about God. He just didn't fit in.

"Can't I just wait in the car?" he begged as they pulled into the church parking lot. "I'll come in when it's time for church."

"No," his mom and dad said in unison.

"Give it a chance. Try to get involved and make friends," his mom added.

Jake sighed. His parents didn't understand what it was like to be outside the clique. At the public school he attended, Jake was popular and had a lot of friends. But it was different at church. There, most of the kids attended church school together or had been friends for a long time. Often Jake felt like there was no place for him in Sabbath school.

A few minutes later he sat down by one of the boys, lost in his thoughts. At first he didn't notice when the teacher asked him a question. The other kids giggled, and Jake's face burned.

"What an idiot," one of the guys mumbled, and the others erupted in laughter.

While the teacher talked to the boy who'd teased him, Jake folded his arms and prayed that Sabbath school would end as soon as possible.

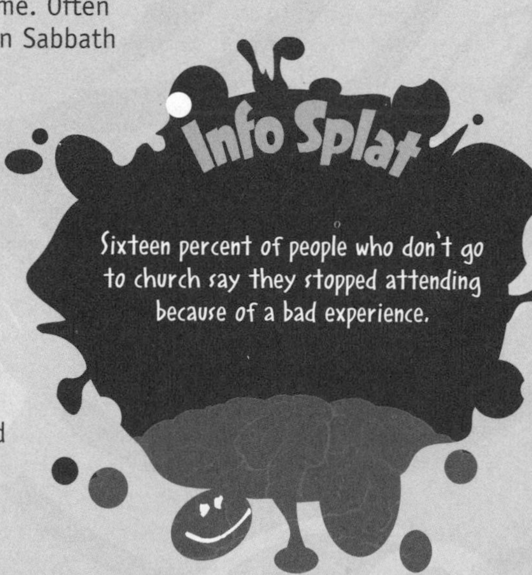

Info Splat
Sixteen percent of people who don't go to church say they stopped attending because of a bad experience.

REACT NOW!

What can you do to help other kids feel welcome at your church? Are you—or others—doing things that could cause someone else to feel uncomfortable?

January 17

~ INCREDI-BIBLICAL ~

My grace is sufficient for you, for my power is made perfect in weakness. 2 Corinthians 12:9.

A TOUCH OF GENIUS

Louis was only 4 years old when the accident happened. He was in his father's harness shop experimenting with a piece of leather when the awl he was using slipped and pierced his eye. Eye injury treatment was limited in 1813, and Louis became permanently blind.

As Louis grew older, he desperately wanted to read, but there were no books for blind people. He had to rely on his sister and friends to read his lessons to him. Then when Louis was 10, he was invited to attend the Royal Institution for Blind Youth. There he discovered that a few books had been created with raised lettering. With his fingers he could make out each letter and read for himself. Unfortunately, because of the massive size of a book necessary to hold all of the large, raised letters, very few books were available. Louis was once again frustrated, and determined to try to find a way to make books available for people like himself.

Info Splat

The muscle that lets your eye blink is the fastest muscle in your body. It allows you to blink five times a second. On average, you blink 15,000 times a day.

At the age of 15 Louis heard about a code of dots and dashes that were used to transmit orders to soldiers. *That's it!* he thought. He created a new alphabet of raised dots, which he taught to his friends. As time went on, others began to see the value of his invention.

Almost 100 years later Louis Braille's contribution still opens doors to education and careers for blind people.

REACT NOW!

Have you ever wondered why God let you go through something really tough? Could it be God wants to use you, too, to help others?

INCREDI-BIBLICAL

He [God] sets up kings, and deposes them. Daniel 2:21.

THE DAY DAD DIDN'T VOTE FOR PRESIDENT

Samantha's neighbor, Mr. Myers, was always open for a good political discussion. Even though the election was over, he still had candidate signs decorating his front lawn, and he was not exactly pleased about the new presidential administration.

On Inauguration Day Mr. Myers was especially vocal. "I can't believe that yahoo made it into office," he complained to Samantha's dad. "We might as well kiss this country goodbye if that's who's going to lead it for the next four years."

Dad didn't say anything. He just smiled.

"Who did you vote for?" Samantha asked Dad when Mr. Myers left.

Samantha's dad shook his head. "I didn't vote for a presidential candidate," he said.

Samantha was confused. "But I thought you told me that good citizens vote."

"I did," her dad explained. "And I do vote on issues that promote life, and religious liberty and fairness—those kinds of things."

"Why didn't you vote for a candidate?" Samantha persisted.

"Well, maybe it's just me," Dad said. "There are a lot of different opinions, even at church. But if I help elect someone into office, I believe I'm accountable in a way for the things they do while they're in office. It's still my responsibility as a Christian to vote for what is right, but as far as leadership in our country, God is the one who knows what will happen in the future. Ultimately, prophecy will unfold as He intends it."

Info Splat
In all of United States history there have been only four presidents who were not members of any church.

REACT NOW!

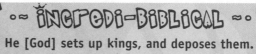

Samantha's father's way of voting is controversial. Do you think it is right or wrong? Why? What do your parents think? This question would make a good discussion.

January 19

~ INCREDI-BIBLICAL ~

So in everything, do to others what you would have them do to you. Matthew 7:12.

NOT-SO-MUCH FUN WITH MICHAEL

"Did you have fun at Michael's house?" Mom asked as Aaron fastened his seat belt.

"Sort of," he said wearily.

"What do you mean, 'sort of'? What happened?"

Aaron sighed. "After I got there, Michael got a call, and talked on the phone forever. Then he checked his e-mail. Then he went and got a snack, and didn't even offer me one. Most of the time I didn't feel like he wanted me there at all."

Info Splat
Ever wonder why McDonald's caters to their youngest guests? Forty percent of McDonald's profits come from Happy Meal sales.

"H'mmm," Mom murmured. "Sounds like he doesn't know about hospitality."

"What's that?" Aaron asked.

"Hospitality means making your guests feel comfortable. It's practicing things like generosity, kindness, and even tolerance." Mom looked over at Aaron. "I'm sorry you had a lousy time. But I think you learned what *not* to do when you have company."

Aaron nodded. "That's for sure."

Here are some tips to make your guests feel welcome:

Think about what would make you most comfortable if you were the guest.

Offer your guest something to drink or eat, *especially* if you are getting something for yourself.

Pay attention to your guest—not your cell phone, computer, or television!

Let your guest know your parents' rules in advance to avoid an embarrassing situation.

Be unselfish—do what your guest would like to do.

Following these suggestions will help you be the "host with the most"!

REACT NOW!

Have you ever imagined how you would treat Jesus if He were your guest?

INCREDI-BIBLICAL

A cheerful heart is good medicine. Proverbs 17:22.

LAUGH IT UP!

Listen to this," Ryan said, calling his brother Jared to the computer. "Grandpa e-mailed me a sound file that is hilarious."

Jared listened while Ryan played the clip. It was a recording of someone laughing. As he listened, Jared started to smile, then giggle. Pretty soon, both Jared and Ryan were laughing just as hard as the person on the recording. It was like the laughter was contagious.

Ryan was laughing so hard he could hardly breathe, and his face was turning red.

"Ah!" Jared put his hand to his stomach. "I think I'm going to be sore from laughing so much."

Have you ever wondered why God created you with the ability to laugh?

Scientists say that laughing is good for your health. It causes your body to produce endorphins that make you feel good, and to make other relaxation hormones that can actually lower your stress level.

Even *anticipating* something funny is good for you. A research team at the University of California at Irvine found that a group of people who were told a week ahead of time that they were going to watch a funny movie experienced reduced levels of cortisol, a stress hormone. And that was just from the *thought* of laughing.

Feeling sad, bored, or stressed-out? Go ahead—laugh!

Info Splat

Apparently, even fake laughing is good medicine. According to Professor Charles Schaefer at Farleigh Dickinson University in Teaneck, New Jersey, 60 seconds of forced laughter can help lift the blues.

REACT NOW!

Do you tend to take things too seriously, or can you laugh when things go wrong? What affect do you think your reaction has on your health?

January 21

~ INCREDI-BIBLICAL ~

For the Son of Man came to seek and save what was lost. Luke 19:10.

RALPHIE, COME HOME

Jenna sat on the curb, shoulders slumped, her eyes raw from salty tears. Every tiny movement of grass caught her attention, and she strained her ears to every sound in the distance.

Ralphie had vanished. Jenna had knocked on every single door in the neighborhood and called his name until her throat was dry, but there was no sign of the little Yorkshire terrier. She even carried a handful of his favorite treats, hoping to somehow entice him home. But he was gone.

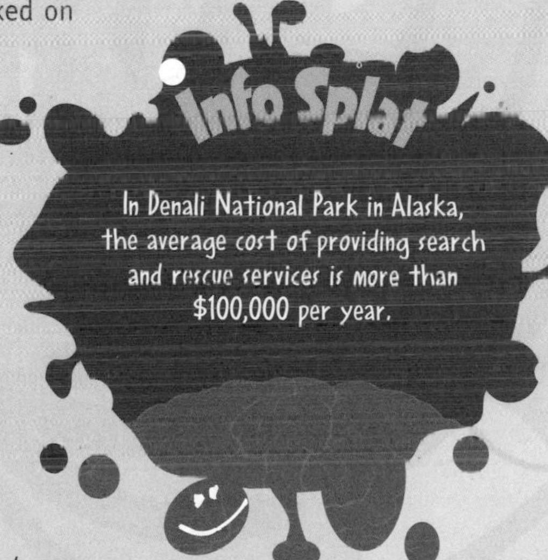

Info Splat
In Denali National Park in Alaska, the average cost of providing search and rescue services is more than $100,000 per year.

As light faded from the sky, Jenna fought against the realization that she might never see Ralphie again. She wandered through the neighborhood, looking in all the same places she'd searched before. Her heart would not let her give up when Ralphie still needed to be rescued.

This must be how God feels about His lost people, Jenna thought. She suddenly felt like she understood God's heart a little bit better—it must be about as broken as hers.

Just before dark, Jenna saw a man walking toward her with a bundle in his arms. "Are you looking for this?" he asked.

"Ralphie!" Jenna ran toward the man, overwhelmed with relief as she saw her terrier's face. "Thank you!" she said gratefully.

Jenna couldn't help feeling sorry for God. He was still waiting for *His* loved ones to come home safely.

If you knew someone was lost, would you help search? What about those who are spiritually lost?

~ Incredi-Biblical ~

See, I [God] have engraved you on the palms of my hands. Isaiah 49:16.

PRICELESS IN GOD'S EYES

How much do you think you're worth?

According to the United States' White House Office of Management and Budget, if you're under 70 years old, your life is worth \$3.7 million. In some cases, the government decides whether or not to enact an environmental protection, such as an anti-pollution regulation, based on the dollar value of the lives it would impact and whether or not the protection would be "worth it."

Magazines talk about business people in terms of their net worth. In other words, how much money or assets a person has left after all their bills are paid.

Television advertisements try to sell us things by telling us we're worth it.

Report cards, sports statistics, video game scores, the number of friends on your MySpace, how many people sit next to you during lunch at school—all of those things can contribute to your own opinion of what you're worth. But these things can be deceiving.

God doesn't measure you the same way that your friends, parents, teachers, or your government does. He measures you by how much He loves you. He created you, and He's re-creating you to look just like Him—inside and outside.

Think about it. The Creator of the universe loves you, He likes you, He's proud of you, and He's stuffed you full of potential. *Now* how much do you think you're worth?

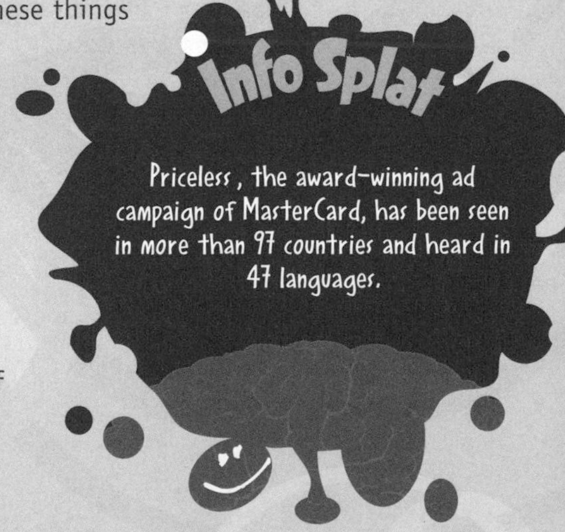

Info Splat
Priceless, the award-winning ad campaign of MasterCard, has been seen in more than 97 countries and heard in 47 languages.

REACT NOW!

Do you ever think negative thoughts about yourself? When that happens, interrupt yourself with conscious thoughts about how much God says you're worth.

January 23

INCREDI-BIBLICAL

They claim to know God, but by their actions they deny him.
Titus 1:16.

MR. PETERSON ON PATROL

He was a grumpy old man with a sour look on his face and a suit that smelled like shaving cream. Every week at church he patrolled the halls, ready to pour out his wrath on anyone he thought wasn't behaving properly.

"Stop running!" he shouted at little kids. "Don't you know this is the house of the Lord?"

"That dress is fit for a prostitute, not for a vessel of God," he'd intone if he didn't approve of a woman's outfit.

One Sabbath Mr. Peterson stood by the door to the sanctuary and refused to let anyone exit during the church service—even if they needed to use the restroom. "You should have gone beforehand. It's time to sit still for worship," he said firmly.

Mr. Peterson thought he was serving God by trying to instill reverence in the congregation. The problem was that he tried to do God's work using the devil's attitude.

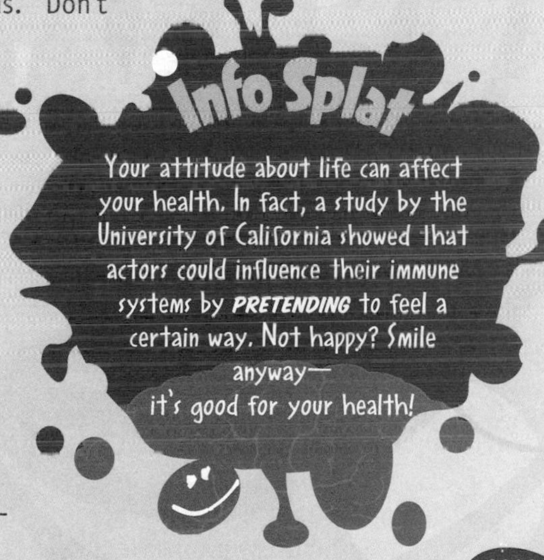

Info Splat
Your attitude about life can affect your health. In fact, a study by the University of California showed that actors could influence their immune systems by **PRETENDING** to feel a certain way. Not happy? Smile anyway—it's good for your health!

Do you know someone who is supposed to be a representative of God, but who is not acting much like God? Sometimes the devil gets church people into a situation where religion is a habit, and their hearts are never really moved by the Holy Spirit.

Don't let these people paint your picture of God. Keep your eyes fixed on Jesus, and make sure *you* never become one of the grumpy Christians.

How can you be a positive influence on a grumpy Christian?

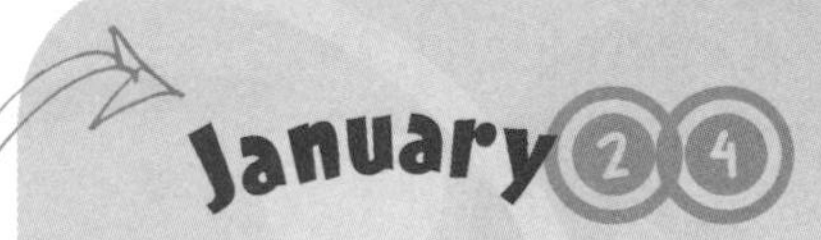

~ INCREDI-BIBLICAL ~

Guard what has been entrusted to your care. Turn away from godless chatter and the opposing ideas of what is falsely called knowledge. 1 Timothy 6:20.

ELLEN AND THE HYPNOTIST

Ellen was discouraged. God had given her amazing visions with messages she was supposed to share with those around her. But when she told others what she had seen, many believed that God wasn't sending her visions. Instead, the rumor was that her visions were the result of hypnotism.

Has it come to this? Ellen wondered. *Those who go honestly to God to plead His promises and claim His salvation are treated as though they've done something wrong?*

One day a famous doctor who specialized in hypnotism came to see her. "You're an easy subject," he taunted arrogantly. "I could mesmerize you myself and give you a vision."

"God has shown me that mesmerism is wrong," Ellen insisted. "We should never yield control of our minds to another human."

The doctor was persistent. To prove that what she had been saying was true, Ellen gave him permission to try to hypnotize her. He tried for a half hour, and finally gave up. Ellen knew that God had helped her resist the doctor's attempts to control her mind.

Today many people believe that hypnotism can help them lose weight, quit smoking, get rid of negative memories, or make other changes that would be helpful for their lives. But hypnotism isn't the true source of healing or change. God is. And we can do anything through His strength.

Info Splat

Do snake charmers really hypnotize cobras? Actually, the cobra sees the charmer's flute as a potential enemy. It rises in a defensive stance and imitates the motion of the flute with its body. The snake isn't hypnotized. It's trying to defend itself!

REACT NOW!

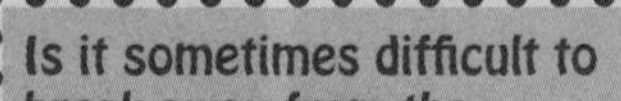

Is it sometimes difficult to break away from the hypnotic grip of the TV? Today, make conscious choices about what you allow to influence your mind

INCREDI-BIBLICAL

Then they cried to the Lord. . . . He brought them out of darkness and the deepest gloom. Psalm 107:13, 14.

HOW ARE YOU TODAY?

As a young person you have a lot happening in your life—school, bumpy friendships, family issues—all of which can sometimes give you the blues. But how do you know if what you're experiencing is *more* than just the blues?

Answer the following questions. (Check "Yes" only if it is something that has lasted **at least** two weeks.)

- Are you almost always in a depressed or angry mood? **Yes**___ **No**___
- Do activities you used to like not interest you anymore? **Yes**___ **No**___
- Have you experienced a major weight loss or weight gain? **Yes**___ **No**___
- Do you sleep too much or too little? **Yes**___ **No**___
- Does your body feel either restless or as if you have zero energy? **Yes**___ **No**___
- Do you feel as if there's no hope and nothing you can do about it? **Yes**___ **No**___
- Do you feel worthless or guilty for no real reason? **Yes**___ **No**___
- Do you have problems concentrating? **Yes**___ **No**___
- Do you think a lot about death and suicide? **Yes**___ **No**___

If you answered yes to five or more questions, you might be depressed. It's important to talk to an adult you trust for help. Whether you have depression or just the blues, remember:

Exercise produces brain chemicals that make you feel happy.

A **well-balanced diet** can help give an unhappy brain a boost.

Talking to a counselor may help you figure out what's making you feel depressed.

Prayer connects you with God and helps relax away the stressors that cause depression.

Don't worry, be . . . Danish? A study of 80,000 people worldwide done by the University of Leicester found that the nation with the highest level of overall happiness is Denmark. The United States ranked twenty-third.

REACT NOW!

What do you do to cheer up when you're feeling down? Is it something that makes you feel good about yourself, or feel worse later?

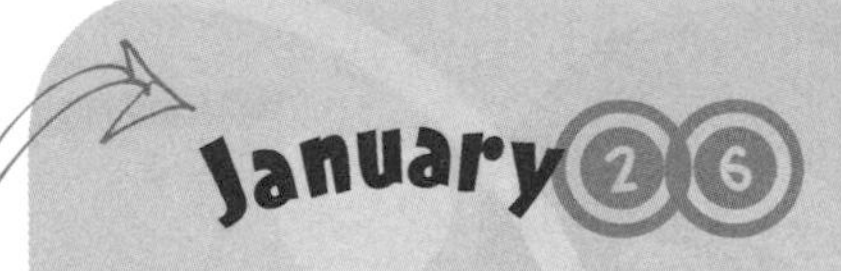
January 26

INCREDI-BIBLICAL

To him who overcomes, I will . . . give him a white stone with a new name written on it, known only to him who receives it. Revelation 2:17.

MELANIE'S DARK SECRET

I'm sick of my name, Melanie thought as she looked down at her notebook. She wrote her name and then drew squiggly lines on it. But nothing she did made it look right.

The name itself wasn't so bad, but the nicknames were. A lot of people called her Mel, which she thought should belong to an old man with gray whiskers growing out his ears. But worse nicknames included Melanoma, Melly Belly, Watermelanie, and Mel Bell.

Next to the nicknames, the worst part about her name was the meaning: Melanie means *dark*. Not *princess*, not *beloved,* not *destined for greatness,* but . . . *dark.*

"You know, you've put me at a great psychological disadvantage here, giving me a name that means *dark*," Melanie joked with her mom. "I know you named me after someone special, but still."

Her mom seemed unconcerned. "It's only temporary anyway." She smiled at Melanie. "You're getting a new name when you get to heaven."

"I am?" Melanie looked up in surprise.

"Yes," Mom said. "It says so in Revelation. God is picking it out for you this time."

Melanie was quiet while she thought of all the cool possibilities. Later, as she studied her Bible, Melanie found a verse that seemed to be just for her. In 2 Corinthians 4:6 she read, "Let light shine out of darkness." She smiled. Melanie may mean *dark*, but her purpose was to shine.

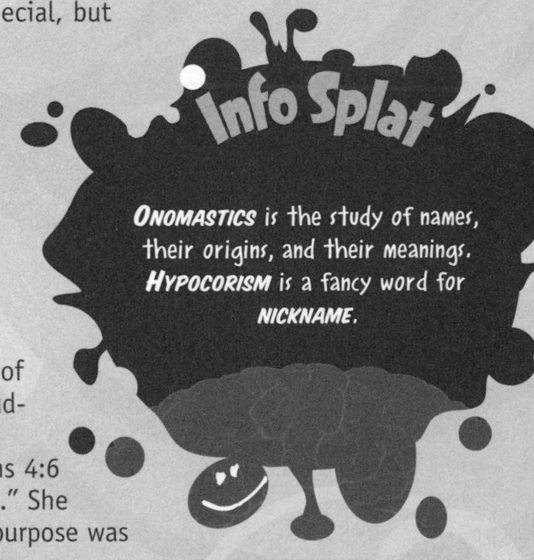
Info Splat
ONOMASTICS is the study of names, their origins, and their meanings. HYPOCORISM is a fancy word for NICKNAME.

REACT NOW!

Do you like your name? Are you looking forward to a new name in heaven?

January 27

~ INCREDI-BIBLICAL ~

Wash and perfume yourself, and put on your best clothes. Ruth 3:3.

THE STINKY TRUTH

OK, so everybody sweats. God actually designed it that way so our bodies wouldn't overheat. Think of it as a sort of . . . personal air-conditioner.

But as you get older and your body changes, your sweat glands start to work overtime. And while the sweat itself doesn't have an odor, the bacteria on your skin do, and that makes a difference in the way you smell. So it's important to adapt your hygiene practices—which is basically a fancy way of saying that you need to pay more attention to keeping your body clean.

Info Splat
The human body has about 2.5 million sweat glands.

Nothing's more embarrassing than having a friend—or worse, someone who's *not* your friend—tell you that a shower should be in your future. Be prepared with the following tips.

1. Take showers often and use good-smelling deodorant. There are scents made for both guys and girls.
2. Wear your clothes only once before washing them again. Hint: if it's on the floor, it's dirty.
3. Keep your room clean. If your bedroom smells like a locker room, so will your clothes!

Brush and floss so your breath is fresh, not frightening.

Keep your nails clean and clipped or filed. It probably won't affect odor, but it's a nice touch.

Let's keep it real. Puberty is weird. But it can also be fun as part of the journey God has for you.

And never underestimate the power of a shower.

REACT NOW!

If one of your friends has a hygiene issue, do you think it would be best to tell them, or pretend you don't notice?

INCREDI-BIBLICAL

**For we are to God the aroma of Christ among those who are being saved and those who are perishing.
2 Corinthians 2:15.**

SOMETIMES YOU ARE THE MIRACLE

The wound on the man's leg was raw and swollen, and the putrid flesh was rotten to the bone. Dolores gasped and looked up at the man's pleading eyes. The evangelistic meeting was over, and many had gathered to ask for prayer, but this was the worst case of illness Dolores had ever seen. When she finished praying, a strange feeling came over her.

"Come back tomorrow," she told him. Dolores went home, but she couldn't sleep. The image of the man's leg came into her mind again and again. "God, what are You trying to tell me?" she asked.

The next day she found a doctor and asked what to do. Then she purchased some supplies, and went to the meeting with the doctor's instructions.

When the man arrived, Dolores cleaned his wound. She could tell it hurt, but he didn't say a word. Every two nights she repeated the process, and by the time the meetings ended, the wound was healing and a ring of healthy skin had grown around its edges.

Through an interpreter, the man told her that he had spent all of his money on his leg. He was almost ready to give up and die, but he prayed, and God told him to go to the meetings, where he would receive help.

Dolores felt tears in her eyes as she understood what God had done. *Sometimes you pray for miracles,* Dolores thought to herself, *and sometimes you* are *the miracle.*

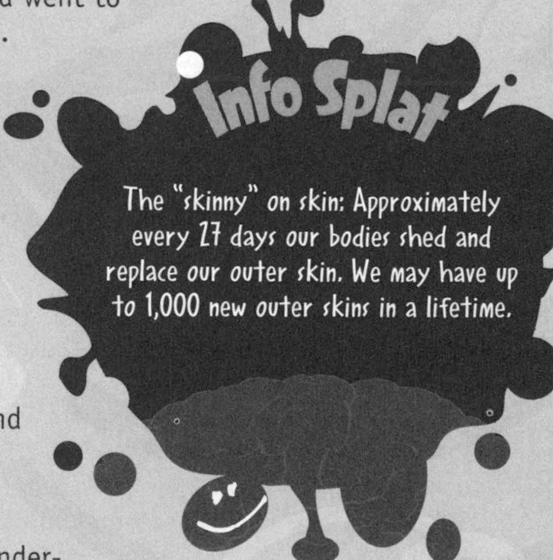

Info Splat
The "skinny" on skin: Approximately every 27 days our bodies shed and replace our outer skin. We may have up to 1,000 new outer skins in a lifetime.

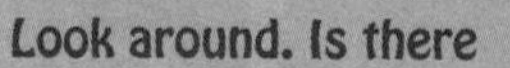

REACT NOW!

Look around. Is there someone who needs you to be a miracle from God as a friend, or a tutor, or a helper in some way? Don't wait—start being that miracle now.

Incredi-Biblical

By his wounds we are healed. Isaiah 53:5.

WOUNDS OF THE HEART

Connor was shocked at the sight of the gashes on Megan's arm. "What happened?" he gasped.

Megan yanked down her sleeve over the wounds, obviously upset that Connor had noticed. "Nothing," she mumbled.

Connor looked closely at Megan's face. "Megan?"

"I did it to myself, OK?" she said, starting to cry. "I don't want anyone to know. Please, Connor. And stop looking at me that way. You don't understand what it's like to be me."

Connor didn't know what to say. He felt sick.

Megan stared away vacantly. "Sometimes I just hurt inside. It's like, so intense, I can't take it. That's why I cut myself. Please don't judge me." Megan looked back at Connor. "My stepdad is a control freak. I don't even want to think about what he'd do if he found out. Probably haul me off to a mental hospital or something."

Connor's thoughts were twisted by confusion as he wondered what he should do.

People who injure themselves are experiencing severe emotional distress. They need to feel loved, heard, and accepted so they can talk about what's causing the pain. They don't need to feel criticized, abandoned, or joked about. If you know someone who is cutting, be a listening friend, and encourage them to talk with someone they can trust about their pain. Most important, pray that God will intervene. He's the healer of outside wounds and inside wounds.

Info Splat

Hope is a powerful thing! According to researchers Zubieta and Stohler, hope uses the same chemical pathway in the brain as an analgesic (such as Tylenol), and can reduce pain and improve health and well-being.

What Bible texts could you use to encourage someone who is suffering from deep emotional pain?

~ Incredi-Biblical ~

For the word of God is living and active. Sharper than a double-edged sword, it penetrates even to dividing soul and spirit. Hebrews 4:12.

NIGHT OF THE SWORD

When Jagger woke up, his heart was pounding inside his rib cage, and his throat was dry. Even though the nightmare was over, his skin tingled with pinpricks of sweat. He could sense a dark presence in the room as he lay in his twisted sheets, staring into blackness.

Overriding his instincts, Jagger slowly sat up and touched his feet to the floor, then stood and walked across the shadowy carpet to turn on the light and pick up his Bible. Opening the pages to Psalms, he read, "Then he rebukes them in his anger, and terrifies them in his wrath" (Psalm 2:5). Something about imagining God rebuking the enemy and giving the evil spirit a taste of his own medicine made Jagger feel less afraid. In fact, when he turned out the light and crawled back into bed, instead of a dark presence he could almost sense warrior angels standing by to protect him.

The next morning he told his dad about the experience. "Jagger," his dad said, eyes bright, "you used your sword of the Spirit—the Word of God."

Jagger sat down, smiling as the realization dawned on him. He remembered reading in Ephesians 6 about putting on the full armor of God, including the sword of the Spirit. Inwardly he vowed to spend more time sharpening that sword—like a soldier preparing for battle—by reading his Bible every day.

Info Splat

Thirteenth-century Japanese swordsmiths were serious about swords. Before forging a blade, they would go through a ritual purification and achieve a state of mind that they believed would breathe their spirit into the sword and give it mythical qualities.

REACT NOW!

What verses from your sword of the Spirit (the Bible) could you use to fight against fear or other negative experiences?

INCREDI-BIBLICAL

A generous man will prosper; he who refreshes others will himself be refreshed. Proverbs 11:25.

WHAT CAN YOU GIVE?

Harvard University is the oldest and (arguably) most prestigious university in the United States. It is world-famous, with a long, proud heritage of educational excellence. Many notable people have received their education from Harvard, including six of our country's presidents and several Nobel Prize winners. Harvard has approximately 18,000 students and 2,000 faculty members. It's also one of the wealthiest institutions of higher learning in the country. But did you know that it started out with only nine students and one instructor?

Info Splat

Harvard University's library has the second-largest library collection in the United States. With more than 14.6 million volumes, only the Library of Congress is larger.

That changed with a generous gift. A 31-year-old minister from Charlestown, Massachusetts, died on September 14, 1638, leaving his library and half of his estate to the newly established college. In his honor, they named the college after him. His name was John Harvard.

If not for his generous gift toward something he cared about, no one would probably remember the name John Harvard. Now his name is almost synonymous with what was important to him: education.

What do you really care about? Is it something that could be of value to your family, your church, or your community? You're never too young to make a contribution of your time, your money, your prayers, or your ideas to something that's important to you. Go ahead. Make a difference.

Do you believe it's really better to give than to receive? Why, or why not?

INCREDI-BIBLICAL

Adam named his wife Eve, because she would become the mother of all the living. Genesis 3:20.

FATHER ADAM

"Who did Adam's sons marry?" Anna asked her Bible teacher after class. Caught by surprise, Miss Chloe asked Anna to repeat her question.

"What I want to know is, since there weren't any other families on earth with daughters for Cain and Seth to marry, who did they marry?"

Miss Chloe smiled. "You're right," she explained, "there were no other families on earth. God had created only Adam and Eve. But the first couple had many children, and eventually the brothers and sisters married each other."

Anna's forehead wrinkled, "But how do you know that? I thought Adam and Eve only had Cain, Abel, and Seth. I didn't think they had any daughters."

Miss Chloe reached for her Bible. "Let's see what Genesis says." Turning to chapter 5, she found the verse she was looking for.

"'After Seth was born,' Miss Chloe read, 'Adam lived 800 years and had other sons and daughters'" (Genesis 5:4). Then Miss Chloe handed the Bible to Anna so she could read it for herself.

Anna gave the Bible back to her teacher with a smile. "I never realized that," she told her. "I think that's the reason I like this class so much. We always find the answers in the Bible."

Info Splat

Adam was 687 when, in man's eighth generation, Methuselah was born. For 243 years Methuselah could have spent time with Adam. Noah was born 126 years after Adam died, but Noah's grandfather Methuselah could have shared stories he got from Adam.

What other types of questions might people ask you that you would answer from the Bible? How can you know where to find your answers?

Incredi-Biblical

Happy are those who find wisdom, and those who get understanding. Proverbs 3:13, NRSV.

THE LAST TEST QUESTION

Lynn tossed her science test on the teacher's desk and announced, "I'm done."

Mr. Chance picked up the test and looked it over, "Your last answer is wrong," he said. "Would you like to take another try at it?"

Shaking her head, brown ponytail flying, Lynn left for her next class a few minutes early. The other seventh graders were not so quick to leave; and when they too were given a second, third, and even fourth chance to redo the missed question, they returned to their desks to rethink their work.

Info Splat
Your brain is amazing. It is as unique as your thumbprint. It uses almost one fourth of the energy that comes from your daily food intake, and weighs around two pounds.

The next day, when the tests were returned, Lynn discovered she had the lowest grade.

"It's not fair!" she told everyone she saw. "Everyone else got to fix their tests, and I didn't."

"What did you choose to do?" Mom asked, reminding Lynn of her earlier decision. "We've talked about this before. Each choice we make has its own consequence."

Lynn stared at her mom. She'd heard it all before, but this was the first time she'd felt so bad about taking the easy way out.

As she worked on an assignment in science class the next day, Lynn found herself stuck on a couple of questions. She wanted to skip the section, but then she remembered what had happened the last time she'd made that choice. Raising her hand, Lynn waited for help.

REACT NOW!

What decisions will you make today and what are some possible consequences?

INCREDI-BIBLICAL

**Nothing on earth is his equal—
a creature without fear.
Job 41:33.**

A PILE OF BONES

"One year the gentle stream experienced a tremendous spring flood," the park ranger explained. "The raging waters overflowed the banks and raced across the land. The rushing water collected living and dead animals, hurtling them downstream until they reached the place where you now stand."

David poked his older brother in the ribs. "Should we tell him what really happened?"

Scott shook his head and whispered, "We could, but he won't believe it."

"But the ranger's story doesn't make as much sense as what the Bible tells us about the Flood and everything dying," David hissed back.

After the lecture the boys walked to the wall of entombed dinosaur bones. The fossilized bones were piled higher than their heads, jutting out at all angles. Some bones were longer than the boys were tall.

"This single bone was part of an unknown dinosaur's leg," David read. "Wow!" he added. "Whatever kind it was, it was huge!"

"I hope there are dinosaurs in heaven," Scott said, running his finger along the giant bone. "I'd really like to know what they were like."

"Me too," David echoed. "They'd be amazing! But if there *are*, I hope I grow a lot more." He grinned at the thought as they continued to explore the ancient pile of bones.

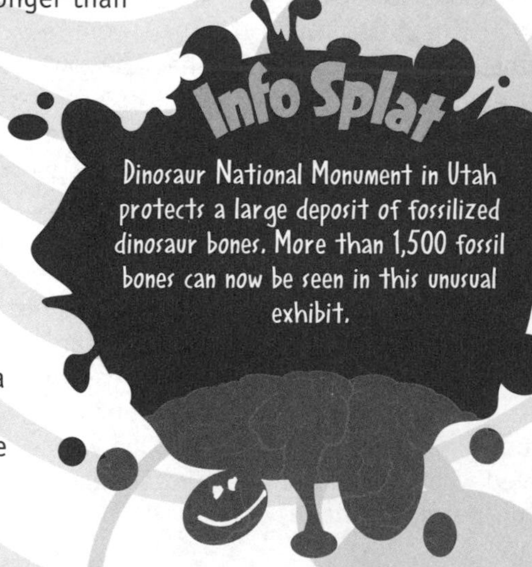

Info Splat
Dinosaur National Monument in Utah protects a large deposit of fossilized dinosaur bones. More than 1,500 fossil bones can now be seen in this unusual exhibit.

REACT NOW!

What do you know about dinosaurs and where they came from? Where does the Bible talk about a worldwide flood?

INCREDI-BIBLICAL

People must learn to devote themselves to doing what is good, in order that they may provide for daily necessities and not live unproductive lives. Titus 3:14.

BIBLE

TEEN MISSIONARIES

The hot, damp air made Adam drip with sweat as soon as he left the airplane. Looking around, he saw a world totally different from the snowdrifts and bare trees he'd left behind. Here, the sun shown intensely on green palms, brown earth, and brightly painted buildings.

"Hey, Adam!" his friend Brittany called. "Over here!"

Adam made his way to where his Pathfinder group stood around their conference director, listening to instructions. Their mission: spend two weeks assisting the visiting doctors and nurses with the medical clinics they'd be holding in several small villages.

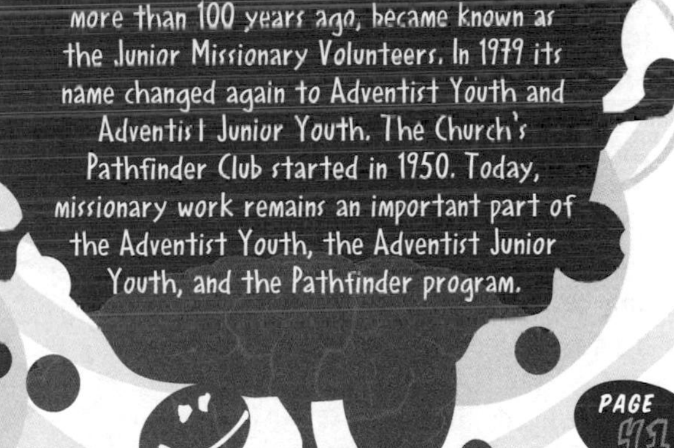

Info Splat
The Missionary Volunteer Society, started more than 100 years ago, became known as the Junior Missionary Volunteers. In 1979 its name changed again to Adventist Youth and Adventist Junior Youth. The Church's Pathfinder Club started in 1950. Today, missionary work remains an important part of the Adventist Youth, the Adventist Junior Youth, and the Pathfinder program.

At the end of each day Adam ached all over from running errands, finding supplies, entertaining little kids as they stood in line, and occasionally pulling teeth.

"I never realized there were people who needed so much help," Brittany told him. She and Adam sat on the steps of a small building, taking a water break while they waited for their next task.

"I know," Adam agreed. "I thought everyone knew to wash their hands and brush their teeth. I never expected I could make a difference."

"Yeah, I thought I'd just go on an adventure. Now I know how much we're actually needed."

"It's fun to truly help," Adam said as he jumped up to fetch supplies for a doctor who'd signaled for assistance.

REACT NOW!

What can you do today in your home, school, or neighborhood to be a missionary for Jesus?

~ INCREDI-BIBLICAL ~

But he was pierced for our transgressions . . . the punishment that brought us peace was upon him, and by his wounds we are healed. Isaiah 53:5.

80 POUNDS OF STUBBORN

Matthew carefully gripped his golden retriever's leash in his hands. "I want to make sure Cindy doesn't get away from me today," he explained to his dad as they left the house. On the trail Cindy was her usual self, pulling on the leash to reach an interesting scent up ahead, or stopping and planting her feet while she smelled something equally interesting that everyone else had passed.

Cindy took off running when they reached the park.

"Wait for me!" Matthew called, taking giant steps to keep up with her, but Cindy wouldn't listen. Matthew tried to stop her, but Cindy strained on the leash, and her weight yanked him forward. The big dog dashed through the weeds, down a path, into some shrubs, and finally across a gravel parking lot. *WHAAP!* Matthew lost his footing and fell.

"Cindy!" he yelled, but she didn't slow a bit. Instead Matthew skidded across the parking lot behind her.

By the time the two finally stopped, blood ran off Matthew's elbows and shins. His hands were scraped, and his face streaked with dust and perspiration.

"Why didn't you just let go of the leash?" Dad asked, finally catching up with the two runaways.

"I was afraid of what would happen to Cindy if she ran off. She might get hurt," Matthew answered, examining his wounds. "I love her too much to let her do whatever she wants."

Info Splat

Between 450 and 850 distinct breeds of dogs exist worldwide. Golden retrievers are trained for search and rescue, arson detection, and drug detection. They also serve as therapy dogs, hearing dogs, handicap assistance dogs, and guide dogs for those who are blind.

Who has had to suffer because of your mistakes? Whom would you be willing to suffer for so they might be kept safe?

~ INCREDI-BIBLICAL ~

**Well done, good and faithful servant! You have been faithful with a few things; I will put you in charge of many things.
Matthew 25:21.**

MATH HOMEWORK

Alan sat with his head on his desk. Would math class never end? Maybe if he thought hard enough he could get his teacher to stop talking about fractions. He was sick of hearing about adding, subtracting, multiplying, and dividing the horrible things.

"Alan, did you get your assignment done?"

Raising his head, Alan stared at Miss Bane with bleary eyes. "Huh? What?" he grunted.

"Is your math finished?" she repeated.

"I'm going to do it at home," Alan informed her.

And he did. The next day Alan turned in his math assignment. It was almost all wrong.

"You need to do this in class where you can get help," Miss Bane said. Alan refused.

Then he began turning in assignments in which he missed only a few problems. Miss Bane hoped he finally understood the math concepts even though he kept insisting on doing his work at home. The day of the chapter test arrived. As Miss Bane graded Alan's paper, she realized he still didn't know how to do any of the work. He had failed the test.

After school the next day Miss Bane spoke with Alan's mother. She discovered that Alan wanted to work on math at home so that he could get his mom to complete his assignment for him. Alan failed his test because his mother wasn't there to do his work.

Info Splat

Sadly, in a recent survey, researchers discovered that four out of five top students thought cheating was all right. Another survey found that more than half of high school students view cheating as acceptable.

REACT NOW!

Is cheating a problem in your class? Do you consider it cheating if your parents do your schoolwork for you? Why?

INCREDI-BIBLICAL

Then what god will be able to rescue you from my hand? Daniel 3:15.

DURA

The fighting reached the palace halls. Sword against sword, dagger to dagger, the combatants struggled to dominate. The king himself was part of the battle. Hearing the cries around him, he wondered who truly fought for the kingdom and who had betrayed their allegiance.

At last, in defeat, the invaders left the palace. Behind them the devastated king wondered where to begin rebuilding. Whom could he trust? He feared that some of his own advisors had shared the secrets of how to gain entry into this fortress. Remembering an old dream, the king had a magnificent statue created. The wood creation towered 90 feet high and was covered in a fine layer of gold. Servants placed it in a huge, open field, and the king required all of his officials to attend its unveiling.

Hananiah, Mishael, and Azariah were some of those required to be present. As the king gave the instructions to bow to his likeness, the three friends had no doubt of whom they served. Yes, they were loyal to their king, but the radiant sculpture was nothing compared to the God of heaven. Even when threatened with fiery death, the three men stood faithful.

In the furnace and out of it, the Son of God is with His servants, yesterday, today, and tomorrow.

Historians tell us that in the tenth year of Nebuchadnezzar's rule he fought some of his army. It is unclear if the test of the idol and the fiery furnace was a test of loyalty after that rebellion.

Info Splat

Nebuchadnezzar's image stood on the Plain of Dura. In Babylonian, ***DUR*** means ***WALL***. An inner and outer wall surrounded Babylon, with a large space between the two walls. It may have been here that the crowd gathered—at the Plain of the Wall.

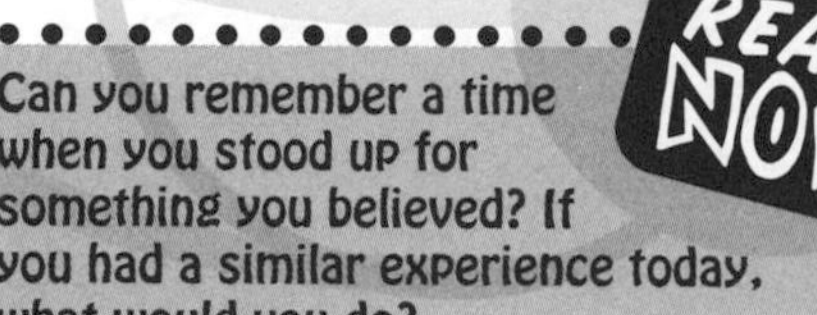

Can you remember a time when you stood up for something you believed? If you had a similar experience today, what would you do?

Incredi-Biblical

Children, obey your parents in the Lord, for this is right. "Honor your father and mother"—which is the first commandment with a promise.
Ephesians 6:1, 2.

THE SURFEIT

Alexander stood on the trail, watching the movement in the ferns off to his left. Suddenly, a few feet from where he watched—frightened, yet fascinated—something broke clear of the camouflaging forest floor and spilled across the path. Skunks!

Should I run? Alexander wondered, but by then it was too late. The black-and-white army had spotted him and was rapidly heading his way. Six noses paraded by; five sniffed at his feet.

Not moving a muscle lest he bring a catastrophe upon himself, Alexander held his breath. Five baby skunks turned back toward their mother as if discussing their findings. Mother Skunk, reluctant to approach the young man, sniffed her children and stared his way.

Abruptly she gave a loud call and dashed back toward the safe covering of ferns. At their mother's command, all the kits turned as one and followed her hasty retreat.

Alexander watched as the family rapidly disappeared into the green of the forest floor. Shaking with relief, he was glad Mother Skunk had decided to flee instead of fight. He was well aware his current well-being was based on the fact that the young animals had decided to obey their mother.

Info Splat

A group of skunks is called a surfeit. When these members of the weasel family feel threatened, they send their sulfur compound spray in a fan-shaped pattern that is up to 15 feet wide.

REACT NOW!

When your parents speak to you, how do you react? Is there anything you should change about the way you respond?

~ INCREDI-BIBLICAL ~

Religion that God our Father accepts as pure and faultless is this: to look after orphans and widows in their distress. James 1:27.

THE THREE BROTHERS

The three African brothers had almost finished supper.

"I'm full," the youngest brother said, and he pushed his leftover food onto the middle brother's plate. With a grateful look the 10-year-old continued eating until he, too, felt full. Getting up, he scraped his leftovers onto his older brother's plate, and the 12-year-old kept eating. When all the food was gone, the oldest brother looked up with a satisfied smile. Taking his plate to be washed, he joined the other children at play.

"Every day I see students in our school throw away food," Mr. Arden told the auditorium full of students. "When I see that happening, I think about the three brothers and how they made sure to share what they had." The students were silent, looking at the screen where they could see a picture of the brothers eating.

"How many of you are 12?" Mr. Arden continued. A number of hands went up. "At 12 years of age, the oldest brother is already the head of the house. The boys' parents died, and they have no relatives to take care of them. The nearby orphanage is full. After school these boys eat the one meal a day some kind people provide for them. Then they go home to a small mud house with a few mats on the floor.

"We can help these boys," Mr. Arden said with a smile. "We can help provide food and even some school supplies. Would you like to do that?"

Info Splat

South Africa is located at the southern end of the continent of Africa. Currently more people die there each year than are born.

How can you find and help people like the boys in today's story?

INCREDI-BIBLICAL

Stop judging by mere appearances, and make a right judgment. John 7:24.

APPEARANCES

Gray hair stuck out from under the dark-red cap of the old woman who leaned on the shopping cart, slowly pushing it into the store. Closely behind her followed a bearded man, his burly arms covered in tattoos, a wallet attached to his belt with a chain. His eyes were on the woman.

Mrs. Vand watched the two from a distance. *Will he try to harm her?* she wondered. *Rob her?* Then as she followed them into the produce section, she heard the man say, "Which do you want? This kind of carrots or the little ones, Mom?"

Instantly, Mrs. Vand's view of the man changed. She watched in admiration as he patiently followed his mother around the fruits and vegetables, helping her make good choices.

Appearances surely can be deceiving, Mrs. Vand thought as she continued her shopping.

The next day Mrs. Vand shared the story with her students. At first they thought it was a good idea for their teacher to keep on eye on the elderly woman. They were surprised to hear that the dangerous looking man was her kind son.

Later that day Chris quietly asked Mrs. Vand, "Do you know who the man was?" Mrs. Vand shook her head. "I think he could have been my father," Chris said. "I don't actually know him, but he looks just the way you described that man. I'd really like to know him."

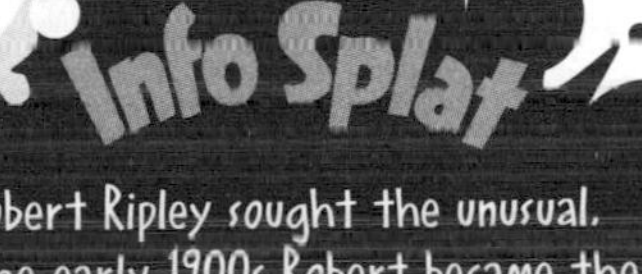

Robert Ripley sought the unusual. In the early 1900s Robert became the most traveled man in the world, visiting 201 countries in his search of the strange. Today you can still see some of his finds at his Ripley's Believe It or Not museums.

REACT NOW!

How can you make judgments that aren't based on appearances? How do you react to classmates whose families are different from yours?

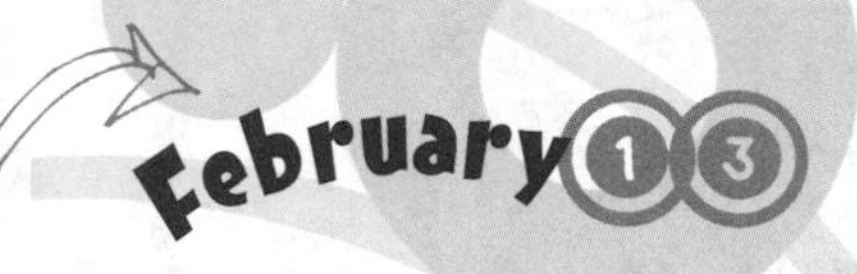

~ Incredi-Biblical ~

And Jesus grew in wisdom and stature, and in favor with God and men. Luke 2:52.

DONNIE'S GOAL

By age 14, Eric had reached six-feet four inches and was the envy of the boys in his school.

"How did Eric grow so tall?" 12-year-old Donnie asked Eric's mom. Donnie was worried, for he was shorter than his younger brother.

Eric's mom thought a moment. "You know, Eric was telling me about an experiment he read in a magazine. The article said that if a child wanted to grow one to two inches taller than expected, he should sleep 10 hours a night in a completely dark room and drink two to three extra glasses of milk a day." Shrugging, she said, "Eric tried doing it. Maybe that helped him a little. But remember, Donnie, your Creator made you just right."

A few weeks later Donnie's mom and Eric's mom were talking. "Donnie has been doing something very unusual," his mom remarked. "He keeps insisting on going to bed early, and we've had to make sure his room is totally dark. And he drinks milk by the gallon."

Eric's mom laughed and explained why Donnie had such seemingly strange behavior.

A half dozen years later Donnie delightedly measured six feet tall. Whether his experiment made the difference, he didn't know. He figured his God-given genes had a lot to do with it. But he had set a goal and worked to reach it. Donnie was very satisfied.

Info Splat

The Bible tells us that the giant Goliath stood nine feet tall. The tallest man in recent times died in 1940 at the height of eight feet eleven inches. And the tallest NBA player? He was seven feet seven.

REACT NOW!
What goals do you want to work toward achieving? What are the steps you need to take toward reaching one or more of those goals?

~ Incredi-Biblical ~

Therefore go and make disciples of all nations, baptizing them in the name of the Father and of the Son and of the Holy Spirit. Matthew 28:19.

A VALENTINE'S DAY TRADITION

In May of 1950, when televisions were just starting to be popular in homes across the United States and Europe, the SDA program *Faith for Today* began broadcasting. It has been on the air every week since then.

Soon people who worked with Faith for Today chose Valentine's Day as a time of special fund-raising. Kids around North America saved quarters in unique containers made especially for this yearly offering. At elementary schools, in Sabbath schools, and homes quarters were saved for the Faith for Today's TV ministry.

Today a special offering will be taken at your church and shared among three Adventist television ministries: Breath of Life, Faith for Today, and It Is Written. The men and women who started these programs believed that they could take the message of Jesus to the entire world. Now—nearly 60 years later—many more TV programs produced by Seventh-day Adventists share God's message of hope and the truths found in His Word. TV stations around the world broadcast programs about Jesus, stories from the Bible, and information about living a healthy life, from diet to exercise. But all these programs have the same mission: telling people about our Friend Jesus.

Info Splat

At the end World War II there were only 7,000 televisions in the United States. Today approximately 98 million households have television sets. If the average household has about two TVs, then the United States has around 200 million.

REACT NOW!

What can you do today to tell other people about Jesus? Why would you share your money to help people you don't know?

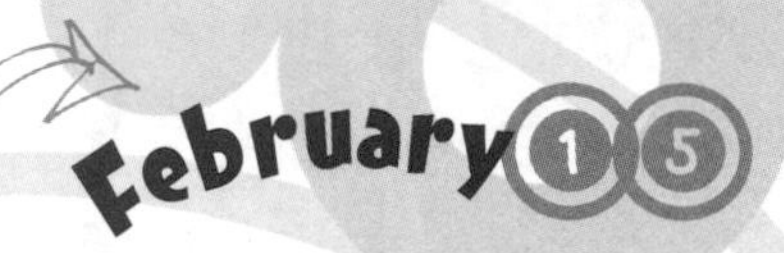

~ INCREDI-BIBLICAL ~

The second is this: "Love your neighbor as yourself." There is no commandment greater than these. Mark 12:31.

WHITE WATER!

Paddle! Put your muscle into it!" yelled the guide.

The rubber raft trembled as it stopped in mid-descent down the little waterfall. Front end down, it was stuck. The group strained against the rushing water, and a dozen powerful strokes later the raft cleared the hydraulic and floated downstream.

"Great teamwork!" the guide called. "You can rest now."

Paddles on their knees, the paddlers stopped to catch their breath. Suddenly a large boulder jutted out into the river ahead of them. Before they could slip past it and around the next bend, the guide reached out and grabbed it.

"Let's wait for the next boat to clear that hole," he said. "With the water this high, the hole's tougher than usual, and the next guide is alone and rowing a bigger boat."

Looking back, the group saw the next raft tip forward over the fall's edge and start its descent. But as their guide predicted, it became trapped in the powerful hydraulic. They watched as the other guide struggled to move her boat out of the backward current.

Suddenly their guide stood up. "Can you hold us here?"

A stocky man near the front gripped the rock as the guide scrambled out of the raft, up the boulder, onto the bank, and toward the falls. Without hesitating, he leaped into the bobbing raft.

The exhausted guide handed her rescuer an oar, and together they generated enough strength to pull the boat out of the current.

Info Splat

Holes are formed when water pours over the top of a submerged object, causing the water downstream to flow backward. This type of water action is known as a hydraulic and can keep boats from moving forward.

People don't have to be in deadly trouble to need our help. In what types of situations can you be of help today?

~ Incredi-Biblical ~

The wisdom of the prudent is to give thought to their ways, but the folly of fools is deception. Proverbs 14:8.

POND WATER AND PARASITES

"I'm not feeling very well," Paul told his mom as they were getting ready to leave for the school's production of Charlie Brown. Paul had practiced Snoopy's facial expressions for weeks and could hardly wait for the performance, but now his stomach hurt.

Mom sent Paul to bed and notified the program director and Paul's understudy. A few minutes later the phone rang.

"I hear Paul's ill," said a doctor friend whose son was in Paul's classroom. Paul's mother explained the problem, and the doctor continued. "Jeff just told me about a dare Paul took during science class this week. Apparently some of his friends dared him to drink a cup of the pond water the teacher had brought in for them to examine under a microscope."

"What?" Mom asked, starting down the hall toward Paul's room.

"Paul took the dare. I think he might be ill because of parasites in that water."

As Mom drove Paul to their town's urgent-care center she asked him how much money he'd won by drinking the water.

"Seven dollars," he moaned.

Mom shook her head. All this pain, suffering, and expense for something that could have been avoided. "Paul, the next time someone wants to make a bet with you or dares you to do something, would you think about it before you act?"

"Yeah," Paul assured her, clutching his belly. "This just isn't worth it."

Info Splat

You can get microscopic parasites by putting dirty hands or other objects in your mouth. By avoiding shared cups, food, and toys, you can also avoid parasites. It is important to wash your hands thoroughly before eating. Experts say you should wash for 20 seconds.

REACT NOW!

What do you do when your friends attempt to get you to try something new?
Whom can you trust to give you good advice?

INCREDI-BIBLICAL

The Lord is . . . the Creator of the ends of the earth. He will not grow tired or weary, and his understanding no one can fathom. Isaiah 40:28.

ANCIENT ARTHROPOD

The long-extinct trilobite fossils are found in the lowermost levels of the Grand Canyon. They are also the earliest fossils found around the world," Mr. Lynd explained to the biology class.

"A trilo-what?" Dorothy blurted. "I don't understand."

The eighth graders were studying about God as the designer and creator of the universe. They had a hundred questions and felt free to ask them.

"A trilobite is classified as an animal such as a lobster or a spider. 'Tri' means three, and 'lobite' means lobes. Today we'd think of trilobites as part of the lobster, crab, and spider families," Mr. Lynd explained. "But here's something else unusual about these creatures. They're found at the bottom of geologic formations—with no fossils found under them.

"Yet trilobites were very complex," Mr. Lynd went on. "It had intricate nervous, circulation, and muscle systems. It also had the most sophisticated eyes of any organism. The eye on the end of its antennae could allow the animal to see, without distortion, underwater. This vision system alone is evidence of being constructed by an exceedingly brilliant designer." Mr. Lynd caught his breath, then continued. "This incredible creature appeared without a trace or hint of an ancestor in the rock layers below!"

Grant waved his hand. "So it sounds like the trilobite was designed, not evolved!"

The class agreed.

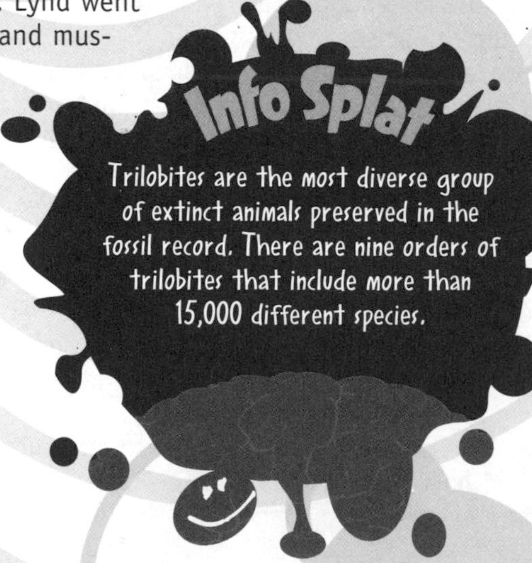

Info Splat
Trilobites are the most diverse group of extinct animals preserved in the fossil record. There are nine orders of trilobites that include more than 15,000 different species.

REACT NOW!

How can you be sure that what you're learning about science from television and movies is true? Where can you find accurate information?

INCREDI-BIBLICAL

For the living know that they will die, but the dead know nothing; they have no further reward. Ecclesiastes 9:5.

THE BACKYARD MISSIONARY

Mom could overhear her sons and a neighbor girl talking on the back deck. Catherine was telling her two friends about a TV program she'd watched the night before. "But she sees them, and they tell her how to find the answers," Catherine repeated.

Is she talking about ghosts? Mom wondered. Then she heard James get up and come into the house. "What's going on?" Mom asked as her older son headed for his room.

"I need to get something," he replied, quickly returning with his Bible. He opened the screen door and rejoined his brother, Mike, and Catherine. Leafing through the Bible, James began to explain why he chose not to watch the kind of TV programs she'd just been describing.

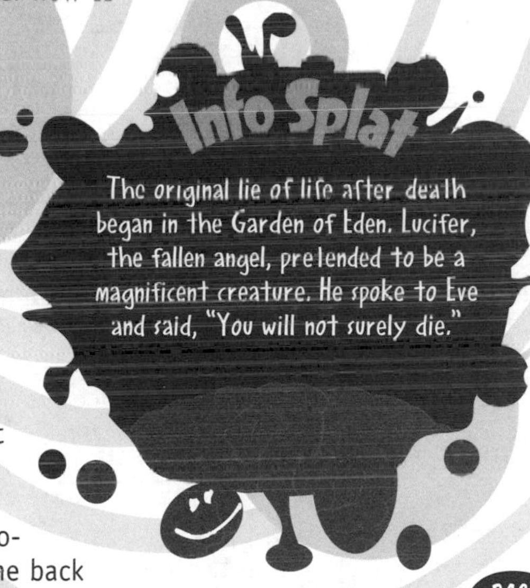

Info Splat
The original lie of life after death began in the Garden of Eden. Lucifer, the fallen angel, pretended to be a magnificent creature. He spoke to Eve and said, "You will not surely die."

First James pointed out Ecclesiastes 9:5. After reading it, he asked, "If dead people don't know anything, how can they come back and talk to us or haunt us?" Catherine just shrugged.

Then James showed her Isaiah's warning to talk to God, not to spirit mediums (Isaiah 8:19). Closing the Bible, James said, "I don't know for sure what you believe, but I think what the Bible says is true."

"Yeah," agreed Mike. "So, Catherine, what do you think?"

"I guess I agree with the Bible," she exclaimed, shaking her head. "That program doesn't know what it's talking about."

REACT NOW!

Where is the idea that people don't really die first mentioned in the Bible?
What's your favorite thing about the biblical truth of eternal life?

INCREDI-BIBLICAL

**And there was evening,
and there was morning—the third day.
Genesis 1:13.**

LOGICALLY SPEAKING

"My dad says he thinks the days must have been longer during Creation week, and that's why scientists say the earth is a lot older then 6,000 years," Brian informed his class.

"That's not right," came Candy's quick reply. "How could days be millions of years long?"

"Yeah, but how can I explain that to my dad?" Brian asked.

"Let's look at the first couple chapters in our textbook." Mr. Jana smiled and opened his Bible to Genesis.

"It does say first plants, next animals, then people, just like evolution," Brian said, frowning. "It could have been a long time between days."

"That doesn't make sense." The class waited while Rachel thought this through. "If the evening and the morning were the first day, how could the earth slow down spinning to make really, really long days and nights? Wouldn't we all float off into space without gravity?"

"And how could a day be millions of years? The side facing the sun would burn, and everything on the side away from the sun would freeze and die," Candy added.

"You've got some great points there." Pointing to his Bible, Mr. Jana said, "A long time ago I decided to believe what the Bible says is true. I think about what scientists say and compare that with what the Bible tells me. If the two don't agree, I choose the Bible and use logic, as you just did, to understand the science."

Info Splat

Through observation astronomers believe that in galaxies like our own, a star will explode, or go supernova, about every 25 years. The remnants from stars going supernova can be measured. Our own galaxy shows remnants of supernovas for about 7,000 years.

Why is it important to believe what the Bible says about the creation of our world? How do you see God's love revealed in the Creation story?

February 20

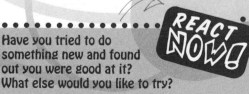

INCREDI-BIBLICAL

So whether you eat or drink or whatever you do, do it all for the glory of God. 1 Corinthians 10:31.

TWO TEENAGE COOKS

The cool autumn breeze felt good to the Pathfinders after their long and sticky bus ride. It had taken several hours to reach the campground, and now everyone's help was needed to set up camp before dark.

"David, Nick," their director said, "you guys have supper duty, right? The rest of us will pitch some tents.

"And thanks, guys, for your help," he added. "I know we usually have extra staff to help with meals, but this time most of them won't arrive until after dark."

Before leaving on the camping trip, David and Nick had decided to make vegetarian chicken noodle soup and sandwiches. The teenagers set to work lighting the camp stoves, getting kettles of water boiling, and determining how long it would take to heat the vegetarian chicken and cook the noodles. The difficult part was adding the seasonings. First they added a little of this and then a little of that. One staff member became their designated taste tester and cheerleader.

After prayer the junior Pathfinders tasted their first bites of David and Nick's soup.

"Mmmm, this is soooo good!" echoed all through the camp. "Can I have some more? This is the best soup I've ever eaten!"

The teen boys served the other club members and staff, offering them second and third bowls of soup. That night they discovered a new skill and found the joy that comes from serving others.

Info Splat

There are more than 2 million Pathfinders around the world. Pathfinders learn about the Bible, nature, crafts, camping, marching, and friends. Building strong friendships with Jesus is the most important part of being a Pathfinder.

Have you tried to do something new and found out you were good at it? What else would you like to try?

~ INCREDI-BIBLICAL ~

Do not let any unwholesome talk come out of your mouths, but only what is helpful for building others up according to their needs. Ephesians 4:29.

THE FIRST CAMP MEETING

If you've attended a Seventh-day Adventist camp meeting, you may have sung the song "I Love Camp Meeting." Or maybe not. But whether you've sung it gustily or have never heard of it, the song reminds us of how the first camp meetings were received.

Way back in 1868, during the first week of September, the first official Seventh-day Adventist camp meeting met in the tiny town of Wright, Michigan. A man named Mr. Root allowed the meetings to be held on his farmland, and soon horses pulling wagons or buggies and horses carrying riders made their way down the country roads toward his farm.

Three hundred people stayed for that week. Most of them lived in the 22 tents the church had provided. Visitors came not from only Michigan but also Wisconsin and as far away as New York. During some meetings more than 2,000 people sat on the ground or on rough log benches to hear God's Word. The meetings were held in the shade under the trees. But two large tents were also set up, just in case it rained.

While James and Ellen White and J. N. Andrews gave most of the sermons, nearly a dozen ministers were there to help encourage the believers. Some towns had just a few Seventh-day Adventists, and camp meeting was a wonderful time to visit with people who held similar beliefs. It was a chance to share experiences and learn new spiritual insights.

Info Splat

J. N. Andrews, camp meeting preacher, became the first official overseas missionary for the Seventh-day Adventist church. The widowed Andrews sailed for Europe, accompanied by his son and daughter. Later, an Adventist university was named after him.

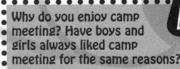

Why do you enjoy camp meeting? Have boys and girls always liked camp meeting for the same reasons?

~ Incredi-Biblical ~

Then God said, "I give you every seed-bearing plant . . . and every tree that has fruit with seed in it. They will be yours for food." Genesis 1:29.

FEED YOUR BRAIN

"Hurry! You're going to be late for school, and you won't have time for breakfast!" Mom calls, frustrated that you aren't out of bed yet.

Why is it so important to your mom that you eat breakfast? For one, she doesn't want you to distract your classmates during that class right before lunch. She knows how loud your stomach can grumble!

Your parents also know you need breakfast to refuel your body in the morning. If you split the word *breakfast* into two words, you get *break* and *fast*. Breakfast breaks the fast that you've been on for the last eight to 10 hours while you've been sleeping.

Without breakfast you can feel tired, restless, or irritable. By midmorning your mood and energy will drop, often when you need to do your hardest thinking. Plus, research shows that if you don't eat breakfast, you often eat more during the day and that often leads to gaining unwanted weight.

Info Splat

The first American breakfast in space was applesauce in a tube. Now astronauts may choose Mexican scrambled eggs, orange juice, sweet rolls, or oatmeal with brown sugar. Food approved by a shuttle dietitian goes through zero gravity testing. If it survives, it's on the menu.

Do you want to eat brainpower food? Choose whole grains, such as bread, cereal, rice, or whole-wheat pasta. You need two to two and one-half cups of grain a day. Add some fruit too, since you need to eat a total of one and one-half cups by the end of the day.

It's true that sugar provides a quick dose of energy, but it's a good idea not to overdo the sweets, because your body stores extra sugar as fat.

REACT NOW!

Do you have any eating habits you'd like to change? What kind of things keep you from eating the things you know are best?

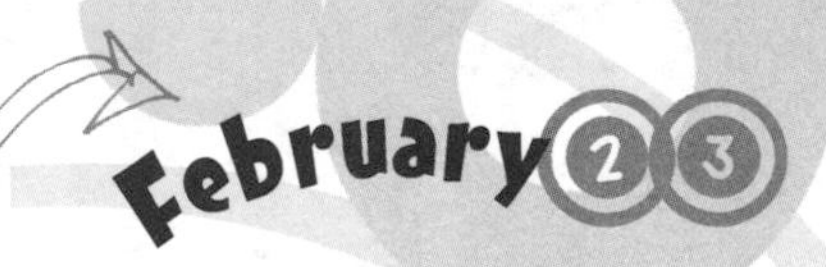

~ Incredi-Biblical ~

If we confess our sins, he is faithful and just and will forgive us our sins and purify us from all unrighteousness. 1 John 1:9.

IN A BAD MOOD

Laura arrived at her new school angry and easily upset when her classmates displeased her. Andrew annoyed her the most. At first he didn't do it on purpose, but soon Andrew began to entertain himself by provoking Laura.

Phhpt! Sitting in the back of the classroom, Andrew shot a spit wad at Laura's neck.

"Hey!" she yelped. "Cut that out!"

Laura was in an especially bad mood, and Andrew wouldn't give it up. The next time Andrew bugged her she yelled at him in class, saying cruel things about his family.

"You don't even know what you're talking about!" he angrily yelled back.

The teacher made the two stop their argument, but the fight was not over. At recess they had to stay in with their teacher while their friends joined another class outside.

For 15 minutes the two sat in angry silence. Finally Laura broke into tears.

"I'm sorry," she said. "I was being really mean. Would you forgive me? I promise I won't act like that again."

A surprised Andrew then sincerely apologized to Laura.

Andrew and Laura kept their promise. They stopped arguing. When Laura ran out of paper, Andrew quickly gave her some of his. If Andrew's pencil broke, Laura was quick to lend him one of hers. Life became much happier.

Info Splat

In one study, rats that were kept in light and dark for 12 hours each for an extended period of time became depressed and anxious. When two hours of darkness were replaced with light, the rats' attitudes improved dramatically.

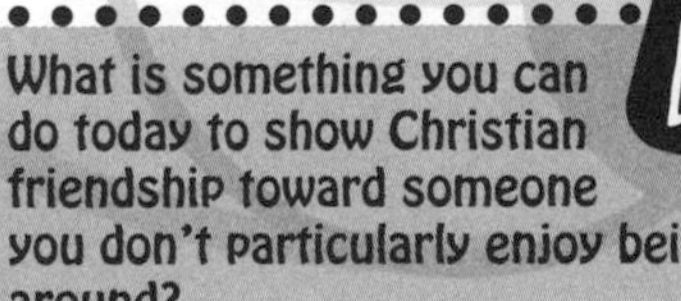

What is something you can do today to show Christian friendship toward someone you don't particularly enjoy being around?

~ Incredi-Biblical ~

Even in darkness light dawns for the upright, for the gracious and compassionate and righteous man. Psalm 112:4.

SKUNKED!

No sooner had Matt begun to drift off to sleep than he was hit with a powerfully bad odor. "What's that?" he yelled though the tent wall.

"I think Cindy just got sprayed by a skunk," Dad sighed. Matt and his brother Scott joined their parents as they crawled out of their tents. Poor Cindy! They'd never seen their golden retriever look so sad.

"Why would a skunk spray her?" Scott asked. "She was just lying there sleeping."

"I don't know," Dad said, "but we need to do something to help her." He went in search of a park ranger while Mom and the boys gathered all of their soap and shampoo. They walked Cindy down to the water hose used for filling RVs. Patiently they washed her fur. Again and again they took turns scrubbing her, rinsing her, and using more soap to lather her body.

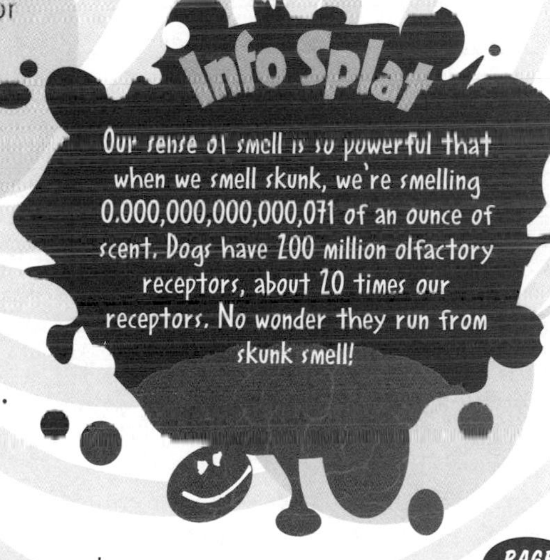

Info Splat
Our sense of smell is so powerful that when we smell skunk, we're smelling 0.000,000,000,000,071 of an ounce of scent. Dogs have 200 million olfactory receptors, about 20 times our receptors. No wonder they run from skunk smell!

"I still don't understand why the skunk sprayed Cindy," Scott moaned during a rest break. "She wasn't doing anything but sleeping."

"I don't understand it either," Mom said, still washing the dog, "but sometimes bad things happen to those who are innocent. I think tonight Cindy was the innocent one who got hurt."

Matt stroked the miserable dog's head and Cindy wagged her tail. She understood that her loved ones were trying to help her.

REACT NOW!

When have you suffered even though you did nothing wrong? What did you do that made you feel better?

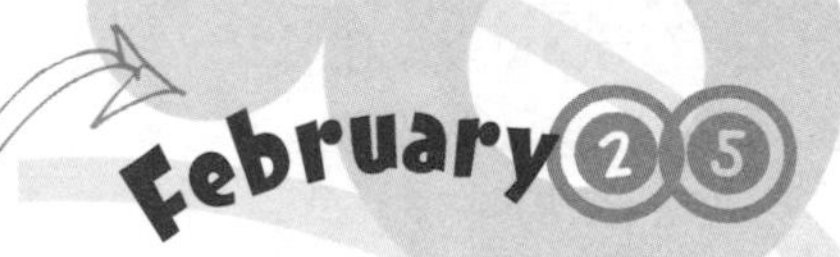

INCREDI-BIBLICAL

The fear of the Lord is the beginning of wisdom, and knowledge of the Holy One is understanding. Proverbs 9:10.

NO BIBLES!

I had my first good Bible study with my students today, Brittany typed from the school library as she e-mailed the message to her family on the other side of the world. *I was amazed at the seriousness of their questions. They are so eager to learn. But when I told them to look in their Bibles for the answers to their questions, they looked down at their desktops and grew silent.*

Brittany, after her first year of college, had answered a call to become a student missionary. She was spending the year in Micronesia, teaching a seventh-grade class.

When I asked the students what was wrong, they answered, "We're sorry, Miss; we don't have any Bibles." I let them look at mine, but I can't believe that no one has a Bible! Brittany looked away from the computer screen, remembering. *Mom,* she wrote, *would you send any extra Bibles we have at home?*

Not only did Brittany's mom do just that—she shared the story at church as well. Families gathered extra Bibles from their homes, purchased new Bibles, and paid to have the precious Word of God airmailed to a class of seventh graders searching for answers. They also sent their prayers across the ocean for the boys and girls who wanted to learn more about their Savior.

Info Splat

There are times the word ***FEAR*** in the Bible means to be in awe of the majesty, power, and position of our divine Maker. It is natural that we would show reverence toward God.

REACT NOW!

What can you do to help other people know more about Jesus? Are you reading your Bible, looking for answers to your questions?

~ INCREDI-BIBLICAL ~

I will come back and take you to be with me that you also may be where I am. John 14:3.

WHERE STARS ARE BORN

People have been looking at the stars in the night sky for as long as there have been people on earth. With the invention of the Hubble Space Telescope, we have the opportunity to see farther into deep space than ever before. Beyond the distortions of earth's atmosphere, the heavens are clearly seen.

Orion, the hunter, is an easily identified constellation in the Northern Hemisphere's winter night sky. The most recognizable three stars are in a straight line representing the hunter's belt, but another set of three stars is known as Orion's sword. The middle star in the sword is actually a great cloud of gas called a *nebula*. In this nebula, stars are born. Is it through this incredible star-filled space that Jesus will someday pass through on His way back to earth?

In one of Ellen White's first books, *Early Writings*, she shares some of what she learned about Jesus' second coming. We're told that the atmosphere will separate and that we will be able to see through the open space in Orion. We will hear the voice of God, and the Holy City will descend from that very spot.

While we don't have all the answers about Jesus' return route, we do have the promise that our Friend will soon come back for us.

Info Splat

The Orion Nebula is the largest complex of gas and dust known in the Milky Way Galaxy. When looking through the dark dust of the Orion Nebula we can see the interior is brilliantly illuminated by hot young stars.

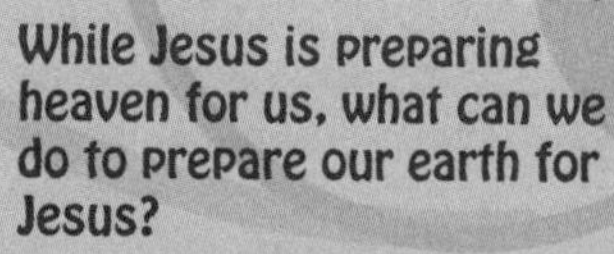

While Jesus is preparing heaven for us, what can we do to prepare our earth for Jesus?

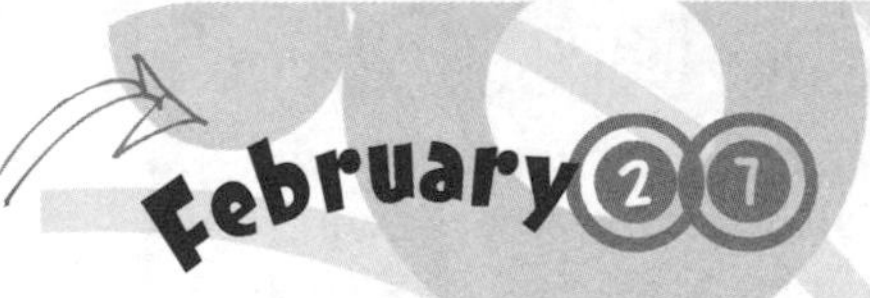

INCREDI-BIBLICAL

My mouth will speak words of wisdom; the utterance from my heart will give understanding. Psalm 49:3.

SPEAKING OF RETAINERS

Jen leaned back in the passenger seat and flipped down the car's sun visor, grinning at herself in the mirror. It was a very good day. The past two years had seemed endless, but her braces came off today! Jen smiled at herself again, then flashed another grin at her mom.

"Remember, Jen," her orthodontist had told her, "to keep your teeth straight you must wear the retainer I'm giving you for a whole year. You need to wear it all the time, except during meals.

"Oh, and one more thing," the dentist said. "Don't be surprised if it takes you about a week to get used to talking again."

Running her tongue across her teeth, Jen nodded, savoring the smooth, straight feeling.

On the way home they stopped at the library. Hurrying in, Jen quickly found the book she needed. "I need thish book for sthcool," Jen told the librarian, surprised at how strange she sounded with the retainer in her mouth. Her words came out slurred and unclear.

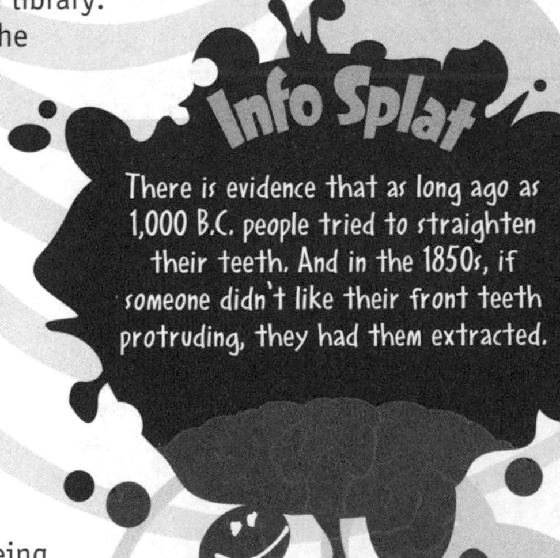

Info Splat
There is evidence that as long ago as 1,000 B.C. people tried to straighten their teeth. And in the 1850s, if someone didn't like their front teeth protruding, they had them extracted.

The librarian nodded politely, but soon Jen realized the woman was treating her like someone with mental disabilities.

There's nothing wrong with me, Jen wanted to explain, but remained silent.

One thing Jen now understood: she would treat other people normally, even when she thought they had a problem. Being treated as "special" or different wasn't very pleasant.

REACT NOW!

Can you remember a time someone misunderstood you? What would you have liked them to do differently? Did that experience change how you treat others?

~ INCREDI-BIBLICAL ~

Grace and peace to you from God our Father and the Lord Jesus Christ. Galatians 1:3.

SPREAD THE WORD!

"No way!" said Jeanna, laughing. "Have you seen this one yet?" She pointed to the *Guide* Web site where the magazine's editor jammed on his guitar. Jeanna and her friend Ryan often checked out the Web site for its cool graphics, amazing stories, and answers to their Bible questions. The Internet was one way they learned more about Jesus.

The ways people hear about God have grown over time. When Jesus was on earth, He shared the good news about His father, forgiveness, and salvation by talking to people. He walked from town to town, teaching friends along the way. Returning home, the listening people shared what they learned with their family and friends.

Paul wrote letters and traveled from city to city, starting new churches and encouraging believers in Christ. Because of Paul's work, people better understood the message of hope and love that Jesus taught. You can learn more about Paul by reading some of his letters in the New Testament.

Info Splat

When the Apostle Paul wrote a letter, he didn't address an envelope, stamp it, and put it in the mailbox. Paul handed the finished message to a trusted friend. Then the messenger walked many miles to hand-deliver the letter.

Nearly 2,000 years later, using the newly invented printing press, James and Ellen White wrote stories and articles to help others understand what the Bible taught. One of the magazines they helped create, the *Adventist Review*, is still printed today.

Now we have the World Wide Web, available in many countries, and we never have to leave the comforts of home or worry about printing costs. The Internet is a new method of telling the world about Jesus' message of love.

REACT NOW!

What do you spend your time looking at on the Internet? How can you use it to tell others about our Friend Jesus?

INCREDI-BIBLICAL

It was he who gave some to be apostles, some to be prophets, some to be evangelists, and some to be pastors and teachers. Ephesians 4:11, 12.

ELIZABETH'S GOT IT ALL

Elizabeth had a singing voice everyone loved to hear. Whenever the church needed to fill a spot for special music, Elizabeth was the first one they asked. Some church members said her voice sounded as if an angel were singing from heaven.

Elizabeth's twin sister, Monica, was proud of her sister's talent. She couldn't deny that Elizabeth had a special gift. But at the same time, it made her feel bad, because she was never asked to give special music. She was never singled out by the music teacher at school. Not only that, instead of being called Monica, she was usually referred to as "Elizabeth's sister."

"I have no special talents," Monica told her Sabbath school teacher. "Why does Elizabeth have everything?"

"She does have many special qualities," the teacher agreed, "but you probably have some that she doesn't."

"Like what?" Monica asked. "I'm not good at anything."

"God has different plans for each of us," her teacher said. "Imagine if every person on earth had a voice like Elizabeth's. Then it wouldn't really be considered a talent, would it?"

Monica shook her head. "I suppose not."

"You don't have to sing in church to serve God," her teacher explained. "You just have to do something with what talents God gave you—wherever He puts you."

Two weeks later, when Monica told the children's story in church, she knew she was using *her* gift for God's glory.

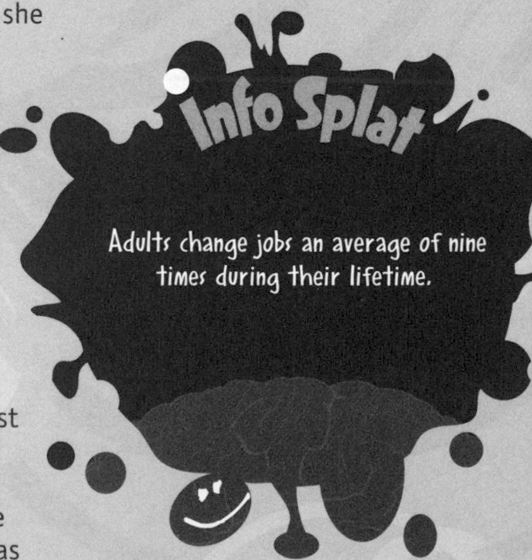

Info Splat
Adults change jobs an average of nine times during their lifetime.

REACT NOW!

Not every talent involves getting up in front of a crowd. Which of your talents can you use behind the scenes?

INCREDI-BIBLICAL

Now faith is being sure of what we hope for and certain of what we do not see. Hebrews 11:1.

WAITING FOR MOM

"See you after school, Tony!" Mom waved as she dropped him off at the entrance. Tony was starting fifth grade at a new school. He was nervous, but his mom promised she'd be there after school to pick him up. They agreed she'd wait for him by the big oak tree.

Tony's teacher helped him settle in with ease. By 3:00, he was convinced this was a good change. He ran out to the oak tree, eager to tell Mom about his day. She wasn't there yet, but he was sure she'd come soon.

He watched as his classmates left, one by one. It seemed everybody had a ride home except him. Where was Mom, anyway? As the minutes ticked away, Tony started to feel anxious. Surely Mom hadn't forgotten him, had she?

She'll be here, a voice inside Tony's head told him. *She promised.*

After a while, he felt tears stinging his eyes. He hung his head, hoping nobody had seen. When he looked up, he saw his mom's minivan. "I knew you'd come!" he exclaimed. "I thought about walking home, but since you told me to wait here I decided against it."

"I'm so glad you stayed!" Mom gasped. "I had a problem and couldn't make it on time. If you hadn't been here, I don't know what I would've done.

"Now let's go home, and you can tell me all about your first day!"

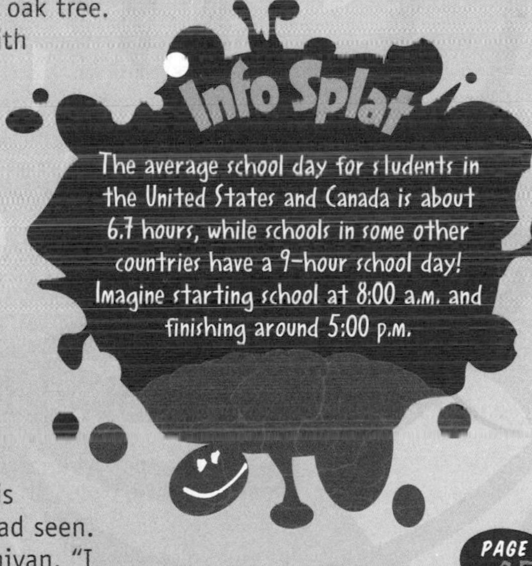

Info Splat
The average school day for students in the United States and Canada is about 6.7 hours, while schools in some other countries have a 9-hour school day! Imagine starting school at 8:00 a.m. and finishing around 5:00 p.m.

REACT NOW!
Have you ever doubted God's promises? What Bible texts can you find that tell us God will always keep His promises?

~ Incredi-Biblical ~

The highest heavens belong to the Lord, but the earth he has given to man. Psalm 115:16.

FEELING THE HEAT

Do you live in a part of the world where the temperature stays below freezing during the winter months? Some of you live in warmer climates such as in Florida, California, or Bermuda. Those who live farther north—such as Canada or the Northern U.S., for example—face much colder winters.

People living in colder climates often wish for a few extra days of sunshine and maybe a little less snow, especially when winter drags into April. In recent years, those wishes have been coming true—but that's not necessarily a good thing.

Earth is warmer than it has ever been. This may be at least in part because of pollution and waste. And while warmer weather might mean a fun day at the beach for you, it could also mean that a polar bear near the North Pole or a penguin near the South Pole is losing its feeding grounds because the ice caps are melting. It could mean the water supply for an endangered desert tortoise is drying up. Or that people can't grow certain foods because the soil is parched.

God entrusted humans with care of the earth, and we must do what we can to preserve it. Don't litter. Always recycle your newspapers and magazines, as well as water bottles and soda cans. If you can, walk or ride your bike instead of having your parents drive you somewhere. What else can you do? Visit www.epa.gov/kids to find out.

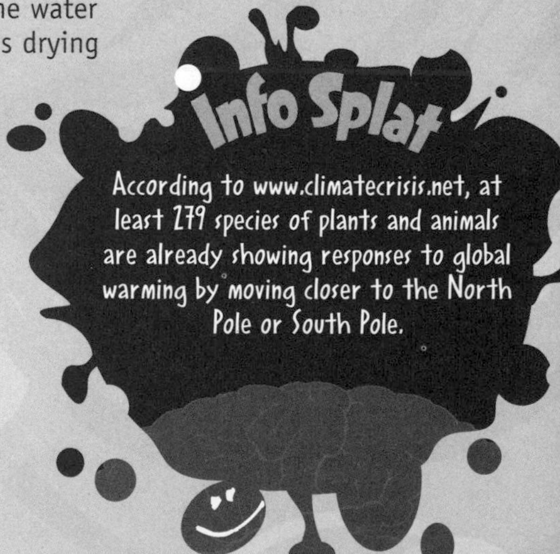

Info Splat
According to www.climatecrisis.net, at least 279 species of plants and animals are already showing responses to global warming by moving closer to the North Pole or South Pole.

REACT NOW!

Think of some small ways you can help the environment. Then get some of your friends or classmates to join you in a project.

March 4

~ INCREDI-BIBLICAL ~

God is able to make all grace abound to you, so that in all things at all times, having all that you need, you will abound in every good work. 2 Corinthians 9:8.

AMY'S NEW WISH LIST

Amy's teacher, Mr. Pedersen, asked his students to write letters to children in Guatemala, wishing them a merry Christmas and telling them a bit about what American children liked to get as presents. "They'll write back in a few weeks," Mr. Pedersen promised the class.

Amy had no problem telling her pen pal what she hoped to get for Christmas, for she'd already given it quite a lot of thought. She wrote that she was hoping to get a new bike and maybe a new CD player. But the letter she received back was quite different from what she expected.

"Dear Amy," the letter began. "Thank you for writing. I hope you also have a very happy Christmas. It is very warm in Guatemala. There is no snow. For Christmas I am hoping I can have some new pencils for school. Also I hope for some shoes for my littlest brother, and a hat for my mother to keep the sun from burning her face when she is working. These would be the best Christmas gifts. Love, your friend, Lupe."

"Is that really all she wants?" Amy asked Mr. Pedersen.

"Not all children have the luxuries we have in America," the teacher answered.

Amy's old wish list went out the window that day, and her mother was surprised when she handed her a new one with just three simple things on it: pencils, shoes for a young boy, and a woman's sun hat.

Info Splat

Water is considered a luxury in some parts of the world. In Africa, millions of people walk for two hours a day to reach a source of fresh water.

REACT NOW!

Many children in other countries struggle with basic necessities. What can you do to help them?

March 5

INCREDI-BIBLICAL

You were taught . . . to put on the new self, created to be like God in true righteousness and holiness. Ephesians 4:22, 24.

"IT'S JUST FOR FUN"

For many stores, Christmas is long gone—but not forgotten. That's because Christmas purchases account for more than 50 percent of some stores' business in an entire year! And one of the top categories of Christmas gifts is electronics.

A few years ago most kids received such toys as dolls, trucks, games, and stuffed animals. These days, a *lot* of kids ask for video games, music CDs, and movies on DVDs.

While many games, movies, and music have wholesome messages, some are packed with negative, even sinful messages. An example is a video game in which the player's goal is to steal a car or beat up someone. Is that something a Christian would do? And if not, is it a game a Christian should play?

Sometimes we think, *This kind of stuff doesn't affect me. I go to church, and I pray and read my Bible almost every day. I'm not like any of the bad characters in those games or movies. This is just for fun.* But everything you and I come in contact with affects us one way or another, no matter how small or great. We *are* changed, for better or for worse, by what we see, hear, and touch. Steady exposure to even imaginary violence will change your thoughts and guide your actions in ways you may not even recognize.

When in doubt, do without.

Info Splat
The Federal Communications Commission, which oversees television content, handed out nearly double the amount of violations in 2006 as it did 10 years ago for things like indecency and profanity.

REACT NOW!

Do you own any questionable items? If you're not sure, ask yourself: Would I play this, listen to this, or watch this if Jesus were sitting next to me?

Incredi-Biblical

You will have plenty to eat, until you are full, and you will praise the name of the Lord your God who has worked wonders for you. Joel 2:26.

WHAT'S FOR LUNCH?

Jeff cringed as he opened his lunch bag. Sure enough, it was pad thai—again! He wished that, just once, he'd open up his lunch to find some plain old macaroni and cheese, or even a peanut butter sandwich. His mom, who'd emigrated to the U.S. from Thailand before Jeff was born, loved to cook dishes from her native country. But Jeff didn't want Thai food.

We're in America! he thought. *Why can't we just eat American food?* There was something else, too. He was afraid his classmates would laugh at him for bringing the strange noodles that smelled like lemons and spices.

Maybe I can make it through the day without eating, Jeff thought. *I can say I forgot to bring my lunch*.

That's exactly what he told his teacher when she asked him why he wasn't eating.

"Well, I can't let you starve!" Miss Kusumpa said. "I'd be happy to share with you."

Jeff's eyes widened as he saw her pull out a plastic dish filled with—pad thai!

"Miss Kusumpa!" he exclaimed as he stared at his blond, blue-eyed teacher. "You're not Thai! Where'd you get this food?"

"My husband is Thai," she replied. "And God blessed me with a husband who can cook! This is one of my favorite dishes."

At that Jeff sheepishly pulled out his lunch and showed Miss Kusumpa what he'd brought. "My mom cooks for me every day," he said, "so I guess God blessed me, too!"

Info Splat

In Mexico, tacos are usually made with soft tortillas. Tacos with hard shells were actually a derivation made in the United States.

How many different types of ethnic foods have you tried? What are some of your favorites?

March 7

~ incredi-biblical ~

Do not repay evil with evil or insult with insult, but with a blessing. 1 Peter 3:9.

THE GRACE OF GEORGE WASHINGTON

Have you ever been at war with someone?

You don't need fighter jets or military strategy to be at war. You might be angry with a friend who betrayed you. Maybe you're jealous of a classmate who's more popular than you. It could be that you're not on speaking terms with some of your relatives.

Whatever the situation, you may have been at war with another person at some time in your life.

War is never a happy circumstance. You'd be hard pressed to find anyone who said they enjoyed it. Yet you'll find war after war threading all through your history books, and that includes the Revolutionary War.

Fought in the 1700s, the Revolutionary War pitted Americans against the British, who believed the American colonies belonged to them. George Washington, before he became the first U.S. president, was a commanding officer during that war. General Washington's British counterpart, William Howe, commanded the British forces. One day Washington's men brought a dog to him that they'd found wandering through their encampment. A tag on its collar indicated it was General Howe's dog.

What would you do if you found something of importance that belonged to an enemy? Would you keep it? destroy it? give it back?

Most people wouldn't willingly surrender their enemy's property, but Washington did just that. Howe may have been his tactical enemy, but Washington thought returning the dog was the right thing to do.

Info Splat

Dogs have served in the military for hundreds, perhaps thousands, of years. They are typically utilized for their strong sense of smell and intuition, which give soldiers an advantage over those who might not have a dog.

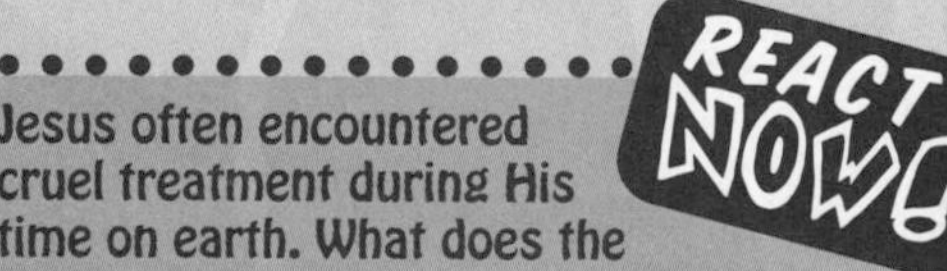

REACT NOW!

Jesus often encountered cruel treatment during His time on earth. What does the Bible say about how He responded to those who treated Him badly?

March 8

~ Incredi-Biblical ~

Do not turn away after useless idols. They can do you no good, nor can they rescue you, because they are useless.
1 Samuel 12:21.

SHAWN'S PERFECT SHOES

Every day Shawn walked to school in his tattered Payless gym shoes. When he arrived, he'd pull a box from his backpack and open the lid to reveal a beautiful, spotless pair of Air Jordans. Taking off the old shoes, he'd stuff them into his locker and carefully put on the Jordans.

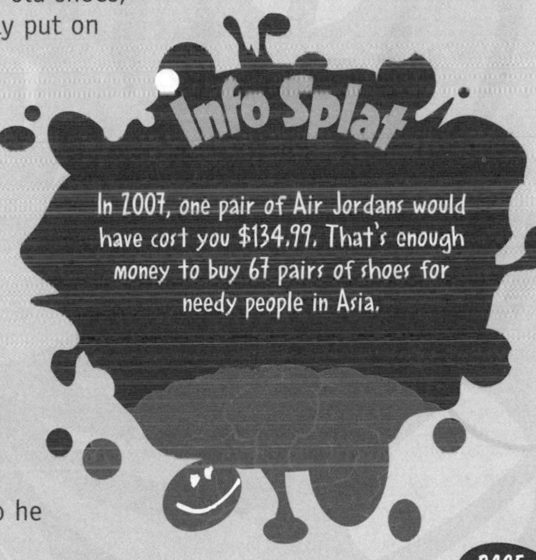

Info Splat
In 2007, one pair of Air Jordans would have cost you $134.99. That's enough money to buy 67 pairs of shoes for needy people in Asia.

At recess the Jordans would go back into their box, and the Payless shoes would come out. Shawn didn't want the Jordans to get scuffed or grass-stained. They were very expensive, and he wanted to keep them in pristine condition.

One day his class was interrupted by an unexpected fire drill. "Everybody line up on the ball field!" his teacher ordered.

Oh, no! thought Shawn. *I can't go out there in my Jordans!* He tried to come up with an excuse for first hurrying to his locker, but nothing good came to mind, so he was herded outside with the rest.

"Ouch!" he yelped as Charisa stepped on his foot.

"I'm sorry," Charisa whispered. "I didn't mean to!"

Shawn looked down at his precious Jordans and recoiled with horror. Charisa had left a large black mark on his brilliantly white shoes!

"Thanks a lot, dummy!" Shawn hissed, not caring that Charisa's eyes had filled with tears.

His shoes were spoiled that day, but it was a little girl who felt the pain.

REACT NOW!

The Bible tells us idolatry is wrong. Is there something in your life that you're wrongly putting on a pedestal? How can you change that?

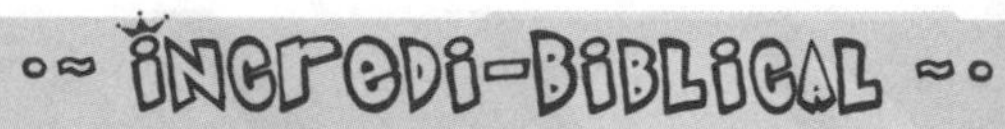

For the trumpet will sound,
and the dead will be raised.
1 Corinthians 15:52, NRSV.

GOODBYE, GRANDPA

Derek trusted the Bible, and knew that Jesus is going to return to earth to raise His faithful followers from the dead and take them to heaven with all who are saved. But that wasn't much comfort the terrible day that he sat in his grandfather's hospital room listening to the *beep-beep-beep* of the heart monitor and the whispers of the adults just outside the door.

Derek's parents were talking with the doctor about Grandpa's condition. He heard the words *organ donor* and *will* come up a few times and knew enough to know they were usually used when a person was dying. Tears filled his eyes, and he gritted his teeth.

It seemed so unfair. Why, Derek wanted to know, did kind, innocent people have to die while lots of criminals lived to an old, old age? Grandpa didn't deserve to be hit by a speeding car as he was crossing the street. *I didn't even get to say goodbye to him,* Derek thought bitterly.

He stepped over to Grandpa's bedside and carefully took his hand. It felt so fragile. Hot, salty tears ran down Derek's cheeks.

Suddenly Grandpa squeezed Derek's hand. Derek gasped.

In that moment he realized that the Holy Spirit had given him a last opportunity to connect with his grandfather, and he knew this goodbye would not be forever. He'd see Grandpa again at the resurrection. "I love you, Grandpa," he whispered.

And *Thank You, Lord,* he prayed. *I'll always look forward to Your second coming.*

Info Splat

Many cities require crossing guards near schools, parks, and other areas where kids are present. If a guard is working on a street you're trying to cross, make sure to follow their instructions.

REACT NOW!

Besides meeting Jesus, what are some of the things you're looking forward to doing when you get to heaven?

March 10

~ Incredi-Biblical ~

God said, "Let us make man in our image, in our likeness." So God created man in his own image . . . male and female he created them. Genesis 1:26, 27.

BE YOUR OWN CELEBRITY!

Have you ever picked up a gossip magazine? You know, a whole booklet of shiny pages filled with pictures of famous celebrities. Did you notice that most of the pictures are of exceptionally beautiful or handsome stars that make average people seem incredibly dull?

Some people think that to be considered beautiful, you must be totally unflawed—brilliantly white, straight teeth, perfectly groomed hair (or carefully spiked and wild), and a gorgeous figure. But how realistic is that?

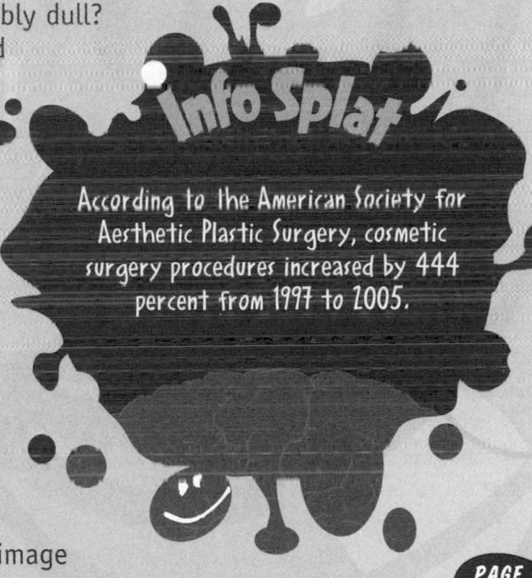

Info Splat
According to the American Society for Aesthetic Plastic Surgery, cosmetic surgery procedures increased by 444 percent from 1997 to 2005.

It's not. But regular people can suffer from the pressure to be perfect, especially when they compare themselves to models and movie stars who spend thousands of dollars on expensive treatments, cosmetic potions—even plastic surgery. Some people become obsessed with perfection, and have made themselves sick or even destroyed their bodies while trying to remake themselves into the image of their favorite star. Tragically, people have even died because they went to such extremes to look perfect.

Don't waste your time comparing yourself to celebrities. They're no more perfect than you or me. They just waste money trying to change it or cover it up. Of course, few admit that. Most they want their fans to think they're simply genetically blessed. (By the way, have you ever heard of Photoshop?)

The truth is that each of us is genetically blessed. Why? Because, as the Bible tells us, God created us in His own image. That's right—you're the spitting image of God! How much more perfect can you get?

Is there anyone besides God whose image you would rather have been molded after? Why?

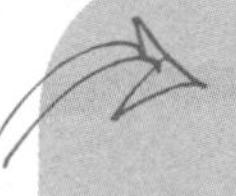

March 11

Incredi-Biblical

All that the Father gives me will come to me, and whoever comes to me I will never drive away. John 6:37.

WHY MR. WONG WAS MAD

Aaron had never seen Mr. Wong so angry.

Aaron's seventh-grade class was in the middle of a Bible lesson, reading the book of Romans when, with a puzzled look on her face, Shabina asked, "Who is Paul?"

Vanessa and some of the other girls sitting nearby started giggling. "*Duh!* Everybody knows who Paul is!" Vanessa chortled. "Haven't you been paying attention at all? Didn't you ever go to Sabbath school?"

More snickers rippled throughout the room. Shabina turned bright red.

Mr. Wong, who had been at the dry-erase board, slammed down the pen he'd been holding. He surveyed the students through narrowed eyes. Aaron almost thought he saw steam coming out of his ears!

Then Mr. Wong told Vanessa and the others who'd laughed at Shabina to stay seated. Everyone else was asked to leave the room.

As the students waited outside, Aaron saw that Shabina had wandered down the corridor. Her back was turned to her classmates. Aaron walked over to her. "Hey," he mumbled, "you really don't know who Paul is?"

Shabina didn't look up, but she shook her head. "My family is not Christian," she answered. "I have never studied this before."

Suddenly Aaron realized why Mr. Wong was angry. How would Shabina ever learn about the love of Jesus if she was mocked by the people who claimed to be His followers?

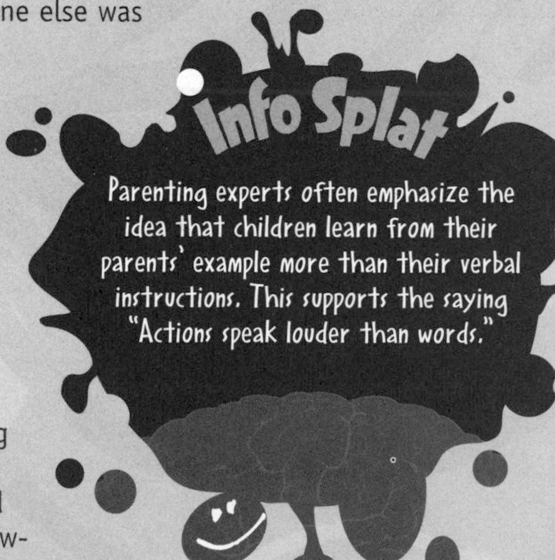

Info Splat
Parenting experts often emphasize the idea that children learn from their parents' example more than their verbal instructions. This supports the saying "Actions speak louder than words."

REACT NOW!

Do you know someone who needs to know about Jesus? What are some ways you and others can share Jesus' love with them?

March 12

~ Incredi-Biblical ~

Do you not know that your body is a temple of the Holy Spirit, who is in you, whom you have received from God?
1 Corinthians 6:19.

LOOKING GOOD!

Americans seems to feel pressured to look more attractive. Do you sometimes worry what your classmates and friends think about how you look?

Body image (how you view your physical traits) plays a major part in how many kids, in both America and around the world, feel about themselves. Having a good body image usually means you'll be happier and healthier, whereas having a negative body image usually means . . . well, you get the picture.

Take this quiz to see if you might have a body image problem.

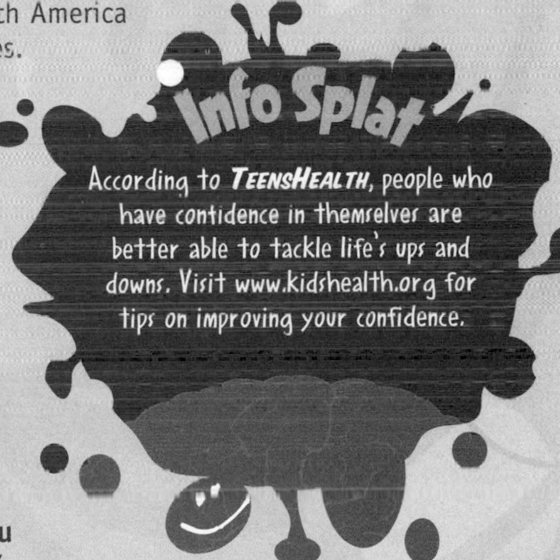

Info Splat
According to TEENSHEALTH, people who have confidence in themselves are better able to tackle life's ups and downs. Visit www.kidshealth.org for tips on improving your confidence.

1. How long do you take to get ready for school in the morning?
- a. Fewer than 15 minutes.
- b. About 30 minutes.
- c. An hour or more.

2. How would you feel if a friend saw you first thing in the morning, before you've brushed your teeth or combed your hair?
- a. Who cares? It wouldn't be the first time, and it won't be the last.
- b. I might feel embarrassed, but I'd find a way to joke about it.
- c. I'd be mortified!

3. What's the worst part about going camping?
- a. The bears and mountain lions!
- b. Sleeping on the ground is sooo uncomfortable.
- c. No showers? Forget it!

Did you choose mostly A's? You're doing great! Mostly B's? So far so good, but remember to stay focused on positive thoughts. If you chose mostly C's, you might have a troubled body image and should consider confiding in an adult you trust.

REACT NOW!

A positive body image comes from knowing that you are taking good care of your body and keeping it healthy. What things can you do to keep your body healthy?

INCREDI-BIBLICAL

Bring the best of the firstfruits . . . to the house of the Lord your God. Exodus 23:19.

FIRST THINGS FIRST

David was looking forward to his baseball team's annual trip to the county fair. Each year the players and parents caravanned to the fairgrounds and spent an afternoon looking at exhibits, going on rides, eating stuff such as corn on the cob and cotton candy, and playing games. This year would be special because David was 12 years old—old enough to explore without the adults.

On the day of the trip David's father gave him a $20 bill. It was payment for the times David had mowed the lawn over the past few weeks. David already had plans for how to spend his money at the fair.

He and his friends looked at exhibits, wandered the midway, rode the Spinout, played darts, and ate popcorn and sugary elephant ears. As the day was winding down, one of David's friends spotted one last adventure. "Hey! Let's go in the funhouse!" he called.

"Cool!" David exclaimed. He dug into his pocket, but he found he had only two one-dollar bills left.

"Uh-oh," he said. "Guys, I can't go. I have only $2 left. You go on without me."

"But the funhouse is only $2," his friend said. "You have just enough!"

David shook his head. He didn't have enough to pay the funhouse attendant and God, too. He knew he owed 10 percent of the $20 Dad gave him to God.

"It's OK," he told his friends. "I'll wait here."

He was sure the funhouse wouldn't be much fun if he spent his tithe to get in.

Info Splat

Tithe paid to the Seventh-day Adventist Church goes to support the General Conference budget. Offerings generally pay for other church needs.

Think of some ways you can make a habit of setting aside tithe so you're not tempted to spend it.

Incredi-Biblical

[Daniel said,] "Give us nothing but vegetables to eat and water to drink." . . . At the end of the 10 days they looked healthier and better nourished than any of the young men who ate the royal food. Daniel 1:12-15.

THE KELLOGGS' NEW FOOD

"Ugh," John said after breakfast. "I feel like I'm oozing with fat."

"I agree." John's brother, Will, pushed his chair back from the table. "What can we do about it?" They were troubled by the typical American breakfast in the late 1890s—heavy, unhealthy foods such as fried bacon, biscuits drenched with fatty gravy, and pastries full of sugar and sodium.

The brothers had grown up in a Seventh-day Adventist family with parents who taught them the basics of healthy living. And that included a diet filled with wholesome fruits, vegetables, and whole grains. Determined to bring healthier food to the breakfast table, they set out to develop a unique product and sell it in stores.

Info Splat

Nutrition experts say breakfast is the most important meal of the day, and yet a majority of people skip it.

Their product turned out to be the first mass produced, ready to eat breakfast cereal. It hit stores in 1906 and revolutionized the way Americans planned their breakfasts. The brothers claimed their corn-based cereal was a better, lighter alternative to the fatty meals many people ate to start their day. The cereal was hugely successful, and you can still find it at grocery stores today. Maybe you've heard of it, or perhaps eaten it: Kellogg's Corn Flakes.

With a little innovation and a lot of inspiration, John and Will were able to spread their message of a healthier lifestyle. Their work continues with the company Will started in Michigan in the early 1900s, the Kellogg Company, which still makes cereals and a whole lot of other products, too.

What do you usually have for breakfast? Is there anything that would make it more nutritious?

March 15

~ INCREDI-BIBLICAL ~

Whoever slanders his neighbor in secret, him will I put to silence; whoever has haughty eyes and a proud heart, him I will not endure. Psalm 101:5.

TONGUES OUT OF CONTROL

"Did you hear that Kristy took money out of Mr. Thurson's desk?" Amanda asked Holly.

Holly gasped. "Who told you that?" she asked.

"I just heard it around," Amanda said. "Everybody's talking about it."

Holly frowned. "How do you know it's true?"

"I heard John and Ray talking. They said they saw her do it."

"Wow!" Holly whispered. "That's horrible!"

During lunch Holly passed the news on to Jackie. "Did you know that Kristy stole money from Mr. Thurson?" she whispered.

"No!" Jackie squealed. "Is she in trouble?"

Holly shrugged. Then, out of the corner of her eye, she saw the school principal watching her. She quickly finished her lunch and got up from the table. Later, when the students were changing classes, Holly saw Kristy following the principal to his office. Holly bit her lip. So it was true.

The next day, after morning worship, Mr. Thurson made an announcement. "Some rumors have been flying around about a person taking money from my desk," he said. "I'd like to put those rumors to rest, as they are untrue."

Holly quickly turned around to look at Amanda, but she looked away, avoiding Holly's gaze.

"You see, I don't keep money in my desk," Mr. Thurson continued. "So I hope this gossip stops right now."

Holly was so ashamed. She couldn't believe she'd condemned someone before finding out the truth.

Info Splat

A study at Knox College in Illinois found that most people gossip as a means of gaining status in social groups.

REACT NOW!

Have you ever gossiped about someone? Be cautious: Once you say something about another person, you can never take it back.

~ INCREDI-BIBLICAL ~

"For I know the plans I have for you," declares the Lord, "plans to prosper you and not to harm you, plans to give you hope and a future." Jeremiah 29:11.

NO MORE LUCK

Cynthia's behavior had been troubling her mother for several days. She seemed nervous and jumpy, unusual for the carefree girl who loved to laugh and was curious about everything. Mom got to the bottom of the mystery when she found Cynthia frantically rummaging under her bed.

"I lost my lucky four-leaf-clover key chain!" Cynthia wailed. "Tomorrow is St. Patrick's Day, and I'm supposed to give my speech in front of the whole class, and I can't do it without my key chain."

Mother pulled her daughter close to her. "Honey, you don't really believe that, do you?"

Cynthia rolled her eyes. "Mom, how else can you explain why I always have better luck when I have my key chain with me? It's obvious, isn't it?"

"It's a bunch of superstition," Mother explained. "Some people believe the universe is made of good luck and bad luck, but we know that's not true, because we know Jesus. The Bible tells us that He has control over everything, and that He knows everything about us. We don't need to listen to superstition, because we can trust Jesus to always do what's best for us.

"And I'm sure that being well prepared for your speech and saying a prayer before you give it will beat any old key chain any day."

"OK, then!" Cynthia exclaimed. "Let's pray right now."

Info Splat

Many professional athletes are so superstitious that they'll sometimes go for days or weeks—even months—without washing a particular item of clothing (such as socks). You wouldn't want to be near someone wearing such smelly things!

REACT NOW!

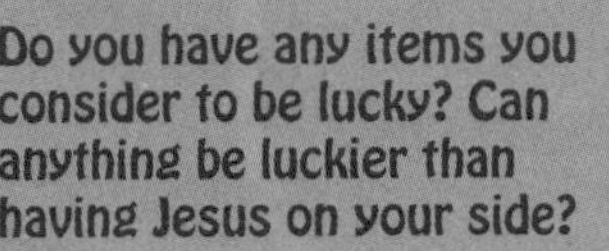

Do you have any items you consider to be lucky? Can anything be luckier than having Jesus on your side?

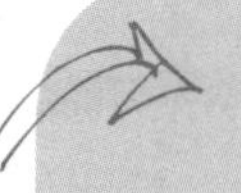

March 17

∘~ INCREDI-BIBLICAL ~∘

Greater love has no one than this, that one lay down his life for his friends. John 15:13.

MR. KIM GAVE EVERYTHING

Father of the year.

That's what some people were calling James Kim.

James, his wife, Kati, and their two young daughters had set off on a road trip during Thanksgiving 2006. They left Oregon, planning to drive south to their home in northern California. But when the Kims didn't show up, family, friends, and coworkers got worried. Days passed as an intense search continued. But there was no word and no clue as to what had happened. At last Katie and the girls were found on an Oregon mountain road. Taking a shortcut, the family was stopped by snow and storm, with very little food or necessities.

The harsh weather made it difficult for them to hang on. The temperature was below freezing, and they had no way to keep warm. They survived for more than a week on crackers and baby food, which they'd brought for their 4-year-old and 7-month-old. Sadly, James died in the wilderness after leaving their car to search for help.

The rescue team that found James's body determined that he had walked for miles, wading through frigid rivers and hiking through deep snow. He suffered from severe hypothermia—when your body temperature dips below normal—and hadn't had a good meal in two weeks. But he forged on, searching for a miracle.

James left clues for the rescuers he hoped were looking for them, and that's what saved his family.

Can you think of someone who died to save you? Of course you can.

Info Splat

According to the Mayo Clinic in Rochester, Minnesota, more than 700 people in North America die from hypothermia each year. Always take precautions when out in the cold.

REACT NOW!

People who have put their lives at risk to help others are often called heroes. How does Jesus fit the label of a hero?

INCREDI-BIBLICAL

For I was hungry and you gave me something to eat, I was thirsty and you gave me something to drink. Matthew 25:35.

BE A STAY-AT-HOME MISSIONARY

In many different sources you will see shocking photos of poor people who are starving and struggling to survive. You've probably seen some of the images—a malnourished child, his ribs sharp as slats through his skin; an elderly woman lying on a mat all day because she doesn't have the energy to get up. While it might be hard to understand the reasons these people have so little, it's not hard to see that they're suffering.

Info Splat
In some poorer countries, many families must live on about $2 a day.

But what can a kid do to help?

I don't have a job, you might say. *I don't have money to buy food for millions of people. Even if I could, how would I get it there?*

You don't have to try to help millions of people. But you can help one. Maybe two. Maybe a few. And there is a way to get help to where it needs to go.

An organization called the Adventist Development and Relief Agency works to help people around the world. But ADRA can't do it alone. It needs donations from people who care and want to help, even in a small way. Some projects, such as providing a hot meal to an elderly person in Asia, cost as little as 25 cents.

Can you spare 25 cents or more to help people in need? If so, ADRA could use your help. Visit www.adra.org and click on The Original Really Useful Gift Catalog.

REACT NOW!

Read 2 Corinthians 8:13-15. What does it say about our responsibility to help people in need?

March 19

~ Incredi-Biblical ~

**Fear not, for I have redeemed you;
I have called you by name; you are mine.
Isaiah 43:1.**

CAMERON'S TOO-LATE RESCUE

Cameron winced as P.J. fell to the ground while the other kids laughed and gave high-fives. When P.J. tried to get up and was shoved down again, Cameron turned away. He didn't want to watch.

He knew he should stand up for his friend. He knew he should tell those other kids to leave P.J. alone, but he couldn't bring himself to march over and confront Anthony—the biggest, meanest kid in the sixth grade. Cameron was afraid Anthony would bully him instead.

Finally, the crowd let P.J. get away. As he headed for the lockers, Cameron sidled up to him. "Hey, man, you doing all right?" he asked.

P.J., his face red and tear-streaked, looked the other way.

"They didn't hurt you, did they?" Cameron persisted.

P.J. kept his back toward Cameron as he opened his locker and grabbed his history book. That made Cameron mad. "Fine! Ignore me if you want," he hissed. "I was only trying to see if you're OK."

P.J. whirled around so suddenly that Cameron jumped back. "Trying to look out for me, are you? Looking out for my best interests?" he growled. "Yeah, you really proved that out on the field!" He slammed his locker shut and headed to class.

Cameron felt a lump rising in his throat. He wished he could have helped his friend, but Anthony was such a mean guy. What could he have done?

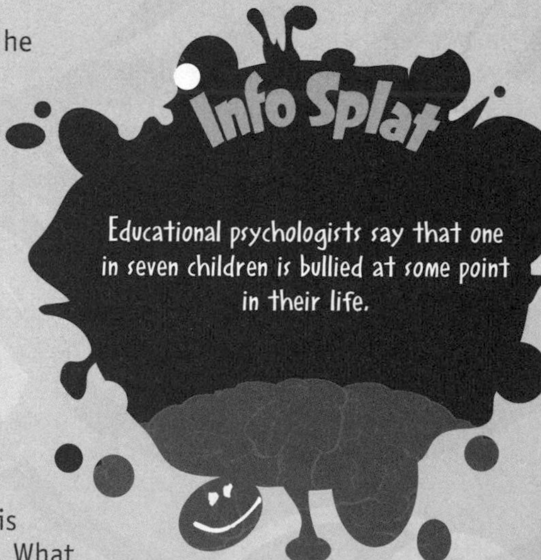

Info Splat
Educational psychologists say that one in seven children is bullied at some point in their life.

REACT NOW!

Have you ever been the victim of bullying or seen someone else get bullied? What are some ways to diffuse that type of situation?

INCREDI-BIBLICAL

Finally, all of you, live in harmony with one another; be sympathetic, love as brothers, be compassionate and humble.
1 Peter 3:8.

BULLIES IN DISGUISE

Bullying is a serious issue, not only for school-age kids, but for adults as well. Bullying can make people feel depressed, worthless, and even suicidal. It should never be an accepted form of teasing.

Do you know what types of behavior qualify as bullying? Read the following scenarios and decide whether they are examples of bullying.

1. Laughing at the clothes a kid wears to school because they're not "in."
2. Encouraging others to ignore a kid so they'll end up a loner.
3. Spreading rumors about someone, whether or not you know the information is true—or even if it *is* true.
4. Always leaving the same classmate for last when choosing teams on the playground.
5. Getting up to leave when a certain person sits down at the lunch table.
6. Watching someone being insulted or picked on, and not trying to make the insults stop.
7. Telling your friends that if they socialize with a particular person, you won't be their friends anymore.
8. Using names such as "nerd," "pizza face," or "fatso" to refer to anyone.

Info Splat

Even adults face bullying. A 2007 study published in the ***Journal of Management Studies*** showed that 30 percent of adults faced bullying at their workplace. For more information on how to recognize and stop bullying, go to www.stopbullyingnow.hrsa.gov.

As you probably figured, all eight scenarios are examples of bullying and should never be used. If you're the victim of bullying—or if you recognize your behavior as that of a bully—get help from a trusted adult.

REACT NOW!

Do you know a bully, or are you a bully? Why do some people get joy out of hurting others? What does it say about them?

~ INCREDI-BIBLICAL ~

Long life to you! Good health to you and your household! And good health to all that is yours! 1 Samuel 25:6.

HEALTHY HISTORY

When the Seventh-day Adventist Church was just beginning, one of the church founders, Ellen G. White, had a vision that inspired her to stress changes in the way people usually ate and lived, and to make healthful living a vital part of the church's mission.

Back then, most people didn't give much thought to their health. The things we know now—that fresh air, clean water, personal hygiene, a nutritious diet, and plenty of exercise are necessary for good health—weren't common knowledge to people living in the nineteenth and early twentieth centuries. Many people worked endless hours, ate poor diets filled with animal fat, often kept their homes dark and airless, and didn't wash on a regular basis—and then couldn't understand why they always felt tired, sick, and depressed.

Ellen White knew that in order for people to fully do God's work, they needed to be strong and vibrantly healthy, so she began promoting better living by preaching and writing about it. Her efforts inspired the church leaders to open a medical institute dedicated to teaching principles of healthful living. It was called the Western Health Reform Institute.

Mrs. White also helped to establish other Adventist hospitals, including Paradise Valley Hospital and Loma Linda University Medical Center, both in California.

Today there are many Adventist hospitals across the world, and each helps to spread the message Mrs. White spoke of so many years ago.

Info Splat

As of 2007 the number one cause of death in North America is heart disease—often the result of a poor diet and inactive lifestyle.

REACT NOW!

What are some things you can do to stay as healthy as possible? Think of three things and try to follow them daily.

March 22

Incredi-Biblical

So the last will be first and the first will be last. Matthew 20:16.

HEAVENLY FASHION

Tyra hid a secret that not even her best friends suspected. Tyra's family was poor. Most of her clothes came from thrift shops. She couldn't remember the last time she'd had something brand-new. Her mom worked two jobs to make ends meet, and there was no room for luxuries.

Each year, after Christmas vacation, Tyra's classmates had lots of fun talking about the gifts they'd received. Tyra always found a way to avoid the question, and sometimes she even made something up. "Oh, I got the most awesome blouse," she once said. "But it's much too flashy to wear to school." She felt ashamed when she said that. She felt like a nobody.

Have you ever had an experience like Tyra's? Or perhaps you know someone who has.

In today's world some people place a great emphasis on what we wear, how we look, and the things we have. It can be difficult to fit in at school if you don't have the latest gear and gadgets. But as hard as it can be, remember that there is Someone who doesn't care what stuff you own. Jesus Himself didn't even have a house to live in! He wandered the streets of Judea and Galilee as a man without a home, and lived with help from others. He didn't mind, though, because He knew that in heaven material possessions don't matter.

It may be hard to convince yourself that new clothes and things don't matter, but Jesus does.

Info Splat

Economic studies have shown that the 10- to 14-year-old age group is the demographic that advertisers are most interested in, because preteens hold a great deal of influence over buying trends.

REACT NOW!

Many of the happiest people don't have a lot of money or fancy things. How can we learn to be happy with what we have?

March 23

INCREDI-BIBLICAL

A new command I give you: Love one another. . . . All men will know that you are my disciples, if you love one another. John 13:34, 35.

THE NEW GIRL

"Dad?" Sam asked as she joined her father on the couch. "Why do some people think it's bad to be Black?"

Sam's father peered over the newspaper he was reading and studied his daughter's puzzled expression. "What gave you that idea?" he asked.

"Well, there's this new girl in my class, and some of the kids are making fun of her," Sam explained. "A couple of them said she's ugly or weird."

"What do you think?" Dad asked.

"She seems OK to me. I guess I don't see what the problem is." Sam paused, thinking. "I've talked to her, and she seems real nice. I'd like to be friends with her."

Dad put down his newspaper and wrapped his arm around Sam. "Some people don't like anyone who looks different from them," he began. "They may even have a lot in common with them, but still make judgments based on the way the person looks."

"But why?"

"That's a good question," he said, "but I don't have a very good answer. People—even grown-ups—can be very unfair. I guess the only explanation is that Satan has poisoned their minds. Do you think God cares what color a person's skin is?"

"Of course not!" Sam exclaimed. "God made everyone."

Her father smiled. "Then we shouldn't either."

Info Splat

In 1791 a brilliant African-American, Benjamin Banneker, was hired to help survey the boundary lines for what would become the city of Washington, D.C. Ironically, it would take until 1965 for African-Americans to be fully assured that their votes would count in elections.

REACT NOW!

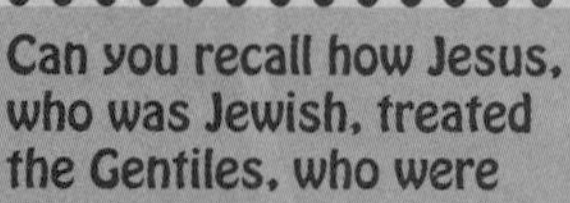

Can you recall how Jesus, who was Jewish, treated the Gentiles, who were despised by most Jewish people? What can we learn from Jesus' example?

March 24

INCREDI-BIBLICAL

Let us acknowledge the Lord. . . . As surely as the sun rises, he will appear; he will come to us like the winter rains, like the spring rains that water the earth.
Hosea 6:3.

IT'S HAPPENING AGAIN!

Springtime is always a wonderful time of year, especially if you live in an area in which winter means snow, ice, and plenty of gray days. In those areas spring is especially welcome because it means the return of green leaves on the trees, the budding of flowers, and wildlife emerging with newly born babies.

Winter officially begins in late December. (Of course, in Canada and some northern states, cold weather comes a lot earlier!) Autumn is when the world prepares for winter's harshness: leaves turn brown and fall off trees, animals settle in to hibernate, and the weather slowly gets colder and colder. By the time winter is in full swing, everything seems, well, dead.

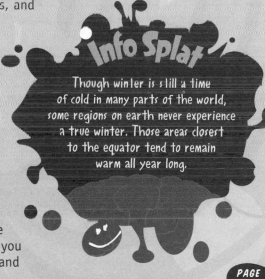

But just as winter puts the world in a period of bleakness, so spring brings life, color, and optimism. You can count on the winter doldrums to arrive every year—but you also can count on spring to revive nature and everything in it.

This pattern is no accident. Winter is a resting period, but spring is always just around the corner. And there is always rebirth in nature: When the geese return from the south, when the robin's nest is full of babies, when the tulips bloom, and the grass is finally green again, we can be sure these are God's gifts to us, reminding us that winter is never forever.

Info Splat

Though winter is still a time of cold in many parts of the world, some regions on earth never experience a true winter. Those areas closest to the equator tend to remain warm all year long.

What is your favorite season? Why do you think God created seasons on earth?

March 25

~ INCREDI-BIBLICAL ~

You are to name him Jesus, for he will save his people from their sins. Matthew 1:21, NRSV.

AN UNFORGETTABLE MISSIONARY

A man was given the opportunity to become a missionary. He had done many good works for God before, but this was the first time he'd been asked to travel to a new region. He was worried about its native people, for they had a reputation of being cold and unmerciful. If they didn't like you, they'd drive you out of their land. He knew that if he traveled to this area, his life would be in danger. But he also knew he was the only one for the job, so he agreed to minister to the people there.

When he first arrived, no one paid him any attention. There was no reason to. He was nobody to them. But he'd come to them on a mission for God, and he was determined that they would hear his message. He prayed often for guidance and wisdom and the power to do great miracles in God's name.

Soon the man had many followers. They were amazed at the truth in the words he preached. They felt hope after hearing his sermons. He made them believe in goodness again.

But many of the nationals were not impressed with him. In fact, some thought he was a madman and demanded that he stop preaching and leave. When he remained, they came up with a plan: they ambushed him, kidnapped him—and murdered him.

Perhaps you've heard of this missionary before. His name is Jesus.

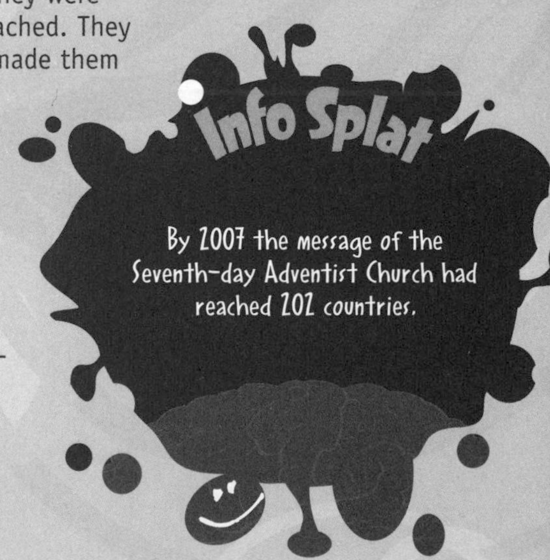

Info Splat
By 2007 the message of the Seventh-day Adventist Church had reached 202 countries.

REACT NOW!

Jesus came to earth to do missionary work. What was His mission, and was it accomplished?

March 26

~ Incredi-Biblical ~

Choose for yourselves this day whom you will serve. . . . But as for me and my household, we will serve the Lord. Joshua 24:15.

HAYLEY'S CHOICE

Hayley was Beat Club's number one fan. She had Beat Club T-shirts, notebooks, and all their MP3s on her iPod. If there was an item out there with Beat Club on it, Hayley owned it.

So it was a dream come true when the local radio station announced that the band would give a concert in her hometown. Her parents had agreed to let her go, and she dutifully saved every penny she earned from babysitting so she could buy the best seats possible.

Info Splat
According to a Princeton University economist, from 2001 to 2006 the average price of a concert ticket rose 61 percent.

But Hayley was crestfallen when Beat Club announced the concert date—a Friday night! She was torn. This was the only date the band would be in town. Surely God would understand if she purposely broke the Sabbath just once and promised never to break it again. Wouldn't He?

If only her parents would tell her what to do, but for once they left the decision up to her. She agonized. This might be her only chance to see Beat Club in person. At last she made a decision, and as soon as tickets went on sale, she bought one for herself and one for her friend Madison.

When the night of the concert arrived, Hayley felt more miserable than she had in her entire life. Immediately after Madison's dad dropped them off at the concert, she knew she'd made a terrible mistake.

What good was it to see Beat Club if all she felt was regret?

INCREDI-BIBLICAL

I am going there to prepare a place for you. And . . . I will come back and take you to be with me that you also may be where I am. John 14:2, 3.

MOVING ON

Michelle felt the familiar itch in her nose and the sting in her eyes as she opened a box filled with photo albums and placed them on her bookshelf. She fought the urge to cry, but the tears flowed anyway. Her family had moved from the big city of Chicago to rural Texas. Chicago was lively! There was always something going on, and it was the only home Michelle had ever known. Texas was mellow, and the people so very different. Michelle wasn't sure she'd ever fit in.

Her parents said it would take time to adjust, but insisted she'd have plenty of new friends in no time. Big sister Heidi was more blunt. "Texas is boring," she said.

Michelle secretly agreed. How could such a foreign place ever feel like home? She'd met a couple of girls her age, but they talked with a drawl, dressed different from the kids in Chicago, and made weird jokes. She felt like an alien visiting another planet.

Have you ever felt the same? Not about your particular hometown. Most of us eventually adjust to a new place and make good friends. But about living in the world in general?

The world can be a difficult place for Christians. That's because earth isn't really our home. Sure, it's a temporary place to live, but Jesus promises we won't be here forever. If you feel as though you don't fit in because you're different, well, there's a reason. It's because you *are* different.

And when the time is right, Jesus will come back to take us to our true home: heaven.

Info Splat

The busiest months of the year for moving companies are June and July. That's because most families wait until their children are out of school for the summer before making a move.

REACT NOW!

Have you ever gone through a big move? Imagine how Jesus must have felt when He moved from heaven to earth!

March 28

~ Incredi-Biblical ~

"In the last days," God says, "I will pour out my spirit on all the people."
Acts 2:17.

FIGHT FOR WHAT'S RIGHT

As you've studied American history in school you learned that the first settlers of the New World left their homeland in search of religious freedom because they were being persecuted in Europe for their religious beliefs. But that was hundreds of years ago. Surely with modern thinking and ideals, no one would have trouble with religious freedoms today—right?

Not exactly. While many religious customs in America are still protected by law, some have been threatened. For example, prayer in public places is sometimes questioned, and lately "a moment of silence" has been the preference. Recently displays of the Ten Commandments in courthouses and other government buildings prompted the U.S. Supreme Court to make a ruling that in many cases those types of displays are unconstitutional and cannot be allowed.

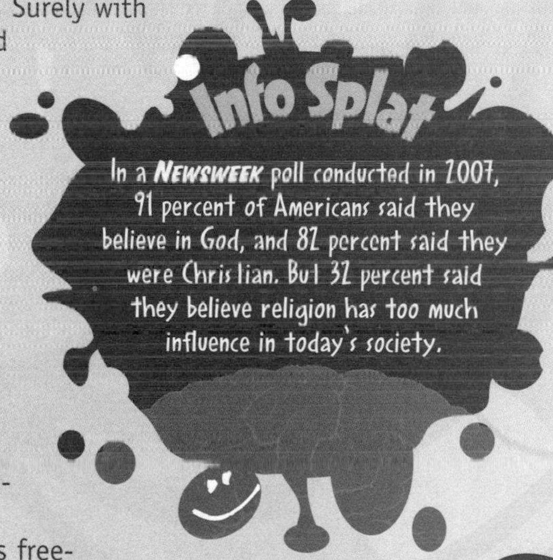

Info Splat
In a *Newsweek* poll conducted in 2007, 91 percent of Americans said they believe in God, and 82 percent said they were Christian. But 32 percent said they believe religion has too much influence in today's society.

And in some other countries, religious freedom is not a right. Many Christians have been persecuted for their beliefs.

The Bible tells us that in the days before Jesus comes again, Christians will be faced with opposition and will have to choose between giving in to pressure and living a life of ease or standing up for Christ and accepting the hardships that will come along with that. But in the end we know that those who choose Jesus will gain eternal life.

Which will you choose?

REACT NOW!

Have you ever felt peer pressure to pretend you're not a Christian? How did you handle the situation? How could you handle it in the future?

March 29

INCREDI-BIBLICAL

No discipline seems pleasant at the time, but painful. Later on . . . it produces a harvest of righteousness and peace. Hebrews 12:11.

WATCH OUT, GINGER!

Maya was superexcited about the pet she'd adopted from the local Humane Society. Ginger, a dwarf hamster, had pretty tan-and-white markings and beady black eyes. She was friendly and curious, too. Maya had fallen in love with her. When she brought Ginger home, she put her cage on a high shelf so Rusty, the family cat, wouldn't be tempted to make her a meal. But Ginger constantly tried to break out of the cage. Maya knew that if Ginger ever got out she was sure to become Rusty's breakfast.

"Why is Ginger always trying to get out?" Maya asked her mom. "Doesn't she know it's unsafe?"

"Well, Ginger is not so different from people," Mom explained. She was at the sink, finishing the supper cleanup. "Like Ginger, we're always trying to do things that aren't good for us. Of course, she doesn't know how dangerous it would be to escape her cage, and we don't always know—or even understand—the danger of sin."

Mom gave Maya a handful of clean cutlery, and Maya put it in a drawer. "Fortunately, we have a heavenly Father who protects us from danger," she reminded her daughter. "Just as you protect Ginger."

Maya nodded. "Yeah, sometimes, when we don't get what we want, we think God isn't listening to us. But maybe He's just doing what's best."

"You're right," Mom agreed. "And it's the same with parents and their kids. We look out for your best interests too." She smiled. "So don't you think it's time for you to clean your room?"

"Aww, Mom!" Maya exclaimed with a twinkle in her eye.

Info Splat

Humane Society adoption centers don't just offer cats and dogs for adoption. You can also find turtles, birds, and even barn animals that need loving homes.

REACT NOW!

Ask your mom or dad to give you an example of something they wanted, didn't get, and later realized was for the best.

March 30

~ INCREDI-BIBLICAL ~

The Lord has heard my cry for mercy; the Lord accepts my prayer.
Psalm 6:9.

PRAYING FOR MARY

Jenny had a prayer request.

Each night when her family had worship together they always finished with prayer. This night Jenny asked her family to pray for her friend Mary.

"Today when Mary and I were walking home from school she told me she'd prayed for her dad to get this new job he'd applied for," Jenny said. "Mary said that he really needed it. She told me, 'I don't normally pray, but I thought I should this time.' I felt so bad for her when I heard that."

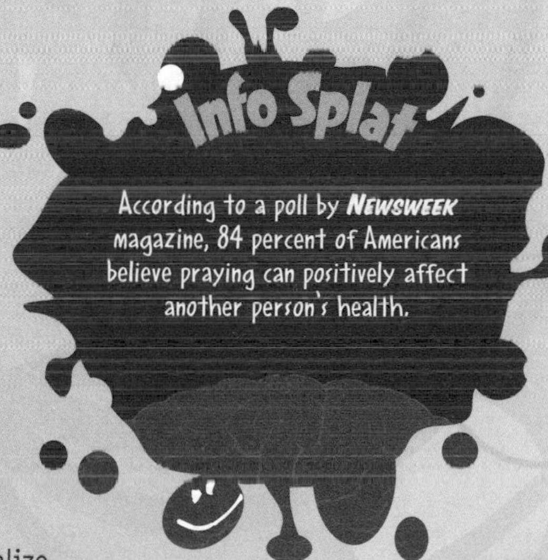

Info Splat
According to a poll by NEWSWEEK magazine, 84 percent of Americans believe praying can positively affect another person's health.

"You felt bad for her at that?" Jenny's mother asked. "Why?"

Jenny sighed. "Well, I thought how sad it is that Mary doesn't pray every day. She doesn't have the comfort of knowing that God is always with her, and that she can ask Him anything."

Mom nodded. "A lot of people don't realize that. They don't know that you can be friends with Jesus."

"I guess so," Jenny said. "But it makes me feel good to know that I can talk to Him whenever I want. Mary's a neat girl, and I felt sad that she doesn't know that."

"Did you tell her?" Mom asked.

"Yes, but I don't know if she really understands. I know that if we pray for her it would help."

"You're right," her mother agreed as she and Dad got down on their knees. "Jenny, why don't you start?"

REACT NOW!

Praying for another person is one of the most powerful gifts you can give. Make a list of people who need your prayers.

INCREDI-BIBLICAL

The body is a unit, though it is made up of many parts; and though all its parts are many, they form one body. So it is with Christ. 1 Corinthians 12:12.

THE ARM BONE'S CONNECTED TO THE . . . LEG BONE

Steven had never felt such pain in his life. It just knocked him down. He'd been playing football with friends, and as Scott tackled him, he heard his right shoulder pop. Steven left the urgent-care clinic wearing an arm sling. His shoulder had been dislocated.

"Does this mean you can't run the 100-yard dash on track-and-field day?" Scott asked.

"Nah," he shrugged. "That's still three weeks away. I'll have time to recover. Besides, I didn't hurt my legs!"

By track day Steven no longer needed his sling, but his shoulder still felt sore. He was sure it wouldn't matter, though, because he didn't need his shoulder to run.

But he was wrong. At the starting line he positioned himself and smiled confidently at his opponents. The race began. Steven took off—and suddenly found out that his shoulder played a big part after all. He pushed with all the strength his legs could muster, but without the ability to pump his arms, he couldn't gain the speed he needed to win. He finished second-to-last.

Injuring just one part of your body part can affect you from head to toe. When God created us, He intended each part of our bodies to work together in harmony. When one part is compromised, it affects them all.

We must remember to take care of our entire body, fingers, toes, and all.

Info Splat

Each year in the United States, emergency rooms see about 6.8 million cases of broken bones. Most people experience a broken bone at least twice in their lifetime.

REACT NOW!

Have you ever been injured? How did it affect your ability to do everyday things? In what way did it make physical activity more difficult?

April 1

~ Incredi-Biblical ~

In the morning, O Lord, you hear my voice; . . . I lay my requests before you and wait in expectation. Psalm 5:3.

WHEN GOD SENT TWO MEN

"#@%&!" Chrissy's hand flew to her mouth as if she were trying to stuff the awful word back inside, but it was too late.

"Chrissy!" her mother said in a strangely calm voice. "We need to talk."

Chrissy and her mom were new in the neighborhood. Chrissy made friends quickly, but it hadn't taken her long to pick up some of their crude language.

"OK," she sighed.

And so they talked. (Mom mainly talked, and Chrissy listened.) Then right after they prayed, Mother said something strange. "Chrissy, go outside and look for two men."

"Who are they?" she asked. "Why are they coming?"

"I don't know, dear," Mother answered. "I just feel impressed that God is going to send two men to help us. I'm going to pray for them to come right now. Would you go outside to look for them, please?"

Info Splat

The first known literature evangelists copied the Bible with their own hands. They were nomadic merchants, selling or giving away Bibles in addition to their other wares. Sometimes this cost them their freedom—or their lives—but the Waldenses courageously shared God's truth.

Chrissy shrugged. "Sure," she said, running outside. About 10 minutes later she saw a car pull up in front of her house. Eyes wide, she watched as two men got out. "Come right this way," she called to them, leading them inside to her mother.

"Where have you been?" Mother asked their visitors. "I've been praying for you two for 10 minutes." She and Chrissy sat down, eager to see what their visitors had.

The men looked puzzled, but opened a briefcase and showed them the *Great Stories for Kids* collection.

"These are beautiful!" Mother exclaimed. Each book was a collection of stories about kids who faced many of the challenges Chrissy did every day. "I've been wanting to read something like this with my daughter." She bought a set for Chrissy and a different set of books for herself.

REACT NOW!

Do you pray to God for His will in your life? Is someone praying for your help? How can you train your ears to hear God's voice better?

April 2

~ INCREDI-BIBLICAL ~

I have fought the good fight, I have finished the race, I have kept the faith. Now there is in store for me the crown of righteousness.
2 Timothy 4:7, 8.

VIDEO GAMES—GOOD FOR YOUR HEALTH?

In 2004 a young boy fighting cancer in California was asked by the Make-A-Wish Foundation for his wish. Ben Duskin said he wanted to design a video game that killed cancer.

No genie came forth to grant Ben his wish, but eventually Eric Johnston, a software engineer at LucasArts, got together with Ben. The two invented a game in which the player fights cancer inside the body playfield of mutating cells.

All the villains battled are ones that Ben has encountered in real life. There are FireMonsters (fevers), VampMonsters (blood problems), Robarf Guards (digestive problems), and QBall (hair loss). Throughout the game the hero rides a skateboard from one level to another while picking up different cancer-killing weapons along the way and collecting shields.

Ben says, "It's not easy to get the shields. They're in the hands of the various monsters, so you have to dodge molten lava, vampire bats, and big smelly green globs of goop."

The game not only teaches a little bit about fighting cancer and the side effects of chemotherapy—it also takes patients' minds off the problems they face. This seems to ease their pain. And that's great, because doctors know that by reducing pain and worry, patients heal faster!

Info Splat

The Make-A-Wish Foundation has granted more than 144,000 wishes since its beginning in 1980. While the cost of each wish depends on circumstances, the average cost of one wish is almost $6,200.

REACT NOW!

How can you fight sin? What do you think will help you heal faster—focusing on your friendship with Jesus or carefully watching out for your sins? Why?

~ Incredi-Biblical ~

The Lord is my shepherd, I shall lack nothing. He makes me lie down in green pastures, he leads me beside quiet waters. Psalm 23:1, 2.

SAVING THE COLD SHEEP

"Shoo! Shoo! Out of the truck," called Bobby.

Bobby Palmer shivered as he helped his younger brother herd their 31 baby lambs into the sheep shed. It was cold that May in the Colorado Rockies, and with almost eight feet of snow on the ground the Palmers had hooked up heat lamps to keep the newborn lambs warm.

Unfortunately, that night the temperature went so low that two lambs froze to death. Bobby was heartsick. "O God, please help us think of something to keep the lambs warm at night," he prayed.

Then his mother had an idea. "Bobby, you and Adam help me herd the lambs up to the back of our home," urged Mrs. Palmer as the sun set in the valley below.

Bobby didn't know what his mother had in mind, but he and his brother helped her drive the lambs through the snow. When they arrived at the back of their mobile home, Mrs. Palmer opened the door and let the lambs inside.

Bobby couldn't believe his eyes. How would he sleep with lambs all over their house? Then he noticed that his father had placed a large piece of plywood on the far side of the utility room. It was a tight fit, but finally the family was able to lead all 29 lambs into the tiny space.

Info Splat

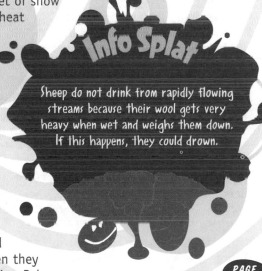

Sheep do not drink from rapidly flowing streams because their wool gets very heavy when wet and weighs them down. If this happens, they could drown.

REACT NOW!

If shepherds of sheep care so much about their animals, imagine how much more Jesus cares for you. How is Jesus leading in your life?

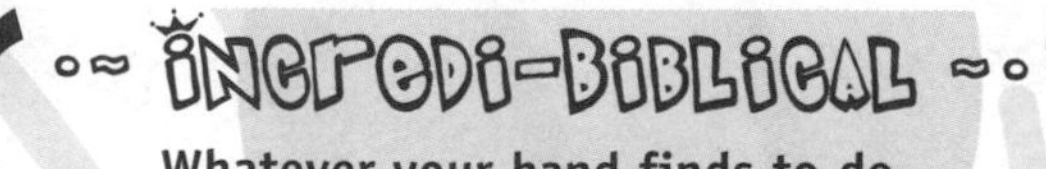

Whatever your hand finds to do,
do it with all your might.
Ecclesiastes 9:10.

CHORE GIRL

Naomi stood in front of the mirror, appearing as a girl might have some 150 years before on the American frontier. Well, almost. She wore a faded print dress, a big blue apron, and—tennis shoes. Wiggling her toes, she grinned at her reflection.

"Now, ladies, we've got work to do, just as our ancestors who would've lived on a farm like this," Mrs. Barkley said. "Have you ever shelled peas?" Before too long, Naomi and Alicia had a pyramid of shelled peas in a large basket by their feet.

"Wonderful!" said Mrs. Barkley as she saw the pile. "You make an excellent team! Now, what do you think chore girls did for a break?"

"They went to recess?" Alicia guessed.

"Nice try," smiled their teacher. "Actually, they found other work to do. I'm going to teach you girls how to make yarn." Naomi groaned, but soon was learning to card wool and spin yarn.

"Wow, Naomi! Great job!" exclaimed Mrs. Barkley. "Some people just have a knack for it, and I think you're one of them."

Naomi was having fun, but she had to admit she'd never worked this hard in her entire life. As she put her own clothes back on, she felt relieved to step back into the twenty-first century. It seemed that every muscle in her body throbbed.

I'm going to think twice about grumbling over my work at home after this, Naomi thought. She realized she had it pretty easy compared to a chore girl living in the 1850s.

Info Splat

Until 1850, shoemakers used virtually the same three hand tools that were used in Egypt during the early 1300s B.C. They were the chisel-like knife, the curved awl, and the scraper.

Even in the Garden of Eden, Adam and Eve worked to care for the plants and animals. Why do you think God created work?

INCREDI-BIBLICAL

You are . . . a people belonging to God, that you may declare the praises of him who called you out of darkness into his wonderful light. 1 Peter 2:9.

WHY RHODA FELT DIFFERENT

Rhoda often felt left out. She was new at the small elementary school, joining the upper-grade students. Although she was smart, the kids in her room often discussed things she didn't know much about. Then one day she began to understand why she felt so alone.

"Students, for part of this morning's Bible class you're going to take a survey," their teacher announced. "Please fill out each answer as it applies to you. Remember, this survey is confidential. You don't have to share your answers with anyone else unless you'd like to."

Rhoda bent her head over her desk and started filling out the survey. One question asked, "Have you ever smoked?" Then, "Have you ever drunk an alcoholic beverage?" and "Does your family have worship?" Rhoda penciled in her answers to each question. Then she read, "Have you ever gone to a movie theater?" She marked "No." Occasionally her family rented a DVD, but she enjoyed reading and riding her horse in her spare time.

At recess Rhoda's classmates stood in line at the drinking fountain, talking about the survey. All of them had seen movies in theaters. Two of them had tried smoking, and she learned that four had tried wine coolers or beer. And in her whole class, she and Ted were the only two whose families had worship together. She began to understand why sometimes she didn't seem to fit in with her classmates.

Info Splat

In the King James translation of the Bible 1 Peter 2:9 says that Christians are "peculiar people." We often think that the word ***PECULIAR*** means strange or a little weird, but it also means extraordinary, remarkable, and special. In other words, ***YOU*** are extraordinary. You are special.

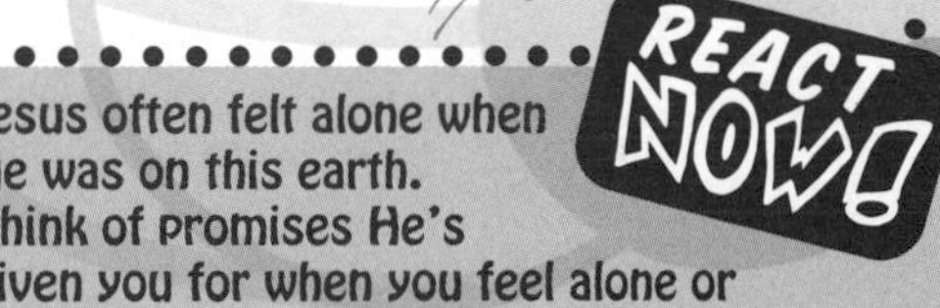

Jesus often felt alone when He was on this earth. Think of promises He's given you for when you feel alone or left out.

INCREDI-BIBLICAL

Carry each other's burdens, and in this way you will fulfill the law of Christ. Galatians 6:2.

WHEN KITES FLY AWAY

Thanks, Mom!" Doland took the bright-red kite in his hands and ran his fingers along the edge, itching to get started. Outside, the wind tossed tree branches back and forth, and the sun shone warm on the field behind his house.

"Let's try it out!" his mother said. In no time they were outside with Doland's new gift. It didn't take long for the kite to gain altitude. Mother watched her son as he made the kite lift and dive through the sky.

Then it happened. A sudden gust of wind snatched the kite out of Dolan's control. Before he knew what had happened, the red object in the sky grew smaller and smaller. His kite was sailing away!

Doland chased the kite through the tall field grass. Finally he saw it land in a cottonwood tree on a faraway hill. He watched in horror as 100 feet of lonely kite string drifted down toward the spool in his hands.

Without thinking, he prayed aloud, "God, please help me get my kite back."

"Wait right here, Doland," Mom called. She jumped into their car and pulled out of the driveway.

Soon he noticed his mother at the foot of the cottonwood tree. She looked like a tiny speck as she shinnied up the tree, retrieved the kite, and climbed back down. When she came home a little later, a red kite and some stronger twine sat on the seat beside her.

Info Splat

The Chinese were the first to build kites about 3,000 years ago. They made the kites out of silk and bamboo. Since then kites have been used for science experiments and even military purposes.

Can you remember a time God answered your prayer by using another person? How can you be an answer to prayer for someone today?

April 7

INCREDI-BIBLICAL

But my God shall supply all your need according to his riches in glory by Christ Jesus. Philippians 4:19.

A NOISE IN THE BUSHES

"Hey! What's that?" asked Brian.

"Peep, peep. Peep, peep."

"Shhh!" Brian held his finger to his lips as he and Jeff crept closer to the sound.

"What do you suppose it is?" whispered Jeff.

"I don't know, but let's find out," Brian urged. Quickly he pulled a branch aside. "Look!"

There beneath the bushes sat a baby bird staring up at the two giants looking down on it. "Peep, peep," it chirped.

"Oh, no. It must have fallen out of its nest," said Brian.

"What should we do?"

"Let's go talk to Ranger Brown."

At the nature center the camp ranger took the bird and asked the boys if they would help him feed it. "Sure! Do you think it will live?" Jeff asked.

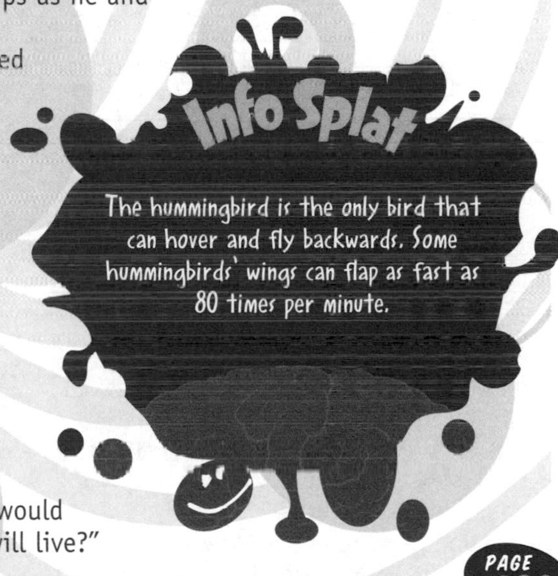

Info Splat
The hummingbird is the only bird that can hover and fly backwards. Some hummingbirds' wings can flap as fast as 80 times per minute.

"Well, this baby bird is one of God's creatures. It's in God's hands. But we'll be sure to give it lots of food."

And they did. The little bird grew and grew. Finally the time came to put it back in the wilderness. Brian and Jeff carefully carried the bird's cage to the bushes close to where they'd found it.

"OK, open the cage," said Ranger Brown.

As the cage door opened, the bird seemed to tiptoe out. Then it spread its wings and flew upward into the tall oaks.

REACT NOW!

As tiny as little birds are, God knows their needs and takes care of them. How has God done the same for you?

INCREDI-BIBLICAL

Have I not commanded you? Be strong and courageous. Do not be terrified; do not be discouraged, for the Lord your God will be with you wherever you go." Joshua 1:9.

FEAR MANOR

Be strong and of a good courage; be not afraid. Doug mulled the words over again and again as he tried to learn that Bible verse. Unfortunately he didn't stop to think about what the words meant.

Doug had a lot of fears, but his biggest fear had to do with people. Especially older people. So naturally, he thought his world had come to an end one Sabbath when his Sabbath school teacher urged his class to go as a group to visit residents in a nearby nursing home.

"We'll make some cards," she said, "and hand-deliver them. Many of the older people there are lonely, and they love visitors. Seeing you will brighten their day."

How much worse could it get? Doug wondered. He soon found out. When the class arrived at the nursing home, he stood in the doorway, looking at the card in his hands. Written on it was a name: Esther Perklin.

He waited, unsure of what to do, as a thin, fragile woman slowly walked toward him. She reached a bony hand toward Doug's sweaty one and said in a quavering voice, "I'm pleased to meet you. I'm Esther Perklin."

Doug was tempted to jerk his hand away, but he was afraid he might hurt her. Instead, he let her lead him to a sofa. She was still holding his hand as they sat down and the class sang a few songs. Soon he began to relax and enjoy the visit. *This isn't so bad,* he thought, watching the look of pleasure light Mrs. Perklin's face. The words of his Bible verse rang in his mind, and he realized that he had no need to fear, for God was with him.

Info Splat

The National Institute of Mental Health estimates that at least 5.3 million Americans experience fear of people. In 1999 the surgeon general reported that the number of people affected by social phobias could be close to 10 million.

REACT NOW!

We all have fears. What's yours? The next time you're tempted to be afraid, remember that God is with you, wherever you go.

~ Incredi-Biblical ~

Then God said, "I give you every seed-bearing plant on the face of the whole earth and every tree that has fruit with seed in it. They will be yours for food."
Genesis 1:29.

HEALTH SELF-TEST: YOU ARE WHAT YOU EAT

If you know the answer, show it—and you can be a healthy poet!

There are eight great secrets to marvelous health. Revealed here is one for you to achieve this wealth.

Fill in the blank.

To stay rich in health, you don't have to be a magician.

Just follow eight secrets. The first has to do with ________________.

(Hint: It's the science of healthy eating. Answer is found in this section.)

Take this quiz to see how well you eat.

A. How many fruits do you eat per day? ______

B. How many servings of protein do you eat? ______

C. How about veggies? ______

D. How many servings of grain do you eat? ______

E. Do you drink milk? ______

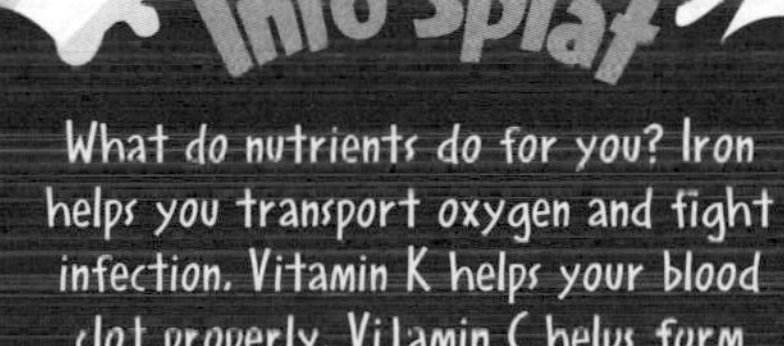

What do nutrients do for you? Iron helps you transport oxygen and fight infection. Vitamin K helps your blood clot properly. Vitamin C helps form tissue that holds your cells together, and vitamin A helps your eyes adapt to changes in light.

(Food Guide Pyramid suggestions: A. 2-4 fruits. B. 2-3 servings. C. 3-5 servings. D. 6-11 servings. E. 2-3 servings. If you don't drink milk, you should eat other foods that contain calcium, such as almonds, tofu, spinach, poppy seeds, figs, haricot beans, kale, sesame seeds, broccoli, soybeans, and cabbage.)

How'd you do? Nutrition is more than just eating the right foods. It also involves avoiding fats, oils, and sweets, which slow your brain and body down. If you're already eating a good variety of fruits, vegetables, nuts, and grains, keep it up! If not, remember that *today* is the best time to adopt a healthy diet.

REACT NOW!

Why does God ask us to eat healthy foods? Try keeping track of everything you eat for at least a day or even a week. Is there anything you'd like to change?

April 10

~ Incredi-Biblical ~

The Lord will guide you always; he will satisfy your needs in a sun-scorched land and will strengthen your frame. Isaiah 58:11.

LOOKING FOR A HOME

I'm sorry, but you can't move here," the man explained.

Toby listened from the car as his parents discussed what to do. They'd purchased land so they'd have a place to park their brand-new double-wide mobile home. Unfortunately, zoning laws forbade mobile homes on that property.

What are we going to do? Toby thought. *I don't want to move.* Toby had grown up in the place they were now living. *I love this neighborhood. All my friends are here.* But there was no choice. His family had to find another place to live.

For a short time they parked the double-wide in a mobile home park. There were no kids there Toby's age, so he was very bored. At night, alone in his bedroom, Toby talked to God. "Why did You let us buy that land?" he asked. "You know what we need. I just don't get it."

But a year later his family moved the mobile home to the country. Now Toby had plenty to keep him busy! Not only did he have chores to do—he had a dog, a cat, a goat, a sheep, a pig, and several other animals. He loved taking care of them. One evening, as he hiked the nearby hills with his dog, Toby realized how thankful he was that things turned out the way they did.

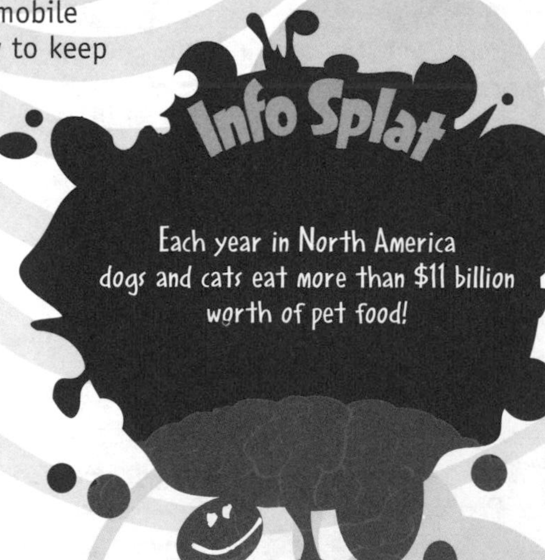

Info Splat
Each year in North America dogs and cats eat more than $11 billion worth of pet food!

REACT NOW!

Think of a time God said, "Wait." If God is allowing a door to be closed for you, look for the one He is opening.

INCREDI-BIBLICAL

The Lord is not slow in keeping his promise, as some understand slowness. He is patient with you, not wanting anyone to perish, but everyone to come to repentance. 2 Peter 3:9.

A BOY NAMED URIAH

For the past few months 12-year-old Uriah had been carefully watching the calendar. Each night he'd taken his pencil and marked an X across that day's date until every box—except today—had a mark. The special day had arrived—October 22, 1844. Soon his family and all the others who eagerly awaited the Lord's return would be safe with Jesus! Soon they wouldn't be teased and ridiculed as they had been during the past year.

"Do you remember when those men smashed all the lanterns in the evangelistic tent?" he reminded his sister as they waited together.

"I'll not forget that." Annie shook her head. "They pushed a pig underneath the tent with us. And if that wasn't bad enough, they lobbed apples at us when we were trapped beneath the canvas."

Uriah could hardly wait. Soon the faithful would go to a place where there was no hate, no crying, no illness, and no dying. They would see Jesus and the angels every day, forever. How Uriah had longed for this day to come.

That night young Uriah and his family searched the skies until the stars finally faded and a new day dawned. But Jesus had not come. The long-anticipated second coming of Christ that Uriah and many others expected on October 22, 1844, didn't happen.

Info Splat

William Miller, a Vermont farmer, preached that Jesus would return to earth on October 22, 1844. Not all agreed or even wanted to hear it! Mobs of angry citizens pelted Miller with eggs and decaying vegetables. But more than 50,000 believed, and around 1 million others watched expectantly.

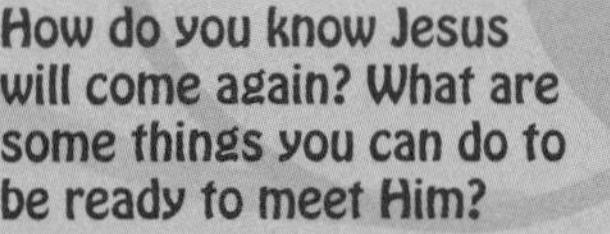

How do you know Jesus will come again? What are some things you can do to be ready to meet Him?

INCREDI-BIBLICAL

Do you not know that in a race all the runners run, but only one gets the prize? Run in such a way as to get the prize.
1 Corinthians 9:24.

NO GOALS, NO SCORE

OK, who thinks they're good enough to get around me?" Pastor Smith challenged the youth group. He stood at the front of the church sanctuary, bouncing a basketball.

Bounce, bounce, bounce. Brian's knees started to bounce in time with the ball. Hearing that sound was more than he could take. Everyone knew he was the best basketball player on the court. Brian stood up, took off his jacket, and side-walked out of the pew. "Let's play ball," he told the pastor.

"OK, your ball first." Pastor Smith bounced the basketball toward Brian.

It was then that Brian realized the church sanctuary was missing something very important for a game of one-on-one. There wasn't a hoop or net to be seen. He looked at the big grin on the pastor's face as the man held out his open hands. Sheepishly Brian tossed the ball back.

"Are there any of you who are playing a game with no goal?" Pastor Smith asked as Brian sat down in the pew. The church was silent.

Brian knew he had done that very thing on several occasions. He listened as Pastor Smith asked, "How can you win the game of life if you have no real goals to reach for?"

Info Splat

When the game of basketball was first played, teams shot the ball into real bushel baskets. At one point, the games got so violent that fences were erected around the court to keep the crowd safe.

REACT NOW!

Make a list of some goals you'd like to meet five, 10, or 20 years from now. After you make the list, pray and plan ways to meet your goals.

April 13

~ Incredi-Biblical ~

**All Scripture is God-breathed and is useful for teaching, rebuking, correcting and training in righteousness.
2 Timothy 3:16.**

WHAT EVA BELIEVED

"Does anyone know what the word *evolution* means?" asked the teacher.

A girl in Eva's grade answered, "It means everything in the world came to be by evolving from something else."

"That's a good definition," said the teacher. "We humans are descendants of ancient apelike creatures. From them all the gorillas, apes, and monkeys we know today descended as well. Yes, Eva?"

Eva had raised her hand. "Mr. Grasty, I don't believe that," she answered truthfully.

"Well, Eva, what do you believe?"

"I believe what the Bible says—that people were created by God, who breathed life into Adam on the sixth day of Creation week, and that He made Eve from one of Adam's ribs."

The class started laughing. Even the teacher chuckled. "Eva, many people see that the Bible is a great literary collection," he said. "But it's just that—an ancient people trying to make sense of things they didn't understand."

Eva's face burned. She felt disheartened that her science teacher would refer to the Bible as some sort of joke book. "There are whole libraries of books that explain evolution," Mr. Grasty added.

"Yes, but God didn't inspire those books to be written," Eva returned. "He did inspire people to write the Bible."

After school Jon came up to Eva. "I think you're right about the Bible," he said. "There's something about it that gets to me like nothing else I've read." He lifted his hand to give her a high-five. "And thanks for speaking up in class."

Info Splat

While textbooks and encyclopedias around the world promote Charles Darwin's theory of evolution as a scientific fact, his theory has never been proven.

Do you sometimes avoid conflict by keeping quiet and not saying anything? Is there a time to speak up?

INCREDI-BIBLICAL

There are different kinds of gifts, but the same Spirit. There are different kinds of service, but the same Lord. 1 Corinthians 12:4, 5.

BRENT'S DOODLES

Hey, would you look at the mess Brent's making!" exclaimed Dan. Brent quickly turned his paper over, but it was too late. His friends had already seen all the multicolored squiggly lines. Giggles erupted from the group.

"Come on! Show us your piece of trash," Dan laughed.

By this time several other kids had crowded Brent's desk to see his squiggles. "Go ahead. Show 'em!" Dan demanded. Brent scrunched down in his chair, and his face grew red. He wanted to disappear.

"What's going on here?" their art teacher questioned.

"Brent is just drawing squiggles," reported Dan.

"Everyone, please find your seats," the teacher instructed. "I have something important to share with you." She waited until each student was at their desk before she spoke.

"Many of you have wonderful talents in art," she told them. "A few may have even taken an art class before, so you draw from a different perspective." She looked toward Dan at that. "You have a different experience from someone who is picking up an art pencil for the first time. But this tells me that you also know there are many styles of art. Judging someone's art by comparing it to your own seems like a poor assessment to me."

Dan shifted uneasily, and turned to Brent. "I wasn't being fair," he admitted. "I'm sorry."

Info Splat

Leonardo da Vinci, an acclaimed scientist, artist, and inventor, was one of the most famous doodlers of all times. In fact, many of Leonardo's inventions were conceived while doodling. Scattered through Leonardo's drawings can be seen oodles of polyhedron doodles.

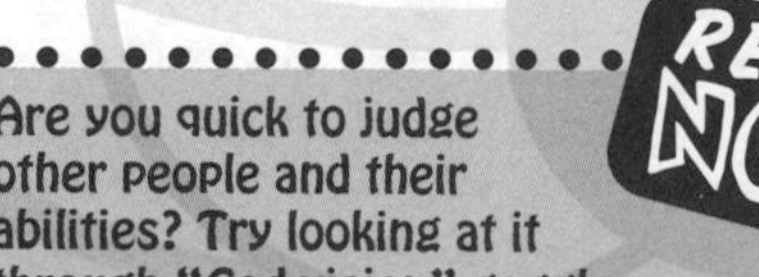

Are you quick to judge other people and their abilities? Try looking at it through "God-vision" goggles.

April 15

~ INCREDI-BIBLICAL ~

**A friend loves at all times,
and a brother is born for adversity.
Proverbs 17:17.**

LOVE THY NEIGHBOR

"God, please help me be a friend," Cindi prayed as she walked over to Sheryl's house. The girls knew each other from school, but Cindi had always felt a little unsure around Sheryl. Sheryl's mom opened the door with a smile.

"Aren't you going to ask why I'm in a wheelchair?" Sheryl questioned after Cindi and she had talked awhile. "All the other kids do."

"Well, I've wondered," Cindi admitted. "But I thought you'd tell me when you were ready."

"It's because someone covered the seat with superglue and I'm the one who happened to sit down in this chair," Sheryl said with a straight face, eyeing her audience of one. Cindi laughed.

"Do you know what spina bifida is?" Sheryl asked.

"No," Cindi said "I've never heard of it."

"Well, it's a birth defect that affects about one in every 1,000 babies born in North America. I happen to be one of those. I was born with problems in my spinal cord. The effect is that my legs don't work."

"But you can still move your arms," Cindi noted.

"And my eyes and my tongue!" Sheryl stuck out her tongue and crossed her eyes.

Both girls laughed. They felt more relaxed as they played several of Sheryl's games together. The time passed so quickly that Cindi could hardly believe it when Sheryl's mom told her it was 5:00.

As she hurried home, Cindi looked toward heaven and prayed, "God, thanks so much for my new friend, Sheryl."

Mothers who consume 400 micrograms of folic acid every day during their pregnancy can reduce the risk of having a baby with spina bifida by as much as 70 percent. Folic acid occurs naturally in greens, dried beans, peas, and some fruits.

REACT NOW!

What does today's text mean for you? Is there someone who needs your friendship this week?

~ INCREDI-BIBLICAL ~

Of making many books there is no end, and much study wearies the body. Ecclesiastes 12:12.

HEALTH SELF-TEST: GET MOVING

If you know the answer, show it—and you can be a healthy poet! There are eight great secrets to marvelous health. Revealed here is one for you to achieve this wealth.

Fill in the blank:

Eat protein for your muscles, and carrots for your eyes,
And so you don't turn into a couch potato, you need to ________________.
(Hint: This activity makes you stronger. Look for the answer below.)

How fit are you?

A. How many minutes do you spend doing a cardiovascular exercise (strengthening your heart by increasing your heart rate) each day? ____ minutes

B. How many days do you do strength training each week? ____ days

C. Does your school have an exercise program? Yes ____ No ____

Recommended answers:

A. For at least four days each week, spend 30 minutes or more doing cardiovascular exercises. This can include walking, running, skipping rope, biking, swimming, or anything else that increases your heart rate.

B. Each week, do three or four days of strength training. If you don't have weights you may use one-pound cans of fruit or vegetables, or fill a one-quart container with water. You can also do sit-ups, push-ups, or any exercise that strengthens your muscles.

C. If you have PE at your school, it will help you stay fit. If you have recess, get involved! Stretch your muscles and put them to use by playing basketball, football, or hopscotch. Or try running a few laps around the playing field.

At the first Olympic Games, contestants were required to speak Greek and be Greek citizens. There were only a few events, and instead of moving to different cities around the world as the games do today, they always took place at Olympia.

One of the most important components of physical fitness is regular activity. What specific things can you do to keep your body healthy and happy?

April 17

~ Incredi-Biblical ~

But I trust in you, O Lord; I say, "You are my God." My times are in your hands. Psalm 31:14, 15.

BIBLE

HOMESICK AT CAMP

Immanuel Cordova quickly found his place with the rest of the group. Although he liked being at junior camp, Immanuel was very shy and wasn't used to being away from home.

"All right, Bisons, let's gather around the campfire," encouraged Mr. Brady. The sponsor sat on one side of the campfire while the kids sat on the other, staring at each other through the flames.

"At the bottom of a deep, dark pit," Mr. Brady began, "Joseph shivered, wondering if he would ever see his father again."

As he listened to the story of Joseph, Immanuel thought he knew a little about what Joseph had gone through. He too was so homesick. Oh, how he missed his family! At the end of the story, Mr. Brady asked, "OK, juniors, when Joseph was sold as a slave and sent far away to Egypt, he was probably pretty homesick. What do you think he did?"

"He prayed," several kids responded.

"That's right," said Mr. Brady. "He prayed to God. Why don't we do the same tonight?"

The juniors bowed their heads as Mr. Brady prayed, "Heavenly Father, thank You that we can be here at camp. We thank You for Your protection. Lord, some of us are a little homesick tonight. We pray that You will be with us as You were with Joseph in Egypt, and we ask this in Jesus' name. Amen."

Immanuel could really relate to the worship that night. He felt the prayer was meant just for him.

Info Splat

Out of the Seven Wonders, only one remains: the Great Pyramid of Giza. The Giza pyramid is made up of about 2,500,000 stones. Each stone weighs between two and 80 tons.

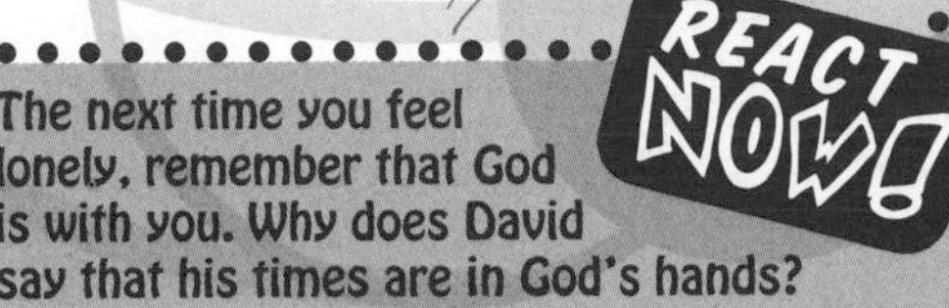

The next time you feel lonely, remember that God is with you. Why does David say that his times are in God's hands?

April 18

~ Incredi-Biblical ~

We wait in hope for the Lord; he is our help and our shield. Psalm 33:20.

WHEN THINGS LOOK MISERABLE

For quite some time Uriah had suffered with an ulcer on his left leg. When he was 4, a fever and infection in the leg had left it shriveled and drawn-up. Now, at age 12, the trouble had returned. His physician, a well-known surgeon, spoke with Mrs. Smith in private. "I hate to tell you this," he said, "but the infection is so bad that the leg has to be removed."

Wondering how Uriah would take this news, his mother stepped back inside his room. "Are you willing to have your leg amputated, Uriah?" she asked.

"Why, certainly," he replied bravely. Then adding a bit of humor, he said, "I guess if I'm going to lose either my leg or my life, I'd rather lose my leg."

And so Uriah's sister and mother held him down on the kitchen table while the surgeon cut off his leg just above the knee. It was a 20-minute surgery—without anesthesia, for there was none in 1845. Tears dripped down Uriah's face as he screamed out in pain.

It was a discouraging time. He'd experienced the terrible disappointment that Jesus did not come, as so many expected. Then, not long afterward, he lost his leg. Even so, a few years later he was readying himself for Harvard College. But God had other plans. Uriah became a poet, a hymn writer, an author, and an inventor. For 50 years he was associated with the office of the *Review and Herald*. He was also the first secretary for the Seventh-day Adventist General Conference.

Info Splat

On May 15, 2006, Mark Inglis climbed Mount Everest. This New Zealander was the first double amputee to climb the tallest mountain in the world.

How has God planned for you? Is there a time God has not promised to be with you?

INCREDI-BIBLICAL

The Lord came and stood there, calling as at the other times, "Samuel! Samuel!" Then Samuel said, "Speak, for your servant is listening." 1 Samuel 3:10.

ME, A PREACHER?

Have you ever thought of stepping behind the podium of your church and giving the sermon? Would you be scared? excited? What if God asked you to do it? Would you do it then?

A few years ago a young girl preached to thousands of people in her country of Brazil. Amazed that a mere child could speak as she did, many were moved to repentance.

In 2006 a 10-year-old boy from Ghana had a preaching spot on two radio programs. He started telling others about Jesus after several years of listening to his father preach.

Jesus is coming back again, and He's calling people your age to help share the good news with others. I think it would be a good idea for skilled speakers to help those kids and teens who have a God-inspired will to preach do it very well.

Of course, you can preach without any formal training. Jesus' disciples didn't have conventional education, and they preached a sermon that brought 3,000 people to the Lord. Jesus Himself wasn't a "trained" preacher. But "everyone who heard him was amazed at his understanding and His answers" (Luke 2:47). He was connected to God, the source of all wisdom.

Yet God may not be asking you to preach up front. He has many other needs as well, and often the loudest sermons people hear come from our actions. In any position we find ourselves, we can preach God's love by our example.

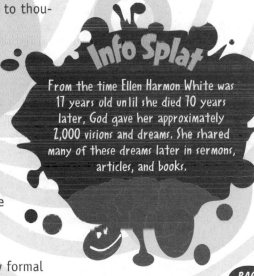

Info Splat

From the time Ellen Harmon White was 17 years old until she died 70 years later, God gave her approximately 2,000 visions and dreams. She shared many of these dreams later in sermons, articles, and books.

How is God calling you? Open your heart to His leading, and He will show you.

Incredi-Biblical

**Call upon me in the day of trouble;
I will deliver you, and you will honor me.
Psalm 50:15.**

WHERE'S THE BRAKE?

"Would you like to drive my four-wheeler?" Tom asked Sarah.

Sarah hesitated. "Sure," she said. She wanted to drive, but she'd never ridden an ATV in her life. Sarah gripped the handlebars and waited for Tom to climb on behind her. As she drove off, she felt confident, but soon she realized that she was speeding toward a riverbank and its 10-foot drop-off.

"Slow down, Sarah!" Tom yelled in her ear. She froze as the riverbank zoomed closer and closer. "SLOW DOWN!" Tom screamed. But Sarah didn't know what to do.

"USE THE BRAKE!" he shouted.

But she couldn't find it. The last thing Sarah remembered before becoming airborne was praying, "Jesus, please save us!"

Sarah and Tom clung to the ATV as they tumbled end over end down the bank to the water's edge. They landed with a thud. They lay motionless. Then Tom sat up.

"Are you OK?" he squeaked.

Sarah blinked a few times. "I think so," she whispered. The two slowly stood to their feet.

"Why didn't you use the brake?" Tom moaned.

"I didn't know where it was," Sarah said sheepishly. "I've never been on a four-wheeler before." Tom groaned and shook his head.

As Sarah rubbed a sore spot on her back, she glanced at the mangled four-wheeler. It looked like she felt, all twisted and bent out of shape. But still in one piece.

"Tom, God protected us," she said. "Let's thank Him."

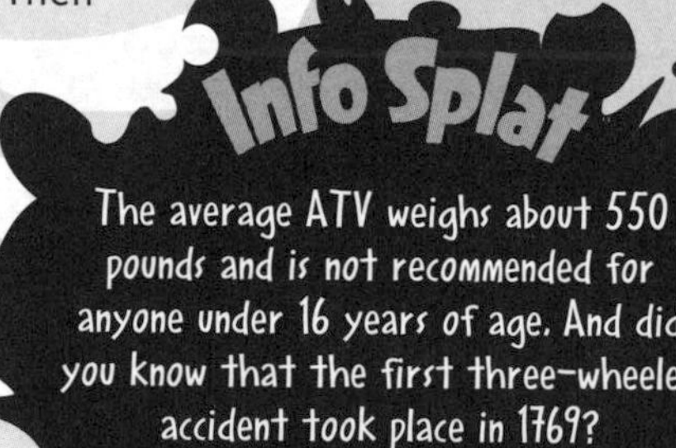

Info Splat
The average ATV weighs about 550 pounds and is not recommended for anyone under 16 years of age. And did you know that the first three-wheeler accident took place in 1769?

REACT NOW!

It's never too late to call upon the Lord, even when you may have chosen to put yourself in a dangerous situation. How do you need Jesus' help today?

INCREDI-BIBLICAL

So I say to you: Ask and it will be given to you; seek and you will find; knock and the door will be opened to you. Luke 11:9.

DEXTER AND THE REALLY COOL ROCKS

God, please help us find some really cool rocks," Dexter prayed as he walked near his younger brother Robert. The boys searched the ground for rocks for Dexter's science class. He needed to collect several types of rocks by the end of the week.

"Is this a really cool one?" questioned Robert, holding up a black rock.

"No, that's just a lump of coal," Dexter smiled. He handed the rock back to his brother.

Then Dexter saw something he had never seen before: a funny rock that looked like a seashell. "Robert!" he called. "I think I found a fossil!"

Robert took no time to run to his brother's side. "A fossil? Let me see!"

"Here," Dexter said, noticing another fossil poking out from among the rocks on the side of the hill. "There's one for you."

"Wow! My very first fossil!" exclaimed Robert.

Dexter and Robert climbed the rocky hill, searching for more fossils. At first Dexter saw only fossilized clams, but after some time he found plant fossils and bone fossils along the embankment. It was like finding hidden treasure.

As he brought several of the fossils to science class later that week, Dexter thanked God for helping him find some really cool rocks.

The largest meat-eating dinosaurs were T. rex and giganotosaurus. They weighed between 14,000 and 16,000 pounds and were 45 feet long. Brachiosaurus, a vegetarian dinosaur, weighed around 140,000 pounds and could grow up to 85 feet long.

REACT NOW!

Is there something you think is too small for God to care about? (See Mark 12:43; Luke 12:6; Luke 17:6.) How is searching for fossils like searching for God?

INCREDI-BIBLICAL

I heard the voice of the Lord saying, "Whom shall I send? And who will go for us?" And I said, "Here am I. Send me!" Isaiah 6:8.

BE A MISSIONARY! BE A VOLUNTEER!

If you like celebrations, you'll be happy to know that this week is National Coin Week, Bike Safety Week, and National Bubblegum Week. It's also National Volunteer Week. Being a volunteer means donating some of your time to help others in need. That's great news! We can all celebrate, because all of us are able to be of help to someone.

What are some ways you can volunteer? If you need some ideas, you might ask your parents or grandparents. Perhaps they know of a friend or neighbor that needs some things done for them. Your teacher, for example, might love some help with classroom chores. Your parents probably would go crazy for a freshly mowed lawn or a spotless kitchen sink. The main thing is that you spend this week thinking about others and helping them out. It's one way you can be a missionary for Jesus.

If you find your brain freezing up on you, here are a few more ideas:

- Help a friend or sibling with their homework.
- Offer to help your mom or dad unload the groceries.
- Visit an older person who doesn't get out much and find out what they need.
- Get a group of people together and sign up to adopt a highway—keep it clean.
- You don't have to volunteer this week only. People need our help all year long.

Info Splat

The Peace Corps is an organization that works with governments, schools, entrepreneurs, education, health, businesses, information technology, agriculture, and the environment. Peace Corps members volunteer in more than 70 countries around the world.

So what are you going to do? You've got God-given talents He's given you to help others.

April 23

INCREDI-BIBLICAL

The woman said to him, "Sir, give me this water so that I won't get thirsty." John 4:15.

HEALTH SELF-TEST: WASHED UP

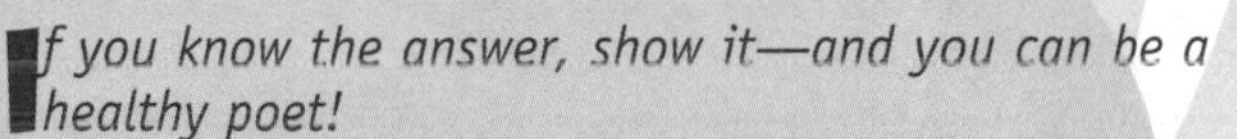

If you know the answer, show it—and you can be a healthy poet!

There are eight great secrets to marvelous health. Revealed here is one for you to achieve this wealth.

Fill in the blank:

As you exercise, you'll need plenty of liquid to help you as you grow:

Vegetable and fruit juice, cow's or soy milk, and especially __________."

(Hint: It's the scientific name for water. If you need help, look for the answer somewhere on this page.)

Inside and outside, how clean is your body?

A. How many glasses of water do you drink per day? ____

B. How often do you shower or take a bath? ____

C. Do you always wash your hands before eating? ____

D. Do you always wash your hands after using the restroom? ____

Answers:

A. Eight is the optimal amount. Most Americans don't drink even four glasses per day. Taking a water bottle to school can help.

B. If you're able, you should take a bath or shower once per day. A daily bath can improve your skin and your mood, and may help with acne.

C. Just do it! Think of the many places your hands have been since you last washed them. Imagine licking some of those surfaces. Pretty gross, huh?

D. If you aren't in this habit yet, start. Avoid getting germs. Wash those hands!

Info Splat

It's a fact that every hour you shed 600,000 particles of skin. This averages one and a half pounds every year. If you live to age 70, you've shed 105 pounds of dead skin.

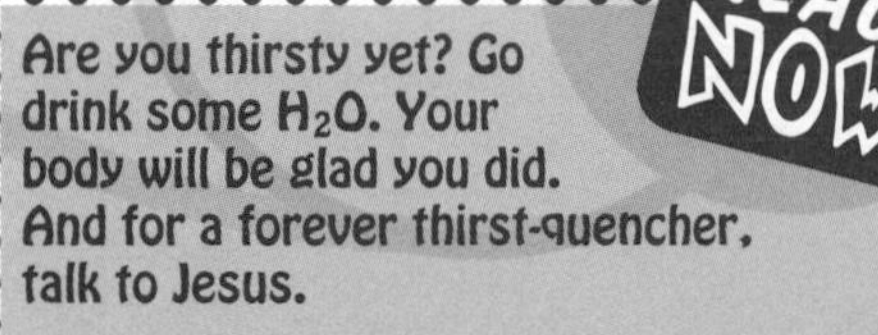

Are you thirsty yet? Go drink some H_2O. Your body will be glad you did. And for a forever thirst-quencher, talk to Jesus.

INCREDI-BIBLICAL

I am with you and will watch over you wherever you go. Genesis 28:15.

IN ALL PLACES

Boy, I wish God were with me, thought Brittany as she sat at her desk waiting for recess. How she wished she could do something right for a change!

"You ready for field hockey?" her friend Heather asked.

"Sure," Brittany said glumly.

During recess Brittany felt even worse. She couldn't keep up with her class, and she kept hitting the ground instead of the puck. *God,* she prayed, *You know I feel as though everything's going wrong this week. You say You're always with me. Please help me believe it. I can't do it without You.* Brittany felt a peace come into her heart.

Suddenly the hockey puck landed right in front of her. Brittany came to life. She zoned in on the other team's goal, where the coach stood poised, ready to block her shot. Brittany aimed, and in a matter of seconds she'd scored her first hockey goal.

"Right on!" yelled Heather. Brittany grinned as her team came up to congratulate her.

"Thank You, God," Brittany whispered. "You let me know You are with me, and then You gave me this goal. You're awesome!"

Brittany learned a lot at school that day. She learned several things in her studies. She learned how to hit a hockey puck and score a goal for her team. But the most important lesson Brittany Lawrence learned that day was that God is always there.

Info Splat

In the game of ice hockey, the puck is sometimes hit so hard that it is sailing at more than 100 miles per hour when it bounces off the glass on the sides of the ice rink.

God is here with you at this moment. Why don't you spend some time talking with Him now?

~ INCREDI-BIBLICAL ~

If anyone would come after me, he must deny himself and take up his cross and follow me. . . . whoever loses his life for me will find it. Matthew 16:24, 25.

WHEN GOD SPEAKS, SO MUST WE

At age 12, Ellen Harmon gave her life to God. Her conversion led her to be baptized a year later, and shortly after this, when Ellen was 13, her family attended some meetings that changed her life. An evangelist named William Miller spoke at the meetings, and young Ellen was convicted that she was not right with God. She realized that she had sins in her life she needed to confess, but wasn't quite sure how to do it.

Jesus is coming soon to take His chosen people home, she thought, *and I must be ready!* Day and night Ellen prayed that she might be prepared for Christ's second coming.

Around this time she received an impression from the Lord. Ellen had always been rather shy and had never prayed out loud at prayer meetings. But now she felt the Lord impressing her that she needed to pray aloud at their meetings.

Ellen tried to avoid doing it. She was too shy. However, every time she went to the Lord in silent prayer, she had a strong impression that she must pray aloud when she knelt with her friends. Eventually she stopped praying in her heart to avoid this deep inner conviction.

Now she felt depressed. She knew what she had to do, but she put it off for three whole weeks. Finally Ellen offered God a short prayer during prayer meeting. At once she felt a sweet peace and joy in her heart, and she praised God for His goodness to her.

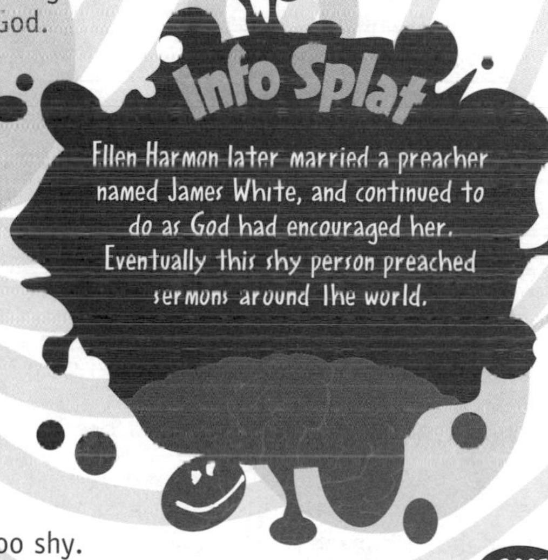

Info Splat
Ellen Harmon later married a preacher named James White, and continued to do as God had encouraged her. Eventually this shy person preached sermons around the world.

REACT NOW!

Has the Lord placed something on your heart? What are you going to do about it?

Incredi-Biblical

Jesus . . . said, "Go home to your family and tell them how much the Lord has done for you, and how he has had mercy on you." Mark 5:19.

CURRENT EVENT

On a gray December day in 2006 he was playing in the yard outside his grandparents' home. Earlier that day the 13-year-old had watched an electric crew repair downed power lines in the neighborhood. Now as he backed up near the open end of a line lying on the grass, he suddenly felt a sharp shock—7,200 volts of electricity burning through his body!

It shot through his baseball pants and into his torso, down his legs to his toes, through his socks, and out his tennis shoes. He still remembers looking down and noticing a blue glow around his feet before he fell backwards to the ground.

"My son's been electrocuted!" his dad shouted on the phone to the electric company.

Amazed, they informed him that by rights his son should be dead. But he was still alive, and they rushed him to the hospital.

Shortly after the incident, he was interviewed by a reporter from the TV Weather Channel. He smiled as he said, "God spared me."

He now warns his friends, "If you see a downed power line, don't assume it's dead. Treat every downed line as if it were live!"

Because of his close encounter with electricity, his family gave him a new nickname. They call him Sparky!

Info Splat

More than 1,000 people are struck by lightning each year in North America, and at least 10 percent die. Did you know it is possible to be struck by lightning even when you are inside your home?

REACT NOW!

How has God showed His great love and mercy to you? Tell someone about it.

~ Incredi-Biblical ~

Children, obey your parents in the Lord, for this is right. Ephesians 6:1.

FAST FRED

Boy, am I getting tired, thought Fred as he pulled the wagon full of food toward home. *I wonder if I could scoot the groceries over a little, get in the wagon, and just coast down the hill to our house.*

He quickly pushed the groceries toward the back of the wagon, where his 6-year-old brother sat, and then hopped in front.

"How would you like to go for a ride?" Fred asked Bill.

"Yeah!" his brother grinned.

"Fred, don't coast down the hill!" he heard his parents call. "You'll go too fast!" But Fred liked to go fast. And fast is what Fred got.

"Slow down!" cried Bill from the back of the wagon.

"SLOW DOWN!" their parents screamed. The wagon flew down the hill and Fred's mother ran after it, watching in horror as the wagonload of boys and groceries careened dangerously through an intersection.

"Jesus, help!" Bill cried.

Mother was getting closer. Soon she ran in front of the wagon and pulled it off into the grass.

BANG! went the wagon into Mother's legs.

CRASH! went the wagon onto the grass.

Fred and Bill fell out, and the groceries spilled all over their neighbor's lawn.

For weeks after that Fred thought of what might have happened. They could have been hit by a car! His mother might have broken her leg. And as he watched her hobble around the house, he wished he had listened.

Info Splat

The three tiniest bones in the human body have one of the biggest jobs. The malleus, incus, and stapes (better known as the hammer, anvil, and stirrup) help you hear.

What's your hearing like when your parents tell you to do something? How can you be a better listener?

~ INCREDI-BIBLICAL ~

When the disciples James and John saw this, they asked, "Lord, do you want us to call fire down from heaven to destroy them?" Luke 9:54.

DIAMONDS IN THE ROUGH

Diamonds do not show their entire luster as rough stones when they are first found. Instead, they must be cut and polished into a variety of shapes to exhibit the brilliance they're known for. The longer the diamond cutter spends on a diamond, and the more precise the cutter is, the brighter the diamond will shine.

For example, the Hearts on Fire diamond is one of the best-cut gems in the world. To get this perfection, diamond cutters spend four times longer creating this diamond than they do on any other diamond. When they're done, the diamond will reflect 98 percent of all its light to your eyes.

Two of Christ's disciples were a bit rough in their approach to witnessing to the world. Their names were James and John. These brothers once suggested to Jesus that they call fire down from heaven to destroy a village that would not let them enter. Because of their rough approach Christ dubbed the two men Sons of Thunder.

Jesus could have expelled them from the group. However, He could see their true potential, and knew that they would be powerful workers for people. To him they were diamonds in the rough. Like the gemstone, at first they didn't appear to have a godly character. They would need to be polished and have their roughness cut away. Then they would reflect His light with much brightness.

Info Splat

What could be the galaxy's largest diamond is not found on earth. According to Travis Metcalfe, an astronomer, the whole core of the white dwarf star BPM 37093 is a diamond with a diameter of about 4,000 kilometers, or 2,485 miles.

Are you a diamond in the rough? Ask Jesus to cut away your rough edges and polish your personality.

~ INCREDI-BIBLICAL ~

He said to them, "Go into all the world and preach the good news to all creation." Mark 16:15.

GO YE

What do you think Jesus meant when He told His disciples, "Therefore go and make disciples of all nations, baptizing them in the name of the Father and of the Son and of the Holy Spirit, and teaching them to obey everything I have commanded you. And surely I will be with you always, to the very end of the age" (Matthew 28:19, 20)?

Some call this familiar text the Gospel Commission. But what does it have to do with you? Many people believe that because it speaks of baptizing, it must be intended merely for pastors and evangelists. While this is partially right, *you* also have a part to play in this great challenge that Jesus gave us not long after His resurrection.

Notice the second part: teaching them to obey everything I have commanded you. All of us have a part to play here. We can set good examples for the people we are around each day—our parents, our friends, our classmates, our grandparents and aunts and uncles and neighbors and . . . all nations. By our lifestyle, we reach them and teach them about Jesus' love.

Don't get caught up with the idea that you're just a kid. Jesus was about your age when He began teaching adults in the Temple. Remember, He says to you, "Surely I will be with you always, to the very end of the age."

Info Splat

When Scandinavian preachers were thrown into prison for preaching that Jesus would come again, God sent His Holy Spirit to children and youth. Because they were under age, the law could not keep them from telling people the news.

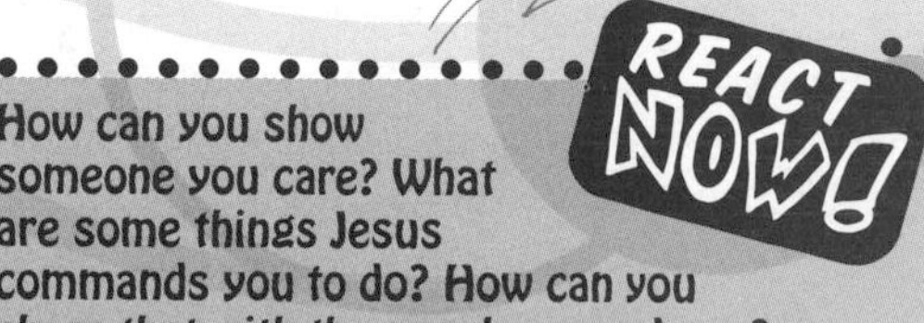

REACT NOW!
How can you show someone you care? What are some things Jesus commands you to do? How can you share that with the people around you?

April 30

~ Incredi-Biblical ~

The day is yours, and yours also the night; you established the sun and moon. Psalm 74:16.

HEALTH SELF-TEST: IT SHINES

If you know the answer, show it—and you can be a healthy poet!

There are eight great secrets to marvelous health. Revealed here is one for you to achieve this wealth.

Fill in the blank:

Step outside and get vitamin D; it's something to give you great might.

If you don't stick around inside all the time, you'll find this in the ________.

(Hint: It's another way of saying "light from the sun." Still stumped? Look on this page.)

What's your sun sense? Answer these questions to find out.

A. How much sunlight do you get each day? _____ minutes

B. Do you protect your eyes from the bright sun? Yes ___ No ___

Answers:

A. Relaxing in the sun is a great way to de-stress and fill up on vitamin D. If you're getting 10 to 15 minutes in the sun every couple days you're doing wonderful. Less? Try to get some more sun. More? Make sure you're using sunscreen or covering up with clothes and a hat.

B. Wearing sunglasses protects your eyes from the harmful ultraviolet (UV) rays found in the sun that can damage your vision. Combined with snow, cold, and wind, ultraviolet rays can cause photokeratitis—or sunburn of your eyes. Also called snow blindness, this temporary but painful problem can last from 12 to 48 hours. So grab your Oakleys, then enjoy the rays!

Info Splat

Sunlight cruising at the speed of light zooms from the sun to the earth—a distance of 93 million miles—in just eight minutes.

REACT NOW!

Go catch some sunlight! Just remember your sunscreen and shades.

INCREDI-BIBLICAL

A righteous man is cautious in friendship, but the way of the wicked leads them astray. Proverbs 12:27.

STEVE'S MISSING HAT

Joy looked enviously at some of the girls in her cabin at summer camp. They were all wearing baseball caps—baseball caps that belonged to guys they liked. At camp this summer, that seemed to be the way a boy announced he liked a girl—he gave her his cap to wear.

Joy really liked Steve, but he didn't even seem to know she existed. Sometimes she daydreamed about wearing his cap—with its Toronto Blue Jays logo. Then one day at the waterfront, while everyone was swimming, she noticed that Steve had taken his cap off and left it lying on the ground. She grabbed it and ran back to her cabin.

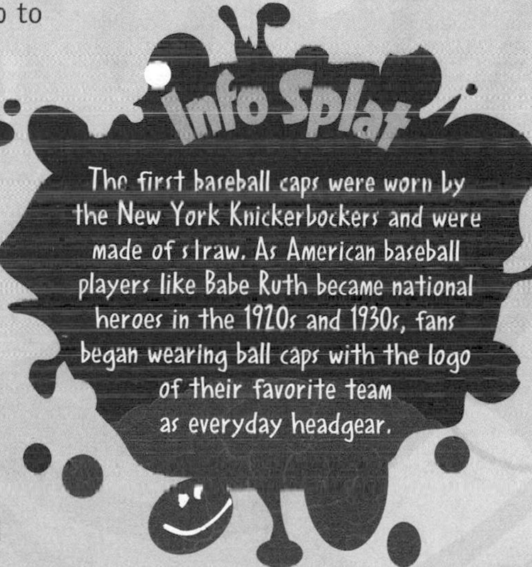

Info Splat
The first baseball caps were worn by the New York Knickerbockers and were made of straw. As American baseball players like Babe Ruth became national heroes in the 1920s and 1930s, fans began wearing ball caps with the logo of their favorite team as everyday headgear.

Soon word was all over camp that Steve's hat was missing and he wanted to find it. Joy kept the cap hidden inside her sleeping bag and didn't dare show anyone. She knew Steve was angry that someone had taken his beloved ball cap.

That night in her sleeping bag Joy looked at the cap by the light of her flashlight. A cap someone gave you as a sign of friendship had a special meaning. If Steve had given her his cap, she'd wear it with pride. But a cap stolen from somebody meant nothing at all. It could be the end of a friendship instead of the beginning.

The next day an embarrassed Joy returned Steve's hat. Without friendship, the cap meant nothing.

REACT NOW!

Do you own something that's meaningful because of your friendship with the person who gave it to you? What do you have that reminds you of your friendship with Jesus?

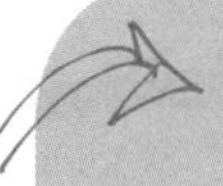

May 2

~ INCREDI-BIBLICAL ~

In Christ we who are many form one body, and each member belongs to all the others. We have different gifts, according to the grace given us. Romans 12:5, 6.

CLARA HEEDS THE CALL

Clara Barton was the youngest of five children in her family. She was a *lot* younger—for all her brothers and sisters were at least 10 years older. But being the baby of the family didn't stop Clara from being useful. When she was 11 years old, her brother David was injured and grew ill after falling from a barn roof. Clara stayed by his side for two years, learning to care for him and giving him all his medications. In the 1800s, when Clara lived, caring for sick people sometimes involved putting leeches on the patient to suck blood—and Clara even learned to do that for her brother!

When still a teen, Clara began teaching school. Later she worked in the U.S. Patent Office. But when the American Civil War was in full swing Clara's early training in nursing became useful once again. She worked as a nurse on the battlefield and discovered how hard it was to get the medical supplies that she needed.

Clara got involved behind the scenes, helping get medical supplies to the armies of both the North and the South during the Civil War. She traveled to Europe after the war and got to see the International Red Cross in action. She was inspired to bring the Red Cross to the United States, and through her efforts the American Red Cross was founded, with Clara Barton as president, in 1881.

Info Splat

In medieval and early modern times, leeches were used in medicine to remove blood from patients since doctors believed that many illnesses were caused by too much blood in the body. Sound crazy? Today leeches still have a use in medicine. They're used to stimulate circulation after certain types of surgery.

REACT NOW!

Sometimes it takes a crisis for people to discover what their true gifts and abilities are. How do you react when things go wrong and people need your help?

~ Incredi-Biblical ~

Don't let anyone look down on you because you are young, but set an example for the believers in speech, in life, in love, in faith and in purity.
1 Timothy 4:12.

RYAN'S WELLS

Ryan Hreljac was just 6 years old when he learned that not everyone in the world had access to clean water. His first-grade teacher told the class that people in some parts of Africa had to walk many miles just to get water. As Ryan's class raised money to help with projects in Africa, and he learned that $70 would build a well, he decided that's what he wanted to do. Ryan worked for four months to earn $70 to dig that first well.

But Ryan didn't stop there. He kept raising money to bring clean water to places that don't have it. Ryan is now a teenager, and the Ryan's Well Foundation he started has raised far more than $1 million. It has supported more than 230 different projects.

Ryan has had the opportunity to travel all over the world, visiting African villages where the money he raised has helped to dig wells. He has traveled to many places to raise money for Ryan's Well Foundation, and has met famous people, including entertainers, athletes, religious and political leaders, and even princes and princesses. Most important, Ryan Hreljac, of Ontario, Canada, has helped show the world that one young person who cares can make a real difference to problems in the world.

Info Splat

More than 1.2 billion people worldwide don't have access to clean water, and most of the world's people must walk more than three hours to get drinking water. Yet Americans flush 6.8 billion gallons of water down their toilets every day!

REACT NOW!

Do you sometimes see problems but feel that you can't do anything about them because you're only one person? Think about one of those problems and plan one thing you could do to make a difference.

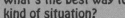

Anger is cruel and fury overwhelming, but who can stand before jealousy? Proverbs 27:4.

BEST FRIENDS . . . FOREVER?

Lauren and Sara had been best friends since sixth grade. Then, in junior high, Sara met Toria at soccer practice and started hanging out with her.

Lauren watched enviously as Sara and Toria came back from the soccer field talking and laughing together. "I'm going over to Toria's house after school," Sara said, even though she and Lauren usually walked home together. "Guess I'll see you tomorrow."

Lauren walked home alone, kicking at stones on the sidewalk and feeling sorry for herself. At home she went to her room and closed the door. She didn't want to talk to anyone. She just wanted to be alone and think about how her best friend didn't have time for her anymore.

Later that evening Sara called, wanting to talk about her visit with Toria. "Next week Mom says I can have you *and* Toria over after school," she said. "Won't that be great?"

Lauren didn't think it was great at all. She wanted things to be the way they'd always been—just her and Sara, best friends forever. But she knew that if she acted jealous, she'd lose Sara's friendship altogether. Somehow she had to find room in their friendship for one more person. She took a deep breath and said, "OK, we could do that." *Maybe*, she thought, *I need to start making some new friends to include too.*

Info Splat

A kind of thick, ribbed, nontransparent glass used to be called jealous-glass. A window made of slats of glass that can be opened to let in air is called a jalousie—the French word for ***JEALOUSY***.

REACT NOW!

Have you ever been jealous when someone took away a friend's time and attention? What's the best way to deal with this kind of situation?

~ INCREDI-BIBLICAL ~

The Lord does not look at the things man looks at. Man looks at the outward appearance, but the Lord looks at the heart.
1 Samuel 16:7.

OUT PAST NEPTUNE

In 1930 a young American astronomer named Clyde Tombaugh discovered an object in the solar system beyond the planet Neptune. This object was given the name Pluto and was considered to be the ninth planet in our solar system.

For most of the twentieth century, schoolchildren learned the names of the *nine planets* in the solar system: Mercury, Venus, Earth, Mars, Jupiter, Saturn, Uranus, Neptune, and Pluto. But as time went on, scientists began to question whether Pluto was really a planet. In 2006 the International Astronomical Union redefined the word *planet* and ruled that Pluto was no longer one of the nine planets. Instead, it was classed as a "dwarf planet" along with two other objects called Ceres and Eris.

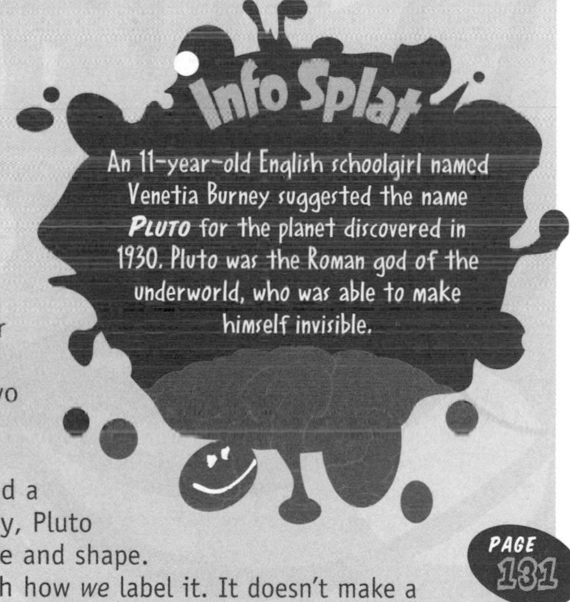

Info Splat
An 11-year-old English schoolgirl named Venetia Burney suggested the name **PLUTO** for the planet discovered in 1930. Pluto was the Roman god of the underworld, who was able to make himself invisible.

Scientists are still arguing over whether or not Pluto should be considered a planet. But throughout all the controversy, Pluto has been in the same place, the same size and shape. Whether we call it a planet has to do with how *we* label it. It doesn't make a bit of difference to Pluto!

Sometimes we label people. Someone might be considered weird, popular, a loser, or a leader. Like Pluto, some of us may wear more than one label in a lifetime. But the reality of who we are doesn't change because of how people see us. It's who we are in God's eyes that matters.

REACT NOW!

What labels have been attached to you in your life? How do you label others? How can we see past people's labels—and our own?

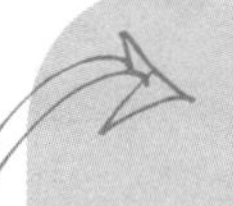

May 6

INCREDI-BIBLICAL

Be still, and know that I am God.
Psalm 46:10.

CALMING DOWN SERGIO

An evangelistic team was having a series of meetings in Costa Rica. The meetings were going well, except for one small problem: Sergio. He was 10 years old, and he just couldn't keep still or be quiet. Sergio had too much energy for his own good. During the meetings, while the evangelist was speaking, he ran around yelling, talking loudly, and getting the other kids excited.

The perfect solution would have been to hold a children's meeting to which all the kids could go while the adults listened to the sermon. But there was no space to hold a separate children's meeting. So when the evangelistic team met for prayer with other teams that were holding meetings in the area, they brought their problem and asked for prayer.

"We'd like you all to pray for Sergio," one of the evangelists explained. "If God could work a miracle in his heart, then our meetings could go ahead without being disturbed."

The next night the evangelistic team was prepared for more running, more yelling, and more disruption from Sergio. But they were in for a surprise. Sergio was like a completely different boy as he sat and listened to the service. Not only was he calm and quiet—he even helped keep the other kids quiet.

God answered prayer by working a miracle in the heart of one 10-year-old boy.

Info Splat

The first European explorer to come to Costa Rica was Christopher Columbus, who arrived on September 18, 1502. He was greeted by the local Carib Indians, who came paddling out in canoes to greet Columbus's crew.

REACT NOW!

Do you find it hard to listen and pay attention in church services and meetings? What helps you to be more attentive during worship?

INCREDI-BIBLICAL

Therefore, since we are surrounded by such a great cloud of witnesses, let us throw off everything that hinders and the sin that so easily entangles, and let us run with perseverance the race marked out for us. Hebrews 12:1.

BIBLE

ALLYSON ON THE RUN

In ninth grade Allyson tried out for track. Just 10 weeks after that first tryout, she came in seventh in the 200-meter dash in a state championship. Allyson Felix had discovered the thing she was born to do: running.

Fast-forward a few years: as a high school senior, Allyson broke the record for fastest time ever by a high school girl in the 200-meter. She even missed her senior prom to qualify for a state meet.

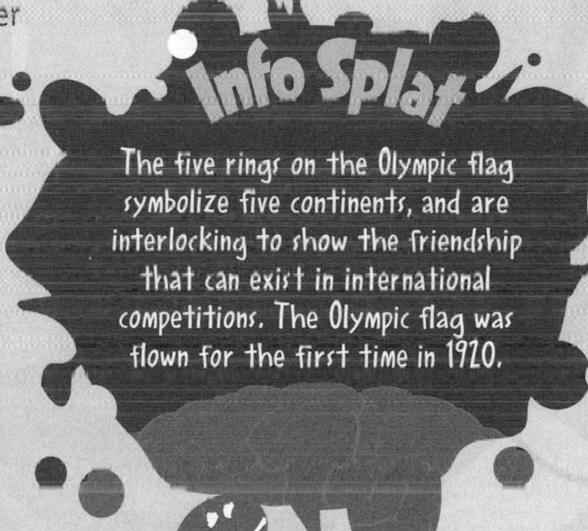

Info Splat
The five rings on the Olympic flag symbolize five continents, and are interlocking to show the friendship that can exist in international competitions. The Olympic flag was flown for the first time in 1920.

In the summer of 2004, 18-year-old Allyson competed in the 200-meter sprint in the Athens Summer Olympics. She set a world junior record in the qualifying round and won the silver medal in the final.

Allyson gives credit to God for helping her through the stress of competition. "I pray a lot," she says. "I always make time to spend in the Word, just talking to God. My speed is a gift from God, and I run for His glory. Whatever I do, it all comes from Him." Studying the Bible and sharing God's love with others are important values for Allyson, who attended Los Angeles Bible Training School at the same time she was studying at a university.

Not everyone can set a world record or win an Olympic medal. But by placing God at the center of our lives, we can all be winners in the race of life.

REACT NOW!

What's your "Olympic event," the thing you believe you have the ability to do well? Ask God to help you develop that skill for His glory.

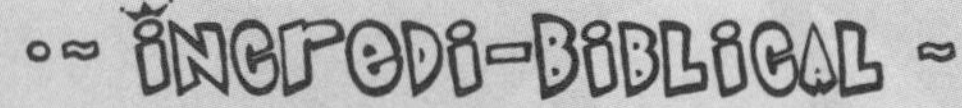

Turn to me and be gracious to me,
for I am lonely and afflicted.
Psalm 25:16.

WELCOME TO CAMP LONELINESS

Derek tilted his head back and looked up at the blue sky above him. It seemed to go on for miles, fringed with spruce and fir trees, and studded with shining stars. The air was full of the tang of wood smoke and the sound of voices singing in harmony. Derek was surrounded by all his friends, yet he felt so alone.

He'd been looking forward all year to teen camp. He and his friends had made plans to be in a cabin together. Though it was the longest and farthest Derek had ever been away from home, he just knew it would be an exciting adventure.

It *was* exciting. Derek loved the swimming, waterskiing, horseback riding, rock climbing, crafts, and campfires. What he didn't expect was to be so homesick. He never mentioned it to his friends or his counselor, for he feared they'd laugh at him. But even though he was having a good time, every evening he thought about how far he was from home. He badly missed his parents, his dog, and even his own comfortable room.

Derek looked up at the stars again and prayed silently. *Lord, I know You've got Your eye on me no matter how far from home I am. Please keep me and my family safe till we're together again, and help me to remember that I'm never alone as long as I'm with You.*

Info Splat
The first official summer camp sponsored by the Seventh-day Adventist Church was held in Australia in 1925.

REACT NOW!

When and where have you been lonely? What can you use as a reminder of God's love and care in situations in which you feel alone?

May 9

~ Incredi-Biblical ~

The Lord has done this,
and it is marvelous in our eyes.
Psalm 118:23.

"SORRY. IT'S A GIRL"

Elizabeth Tudor lived one of the most roller-coaster lives of any young girl in history. When she was born to King Henry VIII of England, she was heir to the throne—even though everyone in the country was disappointed she wasn't a boy! Then when she was just 3 years old, her father had her mother executed for treason. At that terrible event Elizabeth got demoted. She wasn't even Princess Elizabeth anymore; just Lady Elizabeth. Then her father's next wife had a son, which dropped Elizabeth's status even lower.

After both her father and sickly younger brother died, Elizabeth was once more a contender for the throne of England. However, her half sister, Mary, was crowned queen instead, for Elizabeth was considered dangerous. She even spent some time in prison and a few more years under house arrest while her sister ruled the country.

Eventually Elizabeth's moment in the sun arrived. Her sister Mary died, naming Elizabeth as her successor. And so Elizabeth reigned for 44 years and become one of England's most famous and successful monarchs. Through all the ups and downs of her early life she trusted God to work out His plan. It's said that when the news came that she was to be crowned queen, she recited Psalm 118:23: "The Lord has done this, and it is marvelous in our eyes."

Info Splat

In 1588, during Queen Elizabeth's reign, an attempted invasion of England by Spanish ships failed, partly because a severe storm blew the ships off course and sent them up the northern coast of England.

REACT NOW!

Do you ever get discouraged because things don't seem to be working out for you? Choose a Bible verse that you can use, as Elizabeth did, to encourage and remind you that God is working out His plan for your life.

~ INCREDI-BIBLICAL ~

God made the wild animals according to their kinds, the livestock according to their kinds, and all the creatures that move along the ground according to their kinds. And God saw that it was good. Genesis 1:25.

ELEPHANTS TO THE RESCUE

During the devastating tsunami that hit Southeast Asia in December 2004, elephants helped save the lives of several tourists. An 8-year-old girl from Britain was riding an elephant at a tourist resort in Thailand when the water began to recede. The elephant, knowing that something was wrong, ran with the girl on its back away from the water and up toward higher ground. When the oncoming wave caught up with them, the water swirled against the elephant's side, but left the girl unharmed.

In another Thai resort, a group of tourists was awakened before dawn by the sound of screaming elephants. Though the tidal wave had not yet hit, the elephants were agitated and began breaking loose from their chains and charging for higher ground. Neither the elephant handlers nor the tourists knew what was wrong. But they figured that maybe the elephants knew something they didn't, and they followed the elephants inland. As a result, they survived the tsunami.

Sometimes "dumb" animals may be more in touch with the natural world than are we human beings. By listening to the instincts their Creator gave them, animals are often able to survive and avoid disasters. Maybe we should begin paying a little more attention to our animal friends.

Info Splat

Elephants were also used to help with cleanup after the deadly tsunami. They are strong and sure-footed, and their trunks are good at reaching into small spaces and picking up rubble.

Have you ever seen an animal using its God-given instincts to survive? What can we learn from the animal kingdom?

May 11

~ INCREDI-BIBLICAL ~

Even my close friend, whom I trusted, he who shared my bread, has lifted up his heel against me. Psalm 41:9.

BETRAYED!

"You said you wouldn't tell anybody!" Kara yelled, her face hot with rage. Kara had trusted her best friend Jessie with a very troubling secret. Her parents were getting a divorce, and Kara's mom planned to move the family to another city. Kara wasn't ready for most people to hear that news yet, but she just had to talk to someone. So she'd asked Jessie to keep it a secret.

The next day when Kara came to school, all the girls were talking about it. "Oh, Kara, you must feel so bad about your folks splitting up," said Heather, a girl Kara barely knew.

She cornered Jessie in the playground at lunchtime. "How could you do that? I trusted you to keep it a secret!"

Jessie was speechless. "I didn't mean to tell anyone," she blurted. "It just kind of slipped out."

Trust is essential in a friendship. We share our secrets, our fears, our hopes with people we can trust. But trust in a friendship must be a two-way street. We have to be able to trust our friends, and we also must be trustworthy. That means keeping secrets (unless someone is in danger), and being there for our friends when they need us.

A true friendship, rooted in trust, is one of God's greatest gifts!

Info Splat

During the Revolutionary War the most famous traitor in American history, Benedict Arnold, plotted to surrender the American fort at West Point to the British. A monument to him on the battlefield of Saratoga, where he was considered a hero for the American side, does not mention his name.

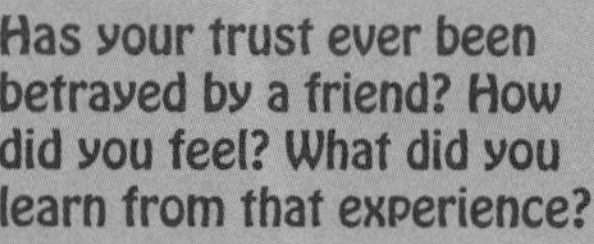

Has your trust ever been betrayed by a friend? How did you feel? What did you learn from that experience?

Incredi-Biblical

As a father has compassion on his children, so the Lord has compassion on those who fear him. Psalm 103:13.

COOL MOMS AND DADS

Emperor penguins may be the most dedicated dads in the animal kingdom. After the male and female penguins mate, the female lays a single egg at the feet of the male. Then Mom penguin takes off on a journey of up to 50 miles across the ice to feed.

The male emperor penguin holds the egg on his feet, covering it with a warm layer of skin and feathers designed to keep the egg safe and cozy. For 65 days the emperor dads huddle together in a group through the icy wind and snow of an Antarctic winter. They take turns standing on the outside of the group, moving into the center when they get too cold. During this time they eat nothing at all.

The chicks hatch near the end of winter, and the mother penguins return just in time to feed their babies. Then the hungry dads get to take off for a long-awaited fishing trip of their own! When they return, both parents feed and raise the baby penguins till they're ready to swim and fish on their own.

Animal parents do a lot for their children. So do human parents. But no parent, animal or human, can match the dedication of our Father in heaven, who does everything for His children.

Info Splat

During the Antarctic winter nearly all animals leave the ice except the emperor penguin—the only animal that spends the entire winter out on the open ice.

REACT NOW!

Take a moment in prayer to thank God for what He has done for you—especially for sacrificing Himself on the cross so that you can live forever.

INCREDI-BIBLICAL

Where can I go from your Spirit? Where can I flee from your presence? If I go up to the heavens, you are there; if I make my bed in the depths, you are there. Psalm 139:7, 8.

BIBLE

GANG WARRIOR FOR GOD

Acacio da Silva Sarmento was headed for trouble. He was a member of a street gang in his hometown of Dili, East Timor. Drinking, stealing, and getting in trouble were everyday activities for Acacio and his friends. Then came the time Acacio was desperate for cash so that he could buy cigarettes. He was searching through everything in the house, hoping to find some money lying around, when he picked up a book. There was no money under the book, but he noticed its title: *Where Are You After Death?*

Acacio was curious. He loved to read, and instead of settling down for a smoke, he settled down in his front yard with the book. As he read, he began wondering about questions that the book raised—questions about God, death, and the way he was living his life.

A few days later Acacio met a Seventh-day Adventist Christian and began asking him some of the questions that were on his mind. "Look in the Bible!" his new friend told him. "The answers are all there."

And so Acacio continued to read. He got a Bible, and sure enough, he found the answers he was searching for. He was drawn to Jesus and felt His love for him. Soon he was baptized as a Christian. Leaving the gang lifestyle behind, he got busy telling others about his new Friend, Jesus.

Looking for money to buy cigarettes, Acacio found a book that led him to God. Sometimes we find the answers we need when we least expect it.

Info Splat

East Timor became a Portuguese colony in the sixteenth century, and was controlled by Portugal until 1975. As soon as the Portuguese left, East Timor was taken over by Indonesia. It became an independent nation in 2002, the first new country of the millennium.

REACT NOW!
Where are some unexpected places in which you've found evidence of God's love and concern for you?

May 14

~ Incredi-Biblical ~

Wine is a mocker and beer a brawler; whoever is led astray by them is not wise. Proverbs 20:1.

BOOZE IS BAD NEWS

The average age at which boys in the United States first try drinking alcohol is 11. For girls, it's age 13. And in Canada 90 percent of twelfth graders report that they have tried alcohol.

If or when your friends try drinking and want to know why you don't, you'll need to know the facts. While "my parents and my church don't allow it" may be reason enough for you, you need some solid facts about alcohol use to tell your friends.

How much do you know about the drug that's used by more young people than any other? Take this quiz to find out.

1. *True or False:* Those who drink a lot, on a regular basis, will find that alcohol affects them less than it used to.

2. *True or False:* If a guy and girl of the same size and body type drink the same amount of alcohol, they both will have the same effect from it.

3. *True or False:* A person who's drunk can sober up by drinking coffee or another drink with caffeine.

4. *True or False:* Drinking is linked to teen deaths by car accident, suicide, drowning, and murder.

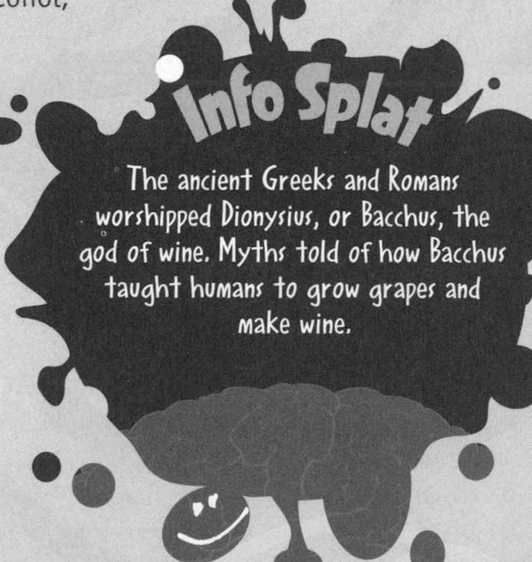

Info Splat
The ancient Greeks and Romans worshipped Dionysius, or Bacchus, the god of wine. Myths told of how Bacchus taught humans to grow grapes and make wine.

Answers:

1. True. Yes, your body soon builds up a tolerance for alcohol—a warning sign that it may be becoming addicted to it.

2. False. The same amount of alcohol affects a woman more than a man because girls' and women's bodies have less water in them.

3. False. The only "cure" for being drunk is time. Your liver and other organs must eliminate the poison from your bloodstream.

4. True.

REACT NOW!

Do any of the kids you know drink? What do you say when you're asked to try it? If that situation hasn't come up yet, plan how you will respond.

~ INCREDI-BIBLICAL ~

Listen, my son, to your father's instruction and do not forsake your mother's teaching.
Proverbs 1:8.

SHAINA'S PROBLEM PARENTS

"If you and Dad really trusted me, you'd let me go to the party!" Shaina shouted at her mom. Then she ran out of the room, slamming the door behind her. She didn't wait to hear Mom's reply. She already knew what it would be.

Mom's so overprotective, Shaina thought angrily. She worried about everything. Bike riding, overnight camping trips, downhill skiing—it seemed that everything Shaina wanted to do worried her mom. Now that Shaina was a high school freshman and her friends were having big weekend parties, Mom worried about that, too.

Info Splat
Teens are most likely to use alcohol and drugs when they are with friends, at parties, or in cars.

"It's no big deal," Shaina assured Dad the next day. "Taylor's parents will be there, and it's not going to be a huge crowd or anything. You've let me go to my friends' houses before." But Dad agreed with Mom. The answer was no.

"You can invite Lisa for a sleepover Saturday night," Mom suggested. "Her parents aren't letting her go to this party either."

In school Monday morning Shaina heard a lot about the party. Some of her friends said it was the most fun they'd ever had. Others didn't enjoy it. Taylor's parents hadn't been there, and some older guys had been drinking and started a fight. "It was kinda scary," Robyn admitted, "and I heard Taylor got in big trouble when her folks got home."

Listening to Robyn, Shaina suddenly thought that having overprotective parents might not be such a bad thing.

REACT NOW!

What kinds of things do your parents say no to? Do you ever disagree with them? Have they ever turned out to be right even when you disagreed?

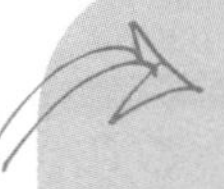

May 16

INCREDI-BIBLICAL

Let us walk properly, as in the day, not in revelry and drunkenness, not in lewdness and lust, not in strife and envy.
Romans 13:13, NKJV.

A SAINT IN THE MAKING

In the early days of Christianity a young man named Augustine grew up in the city of Tagaste in North Africa. At age 17 Augustine, who had a Christian mother and a pagan father, left home to go to school. Like many young people leaving home for the first time, he enjoyed lots of wild parties and found a girlfriend in the city of Carthage. During those years his mother's Christian beliefs were the furthest thing from his mind.

But his mother, Monica, never stopped praying for him. Years later, when Augustine moved to Italy to take a new job and find a wife, his mother went with him. She was still praying that someday he would give his life to God.

One day Augustine felt impressed to take up his Bible and begin reading it. He read Romans 13:13 and was struck by its message to "walk properly, as in the day." He decided to abandon the life he'd been living and become a Christian. After his baptism he returned home to Africa with his mother. Sadly, Augustine's mother died while on that journey, but she died knowing that her long years of praying for her son had finally received an answer. Augustine went on to become one of the most famous and important writers and teachers in the early Christian church.

Info Splat

The city of Carthage, where Augustine went to study, may have once been a center for child sacrifice. Some historians believe that at one time as many as 500 children were sacrificed to appease the gods. However, other historians believe this never happened.

REACT NOW!

Who is praying for you?
For whom are you praying?
How can we keep going even when it seems that God is taking a long time to answer our prayers?

May 17

~ Incredi-Biblical ~

I have fought the good fight, I have finished the race, I have kept the faith. Now there is in store for me the crown of righteousness, which the Lord, the righteous Judge, will award to me on that day. 2 Timothy 4:7, 8.

BIBLE

THE GREATEST REALITY SHOW

If you watch TV these days, it seems that every second show is a "reality show." Instead of using actors to act out fictional stories, the hot trend in TV today is to put everyday people in bizarre situations, then see how they react.

Reality TV shows give people the chance to do everything from surviving on a desert island, to competing in around-the-world races, to facing their worst fears. Reality show contestants might find themselves getting a beauty makeover, eating a bucket of worms, trying out for a singing career, or even finding a marriage partner!

While a few reality TV shows actually help people—such as those that show a team building and decorating a new home for a needy family—most aren't so positive. They focus on getting people to compete and even fight with each other. Makeover shows encourage people to be dissatisfied with their looks and try to change them. Some reality shows make light of marriage, family, and commitment.

Info Splat

People who apply to be contestants on reality shows have to answer questions about everything from their health and their political beliefs to their most embarrassing moments.

As Christians we are starring in the greatest reality show of all time. You might call it *Temptation Planet*. The whole universe watches to see if the people of Planet Earth will choose faithfulness to God over Satan's temptations. And the prize isn't a million dollars or a new home. The prize is eternal life.

REACT NOW!

What kind of TV show is your life most like? If you're the star of your own show, are you allowing God to be the director?

May 18

~ INCREDI-BIBLICAL ~

Lying lips are an abomination to the Lord, but those who act faithfully are his delight. Proverbs 12:22, NRSV.

A SICKENING COMPLIMENT

The history test was harder than Mandy had expected. A lot harder! She stared at question seven with a sinking heart, knowing her answer was all wrong. As for question 8, she didn't even know where to start.

She had studied—she really had. She just found history so much harder than her other subjects. And there sat Josh—across the aisle—busily filling out his test. He looked so confident. Mandy could just tell that he knew all the answers. He wasn't bothering to cover up his paper at all. If she looked—just a little—she could easily see his answer to number 7. He was starting work on number 8 now.

Would it be so wrong? she wondered. She wouldn't exactly cheat—just look for a second to see if she could get an idea. Just to get herself on the right track.

She knew it was wrong. But it was so easy, and she needed the help so badly. Her heart pounding, Mandy looked at Josh's response to number 7 and quickly erased her own, replacing her answer with his. Then she stole quick a look at number 8.

The next day Mr. Silver handed the tests back. Josh got 100 percent. Mandy got 85 percent. "Way to go, Mandy!" Josh said. "You said you thought the test was really hard, but look what a good grade you got!" He smiled at her as he left the room.

Mandy had never in her life felt worse about a compliment.

Info Splat

Sadly, in a 1998 survey of more than 20,000 students, 70 percent of high school students and 54 percent of middle school students said they had cheated on an exam in the past 12 months.

REACT NOW!

Have you ever cheated on a test? How did it make you feel? What are the disadvantages of cheating? How can you avoid the temptation to cheat?

May 19

~ INCREDI-BIBLICAL ~

Therefore, if anyone is in Christ, he is a new creation; the old has gone, the new has come! 2 Corinthians 5:17.

THOSE SHY PANDAS

If you're looking for a pet that's sociable, loves people and other animals, and adapts easily to a new home—don't get a giant panda. (There are probably other reasons you wouldn't want a panda as a pet, but we're just going to talk about one of them.)

Giant pandas are shy creatures who don't like to venture into areas where people live. As people spread out into more and more areas of the panda's native China, this becomes a problem, for the pandas' habitat continues to shrink.

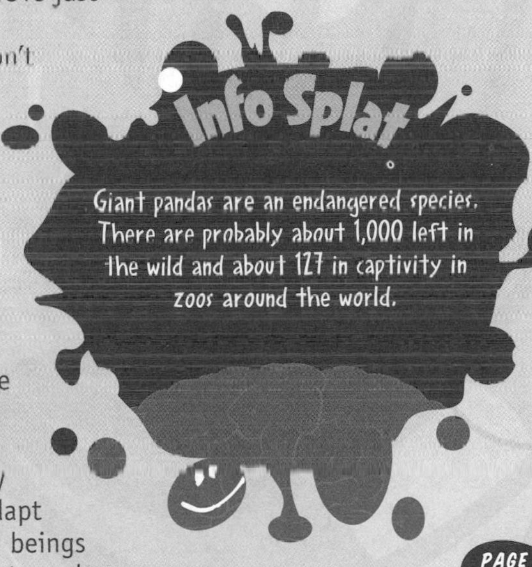

Info Splat
Giant pandas are an endangered species. There are probably about 1,000 left in the wild and about 127 in captivity in zoos around the world.

And like some of us, pandas don't cope well with change. The only thing they really want to eat is bamboo, and when all the bamboo in an area dies off naturally they may starve to death because they're unable to move to where different kinds of bamboo grow.

Life is full of change. We're constantly faced with situations that require us to adapt and accept change. Unlike pandas, human beings have been blessed by God with the ability to make changes and move on to new challenges.

Sometimes we're a little like pandas, though. We may be afraid to try something new, to move to a new place, to make a new friend. Unlike the panda, our biggest fear is often that we'll look stupid if we try something new and fail.

Don't be a panda. Don't let fear of change hold you back from moving forward!

REACT NOW!

What changes are you facing in life in the near future? A move? New school? The chance to meet a new friend or try something different? Ask God for the strength to help you cope with the changes and challenges life throws at you.

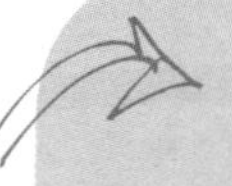

Incredi-Biblical

Though my father and mother forsake me, the Lord will receive me. Psalm 27:10.

A PLACE FOR MAE

Mae's parents gave her up for adoption when she was just a baby. Mae, who had a deformed leg, was born in China, where the government urges families to have only one child. Most parents prefer boys, so many baby girls are given up for adoption, especially if, like Mae, they have a disability.

Sadly, Mae's adoptive parents weren't very kind to her either. At 12 she left school and went to work selling flowers to help make money for them. And when she wanted to go back to school, her adoptive parents abandoned her. Now homeless and living on the streets, Mae searched out her birth parents. When she found them, they sent her away, telling her she was worthless.

Mae's life began to change when a newspaper reporter stopped by her flower stall and interviewed her. After reading her story, someone found a place for Mae to live. Then a Christian doctor made it possible for Mae to attend a Seventh-day Adventist school in the Philippines.

Mae was a Buddhist, but as she began learning about the love of Jesus, she wanted to follow Him. When Mae was baptized as a Christian, her first question to the pastor was "Am I a daughter of God now?" Mae had finally found a place she belonged.

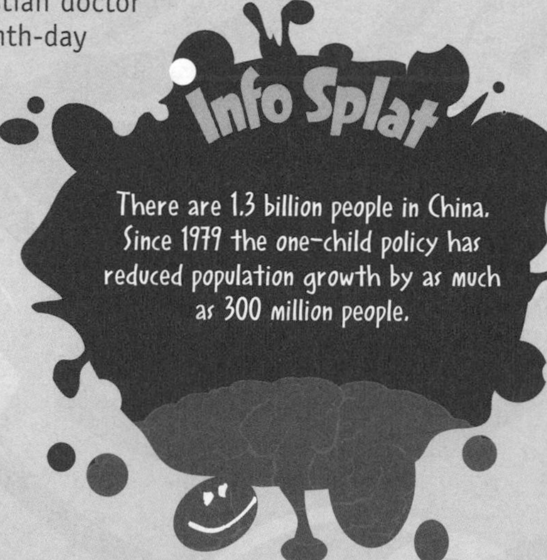

Info Splat
There are 1.3 billion people in China. Since 1979 the one-child policy has reduced population growth by as much as 300 million people.

REACT NOW!

Think about the high value God places on you as His child. How can that help you when other people dislike or reject you?

May 21

INCREDI-BIBLICAL

See, I have engraved you
on the palms of my hands.
Isaiah 49:16.

TATTOOED NO MORE

Tattoos are popping up everywhere. Guys, girls, older and younger people all seem to be getting into the idea of putting permanent designs on their bodies.

From the time he was 8, Joe had tattoos. But these weren't just any tattoos. Like so many kids from the inner city, Joe had tattoos that declared his membership in a gang. While Joe was growing up and in the gang his tattoos were a sign of belonging. But in the world beyond the gang, people looked at him with suspicion.

When Joe was older, he discovered that it was hard for him to get a job. Seeing his tattoos, people immediately figured that he was a gang member—and a troublemaker. So Joe decided he wanted a fresh, clean start in life—with no tattoos.

That's when he found Agape Light Tattoo Removal—a church ministry that removes tattoos from people for free. Lots of people, just like Joe, wanted to erase the marks of their past. A Seventh-day Adventist doctor started Agape Light to help them.

A tattoo that looks cool today might be a lot less attractive a few years down the road. But there's one symbol of belonging that we can always count on. The Bible tells us that we are engraved on the palms of God's hands. It's as if God has a tattoo—one that constantly reminds Him how much He cares for His children!

Info Splat

The word *TATTOO* comes from the Tahitian word *TATU*, which means to mark something. Women in Borneo used to tattoo symbols on their forearm to show that they had a special skill, such as being good at weaving.

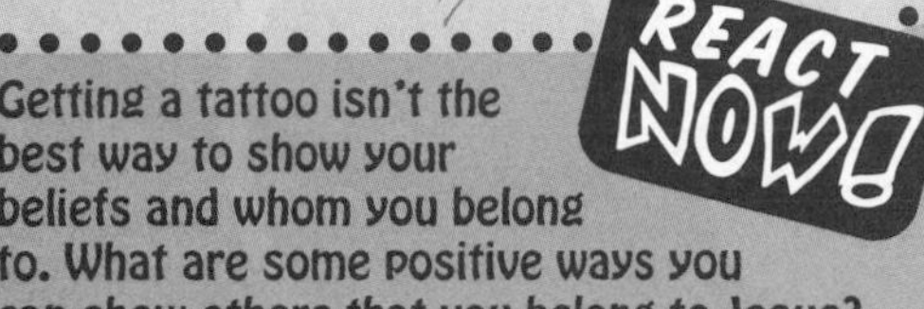

Getting a tattoo isn't the best way to show your beliefs and whom you belong to. What are some positive ways you can show others that you belong to Jesus?

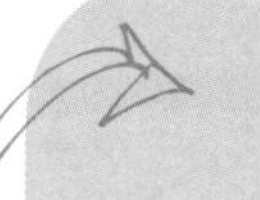

May 22

~ Incredi-Biblical ~

Dear friends, since God so loved us, we also ought to love one another. 1 John 4:11.

FRIENDLY SOCCER

Nick sat at the lunchroom table listening to the guys around him talking and laughing. He felt invisible. The others weren't mean to him; they just didn't seem to *see* him. *It's not their fault,* Nick thought, *it's mine. If I weren't so shy, I'd be able to make friends.*

Nick's family had moved to a new town, and he was in a new school, where he didn't know anyone. It caused him almost physical pain to walk into class every day and quietly go to his seat at the back of the room. At home Nick spent most of his time in his room reading or playing computer games—though Mom insisted that, at least on occasion, he come out and join the family. Mostly, his parents urged him to get out and make friends. *They just don't realize how hard it is,* Nick thought.

As Nick sat staring at his plate of spaghetti, he was startled to realize that Dave was talking to him. "You play soccer, Nick?" Dave asked.

"Um, a little. I used to back home." Nick wanted to kick himself. Why couldn't he just start a conversation?

"You should hang around with us after school. A bunch of us are going to the park for a game. We need a few more guys."

Nick's first thought was to say no. He'd be around a lot of guys he didn't know. But then he changed his mind. "OK, that'd be great," he said. *Dave went out of his way to be nice to me,* he thought. *The least I can do is give it a try.*

Info Splat
The World Cup is the biggest soccer tournament in the world. It is held every four years in different countries, and is watched by billions of people around the world on television.

REACT NOW!

Have you ever reached out to someone who was new, different, or unpopular? Is there someone like that you could reach out to now?

May 23

~ INCREDI-BIBLICAL ~

The eyes of the Lord are on those who fear him, on those whose hope is in his unfailing love. Psalm 33:18.

THE FAITH OF ANNE FRANK

Anne Frank had just turned 11 when the German army invaded the Netherlands, where she lived. During the next two years her life became more and more complicated. The reason? She and her family were Jews. All kinds of laws were passed against Jews. For example, they could not use public telephones or ride trains. They were not allowed in parks that non-Jews went to. And they had to sew a yellow star on their clothes to show everyone they were Jews. Much worse things were ahead, though. Jews were being arrested and sent to labor camps, where hundreds of thousands died.

Info Splat

The word ***HOLOCAUST*** is used to refer to the massive slaughter of Jewish people during World War II. Before World War II the word was used for any great loss of life, especially by fire. The word originally meant ***BURNT OFFERING.***

When Anne was 13, her family went into hiding. Thanks to the kindness of Dutch friends, Anne's family and four others lived for two years in a small attic at the back of an office building. Living in such cramped conditions, in constant fear of being discovered and arrested, was a hard way for a young girl to grow up. Yet in Anne's diary, where she kept a record of all her hardships and fears, she wrote, "Despite everything, I still believe most people are really good at heart."

Their hiding place was discovered in August 1944. They all were sent to concentration camps, where Anne died before her sixteenth birthday. Her father was the only family member who survived.

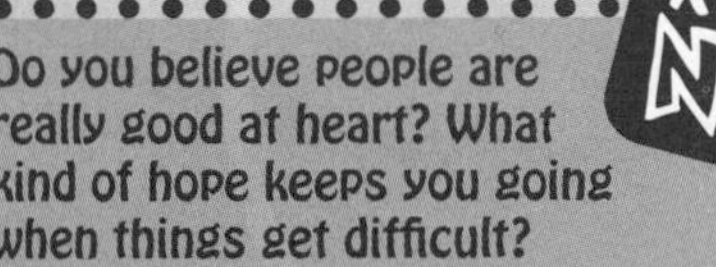

REACT NOW!

Do you believe people are really good at heart? What kind of hope keeps you going when things get difficult?

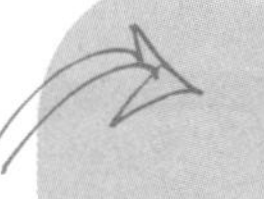

May 24

Incredi-Biblical

I will be glad and rejoice in you; I will sing praise to your name, O Most High. Psalm 9:2.

"You Can't Sing" (Oh, Really?)

George Huff was just a toddler when he realized he could sing along, note for note, with a popular song playing on the radio. Running into the kitchen, little George announced to his mother, "I can sing!"

"Shut up, boy," his mom snapped. "You can't sing. Get out of the kitchen."

But George *could* sing, and soon everyone realized it. Growing up in poverty in a New Orleans public housing project, almost every weekend George found himself with an invitation to sing in churches of different denominations. He describes himself as a nerd in high school, coming from a home too poor to buy cool clothes, but his voice gave him an opportunity to dream of something better. George went to college on a music scholarship.

George wanted a career in music, but by the end of his junior year his scholarship money ran out. He had to quit school and take a job washing dishes in the college cafeteria. Just when it seemed his dreams had reached a dead end, George had the opportunity to audition for the TV show *American Idol*. There he became a top 5 finalist.

After the *Idol* experience George was offered several record deals. He chose one from Word Records and began recording Christian music, using his talents to share the message of God's love with others.

Info Splat
About 2.4 billion CDs are sold every year. Half of these are recorded CDs; the other half are blank.

React Now!

What are your dreams for the future? Think through your goals and whether they can be used to glorify God. Then ask for His blessing to help you fulfill those dreams.

May 25

~ INCREDI-BIBLICAL ~

You shall have no other gods before me.
Exodus 20:3.

COMPUTER GAMES CRISIS

Justin, we need to talk," Dad said as he sat down on the end of Justin's bed.

"What?" Justin's attention was focused on steering his virtual car around the racetrack on the screen in front of him.

"Your mom and I think you're spending a little too much time playing these games."

"Aw, Dad!" Justin said, finally looking up from the screen. "You guys have so many rules about what things I can play, and you know I follow all those rules—no violent games, no fighting games, nothing like that."

"I know, and we appreciate that we can trust you on this," Dad said. "It's not just *which* games you play that worries me, though. It's the fact that you seem to be making computer games number one in your life. You rush home from school and lock yourself in your room to play games."

"I get my homework done!" Justin insisted. "Well . . . most of the time."

"Schoolwork, family, exercise—and God," Dad reminded him. "All those things are a lot more important than computer games. Sometimes it seems as though your games are becoming a false god in your life. They're like something that you worship."

"Dad, don't be ridiculous. I don't *worship* computer games!" Justin laughed.

"To worship something or someone means to put them first, to give them the most important place in your life," Dad explained. "You should think about this some more. And in the meantime, we're going to be setting some limits on your gaming time."

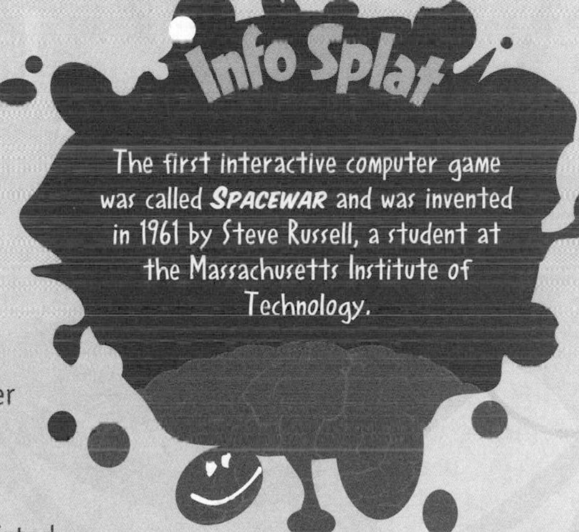

Info Splat
The first interactive computer game was called SPACEWAR and was invented in 1961 by Steve Russell, a student at the Massachusetts Institute of Technology.

REACT NOW!

If you are "worshipping" the thing that takes up most of your time and most of your thoughts, what are you worshipping? How important is your time with God on your list of things to do every day?

Incredi-Biblical

Consider it pure joy, my brothers, whenever you face trials of many kinds, because you know that the testing of your faith develops perseverance. James 1:2, 3.

A STRADIVARIUS "WOOD" BE NICE

Some of the most famous violins ever made were made by Antonio Stradivari in seventeenth-century Italy. World-class violinists today still consider it an honor to own or play a 300-year-old Stradivarius violin. Nothing else sounds quite like it.

Why were Stradivari's violins so great? Nobody knows for sure, but one theory suggests that the weather might have had something to do with it.

Violins, of course, are made from wood. The harder the wood, the better the violin. Slow-growing trees make for harder, denser wood. And the cooler the weather, the more slowly trees grow.

During the years Stradivari was making his violins, Europe was experiencing something called the Little Ice Age. Temperatures were much colder during that time than they are now. Some scientists now believe that because Stradivari's violins were made with very hard, dense wood that grew during the Little Ice Age, they are still making beautiful music today.

We don't always understand the long-term results of the things we do today. Just as violinists today are still playing beautiful music on violins made 300 years ago, choices and decisions you make as a young person will affect your life for years to come. Right now you might experience some tough times—a Little Ice Age of hardship or challenge. But like Stradivari, you can use those hard times to produce something beautiful. With God's help, you can be making beautiful music with your life for years to come!

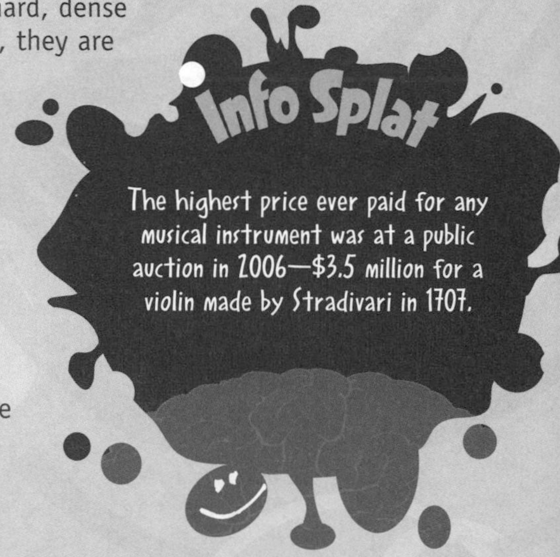

Info Splat
The highest price ever paid for any musical instrument was at a public auction in 2006—$3.5 million for a violin made by Stradivari in 1707.

REACT NOW!

What is one situation you're dealing with now that could affect your life in the future? Ask God to give you the wisdom and strength to make positive choices about this situation.

Incredi-Biblical

Then the King will say to those on his right, "Come, you who are blessed by my Father; take your inheritance, the kingdom prepared for you since the creation of the world. For I was hungry and you gave me something to eat, I was thirsty and you gave me something to drink, I was a stranger and you invited me in."
Matthew 25:34, 35.

TAKE THE WORLD HUNGER QUIZ

The Bible commands us to care for those who are hungry. While you may say "I'm starving!" when you come home at suppertime, most of us have never known real hunger. But millions of people in the world *do* know what it means to be hungry. Tragically, many even die of hunger. Find out how much you know about this problem.

What do you know about world hunger? Choose the correct answer for each of the questions below.

1. How many people in the world don't have enough to eat?
   a. more than 100 million
   b. more than 250 million
   c. more than 800 million
   d. more than 1 billion
2. One child dies from hunger-related causes every
   a. five seconds
   b. five minutes
   c. five hours
   d. five days
3. How many children die every year before reaching their fifth birthday?
   a. 1 million
   b. 11 million
   c. 15 million
   d. 20 million
4. In the developing world, what percentage of children are underweight?
   a. 7 percent
   b. 12 percent
   c. 27 percent
   d. 50 percent

5. *True or False:* The world simply does not produce enough food to feed earth's rapidly growing population.

Answers: 1-c, 2-a, 3-b, 4-c, 5-false.

Even though the world's population has increased 70 percent in the past 30 years, world agriculture still produces enough to feed everyone—17 percent more calories per person than it did 30 years ago. There's enough food out there for everyone!

REACT NOW!

The world's problems of poverty and hunger can seem so huge that we get overwhelmed and feel we can't do anything about them. What is *ONE* thing you can do to help those who don't have enough to eat?

Then you will call, and the Lord will answer; you will cry for help, and he will say: Here am I. Isaiah 58:9.

HELPING THE HEROES

Brother and sister Robbie and Brittany Bergquist were just 13 and 12 years old when they heard about an American soldier in Iraq who ran up a $7,600 phone bill calling home. The story inspired Brittany and Robbie to start a nonprofit organization called Cell Phones for Soldiers.

Between them, Brittany and Robbie's life savings totaled $21, which wasn't enough for many phone calls from Iraq. But once others heard about their plan, donations started rolling in. Not only did people donate money—they also donated prepaid phone cards and used cellular phones. The cell phones were recycled to raise money.

By the time Brittany and Robbie received a National Caring Award two years later, they had raised more than $1 million and sent 80,000 calling cards to U.S. troops in the Middle East. A lot of soldiers were able to talk to their folks at home—all because two teenagers understood the importance of keeping in touch.

Talking to the people we love means a lot. When we're confused or in trouble, it helps to talk things over with a parent, relative, or trusted friend. For a soldier thousands of miles from home, facing the possibility of injury and death, a calling card to home is a precious gift.

We're living on a planet far from our heavenly home, but our Father has a direct line called prayer that's always open for us to use. Are you keeping your prayer line open?

Info Splat

The first cellular phone weighed two pounds and was good for a half hour of talking each time it was recharged. It sold for $3,995.

REACT NOW!

Whom do you trust to talk to when you really need someone to listen? Is God on your list of good listeners? How can you deepen your prayer relationship with Him?

INCREDI-BIBLICAL

"For my thoughts are not your thoughts, neither are your ways my ways," declares the Lord. "As the heavens are higher than the earth, so are my ways higher than your ways and my thoughts than your thoughts." Isaiah 55:8, 9.

POSTER MESSAGE

"Mom, come help me with this!" Toby called from her room.

"In a little while," Mom called back. She was in the kitchen loading the dishwasher while Cheri vacuumed the living room rugs.

"I need help right now!" Toby wailed. "I've finished picking up my room, and I want to get this poster up on my wall *now*!"

Cheri switched off the vacuum and rolled her eyes. "Toby, it's almost sunset," she called to her 7-year-old sister. "We have company coming for supper, and Mom and I are busy trying to get everything cleaned up. We'll help you with the poster later."

"But I need to do it NOW!"

"She just doesn't get it, does she?" Cheri told Mom. "She always thinks whatever *she's* doing is the most important thing in the world, no matter what else is going on. I guess that's just the way little kids think."

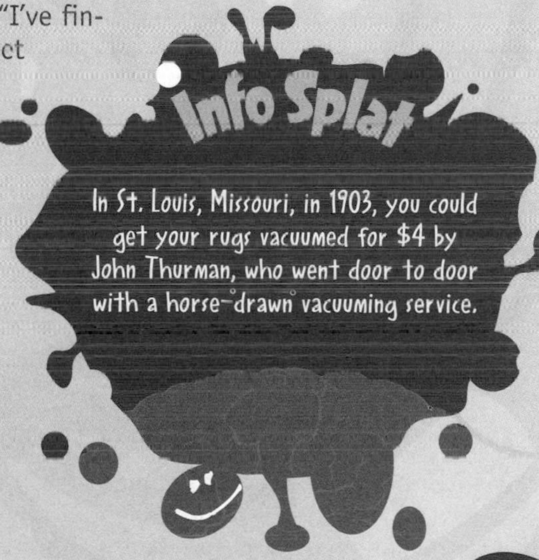

Info Splat
In St. Louis, Missouri, in 1903, you could get your rugs vacuumed for $4 by John Thurman, who went door to door with a horse-drawn vacuuming service.

Mom smiled. "You were like that yourself not too long ago," she reminded Cheri. "Sometimes I think we're all a little bit like that."

"What do you mean?"

"Think about how we often pray," Mom said, closing the dishwasher door. "We beg God for what we want *right now*, and it seems just as important to us as Toby's poster does to her. We don't have any idea what the big picture is or what other issues God is dealing with. Maybe if we did, we'd be a little more patient."

REACT NOW!

Think of a time you had to wait or received the answer "No" to something you prayed for. As you look back, can you see that there was more to the story than you realized at the time?

~ Incredi-Biblical ~

The race is not to the swift or the battle to the strong, nor does food come to the wise or wealth to the brilliant or favor to the learned; but time and chance happen to them all. Ecclesiastes 9:11.

ACCIDENTAL DISCOVERY

The great French scientist Louis Pasteur left his laboratory for several weeks in 1880. While he was away, his assistant, Charles Chamberland, was supposed to inject some chickens with the bacteria for a disease called cholera so that Pasteur could study the effect of the illness on the chickens. But Chamberland didn't do it right away, and by the time he got around to using the bacteria, it was a month old and no longer very effective. Though they were injected, the chickens didn't get sick.

Later Pasteur infected the same chickens with a new, stronger strain of the cholera bacteria. But they still didn't get sick. Louis Pasteur had made one of the greatest accidental discoveries in history! He had discovered that if you infect someone with a very weak strain of a disease, they'll build up immunity and won't get sick when they meet that same kind of bacteria again.

Today Pasteur's discovery is used to vaccinate people against all kinds of infectious diseases. Millions of lives have been saved by vaccination.

Many great discoveries have been made by chance. But Louis Pasteur said, "Chance favors the prepared mind." A lucky accident isn't much good if a person hasn't studied and worked hard. God can work in our lives through all kinds of events, even accidents. But we need to do our part by being prepared and ready to work hard.

Info Splat

Louis Pasteur invented a process to kill dangerous microbes in liquids by heating them, which prevents many diseases. The pasteurized milk you may use on your cereal was named after Louis Pasteur.

REACT NOW!

Have you ever solved a problem or figured something out "by accident"? What kind of preparation did you have to do to be ready for that accident?

May 31

INCREDI-BIBLICAL

Do you not know that in a race all the runners run, but only one gets the prize? Run in such a way as to get the prize.
1 Corinthians 9:24.

THE BIRMINGHAM BOBSLEDDER

When young African-American kids growing up in the city imagine a successful sports career, they might think of playing in the NBA or running as Olympic track stars. Bobsledding isn't the first sport that leaps to most teens' minds.

Bobsled certainly wasn't a sport Vonetta Flowers ever considered while growing up in Birmingham, Alabama. A high school track star, she went to college on a track-and-field scholarship. But a series of injuries stood between Vonetta and her goal of joining the U.S. Olympic track team.

Yet in 2002 Vonetta became the first person of African descent to win a medal in the Winter Olympics when she and her teammate took gold in Olympic bobsled at Salt Lake City, Utah.

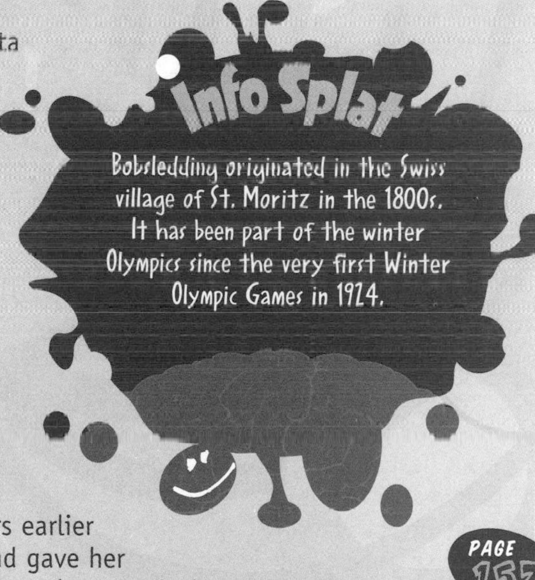

Info Splat
Bobsledding originated in the Swiss village of St. Moritz in the 1800s. It has been part of the winter Olympics since the very first Winter Olympic Games in 1924.

Trying a winter sport was an unexpected detour for Vonetta, but her life had taken a far more important turn a few years earlier when she attended church with a friend and gave her heart to the Lord. Dedicating herself and her talents to God gave Vonetta a new sense of purpose in her life.

After Vonetta won an Olympic gold medal, her very first track coach, who had worked with her from the age of 9, congratulated her with this thought: "God didn't let you win this medal just for you. The Lord let you win so you can look at another young girl from the ghetto and encourage her."

REACT NOW!

Have you ever been scared to try something new? Think about the possibilities open to you when you try a different way of doing something. Then choose one new challenge that scares you a little and, with God's help, decide you'll give it a try.

~ INCREDI-BIBLICAL ~

"Yell a loud *no* to the Devil and watch him scamper. Say a quiet *yes* to God and he'll be there in no time. James 4:7, 8, Message.

ANGER EXPLOSION

Yvette, a sweet little girl with a hot temper, lived with her teacher as a foster child. When she asked to go to a program on the death of Christ at a nearby church, she was allowed to go, but afterward she had a lot of questions about what had happened to Jesus and why.

"Why did the men put Jesus on the cross?" she asked her teacher. "Why didn't He run away? Why didn't He fight back?"

Miss Abbott answered her as best she could, but Yvette became more and more agitated, repeating the questions again and again. Five days later she exploded—yelling, screaming, climbing on furniture, throwing things, and beating on the walls. Nothing would calm her. In desperation Miss Abbott called for police help. As the officer talked with the little girl, she gradually calmed down.

When the child finally caught her breath, her teacher asked, "Yvette, what makes you do these things?"

Yvette looked away, frowning. "I was thinking about the play we watched about Jesus," she said. "It wasn't right for those people to do that to Him. It made me really angry."

Miss Abbott prayed with Yvette and then called a friend to come and anoint the girl and ask God to heal the anger that so often controlled her.

"You know," their friend told Yvette, "James 4:7 reminds me who's got the power. The next time you feel like showing your anger this way, you can ask God for His help. He's just waiting for us to say yes to Him."

Yvette was truly sorry for her actions. She praised Jesus for healing her mind and taking away her desire to be destructive.

Info Splat

In 2006, researchers came up with a name for anger involving hostile or aggressive behavior: intermittent explosive disorder. The general public calls it bad manners, immaturity, and temper tantrums. A reporter for the Roanoke *TIMES* wonders if this is a disorder or simply a lack of self-control.

REACT NOW!

Is anger wrong? In what biblical situations do you see examples of God's anger? What are some good ways to express your anger? What are good ways to help you calm down?

Incredi-Biblical

For God so loved the world that he gave his one and only son, that whoever believes in him shall not perish but have eternal life. John 3:16.

THE SEA WASP

The sea wasp, or box jellyfish, is found in the waters near Australia and Hawaii. This fascinating creature has four eyes but no brain, and its bell or cubelike form is transparent with a pale blue or reddish tint. The sea wasp may be as big as a basketball and have up to 15 tentacles hanging from the bottom corners of its cube. The tentacles, covered with venomous stinging cells, can be up to 15 feet long. When the sea wasp senses certain chemicals on the skin of its prey, it releases the venom into the victim.

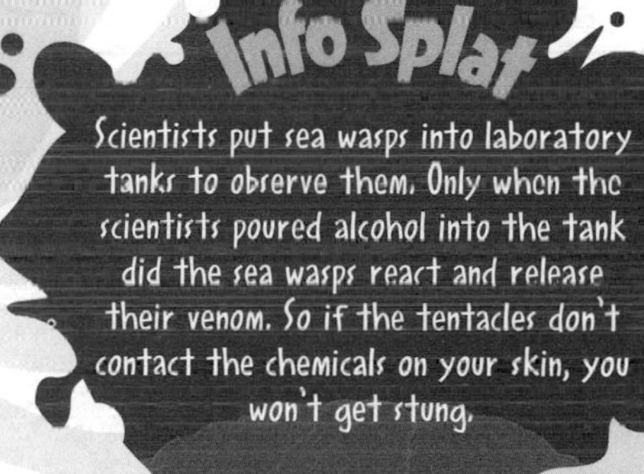

Info Splat
Scientists put sea wasps into laboratory tanks to observe them. Only when the scientists poured alcohol into the tank did the sea wasps react and release their venom. So if the tentacles don't contact the chemicals on your skin, you won't get stung.

If you are swimming and get stung by a sea wasp, you may not make it back to shore. The sting is excruiatingly painful, and death can come in just two to three minutes.

One way to protect yourself from the sea wasp's sting may surprise you: pantyhose. That's right! Sea wasps don't sting through pantyhose, so Australian lifeguards can often be seen with nylons on their arms and legs. Similarly, when we feel the sting of death that Paul talks about in 1 Corinthians 15:55, 56, we can find safety in the covering of Jesus' forgiveness and righteousness.

The sea wasp and Satan's temptations may be hard to see at first, but their sting results in terrible pain and death. Find God's remedy in John 3:16.

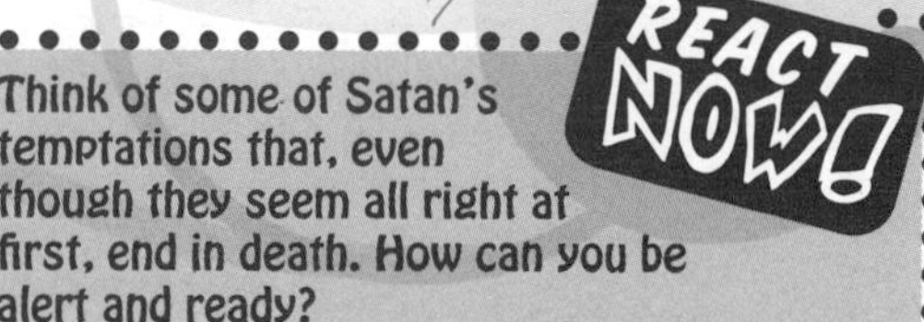

REACT NOW!
Think of some of Satan's temptations that, even though they seem all right at first, end in death. How can you be alert and ready?

~ INCREDI-BIBLICAL ~

Let the little children come to me, and do not hinder them, for the kingdom of God belongs to such as these. Mark 10:14.

DOMINICAN MISSION TRIP

It was Sara's first Pathfinder mission trip, and she was excited. Her club was flying to the Dominican Republic for a week to help at an orphanage.

The Pathfinders settled into their rooms at the orphanage and met some of the children. Even though they didn't speak the same language, the children smiled at the gifts Sara's club had brought: toothbrushes, toothpaste, pencils, and soap. They hugged each other and then started an impromptu game of tag.

On Sabbath Sara went with the other Pathfinders to the orphanage Sabbath school. But across a field she could see a small Adventist church. Slipping from her seat, Sara waded through the grass, crossed the field, and opened the church door.

"Bienvenidos!" a smiling woman said. At first Sara didn't understand, but then the woman motioned for her to come inside.

She didn't want to cause a commotion, so she sat back in the mothers' room to listen. It wasn't long before a small girl came in. Sara took out a pencil and paper and began to draw pictures. Then she'd say the name of what she'd drawn in English, and ask the girl for the name of it in Spanish. Soon five or six pairs of brown eyes watched her draw. Sara had some extra pencils with her, and she gave each child one. Their eyes shone with happiness.

Sara knew that sharing with others brings happiness. It's also one way to show God's love.

Info Splat

In the Dominican Republic, paper currency is printed in peso notes. Most supermarkets either price their goods at an even peso or round off the bill at the cash register.

REACT NOW!

Name three ways you can share God's love with others today. How can you be part of a mission experience while still at home?

**Whatever your hand finds to do,
do it with all your might.
Ecclesiastes 9:10.**

THE HERRIN TWINS

Kendra and Maliyah Herrin were born on February 26, 2002, in Salt Lake City, Utah. They were conjoined twins, joined together at the abdomen and pelvis. They shared some organs and had four arms but only two legs. Together they learned to crawl, scoot around, and even do a somersault, with each girl controlling only one leg.

When they were 4 years old, a team of doctors and nurses made preparations for a special operation to separate them. Seventeen small bags were placed in different places under the girls' skin. Over several weeks saline was gradually added to the bags to stretch the skin so there would be enough extra skin to cover the wounds made during the surgery.

The successful separation surgery took more than 25 hours, 11 doctors, and many prayers. After several weeks in the hospital, Kendra and Maliyah had a happy homecoming.

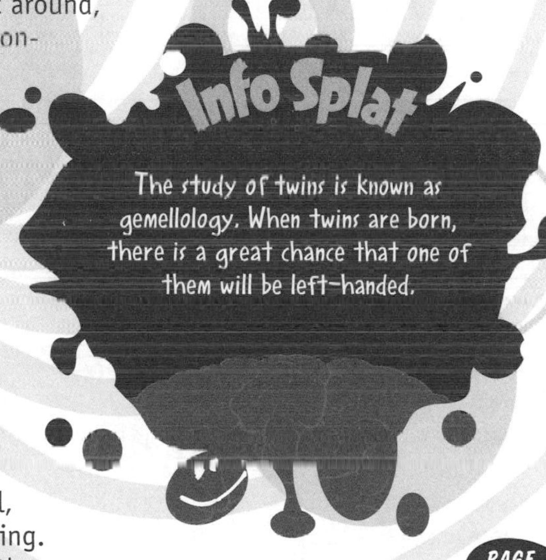

Info Splat
The study of twins is known as gemellology. When twins are born, there is a great chance that one of them will be left-handed.

Now they each have just one leg, but they are learning to use crutches, ride Dora bicycles, and prepare for prosthetic legs. Their medical treatment for different complications continues, but Kendra and Maliyah are sweet and talented little girls who continue to work hard. They put to use the verse "Whatever your hand finds to do, do it with all your might." To read more about the Herrin twins, go to www.Herrintwins.com.

PAGE 161

REACT NOW!

Tell three ways you can show that you work hard without working every minute of the day. How can you be an effective team player?

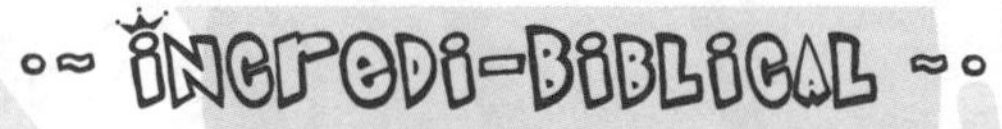

For I have learned to be content whatever the circumstances. Philippians 4:11.

DIVORCE? NOT IN MY FAMILY!

The call to the boarding academy where Kira was in school came on Wednesday evening. "Kira," her dad said, "things are not going the best for your mother and me. I want you to know that we both love you very much, but I will be moving out. I wanted to tell you first."

She'd been expecting it, but the news was still a shock. Her parents—headed for a divorce. Kira's chest felt tight, and tears pricked the corners of her eyes. Even though she'd known that her parents were hurting, she still had a hard time accepting that divorce could happen in her family.

Taking her problems to her heavenly Father, Kira bowed her head. Then she took her Bible and turned to some promises for comfort. Philippians 4:11 and Philippians 4:19 had special meaning. Even when her world was falling apart, she knew she had Someone who would never let her down.

Later that week Kira talked with some friends and family members and took time to think through her reactions. Then she decided to talk with her mom and dad. She needed for them to know that she still loved each of them, and she needed to know they loved her, too. While there would be hard questions to answer and difficult decisions to make, it would help her feelings of self-worth to know that she was loved by both parents.

Kira found comfort in knowing Jesus was her friend in a time of trouble.

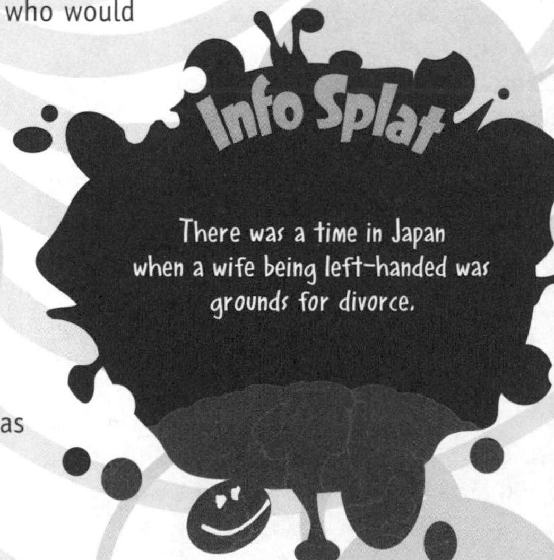

Info Splat
There was a time in Japan when a wife being left-handed was grounds for divorce.

REACT NOW!

How can you help a friend whose parents are divorcing or who is experiencing other significant problems? What Bible promise could you share with them? (Deuteronomy 31:6 and Joshua 1:9 are a good place to begin.)

June 6

~ Incredi-Biblical ~

Do you see a man skilled in his work?
He will serve before kings.
Proverbs 22:29.

HARRY ANDERSON

Harry Anderson was a skilled artist. He went to college intending to study math, but one year when he needed to choose an elective, he picked an art class. His teacher soon realized that Harry had a special talent.

Harry knew it too, and he enjoyed painting. Once during college when he needed work, he saw that a sign painter for a large store wasn't able to make the sale signs one day. "Need some help?" Harry asked, volunteering himself for the job. The manager liked his diligence and hired him on permanently.

After college Harry and a friend went to New York City to try to make a living by painting. But the country was in a depression, and not many people had money to spend on artwork. So Harry worked at a snack shop for a while. Later he moved to Chicago and worked for an art department. He enjoyed sharing ideas with other people and learning new ways to make a picture look alive.

In midlife Harry became a Seventh-day Adventist and was asked to work as a freelance artist at the Review and Herald Publishing Association. Harry painted many biblical scenes to illustrate their books. His most famous image was finished in 1945, entitled *What Happened to Your Hand?* It was done for a children's book, and children around the world still love it.

Harry died in 1996 when he was 90 years old. You can still see some of his work in *Your Bible and You* and *The Desire of Ages*.

Info Splat

Almost all paintings, regardless of style or color, are enhanced by directing light toward them. Some lighting tips include: use brighter lighting during the day, dimmer lighting at night. Always use incandescent lighting, for fluorescent lights cause artwork to fade more.

REACT NOW!

How can a young person show they are diligent and skilled in their business? Do you think others see you are diligent? Does God?

June 7

~ Incredi-Biblical ~

In my Father's house are many mansions; if it were not so, I would have told you. I go to prepare a place for you.
John 14:2, KJV.

CHINA'S CAVE PEOPLE

How would you like to live in a cave? Wang Fengguan does. And he's not the only one there. Approximately 20 families live in the cave with him.

To get from the capital city of Guiyang, China, to the cave, Wang drives for three hours on a paved road, then one hour on an unpaved road that clings to the side of a high mountain. When that road ends, Wang walks for more than an hour up a steep rock path to the cave.

Inside the cave is a village. Using the rock ceiling for roofs, its buildings need only walls. There's even a school inside the cave where some of the adults are learning to read, and villagers pin progress reports to the outside of their houses, where everyone can see them!

Once a week Wang and some of the other cave dwellers go to town. Everything they buy must come up this steep mountain path—food and other everyday necessities, TVs, satellite dishes, concrete, and washing machines. Using the electricity that has been strung over the mountains to them, these people can esaily do a load of laundry in their mountain home.

Unfortunately, each family must live on only 1,000 yuan (US$129) per year. The local government has built homes for them in the valley, but Wang and the others don't want to leave their cave dwellings for the new homes.

Info Splat

The world's deepest cave goes down 5,256 feet and is located in Haute Savoie, France. Mammoth Cave in Kentucky is the world's longest cave system, extending for more than 340 miles.

REACT NOW!

How about you? The people living in this cave may have good reasons for rejecting the home the government has built for them. But how about you? How do you feel about going to live in the heavenly home God has prepared for you?

June 8

~ INCREDI-BIBLICAL ~

The angel of the Lord encamps around those who fear him, and he delivers them. Psalm 34:7.

DANGER FROM A COW

The ringing phone broke the classroom's quiet hum. "Hello?" Mr. Jenkins answered.

"Don't let your students outside. A long-horned cow is running loose," said an excited voice. Startled, Mr. Jenkins looked out a window and saw that it was true. A long-horned cow was running back and forth across the parking lot in a strange manner.

"All right, class," Mr. Jenkins said when it was time to go home. "Before any of you leave, I need to check the parking lot for a cow." Everyone laughed at that, but the teacher assured them it was a serious matter. However, the cow was nowhere in sight, and the students hurried to their rides.

As one of the last carloads of students sat waiting to turn onto the highway, the cow suddenly exploded through the brush and ran wide-eyed into the road, right in front of an oncoming car.

THUNK! The impact threw the cow into the air. It landed with a thud, bouncing off the car and onto the ground. The driver screeched to a stop, so shaken that her legs would not hold her up. Her car was ruined, but she was unharmed and soon able to stand.

"Thank You, Jesus, for taking care of us today," the students prayed. Although the injured cow had to be put to sleep, everyone was relieved and thankful. Their angels had delivered them from danger.

Info Splat

In 1611 the first cow arrived in Jamestown colony in America. A cow chews her cud (regurgitated, partially digested food) for up to eight hours each day. The best cows give around eight gallons of milk each day! That's enough to give 64 people two glasses of milk a day.

REACT NOW!

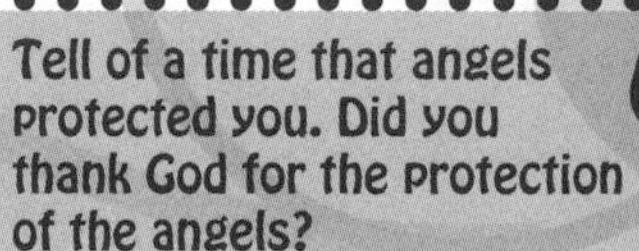

Tell of a time that angels protected you. Did you thank God for the protection of the angels?

June 9

Incredi-Biblical

Watch and pray, so that you will not fall into temptation. The spirit is willing, but the body is weak. Matthew 26:41.

THE KISSING BUG

Did you know that a kiss can kill you? At least one from the kissing bug can. This unique insect can be found in the southern United States and in Central and South America. It likes to hang out with wood rats, opossums, raccoons, and armadillos; and carries a parasite that causes Chagas' disease, a form of African sleeping sickness. The disease can kill children in two to four weeks by weakening their nervous system and heart muscle, finally causing a heart attack. Around 50,000 children die each year because of the kissing bug.

The kissing bug has a flat, narrow body with wings that look like an X when folded over its abdomen. Its mouth is a long piercing proboscis, or sucking mouthpart like a flexible tube. Using this proboscis, the bug sucks blood from the exposed parts of its prey's body. It especially enjoys the lips, eyelids, or ears of a sleeping victim. The kissing bug's nighttime "kiss" is mostly painless but may last from eight to 15 minutes.

Satan is like the kissing bug. He wants to take God's love from our hearts. He likes to work at "night" and enjoys finding the most exposed parts of our lives. He attacks us and works to weaken our connection to Jesus. Will you allow him to succeed, or will you keep close to Jesus today?

Info Splat

Grossed out by your morning breath? Kissing bugs love it. They're attracted to the odors we exhale. They usually feed next to the human body with only their proboscis touching the skin, and they can live three to six months between meals.

REACT NOW!

In what ways could Satan "bite" you today? What can you do to escape? What does it mean to watch and pray?

~ Incredi-Biblical ~

He who despises his neighbor sins, but blessed is he who is kind to the needy.
Proverbs 14:21.

BUDDY BALL

Brittany Colon enjoys sports and loves animals. She also volunteers for Buddy Ball, a program that matches developmentally and physically disabled kids with people who help them participate in sports. Many times a special bond is formed and the young volunteer becomes an adult advocate for the disabled.

Brittany, 11, says that the kids' attitudes are an inspiration to her. Instead of complaining about their problems, the kids are upbeat and happy.

"I am fortunate that God made me healthy, and I want to help others enjoy life," Brittany says, "even if it is only in a small way, like helping them throw a basketball or pushing them around the bases at the baseball game. What's also special about playing at Buddy Ball is that unlike when I play soccer in the leagues, nobody at Buddy Ball is a ball hog. They don't know what it's like to be selfish. It's a whole different world. I am truly blessed each and every time I help out. . . . It is very rewarding, and I highly recommend that all healthy kids out there volunteer their time to make a difference in this world we live in!"

Do you have time that you could volunteer? If you'd like to help someone with disabilities, you can find out more about Buddy Ball and other opportunities by checking in the town where you live or going through an Internet search engine. Jesus needs your hands to do His work.

Info Splat

Best Buddies, a similar program that helps people with intellectual disabilities find friends and jobs, was founded in 1989. It now involves more than 300,000 individuals each year, and volunteers annually contribute services to the community that equal more than $70 million.

REACT NOW!

Are you a friend to the disabled? What can you learn from a person with disabilities? Try sharing God's love with a disabled person today.

INCREDI-BIBLICAL

Even so it is not the will of your Father who is in heaven that one of these little ones should perish.
Matthew 18:14, NKJV.

CHANGING MY WORLD!

Rosetta is out to change her world! For an advanced research paper at school, she wrote about SOS-USA, an organization in Uganda that is making a difference in the lives of displaced children. As she worked on the report Rosetta was dismayed to learn of the decades of conflict and disease in Uganda and the toll it had taken on the children, leaving many of them orphans.

What can I do? she thought. *What would Jesus do?*

Rosetta decided to take action. She began a school club she called Save Uganda. She talked with students and community members about the needs in Uganda. On weekends Rosetta spent many hours at a nearby shopping area sharing what she had learned and seeking donations. She even worked to produce a video about Uganda and its problems. In two years Rosetta collected almost $4,000 to help the children there.

Many people noticed her work for others. In 2007 she became Miss Los Angeles County's Outstanding Teen. She was a runner-up in several contests for those doing volunteer work.

Rosetta saw a need and did something about it. About her we can use the words of Jesus regarding Mary's gift of perfume: She did what she could.

You can do your own research at www.sos-usa.org.

Info Splat

In Uganda the life expectancy is 42 years. About two thirds of the population is less than 18 years of age, with 1.8 million children having lost at least one parent. One in 25 people have a disability.

What service project can you become a part of? Think of some ways you could benefit people in need.

~ INCREDI-BIBLICAL ~

I tell you the truth, whatever you did for one of the least of these brothers of mine, you did for me. Matthew 25:40.

SENIOR PARTY

"How about the church hall?" Kelsie asked.

Her friend thought for a moment. "Sure!" she said, thinking of the possibilities. "That'll be awesome. I'll give them a call."

Kelsie had been looking forward to her senior party all year, but as the day grew closer she became concerned about the kids attending her large school who had disabilities. The room would be too crowded for wheelchairs, and Kelsie was worried they might not even be accepted there.

She decided to organize a special event for students with disabilities. With the help of her friend, she planned the food, decorations, and entertainment. Then she sent invitations to those who might not otherwise be able to attend the school event.

When the special night came, Kelsie's stomach was aflutter. Would the kids like it? Would they have fun? She need not have worried. The church fellowship hall was beautifully decorated, and everyone was dressed in their finest and wearing excited grins. Kids in wheelchairs, and those with slurred speech, paralysis, and blindness, joined arms with Kelsie and others, singing together as they swayed to the music. It was the words of Jesus in Matthew 25:40 come to life—whatever you did for one of [these disabled children] of Mine, you did for Me. Kelsie was bursting with happiness.

Kelsie still has pictures from that night on her wall. She glows as she talks of it. The happiness she shared with others was returned to her when she used her time and talents for God.

Info Splat

Intellectual disabilities are 10 times more common than cerebral palsy, 28 times more prevalent than neural tube defects such as spina bifida, and affect 25 times as many people as blindness. As of 1990, about 7 million people in North America have intellectual disabilities.

REACT NOW!

Is there a lonely person that you could befriend today? Try organizing an event so that everyone would be included, no matter what their disability.

INCREDI-BIBLICAL

For He shall give His angels charge over you, to keep thee in all your ways. Psalm 91:11, NKJV.

PRIEST'S GROTTO

During World War II half of the people living in the Ukrainian village of Korolówka were taken to a concentration camp and the other half to a ghetto. The Stermers were supposed to go to the ghetto, but Mrs. Stermer knew this meant they would be killed. So she told her son, "Go to the forest and find some place for us." He did. A cave!

The family didn't know anything about cave life and had no special equipment to enable them to survive—except for a few friends aboveground. They did have clean water, lots of rooms, and total darkness.

Using candles for three short periods a day, the Stermers learned to get along in the darkness by feel. Sometimes they slept 15 to 20 hours at a time. Miraculously, no one became sick.

Sometimes the men had to leave the cave at night for firewood and other necessities. One night when they'd been out to buy grain, the police saw them and chased them all the way back to the cave. As the men pulled the last large bag of grain through the cave's opening, it became stuck. The police opened fire on the bag, but the Stermers' lives were saved. They plugged up the hole and didn't go out for six weeks.

Finally someone dropped a bottle through the cave opening with a note inside informing them that the German army had withdrawn. Thirty-eight people had lived underground for 344 days.

Info Splat

At 77 miles (124 kilometers) long, Popowa Yama, or Priest's Grotto, is the world's tenth-longest cave. The cave stays at 50°F (10°C). It is so dark inside that you cannot see your hand in front of your face.

REACT NOW!

If you were in a similar situation, how would you feel? Afraid? Peaceful? What would you want to take into the cave with you?

Incredi-Biblical

I have hidden your word in my heart that I might not sin against you. Psalm 119:11.

THE GREAT AMERICAN GPS STASH HUNT

Well, I did it," Dave typed. "I created the first stash hunt stash, and here are the coordinates: N 45 17.460 W122 24.800."

Dave Ulmer, a computer consultant, was the first to take advantage of the 24 satellites around the globe used to pinpoint locations of objects on earth. When the global positioning system (GPS) signals became available to civilians, Dave was ready. He hid a container in the woods, posted its location on the Internet for GPS users to find, and called it the Great American GPS Stash Hunt. Today it's called geocaching.

"Lots of goodies for the finders. Look for a black plastic bucket buried most of the way in the ground. Take some stuff, leave some stuff! Have Fun!" Dave finished, then added, "Stash contains: Delorme Topo USA software, videos, books, food, money, and a slingshot!"

Within three days two people had found the cache and reported back online.

The word geocaching was made from the prefix *geo*, for earth, and *cache,* a word that refers to a hiding place someone would use to store items temporarily. You can go to www.geocaching.com to set up your own account and learn more about the sport.

Geocaching is a great way to get outside, interact with others, use technology in an active way, and even witness. Could something be hidden that would remind the finder that God loves them? What about an encouraging Bible verse?

Info Splat

There's a cache named ghar that has a five-star difficulty rating for terrain. It's under some rocks at the base of a flagpole, in Bagram, Afghanistan. The accompanying note warns: "Areas off path may be mined." I won't be looking for that one.

REACT NOW!

Do you have God's Word hidden in your heart? Find and read one of the promises God has hidden in the Bible.

June 15

~ INCREDI-BIBLICAL ~

May the words of my mouth and the meditation of my heart be pleasing in your sight, O Lord, my Rock and my Redeemer.
Psalm 19:14.

BOUNDARIES

I can't stand Jessica," Carrie stated flatly at the dinner table.

"Why?" Mom asked.

"She's always bossy." Carrie spooned potatoes on her plate and tried to organize her thoughts. "Everything's got to go her way or she gets mad. She has to choose the games we play and the music and the TV shows—just everything!"

"Have you suggested that she take turns in making decisions?" Mom asked.

"Yep! It doesn't help."

Mom passed a dish to Dad. "I have a friend like that," she said with a smile. "In fact, we're very close."

Carrie shrugged. "I thought I knew all of your friends."

Mom laughed. "It's Jessica's mother! Their personalities are very similar."

"How can you be good friends with someone who wants to control you?" Carrie wanted to know.

Mom looked thoughtful. "I've learned to look past her need to control everything. I've learned to look for her good traits."

"Like what?"

"Well, she's a loyal friend. She knows how to make decisions and act on them, which can be good at times. However, she needs to understand that there are limits as to how much she can control. The trick is helping her to understand that you have boundaries."

"How?" Carrie asked.

"First of all," Mom said, "recognize her need to make decisions. For example, you may say, 'Jessica, I don't want to watch that TV show, but I'll be happy to watch *Animal Planet* with you, or we could jump on the trampoline. You choose.' By giving her a choice, she feels in control, but you've established your limits or boundaries. If you are kind but stay firm, she may learn to compromise."

"Boundaries," Carrie mused. "What a neat thought! I think I'll try it."

Boundaries define limits. The purpose of a boundary is to make clear separations between what is acceptable to you and what is not. You need to be able to tell other people when they are crossing your personal boundaries.

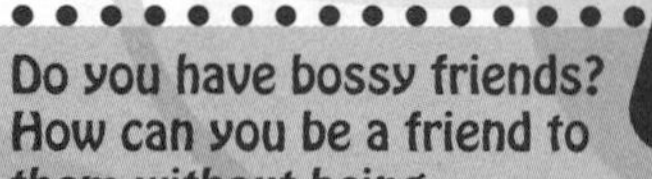

REACT NOW!

Do you have bossy friends? How can you be a friend to them without being controlled by them? What kind of boundaries can you establish in a kind, Christlike way?

~ Incredi-Biblical ~

Even the birds in the sky know the right times to do things. . . . But my people don't know what the Lord wants them to do! Jeremiah 8:7, ICB.

WHY GEESE FLY FARTHER THAN EAGLES

Jesse threw down the crowbar and buried his face in his hands. He had tried all morning to put a new tire on his bicycle, but he couldn't make it snap in place.

"Need some help?" Grandpa asked as he hobbled out the back door leaning on his cane.

You can barely walk, Jesse thought to himself. *How could you possibly help me?* But he said out loud, "No thanks, Grandpa. There must be something wrong with this tire even though it's new."

Just then a gaggle of geese circled the nearby pond and came in for a landing. "Did you know that geese can fly farther than eagles?" Grandpa asked. He leaned forward. "The geese have a secret."

"What is it?" Jesse asked, even though he wasn't very interested.

"When geese migrate, they fly in groups. Did you see that one at the tip of the V? His outstretched neck is like a spear slicing the air, and that causes an upward wind that lifts the birds behind. The others don't have to flap so hard because they're riding on a draft. They soar on each other's strength."

Jesse grinned. "Your point being that if we work together, we can put this tire on."

"Absolutely," Grandpa answered. "I may not be as strong as you are, but I've fixed many a bicycle tire in my days. Shall we give it a try?"

Info Splat

In the "V" formation, the birds in the up drafts can get 70 percent more distance than flying alone. The outer position also gives a better view ahead. The geese stay in the "V" shape because misalignment on drafts increases the workload.

REACT NOW!

Think of a time you did a project with an older person. How is experience better than strength? Why is a group effort better than one person's effort?

~ Incredi-Biblical ~

The grass withers and the flowers fall, but the word of our God stands forever. Isaiah 40:8.

CHAPEL IN THE WOODS

Communist soldiers tramped from house to house, seizing Bibles and anything—and anybody—that taught about God. They burned the items in the public square and killed the Christians or sent them to prison camps. Churches were burned to the ground. Graveyards grew bigger and bigger.

The Communist government in Bulgaria did not tolerate Christianity. While some of the Communist ideals helped the people, it also abused many human rights. Christians struggled together to survive. Then one day someone got a bright idea. "Let's build a church back in the woods behind the graveyard," he suggested. "The Communists will think we're going into the cemetery to visit the graves of our loved ones. They won't know that we're going to worship."

Soon the idea caught on, and builders constructed a small church in the woods. An artist who still remembered the Bible stories painted scenes from the Scriptures on the walls: the Creation, Moses and the Ten Commandments, Jesus healing the sick, and the crucifixion of Jesus. The paintings took two years to complete.

Quietly news of the church spread. Each week believers wove their way through the grave markers and into the church to worship. After some time the Communists took notice of the continual stream of people going to the graveyard and investigated. They discovered the church.

When soldiers found out who had done the paintings, they made sure the man could never again paint pictures of Jesus. They broke his hands!

The Communist government soon fell, but the church behind the graveyard still stands.

Info Splat

It is estimated that at least 100 million men, women, and children have died because of their faith in the Bible. The killing still continues in some countries today.

REACT NOW!

How important is the Word of God to you? Do you love it enough to read it regularly? What would you do if you were forbidden to read it?

June 18

~ INCREDI-BIBLICAL ~

I must be about
My Father's business.
Luke 2:49, NKJV.

KID WITH A CAUSE

Animal lovers from all over the world cried when they heard of the tragic death of Steve Irwin. His TV show, *The Crocodile Hunter*, taught people to respect all creatures, whether slimy or scaly, creepy or crawly. Irwin saw something beautiful in snakes, lizards, spiders, and of course, crocodiles. His father encouraged his interest in animals, and his family built a zoo that attracted millions of people from all over the world. Irwin was killed by a stingray in a freak accident while filming a documentary about the most dangerous animals on earth. One of the animals he lived his life trying to save brought an end to his life.

During his funeral Irwin's 8-year-old daughter, Bindi, stood in front of a crowd of 5,000 and a worldwide television audience of more than 300 million viewers and read a speech she had written.

"My daddy was my hero," she said. "I know that Daddy had an important job. He was working to change the world so everyone would love wildlife like he did. He built a hospital to help animals, and he bought lots of land to give animals a safe place to live." Then Bindi asked everyone to join the fight to help the animals.

At the National Press Club a few months later she told the public she was ready to continue her father's work of spreading the wonder of wildlife. "I'm going to become a wildlife warrior just like he was," she said.

Info Splat

Scientists in the United States have isolated a powerful agent in crocodile blood (called **CROCODILLIN**) that could help conquer human infections immune to standard antibiotics. The discovery was made thanks to the curiosity of Jill Fullerton-Smith, a BBC science producer filming a documentary on saltwater crocodiles in Australia.

Do you have a cause? As Christians, we can be about our heavenly Father's business, just as Jesus was. What does that mean to you?

June 19

~ Incredi-Biblical ~

He who walks with the wise grows wise, but a companion of fools suffers harm. Proverbs 13:20.

THE ODD DOG

The Kelly family loved dogs. They had a German shepherd, an Irish setter, a beagle, and a small mutt. Whenever anyone drove in the yard, all of the dogs would bark loud and long, *Ruff, Ruff, Ruff, Ruff!* They all sounded alike.

One day a neighbor knocked on the door. "I'm sorry to bother you," the neighbor apologized, "but a stray dog wandered over to my house. We can't keep it. Would you like it?"

"I'm sorry, but we have four dogs already," Mrs. Kelly told her. "We don't need another."

"One more won't make any difference," the neighbor pleaded. "If I take this dog to animal control, they might put it to sleep."

Mrs. Kelly couldn't bear the thought of the poor dog being destroyed, so she took pity on it and brought the stray to meet her canine family. Of course, all four dogs said hello in their usual way. *Ruff, Ruff, Ruff, Ruff,* they woofed at the new dog. The stray dog barked back, but its short, quick yelps sounded like *Yap-yip, yap-yip*. The combination was terrible.

Now whenever anyone drove in the yard, four dogs would bark *Ruff, Ruff, Ruff, Ruff,* and one dog would yelp, *Yap-yip, Yap-yip*. As time went on, the Kelly family wondered if they could stand the irritating bark of the new dog. Then an amazing thing happened. One morning when the mailman drove in the driveway and all five dogs barked, they all sounded like this: *Ruff, Ruff, Ruff, Ruff, Ruff*.

Info Splat

Any thought or action repeated over and over builds little grooves or pathways through the brain, just as walking over the same place in a yard will wear a path in the lawn. Within three weeks repetition can form a new habit.

Why did the odd dog change his bark? Do you find yourself using the same expressions, acting like or dressing like someone you hang out with? How does today's text apply to you?

INCREDI-BIBLICAL

Show proper respect for everyone; Love the brotherhood of believers, fear God, honor the king. 1 Peter 2:17.

KING NERO'S TRAGIC LIFE

As a child, Nero's mother let him do mostly anything he wanted. History tells us that he grew up without restraint, and as he became a man Nero was selfish and cruel. He didn't mind killing people to get what he wanted. When he wanted to be king, he killed his young stepbrother. When he wanted a beautiful woman named Poppaea, he tried to please her by killing his own mother. Then he killed his wife and brought her head on a platter to Poppaea.

Later a terrible fire in Rome burned half the city. "Why don't we blame this fire on those Christians?" Poppaea suggested. Once again, Nero listened to her and had thousands of innocent men, women, and children put to death.

Info Splat
Nero was so cruel that he placed human bodies on posts and used them as torches to light the dark street.

But Jesus had once said, "He who kills with the sword shall die by the sword." One day in a mad rage, Nero kicked a pregnant Poppaea in the belly, and she died. It seemed that no one was more vicious than this man.

But despite his evil ways God loved Nero and sent a prisoner to tell him so. As Paul spoke, Nero felt God's presence. Though he didn't give his heart to God, he did release Paul from prison for a time. Wherever he was, Paul continued to spread the gospel of Jesus until his execution under Nero's rule.

In the end, Nero lost his will to live and committed suicide. Without a doubt Nero was a ruthless and corrupt king. Yet he was the ruler when Peter wrote the verse for today's message.

REACT NOW!

Showing respect for people does not mean that we like or accept everything they do. What does it mean? How can you show respect for others?

INCREDI-BIBLICAL

I will give you a new heart and will put a new spirit within you; I will remove from you your heart of stone and give you a heart of flesh. Ezekiel 36:26.

A FATHER'S LOVE

Few people can watch the movie *John Q* without using a box of tissues. In this film, Denzel Washington plays a loving father who must come up with $250,000 to pay for his son's heart transplant—or stand by and watch him weaken and die. John and his family are very poor, and the hospital has no charity. In desperation, John takes the hospital staff hostage at gunpoint and demands that they give his son a heart.

But there is no available donor. When it looks at last as if his son will die, John lies down on the table and prepares to end his own life so that the doctors can take his heart and transplant it into his son. At the very last moment a heart organ is brought in to save the boy.

While this film is not exactly true, it makes one wonder if a father can really love his son that much. The answer is yes. Throughout history, fathers have given their lives for their children.

The most famous and well-known story is true, but there are no hospital records to prove it—just millions of children and adults telling the story of their Savior in heaven who loved them enough to give up His own life so they could live.

Jesus Christ had a choice. His own children decided to follow Satan. He could allow them to die because of their choice, or He could die in their place. Because of His choice to die for us, we can have a new heart.

There were 2,125 heart transplants performed in the United States in 2005. Each year thousands more would benefit from a heart transplant if more donated hearts were available.

REACT NOW!

What happens when God gives us a new heart? What does our new heart symbolize? Why is it important that we ask for this gift?

~ INCREDI-BIBLICAL ~

And this is my prayer: that your love may abound more and more in knowledge and depth of insight. Philippians 1:9.

FRIENDS MAKE THE DIFFERENCE

"I hope you'll like your earliteen class," Dad said as he stopped the car in front of a redbrick church. Robby frowned. The family's recent move meant that he was in a new school and now a new church. He dragged his feet as he and Mom got out of the car while Dad went on to park it.

In his old church his Sabbath school classroom was really big. Its walls were painted a bright-lime green, and the kids used soft beanbags instead of chairs. Of course, the best part was being with his friends. He could picture them now, having a great time.

Info Splat
People with open minds consider themselves to be happier, more content, and have longer-lasting relationships than very opinionated, closed-minded people.

One of the greeters told them the location of his department, and he and Mom found the small room. It had nothing in it but a rug, a table, and several metal chairs. The empty walls were a creamy white.

"This is going to be terrible," Robby complained.

"You can't judge a book by its cover." Mom was always quoting some old saying.

"What's that supposed to mean?"

"Remember your last birthday when you opened the fanciest wrapped package first?" Mom asked with a laugh.

Robby frowned. "Yeah. It was acne stuff for my skin. And I don't have acne!"

"Well, see! The pretty package didn't mean that a great gift was inside. The gifts in the plainer packages turned out to be the best."

Just then the door opened and a boy about Robby's age walked in. He smiled and introduced himself. Before long, three more guys and two girls came in. They were all friendly. The teacher played the guitar while the kids sang, and then the whole group went outside to study their lesson in a beautiful flower garden. Before long Robby felt that he'd been part of the group for years.

REACT NOW!

Have you ever found yourself liking something or someone that you thought you would hate? How could the lesson Robby learned with birthday packages apply to relationships with people?

June 23

~ Incredi-Biblical ~

Surely he shall save you from the fowler's snare.
Psalm 91:3.

THE SNARE

Michael couldn't believe that his first night of summer vacation would find him crammed in a small, camouflaged tent, pitched in marshy wetlands, peeking out a small hole, and swatting mosquitoes. More than anything he wanted to be home playing with his Xbox 360.

At first, capturing birds that preyed on smaller animals with his biologist father sounded exciting, but Michael wasn't so sure now. He did know that they'd learned a great deal as the different birds were identified by age, gender, and size, and then marked by putting special bands on their legs.

Now he watched Dad place a live rat in a trap to lure a hungry hawk. "Here he comes," Dad whispered. "Keep your eyes open and freeze." Even as he spoke a hawk glided in, wings folded and feet ready. As the hawk landed at the lure, his feet were snared in a net. "Gotcha," Dad said quietly. "Let's go and get him."

At home later Dad came in and sat beside Michael as he played a game on his Xbox. "When I band birds," he said, "I play the role of the devil."

"What!" Michael said in surprise. "What do you mean?"

"I study birds to see how I can capture them. I entice them into my snares with foods they like to eat. Satan does that too. He's so good at it that he makes specific traps for different kinds of people. It can be food, friends, TV, or even video games." He turned around to leave. "But unlike the devil, I don't harm the birds."

Info Splat

Teens who play violent video games show increased activity in areas of their brains linked to emotional arousal and decreased responses in regions that govern self-control.

REACT NOW!

How can you recognize the lures and traps that Satan puts out for you? Can certain types of entertainment trap and hold you?

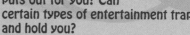

~ Incredi-Biblical ~

When they saw the courage of Peter and John and realized that they were unschooled, ordinary men, they were astonished and they took note that these men had been with Jesus. Acts 4:13.

A FIRE IN THE BONES

Peter knew his sermons would stir up the rulers and invite persecution. He knew he could save his life if he just kept his mouth shut in public, stayed home, and witnessed quietly. But he couldn't stop from telling others about his Savior. His faith was like a fire burning within his bones.

So what's the difference in Peter's faith and the faith of most Christians today? Why don't most of us feel as excited as Christ's disciples did? John 1:14 gives us a clue: "We have *seen* his glory."

How could Peter be afraid of death when he had seen Jesus die on the cross and then a few days later seen Him alive, walking, and talking? Peter actually watched Jesus ascend to heaven, growing smaller and smaller until He was finally enveloped by clouds. And Peter heard the angel's promise that this same Jesus would return to earth.

Peter experienced Jesus!

We can experience Jesus today, even though we can't see Him as Peter and the other disciples did. The Bible and the Holy Spirit can produce the same fire within our bones. We can hear God speaking to us through the Bible. We can speak back to God through prayer.

As we pray and read, we develop faith. Faith is like a small candle igniting within us. As we earnestly seek God, the flame grows brighter and brighter.

Info Splat

It takes about 70 hours and 40 minutes to read the entire Bible at an average reading speed. Between 1815 and 1975, 2.5 billion Bibles were printed. The Bible remains the most widely distributed and influential book in the world.

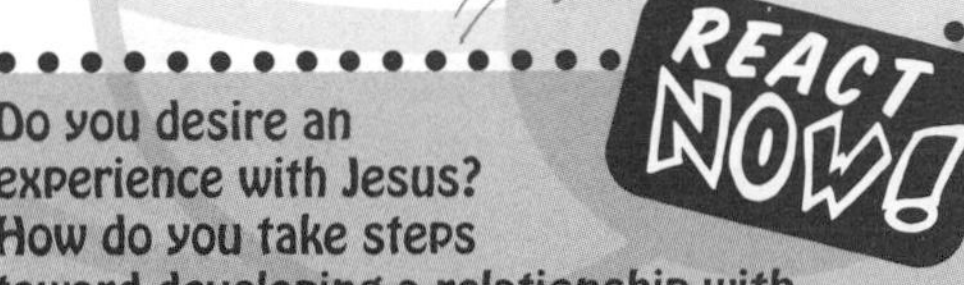

REACT NOW!

Do you desire an experience with Jesus? How do you take steps toward developing a relationship with Him? In what ways has God demonstrated His yearning for a relationship with you?

June 25

INCREDI-BIBLICAL

For as the lightning comes from the east and flashes to the west, so will be the coming of the Son of Man. Matthew 24:27.

BETTER THAN DISNEY WORLD OR NASCAR

John stood in the Bristol NASCAR stadium and watched in awe as a parachutist fastened to a large red-white-and-blue flag floated down from the sky. After she landed safely, tubes of fireworks burst upward on one corner of the field, circling the tracks in quick succession. *BOOM!* All the fireworks exploded at once, filling the air with red, white, and blue sparks. The crowd cheered, the band played, and the Blue Angels roared overhead. The air seemed to be filled with so much electricity that John found himself holding his breath. Could anything be more wonderful?

Then it dawned on him that yes, there will be an event more wonderful than NASCAR or even the precision flying of the Blue Angels. The Bible says that when Jesus comes, the sky will be filled with millions upon millions of bright, shining angels who blow their trumpets and surround the throne where Jesus sits. Around the throne will be a beautiful rainbow with colors more spectacular than any fireworks display.

Every eye on Planet Earth will witness this sight. The graves will burst open, and those who died in Christ will rise. Unfortunately, some people will not be cheering. Those who have refused to believe in Jesus will be screaming in terror and trying to hide themselves from His face. But those who love Him will join that heavenly group and live forever.

And, John thought as he sat down, *unlike NASCAR, my ticket's free—already bought and paid for.*

Info Splat

NASCAR is the fastest growing spectator sport, with races televised weekly in more than 150 countries around the world in more than 30 languages.

REACT NOW!

There is no doubt that one way or another you will see the coming of Jesus, but what will be your reaction? How can it be a wonderful event for you?

June 26

~ INCREDI-BIBLICAL ~

Surely I was sinful at birth, sinful from the time my mother conceived me. . . . Create in me a pure heart, O God, and renew a steadfast spirit within me. Psalm 51:5-10.

YOUR INHERITANCE

It seemed to Keith that everywhere he went someone would say, "You look just like your father," or "You act just like your father." The problem was that Keith's father had a large forehead, short legs, and an explosive temper. Keith wasn't so sure he wanted to look or act like his dad.

We tend to inherit physical and personality features of our parents. You may have the same color of eyes as your mom. You may be tall and skinny or short and stubby like your dad.

It's called heredity. Your parents pass these physical traits to you through your genes. There is nothing you can do about what you inherit. Our parents couldn't do anything about what was passed down to them, either.

You have also inherited a problem called sin. Sin began long ago when the first parents on earth chose to obey Satan instead of God, and has been passed down from generation to generation ever since. Sin affects how you act. Maybe you've developed an explosive temper or a negative attitude. Maybe you have a problem with cheating, impure thoughts, or gossiping. The good news is that Jesus can do something about the sin problem. He died so that He could have the right to live in our hearts and change us into His image!

Now when Keith goes to family reunions and Aunt Sara accuses Keith of acting like his father, he feels hopeful, because that's something Jesus can change.

Info Splat

From the moment of conception, 46 chromosomes with 30,000 genes combined to determine all your physical characteristics, such as whether you're a boy or girl, your facial features, body type, hair color, eyes, and skin. Even more amazingly, intelligence and personality were already in place within your genetic code.

REACT NOW!

What have you inherited from your parents? What traits do you have that do not reflect your heavenly Father's character?

INCREDI-BIBLICAL

Dear friend, I pray that you may enjoy good health and that all may go well with you, even as your soul is getting along well. 3 John 2.

A VISION OF HEALTH

Arnold Schwarzenegger, famous body builder, actor, and governor of California, once said, "Stay away from junk food, get off the couch, unplug the Nintendo, turn off the TV, and go out and get some exercise. A body is a terrible thing to waste."

In 1863, long before Arnold Schwarzenegger was born, Ellen White was given a vision on how to have good health. She was shown that God's children should eat plain and simple foods such as fruits, nuts, grains, and vegetables. Before lung cancer was diagnosed, she was told that tobacco (both smoking and chewing) was a poison. Long before mad cow disease, colon cancer, or high cholesterol was connected with a meat diet, she related that in the last days before Jesus returned, animals would no longer be safe to eat. Long before anyone had ever heard of a diabetic, she was told that large amounts of sugar were not good for the human body. As Adventists began to practice these health principles, they began to live longer and have fewer diseases than other people.

Jesus spent most of His ministry here on earth healing people, and we can follow His example. Because of the vision God gave Ellen White, the Seventh-day Adventist Church has more hospitals and health-related institutions than any other Protestant organization.

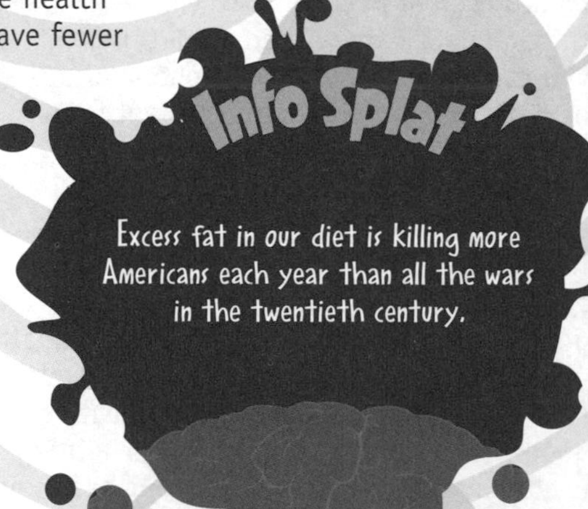

Info Splat
Excess fat in our diet is killing more Americans each year than all the wars in the twentieth century.

REACT NOW!

Why should health be important to everyone? What bad health habits do you have and how could you change them?

June 28

Incredi-Biblical

He died for us that, whether we are awake or asleep, we may live together with him. 1 Thessalonians 5:10.

A CHRISTIAN'S GUARANTEE

Emily watched as her father packed the last of his personal items and closed the suitcase. She felt a sadness in the pit of her stomach that wouldn't go away. Her father was leaving that afternoon and flying back to Iraq.

"This is the last time," he told her. "When I come back, I won't have to leave again."

Emily tried to smile, but she couldn't. "How do I know that you're coming back?" she sobbed. She knew that soldiers like her father were killed every day.

Her father took her into his arms. "Emily, no one is guaranteed a long life here on this earth. But Christians are guaranteed eternal life. We will never be forever separated, because we love Jesus. Jesus can protect me anywhere, but if I should die in Iraq, we will be together again. That is a promise. I stake my faith on it."

That very morning, about four hours' drive away, 33 college students went to classes as usual. Unknown to them, a mentally disturbed student was loading his gun. Before the morning was over, he would take their lives and then end his own. The fate of these students would be forever sealed. They would never have another chance to accept Jesus.

That night as Emily watched the news, she remembered her father's words: "No one is guaranteed a long life here on earth. But Christians are guaranteed eternal life." We will never be forever separated if we love Jesus. You can stake your faith on it.

Info Splat

The Virginia Tech massacre was a school shooting that unfolded as two separate attacks on April 16, 2007. A shooter killed 32 people and wounded many more before committing suicide, making it the deadliest shooting in modern U.S. history up to that time.

How important is *YOUR* faith in God? How can you have peace when there is no world peace?

Incredi-Biblical

Do not store up for yourselves treasures on earth, where moth and rust [and termites] destroy. . . . But store up for yourselves treasures in heaven.
Matthew 6:19, 20.

TERMITES IN THE BANK

It appears that termites have a taste for rich food. Just ask Mr. Dwarika Prasad, of India. Mr. Prasad had faithfully deposited money and investment papers worth $682,000 rupees (US$15,660) in a bank located in the town of Patna. But Mr. Prasad will not see any of his money or investment papers again, because termites ate them!

"I'm shattered," Mr. Prasad said. "I do not know what to do, as I had kept the money for my old age."

The bank had posted signs warning about the termites, but Mr. Prasad had not been to the bank for several months. Bank officials admit, however, that customers were not personally contacted.

What does the bank have to say about the situation? Nothing very hopeful. "The bank is not liable for the deposits kept inside the safe." They have sent Mr. Prasad's letter of complaint to higher authorities, but say he is probably out of luck.

It's all a sad reminder that earthly treasure comes and goes. Thankfully, God has a heavenly "banking system" we can depend on. As we place our complete trust in heaven's "deposit box" each day through prayer, we can face the day assured that God is working for our best interest.

Info Splat

No one knows for sure how long termite queens live, but many are known to live at least 10 years. Some termite mounds suggest some of thier queens may live as long as 40 years.
Source: http://www.utoronto.ca/forest/termite/funfacts.htm

If you were president of the termite-infested bank in India, how would you respond to Mr. Prasad's situation?

INCREDI-BIBLICAL

**I am the light of the world. Whoever follows me will never walk in darkness, but will have the light of life.
John 8:12.**

LET THERE BE LIGHT

From the small four-seater Cessna plane, Rob looked down on the millions of lights dotting the ground. It was like viewing a gigantic Christmas scene from the sky.

"Pretty impressive, isn't it?" the pilot commented.

"I'll say!" Rob agreed. "I'm getting a bird'-eye view of a whole city of lights at one time." Beside him, Rob's grandfather nodded and pointed out the Florida coastline approximately a mile below them.

For the rest of the trip, Rob kept his eyes focused on the lights below. They passed over smaller towns, small farms, and totally dark places, but his eyes were drawn toward the lights the way bugs on a dark night are drawn to a lamppost.

We use light to look at everything around us. We appreciate a simple drawing, computer graphics, gorgeous sunsets, a blue sky, shooting stars, and rainbows—all because of light. But did you ever stop to think that instead of seeing any of these things, we are seeing light? We view the light that somehow left objects far or near and reached our eyes. Light is all our eyes can really see.

The precise nature of light is one of the key questions of modern physics. God thought it was so important that it was the first thing He created on the first day of the week when He said, "Let there be light."

Info Splat

When flying insects encounter a close source of light such as a lantern, the light is perceived stronger in one eye, which makes one wing beat faster. The insect then approaches the light in a spiral path, eventually drawing into the light itself.

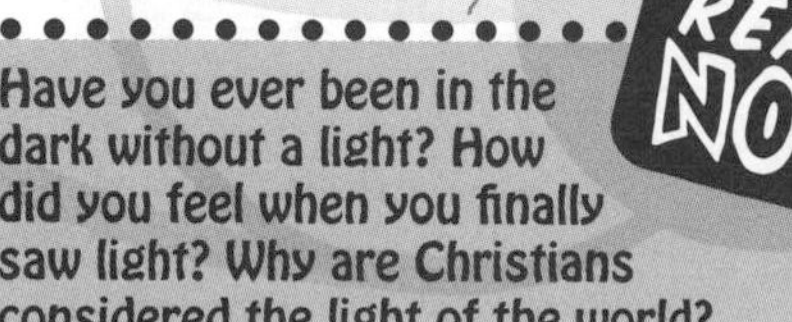

REACT NOW!

Have you ever been in the dark without a light? How did you feel when you finally saw light? Why are Christians considered the light of the world?

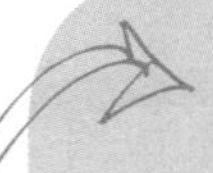

July 1

Incredi-Biblical

Do you think I cannot call on my Father, and he will at once put at my disposal more than twelve legions of angels? Matthew 26:53.

ANGEL GUARDIANS

"Welcome to Sierra Leone, William."

William Lewis smiled as he greeted the other missionaries—D. C. Babcock, T. M. French, and their families. More than anything, Will wanted to share the love of Jesus with the African people, but he had concern for his wife and two small daughters. Tropical diseases had wiped out entire mission families in the past.

Even worse, some of the nationals had warned, "Do not talk to us about your God." But Will had decided to trust his and his family's lives to Jesus, and he was not disappointed.

They'd been at the mission station only a short time when Elder Babcock was called to the home of a dying fetish priest. "I have a confession," said the priest. "One day some men and I plotted to murder everyone in your mission—men, women, and children.

"We came on a moonlit night to kill you while you slept. But when we got to your mission, we saw soldiers guarding the buildings!"

The priest shuddered, remembering. "Guns! Bayonets! We abandoned our plan and ran for our lives! How did you know? Who warned you?"

"No one warned us," Elder Babcock assured him. "What you saw were angels sent by our God, who always watches."

When Will heard the story, he knelt gratefully with the others and thanked God for sending His angels to deliver them. For Will, it was assurance that God was always with them and would bless their work.

Info Splat

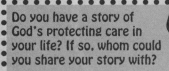

In 1991 a vicious civil war began in Sierra Leone and lasted a decade. During the war two out of every three children were forced to leave their homes. Thousands of children were kidnapped and forced to fight as soldiers.

Do you have a story of God's protecting care in your life? If so, whom could you share your story with?

~ Incredi-Biblical ~

He lifted me out of the slimy pit, out of the mud and mire; he set my feet on a rock and gave me a firm place to stand. Psalm 40:2.

SEAN'S CHOICE

Thirteen-year-old Reg felt unhappy with his life. There was very little spiritual direction in his broken home. In his unhappiness he turned to alcohol and other drugs. Drugs, he felt, were like the one thinq in his life he could control, but he soon discovered that they often left him out of control. Many times he got into trouble and even spent time in jail.

He saw that his own choices kept getting him in trouble, yet he believed there was no way to stop making those same wrong choices. Life looked hopeless.

"Reg, I don't want to see you destroy yourself," a close friend told him one day. Her words shook him. Sean thought seriously about where his life was headed. He knew his choices could easily kill him, and he didn't want to die. The next day he threw away his drugs and joined a support group.

Ellen White wrote that a sinner may choose to resist God's love, "but if he does not resist he will be drawn to Jesus."*

Without the influence of drugs on Reg's mind, God was able to draw him to Himself.

"Would you like to take Bible studies?" a man from a local Adventist church offered one day. Reg began to study, and two years later he was baptized.

Reg believes that God's hand was on him even in the darkest times. He is grateful for the patient, loving way in which God drew him. And he has never regretted giving his life to the One who gives him hope every day.

Info Splat

According to the World Health Organization, about 200,000 people died from drug abuse in the year 2000. That same year, alcohol contributed to the deaths of 1.8 million people, and 4.9 million people died from the use of tobacco.

REACT NOW!

Besides drugs, what are some of the things that can distract us from God's plan to give us hope and a future? How can we avoid these things?

* *Steps to Christ*, p. 27.

INCREDI-BIBLICAL

If you fall, your friend can help you up. But if you fall without having a friend nearby, you are really in trouble.
Ecclesiastes 4:10, CEV.

BRENNA'S NEW FRIEND

Brenna leaned against the outside of the gymnasium building and gazed across the unfamiliar academy campus. This new school was beautiful, but would she make any friends?

She'd had no friends the year before when she had attended a public school. Because she had started school a week late, everyone else seemed to have their friends picked out already. Being very shy didn't help either. "But a whole year without friends," she whispered. What a lonely year it had been!

"Dear Lord," she prayed, "please help me find a friend."

Soon a girl approached her with a big smile. "Are you new here?" the girl asked, her accent hinting that she was an islander from the Caribbean.

"Yeah," Brenna nodded, smiling back at the friendly face.

"I'm DeeDee," the girl said. "What's your name, and where are you from?"

By the time Brenna had answered all of DeeDee's questions, she felt relaxed and welcome at her new school. As the day went on, she found herself able to say "Hi," and talk with some other students. When she went home that afternoon, she had a feeling that things would work out just fine.

She was right. That year she had not one but *three* good friends, and several other casual friends. Her heavenly Father and a kind girl named DeeDee had given her the confidence to make those friends.

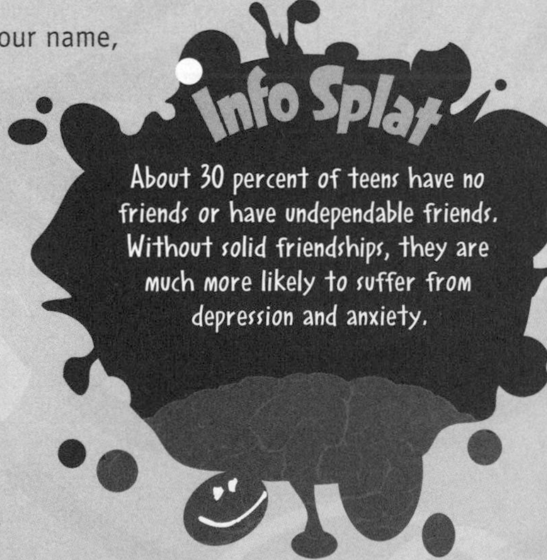

Info Splat
About 30 percent of teens have no friends or have undependable friends. Without solid friendships, they are much more likely to suffer from depression and anxiety.

REACT NOW!

Is there someone at your school who has a tough time making friends? In what ways could you be a friend to that person?

INCREDI-BIBLICAL

And God blessed the seventh day and made it holy, because on it he rested from all the work of creating that he had done. Genesis 2:3.

DISCOVERING GOD'S DAY

"You're worshipping God on the wrong day!"

The words of Rachel Oakes, a visitor to Pastor Frederick Wheeler's church in early 1844, still echoed in his mind. He wondered aloud, "Could it be true?" It was a very troubling thought, but he was determined to find out if there was any truth to it. "Dear God, please guide me," he prayed. Opening his Bible, he began to study everything he could find about the Sabbath. If it was important, the Bible would show him what was right.

To his amazement, he learned that Saturday really was the day God intended as a special day of rest. In fact, God had made that day different from the beginning: At the end of the Creation week He blessed the seventh day and made it sacred. Each seventh day, His children would leave their regular work and spend quality time with Him.

Info Splat

The first Seventh-day Adventist church was formed from members of at least five Christian denominations. Rachel Oakes, who convinced Adventists to keep the Sabbath, was a Seventh-Day Baptist.

Pastor Wheeler's discoveries must have shocked him. How could he have not known? It was part of the Ten Commandments. Weren't pastors supposed to know these things?

His heart must have pounded that Sunday in March of 1844 when he stood in front of his congregation. "I want to speak to you about the seventh-day Sabbath," he began. It took courage to tell his people that he believed Saturday was the true Sabbath.

Over the next few years many others decided he was right about the Sabbath, and eventually his church became the first Seventh-day Adventist church.

REACT NOW!

What truths have you discovered in the Bible? How have you applied your discoveries to your own life?

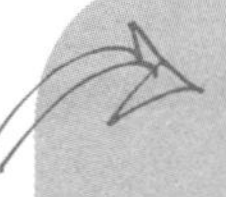

~ Incredi-Biblical ~

For I am the Lord, your God, who takes hold of your right hand and says to you, Do not fear; I will help you.
Isaiah 41:13.

PUT FEAR IN ITS PLACE

What are you afraid of?

Do you fear failing an important test? speaking to new people? a trip to the dentist? family troubles?

Wild weather patterns, terrorism, the spread of dread diseases, and increasing violence might convince us that we have more reasons than ever to be afraid. But God gives us the power to put fear in its place.

Answer the following to find out what you know about this powerful emotion.

1. True___ False___ Fear is always bad.
2. True___ False___ All humans have fears.
3. True___ False___ Often, things we fear don't happen or are not as frightening as we imagined.
4. True___ False___ Uncontrolled fear can take over our lives and make us miserable.
5. True___ False___ God does not want us to be controlled by our fears.

Answers:

1. False. Fear can be a good thing. For example, if you weren't afraid of an escaped tiger, you might walk right up to it and be eaten. This fear equals healthy respect.
2. True. Fear is one of the most common emotions.
3. True. Our imaginations can blow things out of proportion and make us worry about events that may never happen.
4. True. Fear that lasts a long time is sometimes labeled anxiety. About one of every five Americans has an anxiety disorder.
5. True. God invites us to cast all our cares on Him, and that includes our fears.

Info Splat

Ever heard of hair turning gray overnight from fear? It's impossible. But fear can cause a rare condition that makes dark hair fall out quickly. If the person has gray hair, it appears the person has gone gray in a short time.

REACT NOW!

Have you experienced fear that's out of control? Write out a list of Bible promises you can read the next time you're afraid. Memorize as many as you can.

July 6

Incredi-Biblical

Anyone who comes to me but refuses to let go of father, mother, spouse, children, brothers, sisters—yes, even one's own self!—can't be my disciple.
Luke 14:26, Message.

DRESSED FOR A REST

Daniel lived in a small village in West Africa. His parents had died when he was very young, so his grandmother raised him as her son. When he reached school age, she sent him to the nearby mission school.

"I love learning about Jesus," he told Grandmother.

"You stick with numbers and letters," Grandmother told him.

In time, Daniel gave his heart to Jesus. He was an excited new Christian, but his grandmother was unhappy. "I want you to get an education, but I don't like all those strange religious teachings," she complained.

Daniel also had a new habit that bothered her. "Daniel," Grandmother said one day, "I've decided I don't want you to go to Sabbath school and church."

"But I must, Grandmother," Daniel tried to explain.

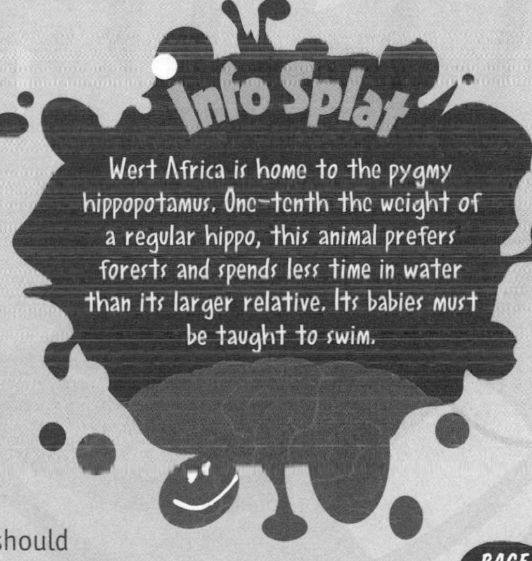

Info Splat
West Africa is home to the pygmy hippopotamus. One-tenth the weight of a regular hippo, this animal prefers forests and spends less time in water than its larger relative. Its babies must be taught to swim.

However, she was determined that he should stay home. "I'm taking away your clothes," she announced on Sabbath mornings. She carefully hid the clothing, thinking that that would keep him from leaving their hut. "How can he go to church without his clothing?" she chuckled.

This made Daniel even more determined to go. When his grandmother was distracted, Daniel went to his room, wrapped himself in a sheet from his bed, and made his escape. Then he dashed away to meet with the other believers.

Even though Daniel loved and respected his grandmother, his allegiance to God meant risking her displeasure. He knew worshiping God at His house was the right thing to do.

REACT NOW!

If one of your friends lost interest in attending church, what would you do? How could you make church more inviting for that person?

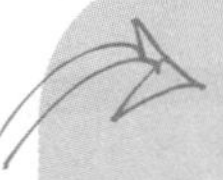

Put on the full armor of God so that you can take your stand against the devil's schemes. Ephesians 6:11.

SNAKES ON THE LOOSE

Behind you!"

Laurie turned to see a fat diamondback rattlesnake slide down the side of a wooden box and slither toward her. Ahead, another venomous reptile slipped to the floor, then another. She grasped her snake stick and slid the curved metal end underneath a serpent's white belly. "Like this?" she asked.

"Good," coached the man. "Keep it balanced."

Laurie cautiously lifted the snake to prevent its fangs from reaching her should it decide to strike. But before she could deposit it back into its box, the man stepped beside her and scooped up another viper that had gotten too close.

"Not bad," he encouraged as he closed the lids over the captured rattlesnakes.

Laurie leaned against the wall in relief. "Thanks, Ross."

During this training exercise, the teen girl had been surrounded by poisonous serpents, yet she had been in very little danger. Why? Because she wore tall, thick snake boots to protect her legs, a snake stick to keep reptiles at a safe distance, and reptile expert Ross Allen to guide and protect her. She had the proper armor, the proper tool, and, most important, the proper instructor.

God's Word warns us about "that ancient serpent called the devil." The Bible offers us the armor of God to shield us and the tools we need to resist temptation. Best of all, it tells us that we can choose Jesus as our instructor, guide, and protector.

Info Splat

A baby rattlesnake's first rattle is silent. When the snake sheds its skin a second time, it receives a second rattle. It takes two or more rattles moving against each other to make the familiar sound.

REACT NOW!

Write out a list of the things that make up "the full armor of God" mentioned in Ephesians 6:14-17. What parts have you put on? How can you put on the armor more completely?

INCREDI-BIBLICAL

I will cleanse them from all the sin they have committed against me and will forgive all their sins of rebellion against me. Jeremiah 33:8.

CHANGE OF HEART

"Jesus loves you very much," the mission teacher said. Quami listened with amazement. He looked around at the other students. He believed that God could love these young ones, for they had never done the terrible things he had done.

"But how can Jesus love me?" he asked.

The more Quami learned about Jesus, though, the more he came to believe that Jesus would forgive him. He was thrilled by the very thought for he desperately wanted to leave his old life behind.

Quami asked to be baptized, but the pastor hesitated. He came from a violent and coldhearted background. Besides, he still smoked a pipe, as he had since childhood.

"Jesus wouldn't want you to smoke," the pastor explained.

"What?" the old man asked. "My pipe is the only friend I have on this earth. Jesus wants me to give that up?"

"Yes, He would," the pastor assured him. "It is bad for you." With that, Quami flung his pipe into the bushes and never smoked again.

"I want to be a 'Jesus man,'" he announced.

The pastor knew that his heart was changed, and soon Quami was baptized.

For decades Quami had served his heathen village by killing human sacrifices. Now he served God as a witness. Whenever possible, Quami stood up at meetings, his heart bursting with joy. "Let me tell you what Jesus did for me!" he would begin.

His new life exceeded anything he could have imagined, because Jesus had forgiven and accepted even him—a former executioner well past 90 years of age!

Info Splat

Almost everyone knows that smoking cigarettes is dangerous to one's health. For teens the risks are greater, but not just physically. Self-destructive attitudes are more common in smokers, and researchers say that teens who smoke have a much greater risk of depression.

Do you have friends who doubt God's love? What knowledge could you share to show His love for them is real? What experiences have you had that show God's love for you?

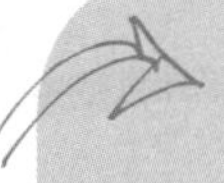

July 9

~ Incredi-Biblical ~

For the Lord himself will come down from heaven, with a loud command, with the voice of the archangel and with the trumpet call of God, and the dead in Christ will rise first.
1 Thessalonians 4:16.

"YOUNG MAN, GET UP"

My son!" the woman wept with every step. "My son, my son."

Her weeping caught the attention of Jesus and His disciples as they approached the gate of the town of Nain.

Blinded by tears, the woman stumbled along in front of the bier on which lay her dead son. It was the custom for the woman to walk ahead of the dead as a reminder that it was through a woman that death entered the world! Yet they must have been loved, for a crowd of people came with her to bury him.

"Look at her, poor thing," they said. "He was her only son."

"Who will take care of her now?" they wondered. As a widow, without any man to support her, she faced starvation and death.

Seeing her, Jesus was overwhelmed by her sadness. "Don't cry," He told her gently. Then He stepped up and touched the bier. "Young man," He said, "I say to you, get up!"

The people were shocked that Jesus touched the coffin, making Himself ceremonially unclean. But they were even more shocked when the young man sat up and began to talk. Luke 7 says that Jesus gave him back to his mother.

We can only imagine this mother's joy and thankfulness. But when Jesus returns to earth, He will do the same for all of His children who sleep. But this time He will give them life that lasts forever.

It's true. God has promised it.

Info Splat

Ancient Egyptians constructed their pyramids in alignment with the constellation containing Polaris, the North Star. They believed that when their pharaoh was buried in the pyramid he would have a straight path to heaven.

Have you ever lost someone close to you? What promises especially give you hope?

~ INCREDI-BIBLICAL ~

The wisdom of the wise keeps life on track; the foolishness of fools lands them in the ditch. Proverbs 14:8, Message.

THINK BEFORE YOU JUMP

David leaned forward on the wooden fence where he and his brother were balanced. Two horses ambled in their direction. "They're awfully big," he muttered. With his eyes he measured the distance from their backs to the ground. It was a long way down, but he had already accepted his brother's dare. If he backed out now, he'd look like a wimp.

"Come on," his brother coaxed softly. "Let's do it." When the animals came close, he caught David's eye. "Jump!"

David leaped onto the nearest horse and grabbed the mane. "Whoa!" he yelled.

The surprised animal bolted only for a moment, seemingly accepting its rider. However, the horse had a surprise of its own. As it trotted toward an orange grove, it picked up speed. Galloping to the fence, it stopped abruptly and bowed its head, tossing its rider into the thorny orange trees.

Yeeeeooowww!

David heard the horses' whinnying laughter as his brother flew from the other horse and landed beside him with a thud. Their clothes were torn and they were covered with cuts from the thorns, but there was something worse.

"Oh, no!" David gasped. As he stood, he found he was covered with hundreds of sand spurs, vicious prickly seeds that stick tight in the skin.

Over the next few painful hours he decided next time he'd consider the consequences before leaping into anything. It would have been better to look wimpy, he decided, than to become a human pincushion.

Info Splat

The first railroads in America featured trains pulled by horses or mules. During the 1820s the Baltimore and Ohio Railroad even tried to power train wheels by having a horse walk on a treadmill inside the train.

REACT NOW!

Have you ever made a reckless decision you later regretted? In the future how can you avoid making dangerous or foolish choices?

July 11

~ Incredi-Biblical ~

Very rarely will anyone die for a righteous man, though for a good man someone might possibly dare to die. But God demonstrates his own love for us in this: While we were still sinners, Christ died for us. Romans 5:7, 8.

CAPE COD'S DARING RESCUERS

Benjamin Kelley peered seaward, squinting as the wind whipped cold rain mixed with snow against his face. A member of the United States Life-saving Service on Cape Cod, he was patrolling the shore for ships in trouble that stormy December night in 1909.

Suddenly he spotted a light offshore. *Perhaps it's a signal from a ship in distress,* he thought. *In any case, those sailors are in dangerous waters.*

Benjamin hurried down the beach toward the light. Soon he could see a ship stranded in the breakers barely 200 feet from shore. "Don't try to leave the ship," Benjamin yelled to the four men on board. "I'll be right back with the lifesaving crew!"

Benjamin and his fellow rescuers hauled a basket-like contraption called a breeches buoy to the scene. They attached it to a rope thrown from the ship and reeled the breeches buoy out to the sailors. One by one each man climbed aboard and was pulled ashore.

In a half hour the rescue was over. It was an easy one for Benjamin and the other rescuers. They hadn't had to risk their lives by launching their wooden rescue boat into the pounding waves.

The motto of U.S. Life-Saving Service was: You have to go, but you don't have to come back. Like Jesus, these brave men were willing to sacrifice their lives to save others.

Info Splat
From 1872 to 1915 there were only two occasions that Cape Cod lifesavers died during a rescue attempt.

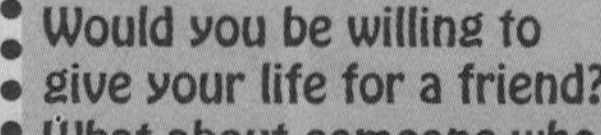

REACT NOW!

Would you be willing to give your life for a friend? What about someone who didn't like you at all? Take some time to think about Jesus' sacrifice for you.

July 12

~ Incredi-Biblical ~

Since we have these promises, dear friends, let us purify ourselves from everything that contaminates body and spirit, perfecting holiness out of reverence for God. 2 Corinthians 7:1.

PLAYING BAPTISM

"Let's have a baptism!"

Tre turned sharply and looked toward the voice. Farther up the creek his cousin Yula and her friends had been splashing in the cool water. But now the girls huddled together, giggling, captivated by Yula's suggestion. "Who's gonna be the preacher?" he heard Ramona ask.

"You can go first," Yula told her, "and I'll be baptized."

Tre turned away. He wanted nothing to do with Yula's "baptism." Baptism was a serious decision, and the thought of the girls making a game of it left a bad feeling in the pit of his stomach. He squatted down and flipped over some rocks in the creekbed, searching for crawdads, but a few moments later a scream shattered his concentration.

Info Splat
Early Christian baptistries were often designed with eight sides because the number 8 symbolized a new beginning.

Upstream he saw the girls dragging Yula's limp body from the water. Tre ran to see what had happened. The "baptism" had not gone well. Yula had lost her balance and struck her head on a stone by the creek bank.

After medical attention and a long rest, Yula was finally back on her feet. She no longer mimicked sacred things and had nothing to do with baptism until she made her decision for Jesus. Tre felt sorry that his cousin was badly hurt, but glad she had learned respect for the things of God.

REACT NOW!

If you were in a situation in which your friends were doing something disrespectful toward God, what do you think Jesus would want you to do?

INCREDI-BIBLICAL

In my distress I called to the Lord; I cried to my God for help. From his temple he heard my voice. Psalm 18:6.

DANGER IN THE STORM

Katchi hugged her drenched shirt and shivered. "This is terrible," she moaned. She'd never been stuck in such a downpour, under such a black sky. Her sister crouched in the front of the boat. "You OK?" Katchi hollered. Her sister nodded, but looked just as miserable.

Their father steered them toward the muddy bank hidden somewhere beyond the dense blanket of rain. *Putt-putt-putt*, the tiny motor spat, barely propelling them forward.

Fierce bursts of wind hammered the stinging rain sideways and thrashed the gray waves into choppy peaks. Lightning strobed around them. They were the highest objects on the lake, a hazardous place to be in a thunderstorm. In an area in which people often died from lightning strikes, the danger was very real.

Katchi couldn't remember ever feeling this much fear. Too frightened even to cry, she hunkered down in the hull. "Dear God, please protect us."

Long minutes later she peered over the side of the boat. Through the rain the shore was almost visible. A short time later the boat groaned onto the bank. "Let's go," Dad yelled. Soaked and cold, but laughing with relief, the three boaters scrambled from their craft and loaded it onto its carrier.

"Thank You, God, for Your mercy and protection," Katchi whispered as the family headed for home.

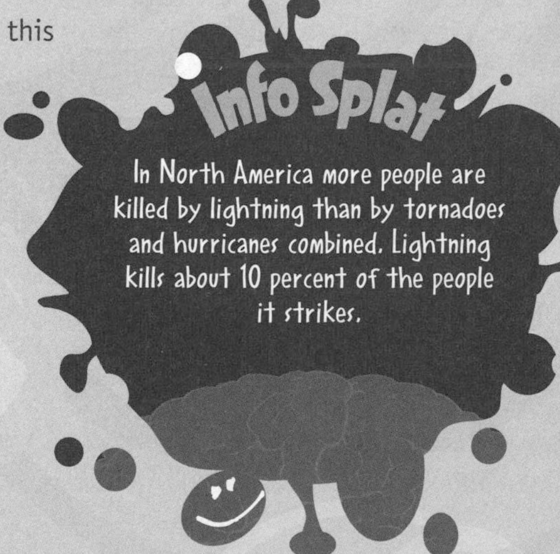

Info Splat
In North America more people are killed by lightning than by tornadoes and hurricanes combined. Lightning kills about 10 percent of the people it strikes.

What experiences have you or members of your family had that show God hears our cries for help?

July 14

~ Incredi-Biblical ~

They will neither harm nor destroy on all my holy mountain, for the earth will be full of the knowledge of the Lord. Isaiah 11:9.

GOD CARES

A pair of dark, long-lashed eyes blinked up at the two sisters and their parents. Huddling around the animal, they caressed the spotted coat and long ears. "He's so soft," whispered one of the girls.

"I didn't know a fawn could be so tiny," breathed the other.

Dad had found the baby alongside the road on his way home from work and knew that something was wrong. "A mother deer wouldn't normally leave her baby in such a dangerous place," he explained. "I believe that its mom is either dead or badly hurt."

Over the next several months they watched the orphan "Bambi" guzzle milk from bottle after bottle and turn from a scrawny infant to a long-legged young white-tailed deer. Eventually he outgrew his milk bottles and his pen. He now wanted wild grasses to eat.

"I'm really worried about Bambi," Mom said. "If he gets hungry enough, it's possible that he'd wander onto the road and get hit."

"We can't let that happen," Dad said.

It was with hope and sadness that they drove Bambi to a forest preserve and turned him loose. "Stay safe, Bambi," they called after him.

They never knew what became of their deer, but Someone knew. The Creator of all the earth watches every one of His creatures. He cares when even one is hurt. He hates what sin has done to them. That's why He promises us a future without sin, suffering, or death.

Info Splat

In spite of their delicate appearance, white-tailed deer can be fierce fighters in mating battles and when defending themselves. Most years, in North America, more people are killed or injured by white-tailed deer than by grizzly bears—mostly by car collisions with them.

REACT NOW!

Read Isaiah 11:6-8. When Jesus creates the new earth, how do you think the animals will be different from animals now?

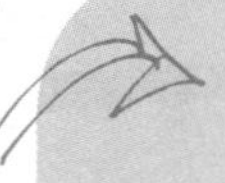

July 15

~ Incredi-Biblical ~

Blessed are the peacemakers, for they will be called sons of God. Matthew 5:9.

THE WAY OF PEACE

William Lewis froze on the African jungle path as a mob rushed toward him. Dozens of angry, shouting men ran alongside their chief as he was carried down the road.

Curious, the missionary stepped out and blocked their progress. Instantly he was surrounded by fierce warriors, their terrible, sharp spears pointed directly at him. "Lord, help me," he breathed, then called out to the chief, "How are you, my friend?"

The chief recognized his voice. "Leave him alone," he called to his warriors. The spears backed off.

"What's all the commotion about?" Will asked excitedly.

The chief responded, "We're on our way to settle a score with another tribe!"

"This will lead to bloodshed," Will warned him. "Your men and theirs. Please let me go to the district commissioner first thing tomorrow. He will help you work things out."

"OK," the chief finally agreed. His warriors were ready to fight it out, but their chief took control. "We must return to our village," he told them.

The next day Will kept his word by contacting the government official. A meeting was set up between the two enemy tribes, and soon they reached an agreement and settled their dispute.

Will saw the chief some time later. "You were right, and I thank you!" the chief told him. "Our tribe has been satisfied, and none of my men had to die."

Now the chief could see wisdom in the way of peace.

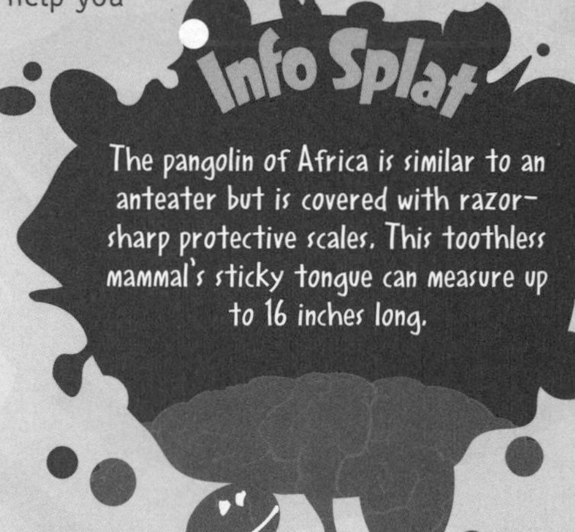

Info Splat
The pangolin of Africa is similar to an anteater but is covered with razor-sharp protective scales. This toothless mammal's sticky tongue can measure up to 16 inches long.

REACT NOW!

Do you know of any rifts between friends or family members? In what ways could you be a peacemaker?

July 16

INCREDI-BIBLICAL

I have brought you glory on earth by completing the work you gave me to do. John 17:4.

BIBLE

CRANKING IT UP

Raspberry Raze," Carla read aloud, writing the name of the lip gloss in her notebook. It was a slow day at Fetzers' drugstore. Carla's dad owned the store, and every summer Carla earned pocket money by working there. Today she had to catalog the merchandise in the beauty aisle. *Not such a bad chore,* Carla thought as she read the different labels.

Her friend Amanda watched as she listed each item. "When do you get off?" Amanda asked.

"Today I can leave after lunch," answered Carla. Amanda's parents were rich and never expected her to earn any of her own money. Eyeing her friend's new iPod, Carla wished her parents felt the same.

"Working for what you want will give you satisfaction and appreciation for the things you have, Carla," her dad had told her. "I can use your help," he reminded his daughter, "and hard work pleases God."

Just then Johnny sped by the beauty aisle, carrying a box. Since he'd started working for Carla's dad, he'd finished one assignment after the other, always looking for more things to do. "You're so annoying," Carla told Johnny.

"I want a stereo," he said, smiling. "And I don't mind the work."

Carla glanced at Amanda. Her iPod wire hung from her ear. Sighing, Carla put the lip gloss back on the shelf and went to find her dad.

"I've finished cataloging the stuff, Dad," she said. "What do you need me to do now?"

Info Splat

According to researchers working on a European Space Agency study, people who rarely exercise their bodies have an increased risk of back injuries. Long-term habits of inactivity will increase the chances of back and health problems.

REACT NOW!

How does God feel about laziness? How are we supposed to treat everything that we do?

July 17

INCREDI-BIBLICAL

"Honor your father and mother"—which is the first commandment with a promise—"that it may go well with you and that you may enjoy long life on the earth."
Ephesians 6:2.

THE BOAT RIDE

Wow, what a great day," Mark exclaimed. Marty nodded as the boys dropped their gear into Tommy's dad's boat.

"It's hot," Tommy said, squinting in the blazing July sun. He peeled off his T-shirt and tossed it next to the pile of gear. Giving the motorboat some gas, he slowly backed it away from the dock.

"We're lucky your dad let us use the boat," Marty told him.

"Yeah," Tommy grunted. He didn't mention how long he'd had to beg before Dad agreed to let him drive the boat on his own.

"Tommy, I'm trusting you with the boat," he'd said. "It's very expensive, and it's not a toy. Plus, you guys could get seriously hurt if you're not careful." He'd reached out and lifted his son's chin with one finger so he could look into his eyes. "Remember, Tom, that means don't go too fast!" Tommy had agreed.

Now Mark turned to him with a big smile. "Let's open it up," he urged.

Tommy looked out at the expanse of clear water before him. There were no other boats around. *Go ahead, do it. No one will know,* he seemed to hear. Then Ephesians 6:1 came to his mind. *"Children, obey your parents in the Lord, for this is right."*

"Come on," Mark echoed. Let's see how fast this thing will go!"

His fingers played with the wheel. *How easy it would be to just push this lever forward . . . and how fun.*

Suddenly Tommy realized what he was about to do.

In 1978 Ken Warby won the title Fastest Man on Water when he drove his homemade boat at a record speed of 317 miles per hour. Attempts to break this record have ended in fatalities, and it has stood for 30 years.

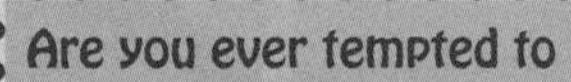

REACT NOW!

Are you ever tempted to disobey your parents? What might Jesus do in this situation? What does God say about this?

July 18

INCREDI-BIBLICAL

I am the Lord your God, who brought you out of Egypt, out of the land of slavery. Exodus 20:2.

A TIME FOR PIONEERS

Today's the day! Sara's eyes flew open as she remembered. It was July 24, 1849, and by now she had almost forgotten the long, tiring trip.

"Just think, dear family. We'll be able to worship in freedom in our own land," Pa had said. Sara's family, like many others, had been forced from their town in Illinois because people hadn't tolerated their beliefs. Listening to Pa, Sara swallowed hard, afraid of the unknown but looking forward to the adventure.

Joining a caravan led by a man named Mr. Young, Sara's family and thousands of others pulled handcarts or drove wagons pulled by oxen or horses. They traveled more than 2,000 miles westward, hitting every bump and rock along the way. They drove over the plains, hundreds of miles of nothing but sky and tall prairie grass, and they journeyed through muddy streams and wide, rushing rivers.

Info Splat

Christians today still die for their faith. In many places in West Africa, when a man embraces Christianity he loses his wives, his wealth, and his children. He is driven away from his village, and sometimes his friends and family pursue and kill him.

Sometimes Sara was so cold that her numb fingers could hardly hold a cup of hot water without spilling it. Shaking, she'd wrap strips of blanket around her feet and bundle her younger siblings in wool blankets.

Finally the caravan had arrived in the Great Salt Lake valley. *It's a desert,* Sara thought as she looked at the bare, dry land, *but it's our freedom land.*

Sara and her family were Mormons, and July 24, 1849, marked the beginning of the Pioneer Days Parade, celebrating their safe arrival in Utah.

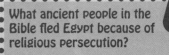

What ancient people in the Bible fled Egypt because of religious persecution?

July 19

INCREDI-BIBLICAL

Therefore, prepare your minds for action; be self-controlled; set your hope fully on the grace to be given you when Jesus Christ is revealed. 1 Peter 1:13.

A TIGHT FIT

Winnie reached for her favorite pair of jeans and pushed her left leg into the pant leg opening. It was the second leg that had her worried. As Winnie pulled them up over her hips and tried to zip them across her tummy she realized there was going to be a gap. Ooops.

Winnie did a few deep knee bends.

"I always have to do a few deep knee bends when my jeans come out of the dryer," Carla, her friend from school, had told her. "No sweat. They always loosen up."

These jeans were not loosening up. Winnie had 20 minutes to meet her friends and get ice cream. *Right, ice cream*, Winnie thought, *just what I need right now*. She sprawled across her bed and lay as flat as she could. With a deep gasp Winnie sucked in her tummy, then pulled the zipper slowly up her belly.

There! she thought with relief. *Finally closed.* Then she sat up. First she felt a sharp pain. Then she looked down at the zipper. *It's broken*, she thought sadly.

Suddenly the sound of Mom's voice floated into her mind. "You need to exercise some self-control," she'd chided her recently. "Whatever comes your way, you just can't seem to say no." Mrs. Barry had been referring to her poor choice of TV programs.

It was that last piece of pie, Winnie realized. She glanced at the clock. The 20 minutes had long been spent. She sighed. *Maybe it was the ice cream on Tuesday and the sundae on Wednesday and the French fries on Friday . . .* and *that last piece of pie.*

"God expects you to have some self-discipline," Mom had added. All of a sudden Winnie wondered if Mom could be right.

Info Splat

There's a holiday called Take Your Pants for a Walk Day, celebrated on the Internet for Ecard and some calendar Web sites. Simply go for a walk. Enjoy nature and all that God has created. When your pants get a little tight around the middle, take them out for a walk. Your pants will thank you.

Do you have any habits that control you? What does God say about self-control? Does God say no to certain behaviors to hurt us, or because He loves us?

~ INCREDI-BIBLICAL ~

The Lord himself goes before you and will be with you; he will never leave you nor forsake you. Do not be afraid; do not be discouraged. Deuteronomy 31:8.

OUTSIDE THE COMFORT ZONE

Jumping off a ledge into the lake below was not Corey's idea of fun. He shivered in the heat as he watched the line of guys shorten ahead of him. One by one, his cabinmates grabbed the rope swing, ran, and tossed themselves over the ledge.

Corey's friend Noah slapped at his neck. "Got another one," he yelled. "These mosquitoes are HUGE!" Corey had met Noah in kindergarten, when Noah dared him to eat paste. Noah was always daring Corey to do stuff. Some of it was OK, like when he dared Corey to run an extra mile in track or when he invited him to attend his church on Sabbath.

"Come on, you might actually like it, Corey," Noah had coaxed. That's what he always said. Usually he was right, Corey had to admit, but cliff jumping?

Now Corey stood at the edge of the cliff, looking at the rope swinging over the deep-blue lake below. *Perfect love casts out fear,* he thought, remembering last week's Sabbath school lesson. *Step out in faith and trust Jesus with your life.*

Corey grasped the thick rope in his hands, said a quick prayer, and rocketed himself off the ledge. As he surfaced seconds later in the cold water, he grinned. *That was awesome!* He heard Noah whooping from the top of the cliff.

"Thanks, God, for being with me," Corey said aloud. Stepping out of his comfort zone wasn't so bad when he had friends like Noah and Jesus.

Info Splat

BASE jumping is a sport like skydiving, except people jump from buildings, antennas (such as unoccupied towers), spans (bridges), or earth formations (cliffs, canyons). This high-risk sport started in 1978 when four climbers with parachutes successfully jumped off El Capitan, a 3,593-foot cliff in Yosemite National Park. It has a fairly high percentage of fatalities.

REACT NOW!

What kinds of challenges make you afraid? What do you do when you are afraid? Is God able to take care of us no matter what danger we may be in?

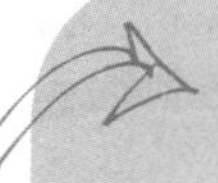

INCREDI-BIBLICAL

If I have the gift of prophecy and can fathom all mysteries and all knowledge, and if I have a faith that can move mountains, but have not love, I am nothing. 1 Corinthians 13:2.

BIG SOFT DINOSAUR

Phillip reached into the box of Rice Krispies and pulled out his prize: a plastic dinosaur. *Cool,* the 6-year-old thought, turning the molded creature around in his hands. Fascinated by the weird-looking animal, he soon absorbed himself in anything he saw about dinosaurs. Then at age 12 Phillip read about Roy Chapman Andrews and his dinosaur hunts in the Gobi Desert. That's when Phillip knew what he wanted to be—a paleontologist.

In 2007 Phillip Currie and a team of paleontologists uncovered the remains of a new dinosaur species. The China dig revealed birdlike bones, and thanks to technologies like CT scans and computers, the studies of the remains may yield new information about dinosaurs.

In recent years cutting-edge approaches to exploration have increased the number of dinosaur discoveries. In March 2005 paleontologists stumbled upon the first soft tissue from a dinosaur. After analyzing the DNA in the soft tissue, scientists answered questions about its environment, its diet, and what caused its death.

Of course, all this knowledge is useless if it doesn't point to something greater. Paul says that even the most incredible things in this world mean nothing without love. The next time you get excited about a new discovery or gift, remember what makes it meaningful: God's amazing love.

Info Splat

Here's another modern discovery: After a journey of 900 million miles, the European Space Agency successfully landed the Huygens probe on the surface of Saturn's largest moon, Titan. The probe's peek at the moon showed that it is orange and spongy, and emits a low whooshing sound.

What makes love so special? What can you do to have God's love in your life?

-~ INCREDI-BIBLICAL ~-

"Love the Lord your God with all your heart and with all your soul and with all your strength and with all your mind," and "Love your neighbor as yourself." Luke 10:27.

BRICKS OF LOVE

Nighttime had fallen on the tiny group. Their 10-day mission trip to Haiti was coming to an end. *It couldn't come sooner,* Matt thought as he stumbled toward his bed and fell across it, feet hanging off the end. "I am beat," he announced to no one in particular, pulling off his sweat-soaked baseball cap.

All day long the group had carried bricks, scraped concrete, and filled walls for the church's new youth center. In Haiti jobs were hard to come by, and poverty led many bored kids to seek out trouble. The youth center would give these kids a place to go and would also teach them skills to make a living.

"You will be serving God and helping others," the pastor had told Matt's group before they left. But so far all they had done was attend a few services, sing, and lay bricks. Lots and lots of bricks!

Matt's Bible lay half open on his bed. He reached over and casually began to flip through its pages.

"Hey, Matt." Isaiah, one of the Haitian kids, walked in the room. "We just want you to know how much your work here means to us." He smiled, laying his hand on Matt's back. "You know, you guys really show us Jesus' love."

Feeling a twinge of guilt, Matt turned and looked into his friend's eyes. They were filled with tears of gratitude.

After Isaiah left, Matt knelt on the floor and prayed.

Info Splat

Much of religion in Haiti involves voodoo and black magic. It's said that in Haiti one finds zombies, or people who have died and then come back to life. However, the Bible assures us that the dead are sleeping in their graves.

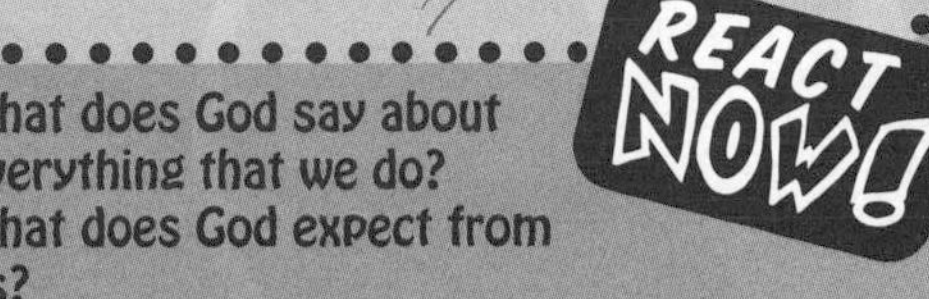

What does God say about everything that we do? What does God expect from us?

July 23

Do not turn to idols or make gods of cast metal for yourselves. I am the Lord your God. Leviticus 19:4.

A LIFE OF PASSION

Anna was relentless. She plastered posters all around youth camp—in the lunchroom, down at the horse barn, in the restrooms, in her cabin, even at the pool. All her T-shirts were covered with pictures of animals, and she wouldn't touch the cafeteria's scrambled eggs. Anna was a devoted animal rights activist.

The kids at camp avoided her. When they saw her coming, everyone found a quick excuse to leave. Everyone except Eric.

"Is that your religion?" he asked Anna on Wednesday as she hung a picture of a dead cat on the camp store's door. The poster was inscribed, "March of Crimes, not Dimes."

"No," said Anna, securing the sheet with small pieces of duct tape. She shrugged. "Maybe. I don't know."

"A few of us are going to be studying the Bible after lunch today," Eric told Anna. "You want to come?" He glanced over her shoulder at the door.

"Guess how many animals are tortured and killed every day?" she countered.

"I don't know," Eric admitted. He took a deep breath. "But what about a man who was tortured and killed though He was innocent?"

"Oh, the Jesus thing," Anna said, then stopped.

"I understand your passion," Eric told her. "I love animals too. There's so much cruelty done to animals—for all kinds of reasons. But I have another passion. Why don't you give our Bible study a try?"

Eric didn't tape up flyers, but Anna could see he believed in his faith by the kind way he treated her. *Why not?* she thought. Aloud, she said, "OK. I'll go."

Info Splat

Like you, Eric and Anna are millennials—people born after 1981. Also called Generation Y, most millennials are tolerant toward multiculturalism, have decided to be their own "decider," and highly value authenticity.

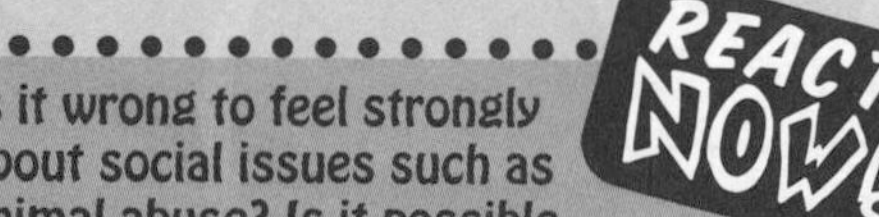

Is it wrong to feel strongly about social issues such as animal abuse? Is it possible to replace Jesus Christ with other philosophies? What should be our first priority?

~ Incredi-Biblical ~

Peace I leave with you; my peace I give you. I do not give to you as the world gives. Do not let your hearts be troubled and do not be afraid. John 14:27.

MOVING DAY

A row of suitcases stood in the hallway of Marta's home. In an adjoining room her mom was supervising the movers. "Are you finished packing?" Mom called to her.

Marta sat on her bedroom floor and picked at the pink shaggy rug. *I don't want to move,* she thought. *I just hate it.* Her cat Cali sat in a patch of sunshine, watching her. "This summer sure stinks," Marta told Cali.

"Consider this an adventure," Mom had said. "You'll make friends in Brightsville, too."

Marta stroked Cali's head. "You don't want to move either, do you?" she whispered.

She thought of Matt, one of her closest friends. "God is with you wherever you go," he'd reminded her just the day before. "God loves you, right? So He wants only what's best for you."

But already missing her friends, Marta had her doubts. She got up and began moving her books from the bookcase to an open box on the floor. When she picked her Bible up off her desk, she noticed a slip of paper sticking out of its pages.

Mom, Marta thought, recognizing the handwriting. She smiled as she read, "Perfect love casts out fear.* I love you, sweetie, and so does Jesus."

"Lord, let me give this move to You," Marta prayed. "I'm afraid of the unknown ahead of me, but I know that You are there for me." She still didn't feel very peaceful, but she knew she could trust God's promises. Her future was in His hands.

Info Splat

According to the U.S. Census Bureau, more than 47 million people, or 16 percent of the population, move each year. On average, individuals move 11.7 times in their lifetime.

REACT NOW!

Have you ever had to face something new that made you feel afraid? What did you do about that fear? What does God say when we are overwhelmed with fear?

* 1 John 4:18

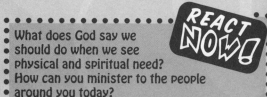

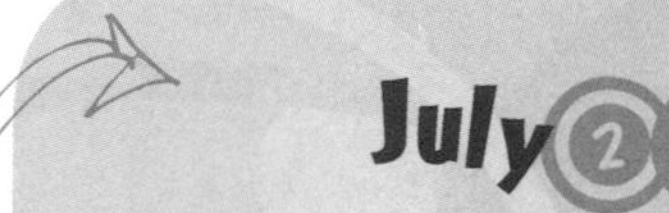

Incredi-Biblical

He who mocks the poor shows contempt for their Maker; whoever gloats over disaster will not go unpunished. Proverbs 17:5.

THE MISSION

"Sir, ya got a penny?" the dirty child asked, hand outstretched toward the minister. William dug into his pocket and fetched a silvery coin. "Here you go, lad," he told the youngster, his voice cracking with emotion.

Since he was a boy, William's heart had ached for the poor in his city of London, England. Beyond his imposing church doors lay a gray, grimy street filled with gray, grimy homeless people. Their empty bellies ached for bread, but if they were fed, he reasoned, they might realize they were hungry for the Word of God.

Surely God would have me to do something for them, William thought.

But when he tried to bring them into his church, he faced strong opposition. "Let them find someplace else," his congregation seemed to say, scowling at the ragged, dirty converts who attempted to join them in worship.

So in 1865 Pastor Booth bravely left his comfortable position and began to fight for the poor. He was at war, building an army to fight poverty and ignorance.

"While women weep, as they do now, I'll fight; while children go hungry, as they do now, I'll fight; . . . while there remains one dark soul without the light of God, I'll fight. I'll fight to the very end!" William Booth declared.

Booth's Salvation Army grew slowly, but today it works with more than 106 nations, ministering where the need is greatest, and guided by faith in God and love for all people.

Info Splat

In 1879 a woman named Eliza Shirley held meetings that inspired William Booth to travel to the United States and formalize his army. In only three years the group had offered services in 12 states. Today the Salvation Army has been active in the U.S. for almost 130 years.

REACT NOW!

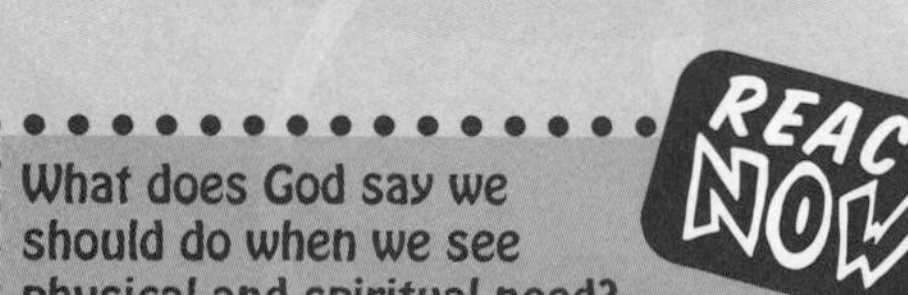
What does God say we should do when we see physical and spiritual need? How can you minister to the people around you today?

July 26

~ Incredi-Biblical ~

Resist the devil,
and he will flee from you.
James 4:7.

TASTY TREATS

Twinkies, frosted flake cereal, and corn chips lined Mary's cart. "What are you doing?" Tim asked his sister as she reached for canned pudding. He'd driven her to the grocery store and knew that Mom had asked her to get their groceries for the week.

Mrs. Smith was strict about her family's diet. "Our bodies are the temple of God, and we should do our best to keep them healthy," she often said, and cooked things such as brown rice and lentils and lots of fresh fruits and vegetables. But Mary was tired of healthy food. She wanted to eat the way many of her friends did. She wheeled down the aisle and put a box of ice-cream sandwiches in the cart.

Info Splat

Some effects of a poor diet include lack of energy, poor concentration, heart disease, and high cholesterol.

Once Tim and Mary got home and unloaded the groceries, Mary ran down the street to Emily's house. "Emily's not feeling well," her mom told Mary. "She's upstairs in her bedroom."

Sure enough, Emily looked a little green. "What's wrong?" Mary asked her.

"I'm not sure," Emily said, "but I started feeling really sick after lunch."

"So what'd you eat?"

"Not much. A peanut-butter-and-jelly sandwich, grape soda pop, a few cookies," Emily recited. "And, I guess, some chocolate bars from the fridge." She shifted on the bed and groaned. "Then for breakfast, when Mom wasn't looking, I had the leftover brownies and ice cream. She'd kill me if she knew."

When Mary left, she knew what she needed to do. "Tim, drive me back to the grocery store, will you?" she asked.

There she plunked two bags of food and the grocery receipt in front of the surprised clerk. "Anything wrong with the food?" he asked.

Mary gave him a big smile. "You bet," she replied.

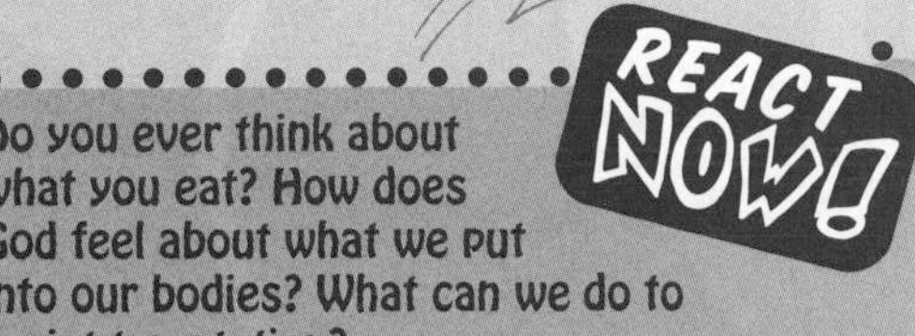

Do you ever think about what you eat? How does God feel about what we put into our bodies? What can we do to resist temptation?

July 27

~ Incredi-Biblical ~

When pride comes, then comes disgrace, but with humility comes wisdom. Proverbs 11:2.

STAR OF THE SHOW

Clayton just knew he was meant to be a star. For some years he'd acted in all the local summer productions, snagging the lead part several times. He'd even had voice and acting lessons. So when tryouts for the Barn Theater production were announced, Clayton was the first to sign up.

A few weeks later Mr. Sang posted the results of the tryouts on the Barn Theater door. Clayton wasn't worried. After all, everyone agreed that he had star quality. But when he looked, his name wasn't there. Clayton checked again. *Denton, Smith, Evens, Wharton,* he read. The list ran on, but there was no Clayton Dunbar.

He turned from the list in shock. *It must be a mistake,* he thought wildly. Suddenly he felt unbearably hot.

"I thought it might be good for you to try your hand at all the aspects of putting on a production, Clay," said Mr. Edwards, the director. "Here, grab that brush and start painting the wall for the first act."

As Clayton slowly picked up the paintbrush, Jack, his friend since grade school, came up beside him. "Hey, it's just like we learned in church," he said. "You know, the body of Christ is made up of many parts, and each one is important." Jack gave Clayton a light punch. "You can't have a whole body if one of the pieces is missing, right?"

Suddenly Clayton felt like a cloud had lifted. "You know what, Jack? You're right!"

Our bodies are amazing examples of humble teamwork. When you pick up a box or a book and your biceps contract, your triceps relax to allow your elbow joint to bend. One flexes; the other chills out.

What lesson did Clayton learn? Have you ever been disappointed in something you expected to happen not happening?

July 28

INCREDI-BIBLICAL

And God said, "Let the land produce living creatures according to their kinds: livestock, creatures that move along the ground, and wild animals, each according to its kind." And it was

Genesis 1:24.

NEW DISCOVERY

Jake wiped his face on the sleeve of his cotton shirt and swatted the mosquitoes from his face. It was early morning in Borneo, Malaysia, and he was already wet with sweat.

"They've got to eat, too," Margaret Altman teased her son.

Jake grunted. "I'm not breakfast," he said.

The two followed the swing of the machete that went ahead of them. "It was over there," their guide told them, pointing to a small clearing on the rain forest floor. He handed Jake's mom a photo.

Looking over her shoulder, Jake saw a small animal, slightly bigger than a housecat, with dark-red fur and a long bushy tail. "What's the big deal?" he asked. "It looks like Sparky back home."

Margaret laughed. "Well, you're right," she said. "It does look a lot like our cat. But this animal is a brand-new species that someone just discovered in the rain forest," she said, eyes shining with excitement. Keep a sharp lookout for one."

That night back at camp Margaret took out her Bible. It was quiet in their campsite. Most of the guides had retired to their tents. Sitting close to their small fire, Margaret read aloud, "'In the beginning God created the heavens and the earth.'

"Imagine, Jake, thousands of years after God made our world, He's still revealing to us all that He has created. Isn't it exciting?"

Info Splat

Finding new animals these days is rare, especially large mammals. In December 2006 the World Wildlife Federation discovered a new mammal in the forest of Borneo. Photographed twice by remote camera, the critter is about the size of a cat and has a long muscular tail.

REACT NOW!

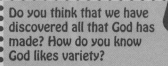

Do you think that we have discovered all that God has made? How do you know God likes variety?

July 29

~ Incredi-Biblical ~

Give thanks to the Lord, call on His name; make known among the nations what He has done. Sing to Him, sing praise to Him; tell of all His wonderful acts.
Psalm 105:1, 2.

SOCCER WITNESS

Dark clouds gathered above the mud house, and the winds began to blow briskly as Carl waited for the summer rain to fall.

"Supper, Carl," his mom called from the kitchen.

He wrinkled his nose. The menu was always the same. Groundnut stew and peanut sauce poured on top of boiled and pounded yam, called *tuo*.

It still felt strange to Carl to be living in the Sahel, in West Africa. His family had served as missionaries there for only three months, and he wasn't too sure he liked it. He missed his house, his school friends, and the kids in his youth group. Right now they were probably getting ready for lunch (and he knew it wasn't groundnut stew!) or playing a quick game of soccer.

He missed soccer. Yes, there were neat things about living in a different country, and he truly appreciated the experience, but he missed the guys at home too. They were there for a reason, though. A good reason. "These people need to hear about Jesus," Dad had reminded him.

"It will change us, too, Carl," Mom had added. "God will use this time to teach us."

Yeah, right, Carl thought as he washed his hands for supper. *All I've been doing is hot, boring work in the fields.*

The next morning as he walked up the path toward the cleared field, Carl was surprised to see his African friends kicking a soccer ball across the dirt.

"What do you need me to do today?" Carl asked as his father came up behind him.

"Get out there and spread the gospel, son," Dad said with a grin. "Play a little soccer."

Info Splat

When visiting with people of other cultures, respect how they live. For example, in northern Togo, don't cross your legs or show the soles of your feet. Throughout western Africa, never shake hands with your left hand; use only your right.

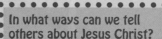

REACT NOW!

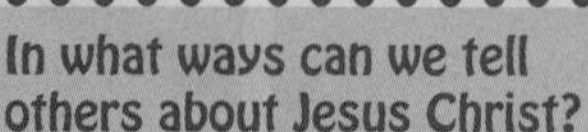
In what ways can we tell others about Jesus Christ?

July 30

~ Incredi-Biblical ~

We have different gifts, according to the grace given us. Romans 12:6.

DIFFERENT IS GOOD

It was Saturday night, and through his bedroom window Brett could see the bright flames of a bonfire over at Jessica's house. Everyone was there. Everyone, that is, but him.

Brett stretched out onto his bed, pushed his glasses up higher on his nose, and reached for the book lying on his nightstand. "Might as well get a jump on this," he muttered. The book was for his physics class he'd begin in the fall, and Brett was engrossed in the subject. He loved physics, math, astronomy, computers, and video games.

"You, my friend, are a geek," Jerry told him one day at school, coming up behind him in the hall. He tugged on Brett's shirt. "Wow! Great threads!" he teased. "Your dad wear this when he was in high school too?"

Brett laughed. He didn't pay any attention to the latest styles.

Now he flipped open the physics book as talk and laughter drifted through his open window. He'd just gone over a page when the phone rang.

"Hi!" said Jessica. He and she had been in school together since kindergarten, but she hung with a different crowd now. "Aren't you coming over?" she asked.

"I don't think so, Jess, but thanks for asking."

"Listen, Brett," she said, a laugh in her voice, "I want you over here *now*."

A minute or two later the doorbell rang. A group of kids from the bonfire stood on the front step—the athletes, the popular kids, and the intellectuals.

Brett smiled, surprised that they'd come after him. "OK," he said, putting his book on the floor.

It was going to be a good night.

Info Splat

Heterochromia, one eye's iris being a different color than the other, is caused by an excess or lack of pigment. This can be inherited or acquired by disease or injury. If inherited, sight in the eye is not affected. The eye looks different but functions normally.

REACT NOW!

Do you think only one group of people should be the acceptable group to hang out with? What does God say about each of us?

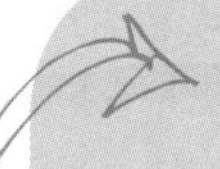

July 31

INCREDI-BIBLICAL

Fruit trees of all kinds will grow on both banks of the river. . . . Their fruit will serve for food and their leaves for healing. Ezekiel 47:12.

BLUEBERRY CURE

Harry scoured the bushes along the path from his house. There! His eyes spotted the plants with the round blue berries. I surely hope these help Marian get better.

"Go, hurry, get some blueberries for your sister," his mother had told him early that morning, pushing him down the path toward the wooded hills. "If you go now, you'll be able to pick while it's cooler, and you'll be back by afternoon."

Marian had been coughing for two days. She was weak, sore, and worn out, and their mother did not know what to do. If Marian wasn't better soon, they'd have to send for the doctor, and Dr. Fields was a day's journey away.

"She needs the juice of blueberries," Aunt Frances told her worried sister. "Harry can find some and gather enough for Marian."

Now Harry pushed his way through the brush, his eyes fixed on his target. *Bingo*, he thought. Reaching out, he plucked the berries from their leafy plants and dropped them into his bucket. He stripped one bush after another, grabbing a berry for himself now and then, but mostly filling the pail as fast as he could. With the berries nicely mounded on top, Harry hurriedly made his way back home.

"Thank you, Harry!" Mother exclaimed when he came through the door. "God is so good. He has once again provided for our needs from His marvelous creation!" Working quickly, she washed, then crushed, the berries. Straining out the juice, she soon had the first cup of blueberry juice ready for Marian.

Info Splat

The pigment that makes blueberries dark blue is a powerful antioxidant. Blueberries may help reduce your chances of getting cancer and heart disease, and help prevent urinary tract infections. Native Americans used tea made from blueberry root to help women relax during childbirth.

REACT NOW!

Do you know of other foods that can help with your health needs? Why do you think God provided these natural medicines?

August 1

~ INCREDI-BIBLICAL ~

I have hidden your word in my heart that I might not sin against you. Psalm 119:11.

TREASURE IN A CAVE

The young Bedouin shepherd looked up at the cave's narrow entrance. After a long day of following his wayward goats to keep them safe, they'd led him here: to the steep cliffs of Qumran, Israel.

Curious, he picked up a rock, threw it toward the cave's entrance—and heard pottery breaking. He wanted to investigate, but it was late. He had to take the goats home. The next day he returned with his cousins to explore the cave. The boys were disappointed that there was no gold among the broken pottery inside the cave, but what they did find on that day in 1947 turned out to be one of the world's most treasured biblical discoveries—the Dead Sea scrolls.

Over the next few years fragments from more than 800 scrolls were found in this and other nearby caves. On these fragments scholars identified parts of every book of the Old Testament except Esther. Several copies of Isaiah were among these fragile scrolls, one thought to be about 1,000 years older than any previously discovered copy of that Old Testament book. It's believed the scrolls were made from around 200 B.C. to A.D. 68.

In all, the shepherds found a previously hidden collection of the world's oldest known copies of the Old Testament. For many people the Dead Sea scrolls prove that God's Word had, in fact, been faithfully copied and unchanged through many, many centuries of time.

Info Splat

Because fragments of the scrolls were sold or divided among many different scholars, publishing and interpreting them has been an ongoing challenge. Scores of articles and books have been written about them along the way.

REACT NOW!

Ever wondered if you can trust a book as old as the Bible? Beyond faith, the Dead Sea scrolls offer concrete proof that you can.

~ INCREDI-BIBLICAL ~

There will always be poor people in the land. Therefore I command you to be openhanded toward your brothers and toward the poor and needy in your land. Deuteronomy 15:11.

HOMELESS IN THE PARK

Jana followed her brother Matt and Pastor Dave along the railroad tracks and toward the tunnel by the park. "Be careful when we get past those trees," Pastor Dave said. "Homeless people camp along there, and they can sometimes be a little rough."

"Rough?" Jana asked.

"Well, some of them use drugs. If they've used recently, they might say or do something you wouldn't like."

Jana felt a tingle of danger, but didn't slow down. It was a bright sunny day, and she knew Pastor Dave would take care of them. Moments later they spotted a group of men, some just teens, clustered around a picnic table. Their clothes were dirty and torn, and their hair looked grimy. They looked surprised to see strangers approaching. Most of them kept their eyes downcast, as if they'd done something wrong by just being there.

"Howdy!" Pastor Dave raised his arm in greeting. A man with a long gray beard waved back.

Pastor Dave turned to Jana and Matt. "Stay here. I'll just be a minute."

Jana watched him walk over to the men. He shook their hands and chatted a few moments, then took out his wallet to give each one a little cash. Jana could see it wasn't much, but the men seemed grateful all the same.

"God bless," the old man said brightly, offering a nearly toothless smile.

"And to you," Pastor Dave returned.

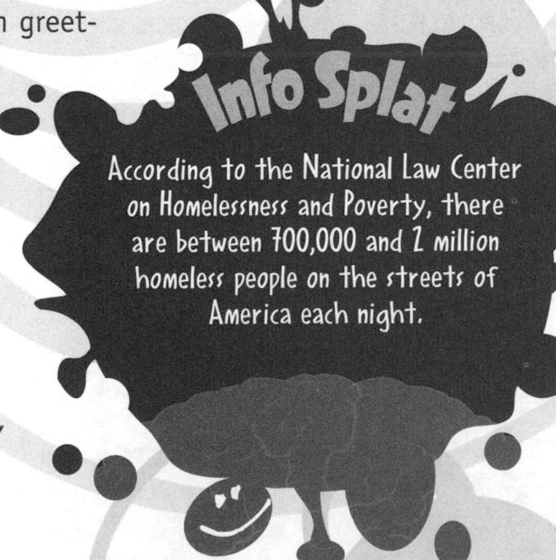

Info Splat
According to the National Law Center on Homelessness and Poverty, there are between 700,000 and 2 million homeless people on the streets of America each night.

REACT NOW!

When you see the poor and homeless, are you quick to judge, or do you see an opportunity to be a blessing?

August 3

~ INCREDI-BIBLICAL ~

[Angels] will lift you up in their hands, so that you will not strike your foot against a stone. Psalm 91:12.

CAR ON THE EDGE

Paige stared at the freeway on-ramp in dismay. They were blocked from Christmas Eve in Bakersfield by a snowbank! Her mother and aunt got out to inspect the snow, kicking at the bank with their boots. "I can drive over it," Aunt Barb said, getting back into the car. "Paige, you watch for cars."

Aunt Barb gunned the car several times, and almost made it over the bank. But on her last try the car skidded, slid to the edge, and stopped—teetering above a steep cliff. Paige cried and braced herself for the fall she felt sure would come.

"I called 911," Mother told them a moment later. "But they said it'll take awhile to reach us."

Paige, Mother, and Aunt Barb waited and waited, but no one came. Finally Mother phoned a friend who contacted his buddies at the fire station.

Info Splat
According to a recent report, 89 percent of teens surveyed said they believe in the existence of angels.

"If we touch it, that car will go right off the cliff," one of the firefighters said an hour later. His eyes narrowed in concern. "We'd better call for some more help."

When a police officer arrived and called a tow truck, Paige heaved a sigh of relief. *Soon this will be over!* she thought.

Ninety minutes later, as the tow truck lifted the car to safety, a young fire officer shook his head in disbelief. "The only thing holding you up was a small rock wedged against the tire," he told them.

But Paige knew that God's angels had held the car in place.

REACT NOW!

Have you ever been rescued by an angel? If you were in danger, would you trust God to send help? What if He didn't?

~ INCREDI-BIBLICAL ~

He guarded him as the apple of his eye, like an eagle that stirs up its nest and hovers over its young, that spreads its wings to catch them and carries them on its pinions. Deuteronomy 32:10, 11.

THE EAGLE'S TEST

Soaring high, the female eagle considers which male will be her mate. She cares nothing about finding a handsome, shapely bird. No, his vital feature must be strength. She's looking to the future, knowing their babies must learn to fly from a great height.

For that reason, the female puts her prospective suitors to the test. When a male makes a bid for her attention, she chooses a small stick and flies high, dropping it for him to catch on his back. If he drops it, he's rejected. If he catches it, she finds a bigger stick and drops it from a lower height. This continues as long as he keeps catching them, until she drops the heaviest stick she can carry. If he catches that one, he becomes her mate for life.

Why such a strange test? Eagles build their nests in high, rocky cliffs. When parents teach an eaglet to fly, they push it from the nest, and the baby can fall hundreds of feet while it struggles to use inexperienced wings. Papa eagle must swoop down and catch the baby on his back at the last second to carry it back to the nest for another try. If a male can save a big heavy stick, he can probably save a frightened eaglet needing a lift.

Info Splat

Wild eagles live up to 40 years, which means a pair of eagles can be mates as long as some people stay married. In 1782 the United States chose the bald eagle as its national symbol, partly for its strength.

REACT NOW!

Like the eagle, God faithfully catches His children as they learn new things. When you choose your life mate, what godly traits will you look for?

August 5

~ Incredi-Biblical ~

For the Lord your God will bless you in all your harvest and in all the work of your hands, and your joy will be complete. Deuteronomy 16:15.

MEXICO ADVENTURES

Christie dunked her hands in ice water to cool off and then continued to hammer nails, amazed she could work in such heat. The mission trip had been an adventure from the beginning. She remembered her first night here in Tijuana, Mexico. Bees had invaded her youth group's crude sleeping structure, and everyone moved outside to sleep on a cement platform under the stars.

At the end of the day Christie lay in her sleeping bag, staring up at the night sky. "I thought this was going to be relaxing!" she whispered to her friend Deanne.

"I know," Deanne whispered back. "And I'm so hungry for something besides sandwiches! But I'm glad we came and can help a little."

Christy agreed. She'd never seen such poverty. The main part of Tijuana had paved streets and brightly colored buildings, but the teens worked in the outskirts, where small children roamed dirt roads alone and the only homes were plywood shacks with ragged cloth roofs. The church Christy's group was constructing would be the neighborhood's only real building. It would hold about 20 worshippers.

On Sabbath morning the students and adults filled the little church for the commemorative service. It had been a long week of sacrifice and discomfort. But the trip also brought a joyous sense of satisfaction none of them would soon forget.

Info Splat

Situated just south of San Diego, California, Tijuana is the world's busiest border city. Approximately 300,000 people cross this border between the United States and Mexico every day.

REACT NOW!

When God asks you to pitch in and help someone less fortunate, do you grumble? Or do you do your work with joy?

Incredi-Biblical

For you have spent enough time in the past doing what pagans choose to do. 1 Peter 4:3.

WHAT'S YOUR TV IQ?

Nearly every American home has at least one TV, and cable channels, satellite dishes, and DVD rentals fuel our appetites to watch more. This quiz offers an honest look at TV:

1. American children spend almost as much time watching television as they do attending school. True____ False____
2. Bedroom TVs can affect: (a) your bedtime, (b) your ability to fall asleep, (c) sleeping enough hours, (d) all of the above
3. For young viewers, increased TV causes increased: (a) obesity, (b) pressure on parents to buy things, (c) anxiety/aggressiveness, (d) all of the above
4. Advertisers place their products within television shows to increase sales. True____ False____

Answers:

1. True. Kids average about 25 hours per week watching television, almost equaling classroom time.
2. d. Bedroom televisions are bad news, producing all kinds of sleep problems. These include later bedtimes, taking longer to fall asleep, and sleeping fewer hours.
3. d. Couch potato kids tend to eat more and gain more weight; children's commercials purposely entice kids to ask for more stuff; kids see an average of 12,000 violent acts on television per year, causing many to feel anxious and sometimes act more aggressively.
4. True. Television "product placement" is popular. When viewers see their favorite stars using a product, they tend to want to use it too, which boosts its sales. An example is the *American Idol* judges drinking Coca-Cola from Coke glasses instead of drinking water.

Info Splat

Thirty years ago viewers had less than 10 channels to choose from; now, hundreds are available. If you added all the hours the average 65-year-old American watches TV over their lifetime, it would come to about nine years of solid TV time.

REACT NOW!

Next time you feel the urge to channel-surf, ride your bike, take a walk with your family, or read a book instead.

August 7

Incredi-Biblical

A gentle answer turns away wrath, but a harsh word stirs up anger. Proverbs 15:1.

OUT OF CONTROL

Conner ducked to avoid the basketball coming right at him, but he was a second too slow. It smacked him in the shoulder. Both skin and muscle stung with pain.

"What'd you do that for?" he snapped, unable to control his temper.

"Sorry," Justin called out, a lopsided grin on his face.

"No, you're not," Conner shot back.

Against his will, angry feelings welled up inside him. In a moment he found himself rushing at his friend like a raging bull, his head barreling toward Justin's midsection. He was shorter than Justin and much skinnier, so contact was swift but didn't seem to have much effect.

With a sigh Justin wrapped his arms around Conner in a bear hug. Though Conner fought, he held him tight, but not tight enough to hurt him.

Undaunted, Conner tried to pummel Justin's back with his fists, but his grip kept him from doing any real harm. Finally Conner grew too tired to fight, and stopped.

"I told you I was sorry," Justin repeated gently, releasing him.

Conner could see he meant it.

"That really hurt," he said stubbornly, pointing at the ball. But deep down he was ready to put the argument to rest.

"I know," Justin agreed. "Here," he added, handing him the ball. "You take the first shot."

Pretty soon the game was back on, and Conner's anger floated away on the stiff afternoon breeze.

Info Splat

In the Middle East, where Israeli and Palestinian youths have little in common, the game of basketball is being used to bring the two groups together for some peaceful teamwork and fun.

REACT NOW!

When you're angry at someone who refuses to fight back, how does that make you feel? Is your anger "turned away"?

Incredi-Biblical

He said to them, "Go into all the world and preach the good news to all creation." Mark 16:15.

CHAMPION OF THE BIBLE

Born in 1320, John Wycliffe was many things, including a highly educated theologian, a professor, and a church reformer.

For years Wycliffe worked for reform in the English church. When he compared it to the early Christian church established by Christ's apostles, the English church appeared far too wealthy and worldly. Wycliffe also did not believe that the authority given the pope was biblical.

Wycliffe worked hard to bring about change in the church through writing books, letters, and tracts, and doing public speaking. When those didn't work to his satisfaction, he decided the only way to bring about real change was to make the Word of God available to people so they could read and judge for themselves.

To make that happen, in 1378 he defied the church by enlisting both friends from work and professional scribes to help him translate the Latin Bible (called the Vulgate) into the first-ever handwritten English Bible translation. A printed English translation wouldn't happen for about another 130 years—not until the invention of the printing press.

Of course, Wycliffe's translation infuriated the Catholic Church, since they taught the church had sole authority to explain the Scriptures. But Wycliffe believed that the only real authority that Christians should live under is the Bible, which must therefore be made available to them in their own language.

According to Wycliffe International statistics, the Bible has now been translated, at least in part, into more than 2,000 languages.

Info Splat

The Catholic Church had their day of "punishing" John Wycliffe. In 1428 Pope Martin V commanded that Wycliffe's bones be dug up, burned, and thrown into a river—more than **40 YEARS** after his death.

REACT NOW!

Do you have an idea to help spread the gospel to people who have never heard of Jesus? Every Christian needs to do their part.

August 9

INCREDI-BIBLICAL

**The clever see danger and hide;
but the simple go on, and suffer for it.
Proverbs 22:3, NRSV.**

DANGER IN THE NEIGHBORHOOD

Jake and Zack left the eighth-grade classroom behind and walked three blocks to Zack's house. Zack had spent the night lots of times at Jake's house, but this was Jake's first time sleeping over at Zack's.

When they were almost home, they passed some guys about their age standing on the corner. They were all smoking, and one guy was playing with a small knife. Their eyes narrowed as the boys came close.

Jake felt nervous. He wondered if he should say hi or even wave as they walked by. In the end, he breathed an open-eye prayer for God's protection and turned away, walking a little faster. But as they left the guys behind, one suddenly turned and yelled something at Zack. Zack looked back and shrugged, showing he couldn't get into it right then.

"They're always trying to get me to join their gang," he explained as they got out of earshot.

Gang members can be identified by certain colors worn somewhere on the body, certain clothing styles, types of graffiti, hand signals or gestures, and certain types of writing or codes.

"That's a gang?" Jake whispered. "You have gangs in your neighborhood?"

"Yeah," Zack sighed. "We've lived here since I was little, and it was a nice place, you know? Then the gangs started last year. Mom wants to move, but Dad thinks we should stay. He says we wouldn't get enough for the house to buy one someplace else. Anyway, I'm not allowed to walk around here at night anymore." He shook his head. "It stinks."

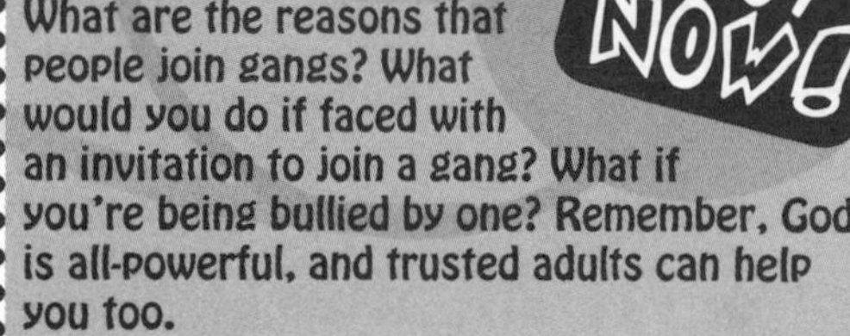

What are the reasons that people join gangs? What would you do if faced with an invitation to join a gang? What if you're being bullied by one? Remember, God is all-powerful, and trusted adults can help you too.

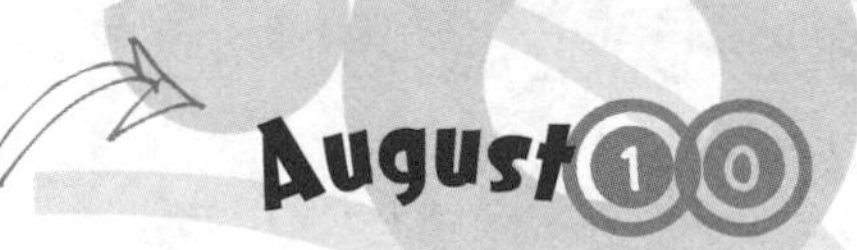

INCREDI-BIBLICAL

Therefore each of you must put off falsehood and speak truthfully to his neighbor, for we are all members of one body.
Ephesians 4:25.

THE BLUE RIBBON

Cassidy grabbed her backpack and puppet, casting one last indecisive, guilty glance at Marcy's collage in the corner. Marcy had called Cassidy the night before.

"I accidentally left my art project at your house," she'd said. "Can you please bring it to school tomorrow for the art contest?"

Cassidy had promised she would, but now . . . she closed the front door behind her, leaving without the project. It was wrong and dishonest, but she knew her puppet would never win against Marcy's collage in the competition.

At school Cassidy rushed to tell Marcy she'd forgotten to bring it. She apologized, but Marcy was upset and looked suspicious. By now, caught in her dishonesty, Cassidy felt awful, but it was too late. The judging was about to start.

When her puppet earned a blue ribbon, her victory tasted bitter, especially when Marcy, almost in tears, came and congratulated her. Cassidy felt so guilty that she could hardly bear having Marcy around. Also, she wondered if Marcy *knew*. And if she did, would she ever speak to her again?

After school, instead of showing off her ribbon, Cassidy went straight home and into her room. Shutting the door, she saw the collage where she'd left it in the corner. Heavyhearted, she pinned the blue ribbon to Marcy's art project and cried.

Tomorrow she'd take the collage to school, admit what she'd done, and give Marcy the ribbon. Maybe then they could be friends again, if it wasn't too late.

Info Splat

In 2006 Paul Kinsella dropped 100 identical wallets in public places to test people's honesty. Three quarters of the wallets were returned with all their contents. But he found that people under age 30 were less honest than others. Only 56 percent of the young people returned the wallets.

How important is honesty to you? When have you seen dishonesty hurt someone you cared about?

~ Incredi-Biblical ~

The wolf will live with the lamb, the leopard will lie down with the goat, the calf and the lion and the yearling together; and a little child will lead them.
Isaiah 11:6.

UNLIKELY PALS

When Jayla brought Sunshine home, she wondered how her new bird would get along with her brother's kitty, Sadie. The family's other pet, a garden snake named Jaws (who ate live goldfish whole), didn't like Sadie at all, and the feeling was mutual. The kitten would lie on top of Jaws' cage until it coiled up in a corner, trying to hide. But Sunshine and Sadie were both young, so Jayla hoped the two "babies" would bond.

When Jayla introduced Sadie and Sunshine, she held the bird at a careful distance. Sadie, this is my pet," she said in a gentle voice. "You mustn't scare him by trying to hunt him down. And whatever you do, don't eat him!"

Sadie tilted her head and looked at Sunshine with great suspicion. But when Jayla petted Sadie while still holding the bird, she purred and seemed to understand.

For the first few days Jayla let Sadie in her room only if Sunshine was safely inside its cage. But then she started letting them spend a few minutes together outside the cage. In time they became good friends and enjoyed looking out the window side by side.

They were an unlikely twosome that made people smile, offering a glimpse of heaven, where all animals, even those who are natural-born enemies on earth, will live together in peace.

Info Splat

As hunters, cats are the natural enemies of mice, rats, bugs, insects, a variety of small animals, and of course, birds. In turn, cats worry about larger species that might decide to eat them, such as coyotes and large owls.

Is someone in your life considered an enemy? Jesus can help you live in peace with that person.

INCREDI-BIBLICAL

Do not make idols or set up an image . . . for yourselves, and do not place a carved stone in your land to bow down before it. I am the Lord your God. Leviticus 26:1.

GOD OR BUDDHA?

Tom sat staring at tomorrow's lesson plan, his mind far away. As the Bible teacher for a Seventh-day Adventist school in Thailand, one of his responsibilities was to introduce Jesus to his students.

He loved teaching and talking with his students outside of the classroom, but it was challenging, too. Beyond the school grounds evidence of the predominant religion was everywhere. Villagers bowed to tiny one-inch gold statues of Buddha and made offerings to others that stood 80 feet high.

Yet daily Tom taught his students about God, stressing His displeasure at the worship of idols such as Buddha. "If I carve an image out of a rock, is that rock going to help me at all?" he asked them. "If I melt some medal and pour it into a mold, will the object that comes out of the mold be able to help me?" And through the Bible and personal experiences, Tom continued to introduce his students to the God of heaven. Yet, as time passed, he wondered if he was making a difference. With family and religious culture so important, it seemed unlikely his students would challenge ancient customs.

Then Tom had a wonderful surprise. Lily, one of his students, stayed after class to talk to him. "I went to the festival, where everyone bowed down to Buddha," she told him. "The whole family bowed, but I didn't. I stood in the back."

She went on to say that she now prayed to God in her room with the door closed, so no one in the family would see. "I respect God now," she said, "not Buddha."

Tom smiled, praising God that this student courageously rose to the challenge of putting our living God first.

Info Splat

The Buddhist religion was started by Prince Siddhartha Gautama of Nepal almost 600 years before Christ. Eventually he became known simply as Buddha, which means the enlightened one. As of 2004, Buddhists made up about 6 percent of the world's population.

If you had to publicly choose between honoring God and your family's traditions, which would you choose? Is God above all else, even your family?

~ Incredi-Biblical ~

Your beauty should not come from outward adornment . . . Instead, it should be that of your inner self, the unfading beauty of a gentle and quiet spirit, which is of great worth in God's sight.
1 Peter 3:3, 4.

THE PERFECT LOOK

Our culture is saturated with airbrushed, surgically enhanced, unlikely images of beauty, making girls wish they were thinner, boys want bigger muscles, and both expect more perfection in the opposite sex. If you think you know what some kids are willing to do or risk to achieve perfection, try this quiz.

1. According to a popular teen magazine, what percent of girls ages 6 to 12 have been on at least one diet?
   a. 10 b. 25 c. 35 d. 50
2. When teenage boys use anabolic steroids to beef up their bodies, they run the risk of which side effect?
   a. lack of bone growth
   b. liver damage
   c. increased aggression
   d. all of the above
3. According to statistics, the number of teens ages 18 and less having plastic surgery went from 60,000 in 1997 to how many in 2003?
   a. 100,000 b. 150,000 c. 200,000 d. 225,000

Info Splat

If a Barbie doll's measurements were proportionately transferred to a woman, she'd have a 38- to 40-inch bust, 18- to 24-inch waist, and 36-inch hips, and weigh about 110 pounds—not exactly a comfortable body to walk around in.

Answers:
1. c. The magazine also reported that between 50 and 70 percent of girls in that age range with normal weight think they're overweight.
2. d. The National Institute on Drug Abuse reports all these and more are possible, some being irreversible.
3. d. The American Society for Aesthetic Plastic Surgery reports a significant rise in all types of teen surgeries, including chemical peels for acne, nose jobs, breast reductions or enlargements, and liposuction to remove excess fat.

REACT NOW!

If you're upset about your self-image, check out nature. See how different, yet equally beautiful, the flowers and plants are just the way God made them.

~ INCREDI-BIBLICAL ~

The righteous give generously. Psalm 37:21.

A DRESS FOR JENNY

Jenny walked toward English class with a heavy heart. She'd just found out the girls in her class would wear white dresses to escort the graduating class in their upcoming ceremony. But she didn't own a white dress, and she knew her family couldn't afford to buy one for her.

"Why the long face?" Mrs. Harris, the school librarian, slipped an arm around Jenny's shoulders and gave a gentle squeeze.

Jenny sighed, and explained. "Maybe I could just watch from the audience and not take part. It really wouldn't matter."

"Oh, no," Mrs. Harris scolded with a smile. "We can do better than that. Give me a day. I'll think of something." And sure enough, the next afternoon she told Jenny that a woman from church had volunteered to take her shopping.

"But I don't even know her," Jenny moaned, mortified.

"That doesn't matter a bit," Mrs. Harris assured her. "Eleanor Hamlin is excited to do it. All her grandchildren are boys, so this is a true treat for her."

On graduation day Jenny took her place with the junior honor guard as the seniors marched up the aisle. She looked around at the other girls' dresses. They were all pretty, but none were as special as hers.

Jenny gave her two helpful "angels" extra big smiles, and silently thanked God for giving her the perfect dress for a perfect day.

Info Splat

The first academic graduation took place in 1432 at the University of Oxford in Oxford, England. A hundred years ago diplomas began being printed on parchment paper. Before that, they were handwritten on sheepskin.

If someone in your church offered to help you with a personal problem, would you accept their help? Letting others give to you allows God to bless you both.

August 15

~ Incredi-Biblical ~

But let all who take refuge in you be glad; let them ever sing for joy. Spread your protection over them, that those who love your name may rejoice in you. Psalm 5:11.

CONSCIENTIOUS HERO

World War II was a time of heroism and sacrifice. In all, nearly 300,000 U.S. soldiers died in battle, and more than 600,000 were wounded. But one serviceman stood out from the rest.

Desmond Doss, a Seventh-day Adventist, went to war as a conscientious objector, willing to serve but unwilling to fight. In his case, that meant serving as a medic in the battlefields of Okinawa—working without a gun, which earned him ridicule from the other soldiers.

In May of 1945 the ridicule stopped when Doss's battalion scaled a 400-foot cliff under heavy Japanese fire. Seventy-five soldiers were wounded, and the battalion decided to retreat. For several hours Doss remained under Japanese fire, carrying the wounded one at a time to the cliff's edge, then lowering them on ropes to safety. Many hours and lots of prayer later Doss brought down the last injured man. Then, finally, he lowered himself out of harm's way.

Days later Doss surprised his comrades again. While aiding wounded soldiers through a night attack, he himself was seriously hurt, forced to tend his own wounds. Another round of fire injured him further. Other medics tried to carry him, but he crawled 300 yards to reach aid, insisting that a more seriously wounded soldier be carried in his place.

Doss was awarded the Congressional Medal of Honor for his bravery, the only person in World War II to receive this honor for noncombat achievement.

Info Splat

To be a conscientious objector, those otherwise qualified to serve in the military must demonstrate religious or moral beliefs preventing them from bearing arms or going to war. World War II produced about 37,000 conscientious objectors. Since the beginning of the Iraq war, hundreds have applied for CO status.

REACT NOW!

In 2004, a film titled ***THE CONSCIENTIOUS OBJECTOR*** documented Desmond's remarkable achievement. Do you have to be in the military to be brave for God?

INCREDI-BIBLICAL

Satan himself masquerades
as an angel of light.
2 Corinthians 11:14.

THE SPOOK OF TREYMOUR HOUSE

Willy and his friend Robert heard rumors that the Treymour house was haunted. Several people had seen a mysterious light coming from the old place. "Let's go and see for ourselves," Willy suggested. So that evening the two friends hurried toward the Treymour house. Sure enough, a strange glow radiated from the decaying eaves. And outside on a ledge of rotting wood sat the spook—a shapeless blob of greenish light.

Willy and Robert stared, speechless. Willy had been taught that there were no such beings as ghosts and goblins. But the eerie figure was so real!

Two years passed before the mystery was solved. One damp night Willy was walking through the forest when he saw two greenish eyes staring at him. He froze, certain that a mountain lion was about to spring. Then he remembered the spooky glow at the Treymour house. These "eyes" looked just like it. Heart pounding, Willy reached toward the glow and found it was only a decaying log.

Willy's spook was foxfire, a fungus that grows on rotting wood, especially in damp conditions. The fungus contains a chemical called luciferin that reacts with an enzyme, producing a glow that can last for days.

Willy was right—ghosts and goblins don't exist. Many apparently supernatural phenomena have ordinary explanations. But Lucifer, the fallen angel now known as Satan, sometimes creates real supernatural appearances to fool people. Knowing the Bible's truth will keep you from being deceived.

Info Splat

Earthquakes sometimes create bright flashing lights in the sky, fireballs several feet across that pop up out of the ground, and other strange lights. Reports of these earthquake lights go back to 373 B.C. Some scientists believe that balls of light caused by smaller strains in the earth's crust could explain many UFO sightings.

REACT NOW!

Have you ever seen something you couldn't explain? Read Willy's story and other bizarre tales in ***GUIDE'S GREATEST MYSTERY STORIES.*** Get it at www.adventistbookcenter.com.

~ INCREDI-BIBLICAL ~

In everything, do to others what you would have them do to you, for this sums up the Law and the Prophets. Matthew 7:12.

SOCCER LESSON

Tate grabbed a soccer ball and looked across the field. The other boys had chosen teams for softball, but he had another idea.

A new boy, Jonathon, had joined their class in midspring. He had carrot-red hair, generous freckles, and a shy smile. The teacher said he'd moved from a farm in Idaho because his mother had died, and she had told the class be nice to him. But for some reason Jonathon hadn't made any friends yet.

Tate could feel God leading him to do something about that. With determined steps, he walked to the far corner of the field where Jonathon sat by himself. "Hey!" Tate called. "Want to play soccer?"

"I guess," he answered. "I've never played before."

"Never?" Tate was shocked. "Don't they have soccer where you're from?"

"No," he said. "We mostly worked with animals for fun. You know, ropin' cows and ridin' bulls. Then, of course, I had my own horse to take care of."

Tate thought about this for a moment. He'd never even been on a farm, and had ridden a horse only once. "I guess I'll have to show you how to play soccer, then. Come on."

Tate demonstrated kicking the soccer ball with both his foot and knee, then butting it with his head. Jonathon gave it try. After some misses and wild kicks, the ball flew in a graceful arc.

"I did it!" he laughed. "Wow! I did it."

All too soon recess was over, but their friendship was just beginning.

Info Splat

The Random Acts of Kindness Foundation formed in 1995 as "a resource for people committed to spreading kindness." It suggests creative new ways to bring kindness to others.

REACT NOW!

Do you know someone who needs a friend? It pleases God when we're willing to treat someone with the same friendly kindness we ourselves would want.

Incredi-Biblical

It is I who made the earth and created mankind upon it. My own hands stretched out the heavens; I marshaled their starry hosts. Isaiah 45:12.

ROCKS FROM HEAVEN

Ben ran to the hot tub, making a splashing entrance. It was already jammed with people: his best friend, Zane Lewis; Zane's parents and his little brother Alex; and Ben's mother. Alex was craning his neck to look up at the night sky. It was already dark, and according to the weatherman, in a few short minutes there would be a meteor shower.

"What makes a meteor?" Alex asked.

Mr. Lewis rumpled his son's dark hair. "Good question, buddy," he said. "It's when a meteoroid flies into our atmosphere and gets so hot that it turns into a flaming streak in the sky."

Alex pondered that, and then asked, "What's a meteoroid?"

"It's a space rock, or a piece of comet or asteroid."

"Wow," Zane said, elbowing Ben. "That's cool . . . rocks falling all the way from space to us."

Ben watched his mom getting her binoculars ready. "Mom, could a meteoroid come all the way from heaven?" he asked.

They all sat quietly for a few more minutes, thinking about stars and comets and rocks possibly falling from heaven.

All of a sudden, the first brilliant meteor flashed across the velvet sky, almost too quickly to see. Then another, and another, until the heavens were ablaze with hot streaks of light trailing in every direction. Some looked almost close enough to touch.

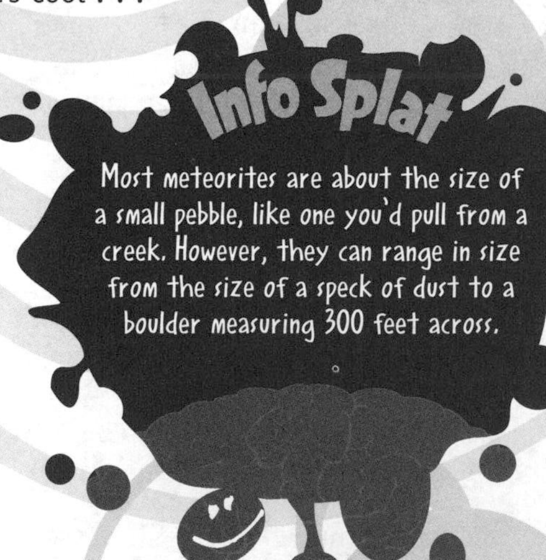

Info Splat
Most meteorites are about the size of a small pebble, like one you'd pull from a creek. However, they can range in size from the size of a speck of dust to a boulder measuring 300 feet across.

REACT NOW!

If you want to see the heavens in action, there are books and Web sites with times and dates for meteor "shows" all through the year.

INCREDI-BIBLICAL

Let me understand the teaching of your precepts; then I will meditate on your wonders. Psalm 119:27.

THE TEACHER TESTED

When Jamey needed a break from college, he volunteered to teach Bible at a small Seventh-day Adventist school on the island of Pohnpei, in Micronesia. One day, he gave the class an unusual assignment.

"Visit a church of any denomination," he told the class, "and ask the priest or pastor to explain what happens when you die. Then get Bible verses to support their answer."

When all the assignments were turned in, Jamey read them out loud, confident he'd be able to explain away any answers that didn't jive with his faith. Most were easily explained, but one was not. He had to take the paper home and, for the first time ever, go back and study to discover the biblical reasons he believed that death is a sleep that lasts until Jesus returns to earth.

"This experience made me more grounded and knowledgeable in my faith," he says. "I realized I'd look pretty foolish if I couldn't defend and explain my Adventist beliefs."

That assignment turned out to be a pretty tough lesson for the teacher, but Jamey was encouraged. "I came out of it feeling proud of my church," Jamey said. "What we believe the Bible teaches makes the most sense out of everything I've ever seen."

Jamey eventually returned to his college studies, and now is a youth pastor in southern California.

Info Splat

A survey revealed that three out of five American teens believe the Bible is accurate in every way. However, two thirds saw Satan as a nonliving symbol of evil, and six out of 10 thought good deeds could earn them salvation.

REACT NOW!

If you had to defend your church's beliefs, could you? Try taking one doctrine and see what biblical evidence you can find to support it.

~ Incredi-Biblical ~

Finally, brothers, whatever is true, whatever is noble, whatever is right, whatever is pure, whatever is lovely, whatever is admirable—if anything is excellent or praiseworthy—think about such things.
Philippians 4:8.

MOVIE RATINGS QUIZ

Judging a movie by its rating can bring disappointment and an unhealthy viewing experience at show time. Do you know what movie ratings mean and how they got there? Try this quiz and find out.

1. Who assigns ratings?
   a. clergy b. federal government c. parents d. all of the above
2. PG means:
   a. parents should investigate films before children view them
   b. some violence and brief nudity is allowable
   c. drugs aren't allowed
   d. all of the above
3. PG-13 means:
   a. an expletive can be used once, not more
   b. content is never as graphic as an R-rated film
   c. mature content is allowed if those making the rating believe the story warrants it
   d. all of the above
4. Before ratings started in 1966, all movies were wholesome.
   a. true b. false

Very early films (prior to 1922) sometimes contained images that would now earn them a PG, PG-13, or even an R rating, though at that time children of any age could view them without parental consent.

Answers:

1. c. Anonymous parents of young children, unaffiliated with moviemaking, rate the movies.
2. d. All of these are true. A PG rating is never a green light for all young viewers, since some adult content that used to earn an R rating is now OK for PG.
3. a. In this rating it's OK for young viewers to hear cursewords once but not twice. On the other hand, PG-13 films can have R-rated content, but only if two thirds of the raters believe most parents would agree with the PG-13 rating.
4. b. Pressure for studios to clean up movies first came in 1922, when churches and other groups declared Hollywood films indecent and immoral.

REACT NOW!

The next time you choose a film, first read a Christian review or talk with your parents to help you decide if it's something you want to spend time watching.

August 21

INCREDI-BIBLICAL

The grass withers and the flowers fall, but the word of our God stands forever. Isaiah 40:8.

FADED FLOWERS

Zoë watched her mother's smile fade. They were almost home when they spotted two little girls running from her prized flower garden, their arms loaded with fresh blooms.

"They're just flowers," Zoë reminded her.

"Yes, but they're our flowers. And those girls just come and pick them all the time without asking. Pretty soon the garden will be bare!"

Mother parked the car and strode purposefully to the girls' tiny house a little ways down the street. Zoë followed a short distance behind. A tired-looking young woman answered Mother's knock, wiping her hands on a shredded dish towel. "May I help you?" she asked.

When Mother explained what she'd seen, the woman looked embarrassed. "I'm so sorry," she exclaimed. "Girls! Come here, please."

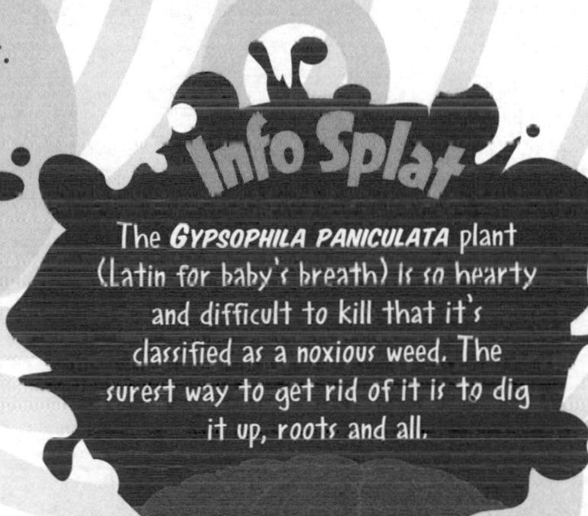

Info Splat
The *Gypsophila paniculata* plant (Latin for baby's breath) is so hearty and difficult to kill that it's classified as a noxious weed. The surest way to get rid of it is to dig it up, roots and all.

The girls came sheepishly around the corner from the backyard. "This lady tells me you helped yourself to her flowers without asking. Is that true?"

They both nodded, mouths clamped shut. Then following their mother's orders, they returned the ruined, limp blossoms and tearfully apologized.

The next day when Zoë and her mother went outside to work in the garden they found the flowers floppy and looking sick. They immediately watered everything, but the plants never perked up. Within a few days the entire garden of sweet peas, delphiniums, petunias, and baby's breath was dead.

"What happened to your garden?" Zoë asked her mom.

"I'm not sure," she sighed wistfully. "One thing I know without doubt, it surely is bare now."

What other ways could Zoë's mom have handled the situation? What would you have done?

~ INCREDI-BIBLICAL ~

If we live, we live to the Lord; and if we die, we die to the Lord. So, whether we live or die, we belong to the Lord.
Romans 14:8.

WILLIAM THE REBEL

When William Hunter was just 19 years old, his faith and courage were tested in ways few people can relate to. Hunter was living and working in London as an apprentice silk weaver when Queen Mary Tudor took the throne in 1555. The queen, a Catholic, made it law that every person in England had to practice Catholicism and attend Mass.

Hunter did not agree with all the teachings of the Catholic Church, and so didn't go to Mass. For publicly denying the church and breaking the law, he was fired from his job.

After returning to his hometown of Brentwood, Essex, Hunter began reading the Bible for himself, something that Catholics didn't do at that time. When a local priest found out, he sent Hunter to be interrogated by the Bishop of London.

For his Protestant beliefs, clear denial of England's official church, and refusal to give up reading the Bible Hunter was imprisoned for nine months. While in prison he endured harsh punishments and constant offers of bribery. And when it became clear that he would not repent, Hunter was sent home to Brentwood. There he was burned at the stake for his unshakable faith.

A monument now stands in the town in his honor, with this inscription:

"William Hunter, Martyr. Committed to the Flames March 26th MDLV. Christian Reader, learn from his example to value the privilege of an open Bible. And be careful to maintain it."

Hunter's accuser, Sir Anthony Browne, built the Brentwood School on the site of Hunter's execution in 1557, two years after Hunter's death. Nearly 500 years later the school continues to thrive as an educational facility for both boys and girls.

Do you value the privilege to read your Bible whenever and wherever you please? Remember William Hunter. Don't let that privilege go to waste!

INCREDI-BIBLICAL

For our struggle is not against flesh and blood, but against the rulers, against the authorities, against the powers of this dark world and against the spiritual forces of evil in the heavenly realms. Ephesians 6:12.

THE "THING" IN MIKE'S ROOM

Mike waited until the dorm hallway was empty to use the pay phone. "Hey, Mom, it's me," he said tiredly. "That thing was in my room against last night."

Mom was quiet. "Did you ask God to make it leave?"

"Uh-huh."

"And?"

"It laughed."

"OK, let's pray together now for God's protection. But promise me you'll talk to the school youth pastor—today."

That afternoon Mike found the young pastor in the gym. "What can I do for you?" he asked, disarming Mike with a friendly grin.

Mike explained that for the last several nights, after the lights were off, he'd felt someone watching him while he tried to sleep. When he opened his eyes, a dark, shadowy "figure" would be sitting in the chair by his bed, staring.

The pastor asked some pretty personal questions. "What do you do in your free time?" he wanted to know. Then he asked, "Have you fully given your heart to the Lord?"

It was hard letting go of secrets, but slowly Mike revealed that within months of his baptism two years before, he'd let drugs and other things turn his life away from God.

The pastor explained how those wrong choices had invited the nightly apparitions, and asked Mike if he wanted to pray for God's forgiveness and help. Mike agreed. Afterward, they made plans to meet again.

That night the chair stayed empty, and Mike slept peacefully at last.

A reported seven million American teens, age 13 to 18, say they've seen or heard angels or demons. About 75 percent have dabbled in witchcraft and psychic phenomena, while less than a third of evangelical teens have experimented with the occult.

If you've experimented with the occult, the time to stop is now. Ask someone you trust to pray with you for God's protection and forgiveness.

INCREDI-BIBLICAL

Be kind and compassionate to one another, forgiving each other, just as in Christ God forgave you. Ephesians 4:32.

FORGIVENESS IS SWEET

The instant Kyle nabbed the soccer ball to make a play he was surrounded by guys, all pushing and shoving for the ball. Then he felt himself pinned against the gym wall. There was a stab of pain. Someone had wrenched his arm, hard. The ball slipped out of his grasp, and the crowd took off, leaving him hurt and alone.

Kyle brushed himself off and headed for the lunch area. He was through with soccer for the day, and his feelings were as bruised as his arm. Why would someone intentionally hurt him for a ball? But before he could finish that thought, a guy came from behind and shoved him forward. He hit the grass facefirst.

He pushed himself up and brushed off the dirt, not even looking back to see who did it. Instead he went straight for the nearest bench and buried his face in his hands, hiding unwanted tears. A couple of minutes later a teacher sat beside him, asking what was wrong.

Kyle told her, and after a few minutes she brought two guys over to face him. Ross refused to apologize. He angrily blamed the arm-pulling on others, dismissing what witnesses said. But Nathan looked sadly at Kyle's tears.

"I didn't mean to push you into the grass," he said. "I'm sorry."

Looking up, Kyle gave Nathan a nod. Those words meant so much. "It's OK, I forgive you." And he wiped his tears away, ready to face the next class.

Info Splat

Studies have shown that forgiving others brings physical benefits to the forgiver, including less stress, improved heart rate and blood pressure, decreased levels of pain, and increased happiness. Forgiveness was also found to strengthen relationships by ending arguments faster.

When you've been hurt by someone, are you quick to forgive? God's forgiveness of your sins depends on your willingness to forgive others.

~ Incredi-Biblical ~

The Lord said to Moses and Aaron, "Say to the Israelites: 'Of all the animals that live on land, these are the ones you may eat.'" Leviticus 11:1, 2.

PIGS, BUGS, AND OTHER DELICACIES

God gave the Israelites guidelines for healthy eating. (For more details, look up today's verse and read on.) Find out some reasons for these guidelines by testing your food IQ.

1. Sea creatures without fins and scales have:
   a. faulty digestive tracts
   b. small bodies
   c. light coloration
   d. appetites for decayed flesh
2. Pigs could be harmful because they:
   a. smell really bad
   b. like rolling in mud
   c. have wormy flesh
   d. are fat and gross
3. Cute little bunnies are banned because they:
   a. eat dangerous veggies
   b. are prone to fevers
   c. are too precious to eat
   d. don't drink enough water
4. "Bugs" you can eat:
   a. grasshoppers b. spiders
   c. worms d. bees

Info Splat

Insects are big business. Some candy companies now offer sweet winged treats such as fancy chocolate-covered crickets and colorful cricket lollipops, with real crickets in the middle! Want some?

Answers:

1. d. Unclean sea critters are scavengers, not predators. They wait for sea life that's already dead and decaying to fall to them instead of chasing live, healthy prey. If these fish and shellfish eat critters that died from disease, they could pass that disease on to the human that eats them.
2. c. Modern health practices dictate cooking pork well done to kill the worms in their flesh, which could be fatal to ham-hungry humans.
3. b. Bunnies can actually carry tularemia, or rabbit fever, which is very harmful to humans and sometimes fatal. Even handling a dead rabbit can spread the disease.
4. a. While there are a number of bugs classified as clean, the Bible specifically mentions grasshoppers. (John the Baptist ate locusts, a type of grasshopper, with wild honey.)

REACT NOW!

If the smell of barbecued pork ribs or deep-fried shrimp is tempting, remember what might be inside! A mouthful of wormy, diseased flesh isn't worth it.

~ Incredi-Biblical ~

Jesus said, "Let the little children come to me, and do not hinder them, for the kingdom of heaven belongs to such as these." Matthew 19:14.

WORTH THE COST

Katie was excited. At 14, she was finally on her first mission trip. She'd traveled to Baja California, Mexico, with eight others from her school. They helped build a much-needed day-care center next to an orphanage that housed about 100 children. The center would provide child care for parents tempted to drop their children off at the orphanage while they worked.

Some days Katie knocked down walls, moved furniture, and cleared rubble from what would soon be a playroom with toys. Other times she worked in the orphanage cooking lunch for everyone. But her favorite job was playing with the children, and it hurt her to see little kids wandering the streets outside the orphanage, alone.

"I have a passion for helping kids," Katie says. "I wanted to help because if the parents don't have a place to take their children, they'll be in the streets all day and [may] get into gangs at an early age."

Katie says that she'd wanted to go on a mission trip since third grade, but helping people far away costs money. For the trip to Baja she had to raise $250 to pay her own way.

"It was worth it!" she says. "I was having a hard time with God before the trip. The world was tempting me, and it seemed that everyone else was better off than I was. Mexico made me realize that helping someone less fortunate is what feels good."

Info Splat
There are about 2 million orphan children in Mexico. Tragically, many of them end up living in the streets, trying to survive on their own.

REACT NOW!

Feel discontented with life? Share what you have with someone who has even less, then reflect on the experience.

Incredi-Biblical

He [Jesus] humbled himself and became obedient to death—even death on a cross! Therefore God exalted him to the highest place. Philippians 2:8, 9.

A PRINCE OF PEACE

It was unlikely that Prince Bhumibol would ever be the king of Thailand. His uncle was reigning when he was born, and his father and older brother were in line for the throne. But Bhumibol's father died when the boy was only 2, his uncle died, and his older brother became king.

The prince was in Switzerland studying engineering when his brother unexpectedly died. Suddenly the 18-year-old college student became His Majesty King Bhumibol Adulyadej of Thailand.

Like the Thai prince, Jesus had an opportunity to become an earthly king. After He fed more than 5,000 people with bread and fish, they were eager to claim Him as their ruler. But Jesus knew that His purpose was not to become a powerful dictator, but to die as our Savior.

King Bhumibol used his power to serve his people. He started free medical clinics and helped poor farmers find better methods of growing crops. He kept the country unified in times of crisis, preventing war and violence.

In June 2006 Thailand celebrated the king's sixtieth year of rule. At that time he was the world's longest-reigning monarch. Nearly 1 million people came to hear his anniversary speech, cheering and waving flags to honor their beloved king.

"The king is the most important person in the world to me," said Sahataya, a 21-year-old student who attended the celebration. "I would die for him."

The king with the shortest reign on record is Dom Luis III of Portugal, who was technically king for about 20 minutes. He was fatally wounded when his father was assassinated in 1908.

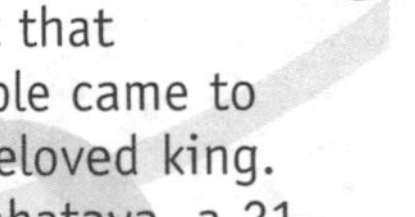

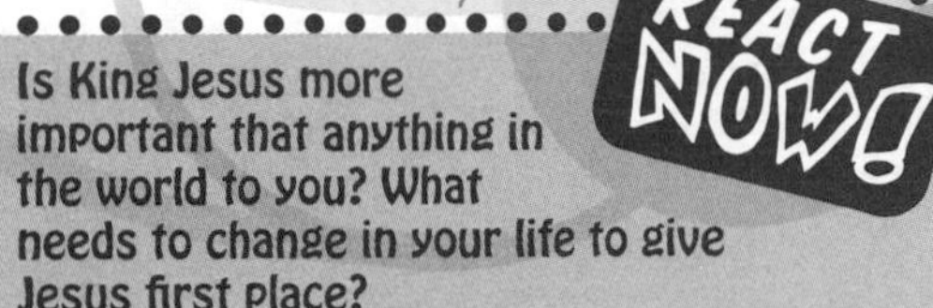

Is King Jesus more important that anything in the world to you? What needs to change in your life to give Jesus first place?

Incredi-Biblical

The Israelites generously gave the firstfruits of their grain, new wine, oil and honey and all that the fields produced. they brought . . . a tithe of everything. 2 Chronicles 31:5.

THE SABBATH TITHE

Ali struggled to finish her math assignment before the sun went down. Soon it would be Sabbath. "Is this right?" she asked Linda, her tutor.

Linda looked at Ali's paper and made a few notations. Then she slipped the lesson inside a folder.

"You marked some wrong," Ali said, looking discouraged. "Aren't we going to fix it?"

"Not now," Linda said, pointing out the window. "It's time to stop. But before I go, I want to show you something."

She took some paper and wrote out a division problem. "See this?" she asked.

Ali nodded, but couldn't see anything special about it.

"I multiplied seven days by 24 to find out how many hours are in a week," Linda said. "Then I took that number, 168, and divided it by 10, which equals 16.8."

"So? What does that show?" Ali felt as puzzled as ever.

"Well, 16.8 is exactly one tenth of one week in hours. It's a tithe amount. If I subtract 16.8 hours from a single 24-hour day, that leaves 7.2 hours to sleep. And so, allowing for sleep, a weekly tithe of my time adds up to about one regular Sabbath."

"Wait a minute," Ali said, amazed. "Let me see that again."

That Friday Ali's math lesson demonstrated more than arithmetic. It also showed how perfectly God's ordinances fit together with the world around us, all for our good.

Info Splat

In ancient times, each Sabbath traditionally ended when three stars could be seen by the naked eye in the evening sky. Many Sabbathkeeping Jews still hold to that tradition today.

Can you think of other things in your life you could tithe for God besides money and time?

~ Incredi-Biblical ~

And afterward, I will pour out my Spirit on all people. Your sons and daughters will prophesy, your old men will dream dreams, your young men will see visions.
Joel 2:28.

AN ORDINARY GIRL

According to Arthur L. White, Mrs. Ellen White is "the most translated woman writer in the entire history of literature, and the most translated American author of either gender." Despite such accomplishments, when she was a child there was little reason to believe she'd have such a remarkable life.

Ellen grew up in the early 1800s on a farm in Gorham, Maine, with her parents, twin sister Elizabeth, and six siblings. After the family moved to nearby Portland, she assisted her mother at home and helped her father make hats. By all accounts, she was happy and healthy until an accident changed everything.

When she was 9 years old, one of Ellen's classmates threw a rock at her on her way home from school. The rock injured Ellen's face, particularly her nose. Walking home, she soon fell unconscious and stayed that way for three weeks. Her formal education ended, and it was thought she might not live long.

Info Splat

Despite her early brush with death, Ellen White lived to age 87. In her lifetime she helped the Adventist movement grow from a few people to more than 100,000 members worldwide. Today, the Seventh-day Adventist Church has more than 10 million members.

Of course, Ellen did live, and at age 12 she gave her heart to the Lord. Three years later she was baptized in the Casco Bay in Portland, Maine, and became a member of the Methodist Church.

In the years that followed, Ellen and other members of her family attended Adventist meetings, prompting her to work to win other young souls for Christ. At age 17 she reported her first vision and eventually went on to write more than 5,000 periodical articles and 40 books.

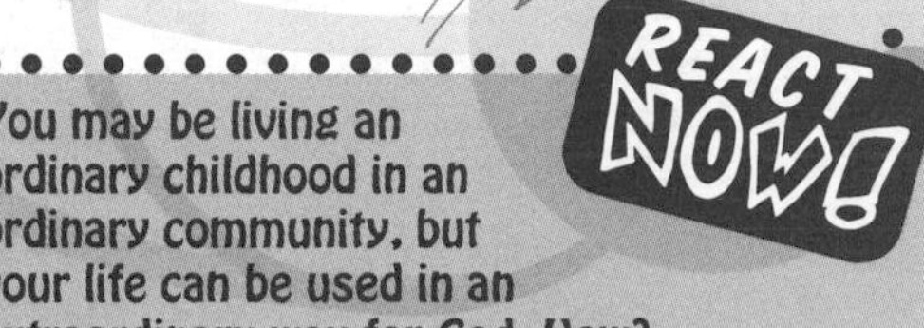

You may be living an ordinary childhood in an ordinary community, but your life can be used in an extraordinary way for God. How?

~ INCREDI-BIBLICAL ~

Shout for joy, O heavens; rejoice, O earth; burst into song, O mountains! For the Lord comforts his people and will have compassion on his afflicted ones. Isaiah 49:13.

LIFE GOES ON

Willie sat with his hands over his face and wept. Earlier that morning his father had died while lifting a heavy sack. His heart just quit working.

From his room Willie heard his mother call all five children to gather in the kitchen. "Well, it's just us now," she told them tearfully. "You know that the country's in a depression, and without your papa providing, I don't know what we'll do. The only work I can do is laundry and scrubbing. That doesn't bring in much." She mopped her wet eyes with a cotton hanky. "I'm not sure I can go on without your papa."

Willie's head jerked up. What did she mean? Didn't she want to live anymore? What about him and his little brother and sisters? Just then Aunt Lila opened the door and walked straight to Mother.

"Come, Lizzie," she said quietly. "Let's walk. Willie, you stay with the others."

Mother and Aunt Lila walked arm in arm through the meadow, toward the blackberry-covered fence along the woods. They talked as the afternoon sun cast a fuzzy glow on their long white dresses. When they finally came back, Mother's eyes didn't look as lost as they had before.

"Your mother's had a change of heart," Lila said. "The Lord and I convinced her that life goes on no matter what, because He's still here watching over us, making plans."

Willie hugged his mother tight. With God's help, they would all be OK.

Info Splat

After a death in the family, survivors typically go through five stages of grief: denial, anger, bargaining, depression, and acceptance. These stages will overlap, and may even occur in a different order. Depression from loss can sometimes lead to thoughts of suicide, the third-leading cause of death for people ages 15 to 24.

REACT NOW!

If someone you loved passed away, would the future look hopeless? What promises has God given us for tough times?

~ Incredi-Biblical ~

Make it your ambition to lead a quiet life, to mind your own business and to work with your hands, just as we told you, so that your daily life may win the respect of outsiders and so that you will not be dependent on anybody. 1 Thessalonians 4:11, 12.

NOT MY JOB

Brittney took the last bite of her sandwich and stood to leave, signaling the rest of the cheerleading squad at the table to do the same. Her friend Tammy grabbed empty milk cartons and crumpled napkins, but the others left the area a mess, including piles of trash and two drippy, sticky cafeteria trays.

"Let's go to the front lawn," Brittney said. "We can practice that new cheer and work on our pyramid."

It was a gorgeous day, and their cheers mingled happily with the sweet smell of the newly cut grass. Pretty soon the girls' thoughts were far away from lunch, focused on more important things. Then the lunchtime aide sauntered outside.

"Girls, come back and clean up your mess. All of you," she instructed.

"I didn't leave a mess," Brittney argued, sure she'd tossed out her trash.

"I appreciate that, but you ate at the table with the others, and you all left the mess behind. Now go clean up after yourselves."

Feeling irritated at being interrupted, Brittney led the way back to the lunch tables. Behind her Tammy grumbled that the janitor should clean up the mess, since that was his job.

The aide heard Tammy's remarks. "Tammy, don't depend on the janitor to clean up after you," she said. "That should be the work of your own hands."

The grumbling stopped, and in no time the table was clean. Soon the girls were practicing cheers again.

Info Splat

A Web site devoted to school cleanliness says germs can live up to 72 hours on most surfaces. That includes water faucets, desks, and even lunch tables. Since millions of germs can live on those surfaces, cleaning up is very important.

REACT NOW!

Do you ever leave your work for someone else to finish? Doing your own work is a thoughtful way to put other people first.

INCREDI-BIBLICAL

The fool says in his heart, "There is no God." Psalm 14:1.

GENIUS GETS BONKED

Sir Isaac Newton is considered to be a seventeenth-century genius in the world of science and mathematics. After getting bonked on the head by an apple that fell from a tree, he made amazing discoveries about gravitational pull and the laws of motion. He developed calculus and even invented a reflective telescope. Today classrooms all over the world study science through Newton's observations.

But what a lot of classrooms don't talk about is the fact that Newton was amazed by God. He studied the Bible very carefully, and actually wrote *more* pages about his discovery of God than he ever wrote about science. Newton tested his religious theories with the same zeal as his scientific theories. The more he uncovered about science, the more he learned about God.

Many scientists today believe that everything happened by chance, and that there is no God. Newton, however, completely disagreed. In fact, he said, "This most beautiful system [the universe] could only proceed from the dominion of an intelligent and powerful Being."

Too bad so many classrooms today remember Sir Isaac Newton only for his scientific discoveries. The Bible says that God revealed Himself to us in the things He created, so that there would be no excuse for us not to know Him. If we open ourselves to studying the amazing complexities of nature, we'll discover as Newton did that there's evidence of God everywhere.

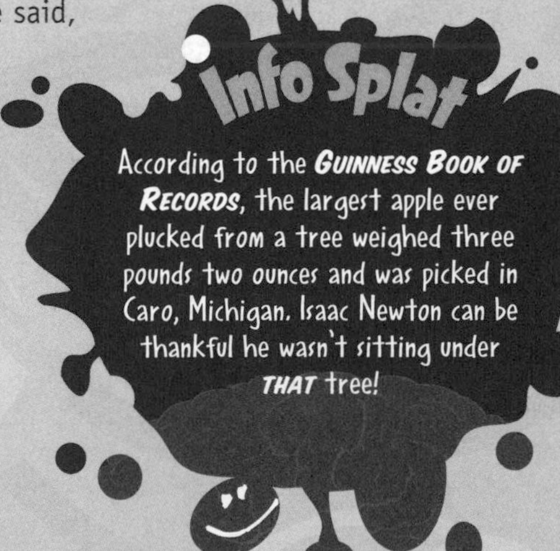

Info Splat
According to the GUINNESS BOOK OF RECORDS, the largest apple ever plucked from a tree weighed three pounds two ounces and was picked in Caro, Michigan. Isaac Newton can be thankful he wasn't sitting under THAT tree!

REACT NOW!

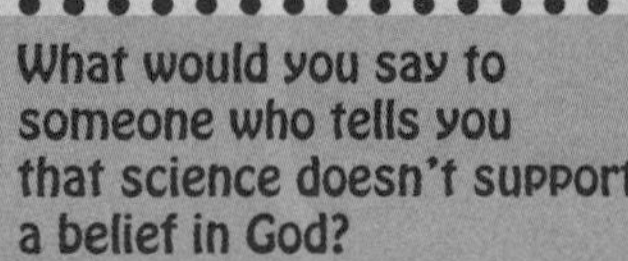

What would you say to someone who tells you that science doesn't support a belief in God?

~ INCREDI-BIBLICAL ~

Everyone must submit himself to the governing authorities. Romans 13:1.

BIBLE

MISSION AT CHURCH

Maria had never thought of herself as a rebel. But this was different. A new family that had never gone to church before started attending Maria's small church. Their daughter was a few months younger than Maria, and technically not old enough to be part of the youth group. That meant she had to attend the only other kids' class, which was for much younger children. Maria knew that Nikki wouldn't want to keep attending a church where she had to go to Sabbath school with babies, so she tried to convince the youth leader to allow Nikki into the group. He refused.

"She's only a few months too young," Maria explained. "She's *almost* old enough."

"Rules are rules," he said.

"But this might make the difference between whether she comes to church or not," Maria insisted.

The youth leader wouldn't budge. All week long Maria tried to figure out what to do. Finally she came up with a solution. If Nikki wasn't allowed to attend the youth group, Maria would go with her to the younger kids' class. There was no rule against that. So she did. And when the other youth group kids found out, they all decided to attend the younger kids' class with Maria and Nikki.

Well, at that the youth leader saw he wasn't going to have a class at all. So he finally changed his mind.

Maria didn't intend to lead a rebellion. She just wanted to do what was right.

Info Splat

Joan of Arc is considered a heroine for battling to lift English domination from the French people. She was only 17 at the time.

REACT NOW!

Do you think that what Maria did was disrespectful to the youth leader, or do you think she did the right thing? What would you have done?

INCREDI-BIBLICAL

These should learn first of all to put their religion into practice by caring for their own family . . . for this is pleasing to God.
1 Timothy 5:4.

MOM IN SCHOOL

"I've decided to go back to school," Mom announced to Rachel and Evan at dinner. Rachel's younger brother, Evan, stopped his fork halfway to his mouth and looked at his mom. "Really?" he asked, surprised.

"Yeah," Mom said, flashing a smile at Dad. "I always thought that someday when you kids were older, I'd go back and finish what I started."

"Mom, that's cool," Rachel told her. "I guess *all* of us will be doing homework now."

Mom laughed. "Yes, that's true. To quote Solomon, 'Wisdom is supreme. Therefore get wisdom!' "

"Of course, the rest of us will have to pitch in around here," Dad said. "Mom will have less time to do housework and cooking, so we're going to help her. A team effort."

Rachel didn't mind that Mom was going back to school, even though it meant more housework. In some ways she felt closer to her mom because they had even more in common. The day that Mom graduated was special for the whole family. Mom had received the highest scores on her final exams, and everyone was proud of her.

"You did it, Mom!" Rachel exclaimed.

"No, *we* did it," Mom corrected her. "I couldn't have done it without my team."

Info Splat

Mary Fasano is the oldest person known to graduate from college with a bachelor's degree. She graduated from Harvard at the age of 89.

How can you show support and encouragement to the people in your family who care for you?

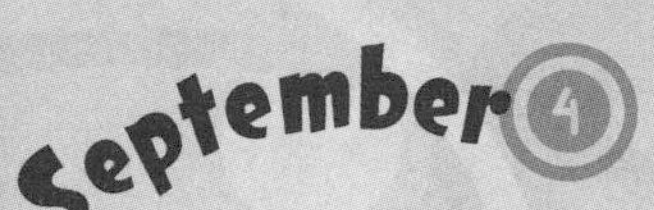

Incredi-Biblical

He [the Lord] whistles for those at the ends of the earth. Here they come, swiftly and speedily! Isaiah 5:26.

A WONDERFUL WHISTLE

Michelle was lost. She sat down on a bench and searched the faces in the milling crowd for someone she recognized, but her mom, dad, and younger brother were nowhere to be seen.

Great, Michelle thought as she looked around at the confusing maze of World's Fair technology exhibits, massive art structures, and wide-open pavilions. *How in the world did we get separated? I'll never find my way out of here.*

Michelle knew it was best to stay in one place rather than wander around, so she waited on the bench under a flower basket and impatiently watched the sun change positions in the sky. Suddenly she heard a familiar sound. She sat up and listened, tuning her ears to a distinctive whistle that echoed in the distance—a high, rising note that peaked, then cascaded sharply.

"Mom?" Michelle called, standing up and quickly scanning the mass of people revolving around her. The whistle came again, and Michelle turned to see small dots on the other side of the pavilion that resembled her parents.

Michelle pushed her way through the crowd until she reached the other side.

"There you are!" Mom said with relief.

"I heard you whistle," Michelle laughed, happy to find her family.

"I'm surprised you could hear me over all this noise," Mom told her.

"Well, I've been listening to your whistle since before I can remember," Michelle shrugged. "I guess I'm sort of tuned in to it."

Info Splat

Puccalo is the term used for the advanced art of mouth whistling. Different from casual whistling, puccalo is considered a musical instrument that players can master to perform many kinds of music—from classical and jazz to blues and rock.

PAGE 253

REACT NOW!
Does your family have a special call or whistle that you recognize? Are you tuned in to God so that you recognize His voice?

Incredi-Biblical

Blessed are you when people insult you, persecute you and falsely say all kinds of evil against you because of me. . . . Great is your reward in heaven.
Matthew 5:11, 12.

A PENMAN IN PRISON

John Bunyan just wouldn't stop preaching. And in England in 1660, unauthorized preaching was against the law.

Time after time John was brought before the tribunal, where he was laughed to scorn and treated badly. "Your gift isn't preaching—it's fixing kettles!" they said, making fun of his family trade. "We'll let you go if you stop preaching. If you don't stop, we'll banish you from England. And if we find you in England after that, we'll stretch your neck!"

But John could not be convinced to stop sharing the gospel. "If you let me out today," he told the tribunal, "I'll preach again tomorrow."

And so he was thrown into prison. Year after year John waited in a dark dungeon. While there, he preached the gospel to the other prisoners and spent time writing a book—an allegory about the Christian's journey of life. Twelve years passed before John was finally released to be with his wife and six children.

Though John had little education, the book he wrote there, *The Pilgrim's Progress*, is still popular among kids and adults today—more than 300 years later! It has been translated into more languages than any other book except the Bible.

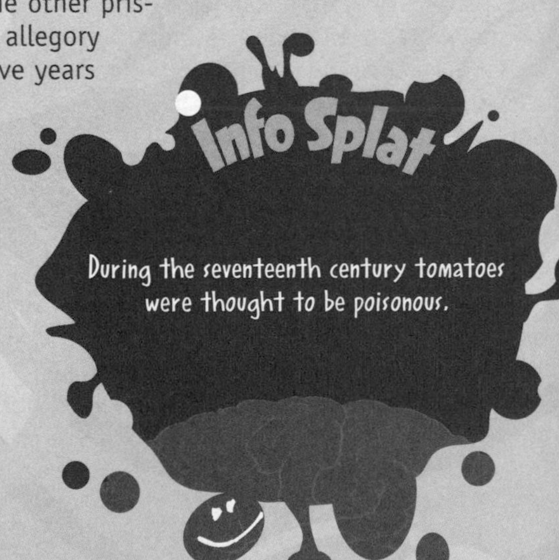

Info Splat
During the seventeenth century tomatoes were thought to be poisonous.

REACT NOW!

Has anyone ever made fun of you for what you believe? How did you react?

September 6

~ INCREDI-BIBLICAL ~

Be self-controlled and alert. Your enemy the devil prowls around like a roaring lion, seeking someone to devour.
1 Peter 5:8.

WHITNEY'S SNEAKY REQUEST

Arianna, you're my best friend, right?" Whitney asked.

"Only since forever," Arianna answered. "What kind of question is that?"

"Well, I have a secret, but you've got to promise you won't say anything to anyone."

Arianna rolled her eyes. "Whitney, I've never told any of your secrets. I'm not that kind of friend."

"Good." Whitney plopped down on the bed and put her face between her hands. "I met somebody online."

"What—do you mean?"

"I met someone—this guy," Whitney said. "He sent me his pictures, and he's so hot! He asked me to meet him at the mall this Sunday, so I told my mom you and I were going to the mall together so she'd drop me off. You've got to cover for me, OK?"

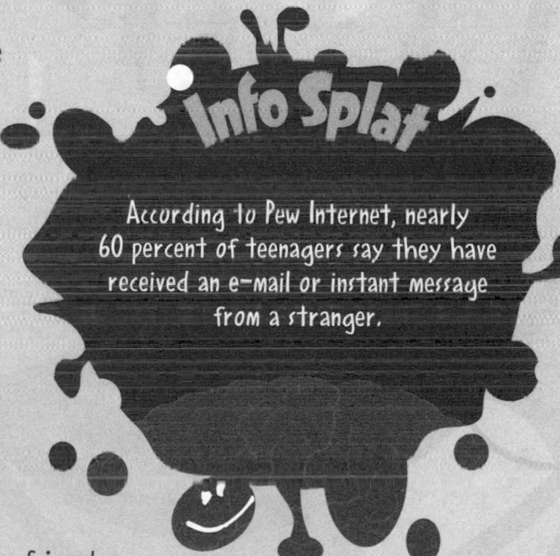

Info Splat
According to Pew Internet, nearly 60 percent of teenagers say they have received an e-mail or instant message from a stranger.

"Whitney, I can't . . ."

Whitney glared at Arianna. "Are you my friend or not?"

"Yes," she said slowly.

All weekend Arianna felt miserable. She knew it wasn't safe for Whitney to meet this stranger. She also knew that if she said anything to get Whitney in trouble, their friendship would be over. Forever.

"You OK? You're awfully quiet," Mom asked as Arianna stared out the window.

The girl sighed deeply. She could never forgive herself if something bad happened to her friend. "Mom, there's something I need to tell you," she said.

REACT NOW!

When you're online, are you careful to make choices that keep you and your family safe?

Every good and perfect gift is from above, coming down from the Father. James 1:17.

A TREASURE CALLED YOU

Each of the kids in the Gonzales family was different: Kelli was the smart one, Eddie was the athletic one, and Tina was, well, just *Tina*. "I wish I were good at something," Tina told her mom one day while they were folding laundry together.

"What do you mean?" Mom asked.

"Well, I feel as though I'm the only one who doesn't have a special talent. I have a smart sister and an athletic brother, and I'm just the boring one." Tina shrugged her shoulders and tried to keep from letting Mom see her start to cry.

"Tina," Mom said, putting down the T-shirt she was folding and taking Tina by the shoulders. "Look at me, honey. I could list a thousand things that are wonderful about you. You're great with animals. You have a soft heart. You have an amazing imagination."

"Thanks, Mom, but you're sort of obligated to say nice things. I just wish that I had a really special talent that would set me apart from everyone else."

Tina's mom smiled at her. "I see," she said. "Tina, don't worry. God *has* put special talents in you. You've only had 11 years to unpack them. Keep exploring the things you love, ask God to show you, and see what happens."

Tina picked up a pair of jeans to fold. Maybe her mom was right. Maybe someday she'd discover a treasure chest—inside herself.

Info Splat
A caterpillar grows to about 27,000 times the size it was when it first emerged from its egg.

REACT NOW!

What special gifts do you have? What is the purpose of the gifts God has given us? (See 1 Corinthians 12:7 for a hint.)

September 8

INCREDI-BIBLICAL

God blessed them and said . . . "Rule over the fish of the sea and birds of the air and over every living creature that moves on the ground." Genesis 1:28.

WHAT CAN YOU DO?

"That is so disgusting!" Jessica looked into the swirling vat of salmon eggs and felt her stomach leap into her throat. It was an unfortunate coincidence that lunchtime was scheduled right after their fish hatchery field trip. As wildlife science students, the whole class was expected to participate in the harvesting of the eggs and the milt, which were then mixed together and the fertilized eggs carefully cared for until the fish were hatched.

"I think it's cool," Andrew countered. "Can you believe that we're actually helping to create a whole batch of little fish?"

"What difference does it make?" Jessica complained with a wrinkled nose. "They're just fish."

"Actually, it's a big deal," Andrew said, looking offended. "God pretty much gave us the responsibility when He created them."

"I don't think *this*"—Jessica pointed with her thumb at the salmon that had given their lives in the process—" is what God had in mind."

Andrew looked at the pile of dead salmon. "I don't think so either. It's more like a plan B. But they do need our help, or eventually they'll be gone. All of them."

Jessica stared at the fish eggs, trying to feel some sort of attachment to them. It wasn't happening.

"Relax," Andrew said as though he had read her mind. "You don't have to be a fish scientist to take responsibility for keeping this species of fish alive. You can help just by being careful about what chemicals you put down the drain. A lot of things poison the water—and things that live in it, you know."

Info Splat

Salmon live in the sea until they mature, then return to the same freshwater location where they hatched to lay and fertilize eggs before they die. Some salmon travel more than 1,000 miles, and no one is positive how they know the way.

What can you do to help take responsibility for the fish and other animals God has trusted us with?

INCREDI-BIBLICAL

Share your food with the hungry and . . . provide the poor wanderer with shelter. Isaiah 58:7.

MARK SERVES IT UP

Mark didn't really want to go at first. *Spend the afternoon making sack lunches for homeless people?* he thought. *When I could be on the basketball court or in the swimming pool or riding my bike around the neighborhood?*

Mark's friends in the youth group finally convinced him to go along, and he soon found himself on an assembly line of bread, peanut butter, jelly, fruit, and chips. After a while, Mark realized he was pretty good at making sandwiches, and the time flew by as he and his friends handed out sack lunches to homeless people under the supervision of their youth leader.

Much to his surprise, Mark found out that some of the people used to have good jobs, but because of an injury they couldn't work, and had lost their homes. Some could not support themselves because of a mental illness that prevented them from being able to hold a regular job. Some of the homeless were kids Mark's age or younger.

Mark thought about how hungry he felt after spending the afternoon playing ball. He always went to the refrigerator for a snack. The people he was serving didn't even have refrigerators. Right now they were depending on *him* for food.

After the youth group cleaned up the food preparation and got back on the bus, Mark leaned back in his seat and took a deep breath. He was very glad he'd come.

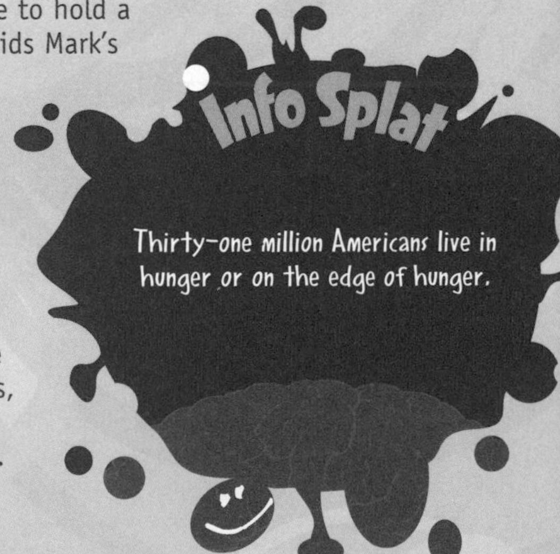

Info Splat
Thirty-one million Americans live in hunger or on the edge of hunger.

REACT NOW!

What kinds of things do you do to make a positive contribution to your community and to honor God?

INCREDI-BIBLICAL

**Since we are surrounded by such a great cloud of witnesses, let us throw off everything that hinders . . . , and let us run with perseverance the race marked out for us.
Hebrews 12:1.**

YOU'RE BEING WATCHED!

Today reality TV shows are on every channel. If you want to watch someone remodel a house, have plastic surgery, survive in the wilderness, or live with famous parents, all you have to do is turn on the television.

But did you know that the *ultimate* reality show of all time is on right now? That's right. And it's a makeover. Beings all over the universe are tuning in to watch; and you're in it. Your life, the decisions you make every day, the connection you have with God—all of those things are intensely interesting to those who are watching. Even angels long to look into these things (1 Peter 1:12). Why?

Info Splat
The longest-running reality television series is ***Cops***. It premiered on March 11, 1989, and has aired hundreds of episodes since then.

The Bible says that God is allowing us to help Him prove Himself. God intended that through us, His wisdom would unfold so that the "rulers and authorities in the heavenly realms" would see what He accomplished through Jesus. He is giving us the ultimate makeover back into His image, refreshed with His character in us, and the entire universe is anxiously waiting to see "the reveal."

How is your "episode" going? Are the viewers disappointed, or cheering your decisions? If you want to let God use you, all you have to do is pray the prayer that David prayed: "Create in me a pure heart, O God, and renew a steadfast spirit within me" (Psalm 51:10).

REACT NOW!

Do you act differently when others are watching, or the same as when you are alone?

INCREDI-BIBLICAL

Religion that God our Father accepts as pure and faultless is this: to look after orphans and widows in their distress. James 1:27.

STACKING WOOD

Amber grabbed her bathing suit and towel and ran outside to where the youth group leader's van was waiting. The sun was hot, and Amber couldn't wait to get out on the sparkling lake with her friends in the ski boat. But before they got started their leader had something to say. "Listen up, please. Everybody knows Mrs. Smith, right?"

Amber nodded. She was an 80-year-old widow from church who walked with a cane.

"Well," he continued, "I just found out that someone donated firewood to her. It's enough to keep her warm all winter, but she desperately needs help hauling it. What would you guys say about helping her for a couple of hours before we go to the lake?"

Hauling firewood in the hot sun didn't sound like fun to Amber, but she agreed to help with the rest of the kids. The job went even faster than expected. They set up an assembly line, and soon all the firewood was stacked neatly under Mrs. Smith's carport. Her eyes were misty with gratitude, and she prepared a thank-you of ice-cold lemonade.

Waterskiing seemed twice as much fun that afternoon, and the group decided that next time before going to the lake, maybe they'd stop over and help Mrs. Smith with some yard work first. It felt good to be needed.

Info Splat

Now, that's teamwork! In Laguna, Brazil, dolphins help fishermen catch fish. The dolphins drive the fish to the shore, right into the fishermen's nets. Any fish that escapes the nets becomes dolphin dinner!

Can you think of anyone in your church or neighborhood who could really use some help?

~ INCREDI-BIBLICAL ~

What, then, shall we say in response to this? If God is for us, who can be against us? Romans 8:31.

AN EARTHSHAKING MESSAGE

At the General Conference session in Minneapolis, Minnesota, in 1888, two different men presented the same message. When church leader Ellen White heard it, she excitedly called it the third angel's message—the last message to be given to the world before Jesus comes.

But other church leaders were not happy about it. In fact, they rejected it.

What was the mysterious message given by the two men, Elder Jones and Elder Waggoner? Why did it delight some people, and upset others?

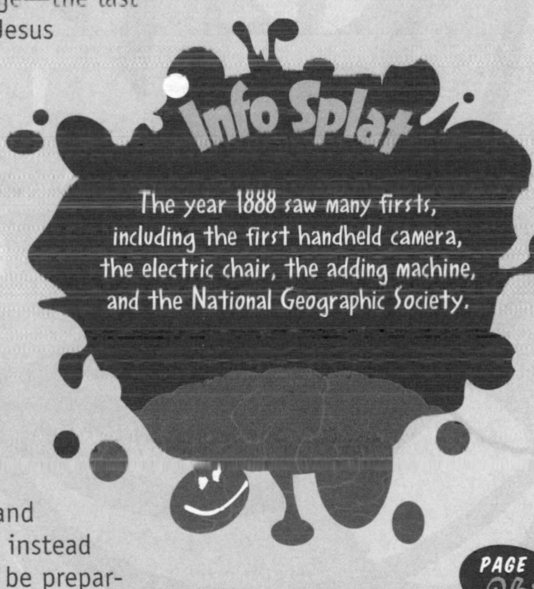

Info Splat
The year 1888 saw many firsts, including the first handheld camera, the electric chair, the adding machine, and the National Geographic Society.

Elders Jones and Waggoner preached that it's easy to be saved, and hard to be lost! All we need to do is accept Jesus' righteousness through faith, and let God take responsibility for doing the work of removing our sin. This process, they said, restores the image of God in His people, and paves the way for Jesus to come soon. So instead of getting prepared for death, people can be preparing to go to heaven without dying! It was good news, like a spotlight on God's Word.

Can you imagine what could have happened if the leaders had not rejected the message? We might be in heaven right now! God hasn't given up, though. The leaders in 1888 may have missed out, but now it's *your* turn. God is counting on you to be part of the generation that finishes His work. Are you up to the challenge?

REACT NOW!

If God called you to deliver a message that would be unpopular, how would you respond?

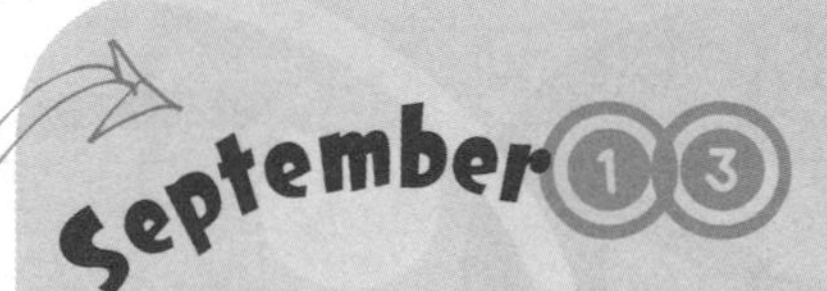

~ INCREDI-BIBLICAL ~

For you created my inmost being; you knit me together in my mother's womb.
Psalm 139:13.

MITCH WANTS MUSCLES

Karie hated the way her ears stuck out through her hair. Everybody else's hair fell straight to their shoulders, but hers took a detour around her stand-out ears.

Mitch was pretty sure his eyes were too big for his head. He also wondered if he could mentally force some of the casserole he ate for dinner to find its way to his pathetic muscles.

There are probably things about the way *you* look that you don't like, too.

Relax. As you become a teenager, it's natural that you'll become more aware of yourself—especially as your body begins to change and do things it's never done before. But spending a lot of time in front of the mirror worrying about what you don't like is a waste of time. Get out there and live your life! Don't forget that you're in a change mode. You're not done yet.

Also, take some comfort in knowing that you notice those things much more than anyone else does. Most other people are too wrapped up in what they look like and their own imperfections to be focused on yours. So don't take yourself too seriously.

You may not have much control over what your body does, but you do have control over who you choose to be. You can either be the nice guy with the big nose, or the jerk with a big nose. It's up to you.

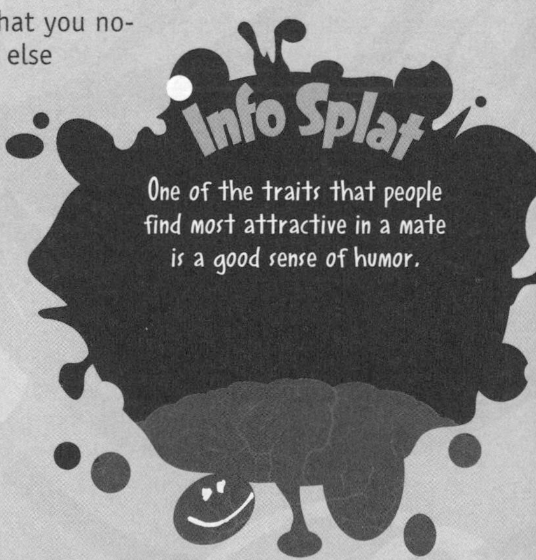

Info Splat
One of the traits that people find most attractive in a mate is a good sense of humor.

REACT NOW!

What positive qualities do you have that make other people enjoy being around you? Are they physical qualities or character qualities?

INCREDI-BIBLICAL

They have eyes to see but do not see and ears to hear but do not hear. Ezekiel 12:2.

ARE YOU LISTENING?

Ling opened her brown bag and poured the contents onto the cafeteria table. Normally by lunchtime she was ravenously hungry, but today not even her favorite sandwich looked tempting.

"Hey, Ling!" Ashley flung her hair over her shoulder and sat down across the table with her lunch tray. "What's the matter? You haven't touched your food."

"I don't feel like eating," Ling said softly.

"I totally know how you feel!" Ashley exclaimed, swirling her French fries in a pool of ketchup. "I felt that way the other day after I played soccer. My mom made dinner, and I was, like, 'No, thanks.'"

"I actually got some bad news this morning." Ling felt a tear at the corner of her eye, and she dabbed it away with her fingertip.

Ashley waved at someone across the room. "I hate bad news," she said. "Hi, Jason! Come sit over here!"

"It's about my grandfather," Ling continued.

"Oh, really?" Ashley said, taking a sip of her drink. "I haven't seen *my* grandfather in years. He moved to Florida when I was little and never came back."

"Are you even listening to me?" Ling shook her head as she stood and scooped her lunch into her backpack. "Just forget it."

Ashley looked surprised. "What do you mean? I heard everything you said."

Ling sighed. "Yeah, but you weren't *listening*."

Ashley shrugged as Ling walked away. "What's the difference?"

According to a study done by Wayne State University, only one out of five students attending a college lecture are actually paying attention to the professor, and only 12 percent are actively listening. The rest are thinking about something else.

REACT NOW!

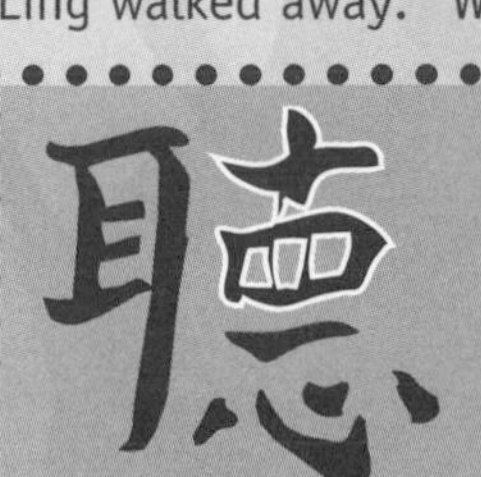

The Chinese character for the word "listen" is an excellent example of what true listening involves. Next time you listen to someone, follow the Chinese model by listening with your ears, your eyes, your undivided attention, and your heart.

Incredi-Biblical

He sends you abundant showers, both autumn and spring rains as before. Joel 2:23.

RAIN IN THE FORECAST

In the East, farmers depend on two rainy seasons. The autumn rain (or former rain) is gentle. It comes just after farmers have planted their fields, and helps awaken the little seeds to produce the first green shoots. The spring rain (or latter rain) is heavy. It comes just before harvest, and helps the crop get ready for harvest.

Can you imagine what would happen if the *heavy* rain fell on the newly planted seeds? Instead of sprouting and implanting their roots in the soil, they'd be washed away. God uses this example to explain how He gives us the Holy Spirit—the "former rain" first, and the "latter rain" afterward.

People often pray for the latter rain—the heavy outpouring of the Holy Spirit. But just like the seeds in the farmer's field, we first need the former rain to help us grow and get ready *before* God can give us the downpour.

The former rain is the same power Christ's disciples were given that enabled them to heal the sick, raise the dead, and speak foreign languages. It's what God wants to give everyone now—including kids. God says that He will pour out His Spirit on sons and daughters, and they will prophesy. He's talking about *you*. How exciting is that?

Stay connected to God by asking for the Holy Spirit every day. When the heavy downpour comes, be ready—firmly planted and growing!

Info Splat

The trees of a tropical rain forest are so densely packed that rain falling on the canopy can take as long as 10 minutes to reach the ground.

How does it make you feel to know that God has exciting plans for you?

September 16

~ Incredi-Biblical ~

A thousand may fall at your side, and ten thousand at your right hand, but it will not come near you. Psalm 91:7.

INVISIBLE IN KENYA

Morning light was just beginning to crawl through the door of her hut when Janet heard the screams. Heart racing, she leaped up and ran outside to find her village overtaken by chaos and terror. Tongues of orange fire and black smoke rose from the huts, and gunfire cut screams short. Men were raiding the homes, taking what they wanted, and destroying or killing the rest. Fear crushed Janet's chest. She gasped, hardly able to breathe as she realized that her village was under attack by shifters!

Janet pressed her back up against her family's hut, knowing there was no place to hide where the shifters could not find her. "God," she prayed. "Please help me! There is no one to save me from the shifters but You. Please make me invisible."

When Janet opened her eyes, she saw that the shifters had finished with her neighbor's hut. It was burning, and they were moving on to their next target. She stood perfectly still as they strode toward her, closer and closer, then tramped past her as if she weren't there. Janet watched in disbelief as the men disappeared into the bush. She and her hut stood untouched amid a smoking village.

"God made me invisible," she breathed. "He answered my prayer!"

Today Janet is one of the oldest members of the Kiengu Seventh-day Adventist Church in Kenya.

Info Splat

Science fiction often provides ideas for real scientists. That's why a group of scientists at Duke University are extremely interested in the electromagnetic qualities of artificially structured materials, or meta-materials. These materials provide the possibility of creating invisibility cloaks through transform optics.

REACT NOW!

Sometimes people pray for things that God does not give them. Why do you think this happens?

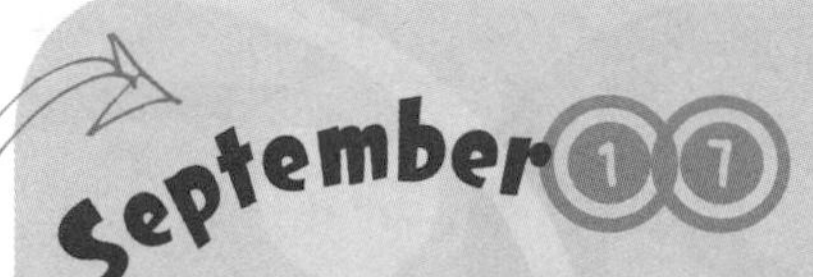

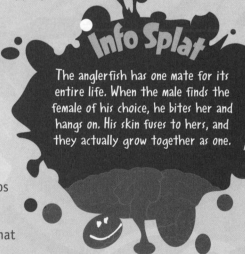

INCREDI-BIBLICAL

Do you not know that your body is a temple of the Holy Spirit, who is in you? 1 Corinthians 6:19.

A PURE FUTURE

So, have you ever, like *done* anything with a guy?" Kelsey lowered her voice to a whisper midsentence and leaned secretively toward Sierra.

Sierra felt her face burning. "Well . . . no."

Kelsey seemed shocked. "You've never even kissed a guy? Or held hands, or . . . anything?"

Sierra shook her head. "No. Have you?"

Kelsey looked smug as she described the details of her experiences. Sierra wasn't sure what to think. She was curious, and what she was hearing was pretty interesting.

It's normal to have questions about boy/girl relationships, so you shouldn't feel guilty for being curious. Just keep in mind:

The info your friends give you may be inaccurate. If you want truth, ask your parent or another appropriate adult.

When it comes to making decisions about purity in relationships, think with logic, and not with your feelings. Make firm decisions now, *not* when the opportunity arises.

Understand that marriage, including the physical part, represents spiritual intimacy with God, so choosing to be involved with someone you're not married to is sort of like worshipping idols.

Maintaining purity in your relationships with the opposite sex means having a clean conscience before God and someday sharing a special bond with your spouse that you have with no one else on earth.

The good thing about God is that nothing about you will surprise Him. Share your feelings with Him, even the ones you're not sure about. He can handle it. And He'll guide you.

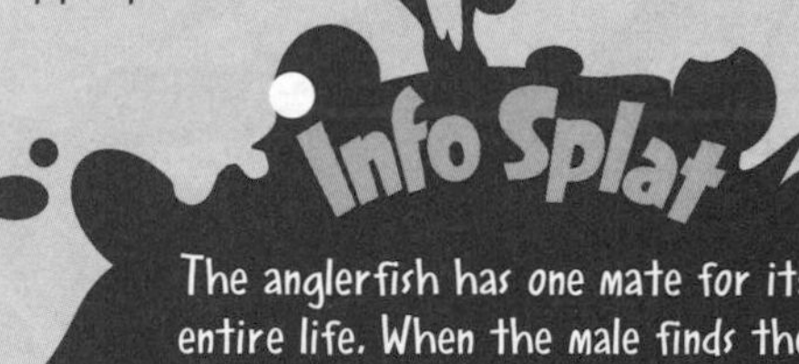

The anglerfish has one mate for its entire life. When the male finds the female of his choice, he bites her and hangs on. His skin fuses to hers, and they actually grow together as one.

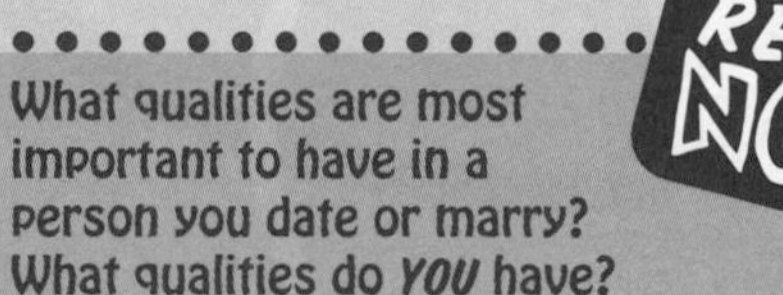

What qualities are most important to have in a person you date or marry? What qualities do *YOU* have?

INCREDI-BIBLICAL

"From one New Moon to another and one Sabbath to another, all mankind will come and bow down before me," says the Lord. Isaiah 66:23.

A DAY TO REMEMBER

Tracie loved Sabbath.

There was something special about the sense of purpose on Friday afternoon as her whole family worked together to be ready for it. Tracie and her sister cleaned their rooms and finished their other chores, Dad mowed the yard and took out the trash, and Mom ironed their church clothes and cooked.

By the time the sun turned pink in the western sky, the family would be sitting down to their traditional Friday night taco dinner. Afterward, they'd sprawl on the floor or the couch while Dad read to them from a special storybook. The *air* even felt different on Sabbath, with a kind of energy that made Tracie feel that somehow God must be closer to them during the Sabbath hours.

Sabbath morning they'd drive to church in the early-morning light, watching to see who could spot the first hot-air balloon drifting over the Napa Valley.

After church they usually had a whole crowd of company, and the kids would have a blast playing in the woods or going on a hike. Sometimes they'd have a sing-along in the living room around the piano, or drive to the ocean for the afternoon, or visit Elmshaven—Ellen White's home during the last years of her life.

They always said goodbye to the Sabbath by singing together while the sun set over the hills. At the day's end Tracy could hardly wait for Sabbath to come again.

Info Splat

Italian, French, Spanish, Portuguese, and Romanian are among the world languages in which the word for Saturday actually means Sabbath.

What makes Sabbath special for you?

INCREDI-BIBLICAL

Do not cut yourselves for the dead or put tattoo marks on yourselves. I am the Lord. Leviticus 19:28.

MARKED WITH GOD'S LOVE

Brian sat still as the barber cut his hair. Then out of the corner of his eye he saw a dark-skinned man take a seat across the room. Brian shifted his gaze to the man, and was surprised to see that the man's face was pale. What Brian had thought was dark skin was actually ink from the many tattoos covering the man's arms.

While some people would never get a tattoo, others have them all over their bodies. Some get tattoos to commemorate a life event or a special someone, while others have their astrology sign inked on their body. The tattoos of some people show their tribal ancestry, while the tattoos of others show they belong to a certain gang. And, of course, many people get tattooed simply because they think it looks cool.

No one is sure exactly how or when the art of tattooing began, but history shows that it has been around for thousands of years. In fact, scientists have discovered 5,000-year-old mummies with tattoos. According to their design and placement, the tattoos are thought to be rites of passage into adulthood, marks for protection, status symbols, or images of dead people.

Did you know that tattoos are mentioned in the Bible? God told the children of Israel not to tattoo themselves. After God rescued them from slavery, He gave them protection, a sense of identity, and the special hope that they would see their dead loved ones again. A tattoo showing allegiance to or dependence on anything else would have been a slap in the face to God. Even a tattoo that represents God is meaningless, because God wants to write on our *hearts*, not our skin.

You belong to God. And instead of putting a tattoo on you to show ownership, He's stamped you with His own image. Now, *that's* special.

Info Splat

Some tattoos can be removed using laser light that breaks up the pigments of color in the skin, enabling the ink to be removed by the immune system. But a tattoo is a scar filled with ink. Even when the ink is gone, the scar remains.

As a Christian, do you wear what you believe on the outside, the inside, or both?

INCREDI-BIBLICAL

**We will all be changed—
in a flash, in the twinkling of an eye.
1 Corinthians 15:51, 52.**

WHO'S TO BLAME?

Kylie was in shock when she and the rest of the teen group went into the nursing home. All around her were people who inspired her sympathy. Some had mental disabilities, some were paralyzed and attached to machines, others were cramped in arthritic positions and confined to wheelchairs. Kylie swallowed hard and attempted to smile as she went from person to person, trying to be cheerful and to pretend she didn't notice the acrid odor of urine.

Info Splat
According to a Fox news poll,
92 percent of Americans believe in God.

As the kids got back into the van to leave, Kylie felt furious. "All my life I've heard, 'Oh, God created you just how He wanted you to be,' or 'God doesn't make junk,'" she fumed. "If that's true, then God wants all these people to be sick and deformed!"

The whole van was silent. Finally Pastor Joe spoke. "You're right," he said simply. "God meant for all of us to be tall, good-looking, with perfect skin, perfect hair, nice teeth, and healthy muscles. But sin has gradually morphed us into what we are, and what those people in that home are. Don't be mad at God, Kylie. Be mad at Satan. He did this."

Pastor Joe paused. "But God will eventually turn us back into who He meant for us to be. If we let Him work on our hearts and minds until they're perfect, He'll also give us new, perfect bodies."

"I hope it happens soon," Kylie whispered, her heart still sad.

REACT NOW!

What was Jesus' purpose when He came to earth? (See 1 John 3:8 for a clue.) What can we do through Jesus?

INCREDI-BIBLICAL

Baptism . . . [is] not the removal of dirt from the body but the pledge of a good conscience toward God. It saves you by the resurrection of Jesus Christ.
1 Peter 3:21.

BAPTISM IS THE BEGINNING

Mandie and Nora did everything together. Though they were cousins, they were also best friends. They knew each other's secrets, news, and dreams for the future. They even decided to be baptized together. Their grandfather would do it during a family reunion.

The night before the big day the two girls sat by a campfire under the velvet Colorado sky. Grandfather went over each of the Bible's basic teachings with them, to make sure they understood them and what baptism truly meant in their commitment to God.

"The most important thing to remember," he said quietly, "is that baptism isn't a graduation ceremony. It just signifies the beginning of an amazing friendship with God. You will have to make the decision to be close to God every day. Sometimes many times a day."

As Mandie watched the glowing sparks fly up into the air, she deeply sensed that her decision to be baptized was probably the most grown-up decision she'd ever made.

The next day when Mandie and Nora stood in the lake water next to their grandfather, Mandie looked at her family and at Nora—her cousin and best friend. Silently she told God she wanted a friendship with Him that was like hers and Nora's—nothing hidden. Her secrets, her news, her dreams for the future, would all be open to God.

Info Splat
The water we have right now on earth and in our atmosphere is all the water we will ever have!

REACT NOW!

Have you been baptized? If not, is it a commitment you'd like to make with God?

He who was seated on the throne said,
"I am making everything new!"
Revelation 21:5.

NATE GETS STUCK

Ouch!" Nate pulled off his gardening glove to find that a thorn had pierced his thumb. He examined the puncture site, and wiped the tiny drop of blood on his old jeans. "I hate pulling weeds!" he said to his dad.

Dad sat back and wiped his brow. "Me too," he admitted. "But it's part of the curse, I guess."

"What curse?" Nate took a sip from his water bottle.

"Well, when sin entered the world, people were cursed, but so was the ground. Remember, God said, 'Cursed is the ground because of you; through painful toil you will eat of it all the days of your life. It will produce thorns and thistles for you'" (Genesis 3:17, 18).

Nate shook his head and laughed. "How do you remember all that?" he asked.

"I guess I think about it almost every time I hack out these weeds," Dad laughed. "But the Bible says that creation will be rescued just like us. I think it's interesting that when Jesus died on the cross for us to lift the curse of sin, He wore a crown of *thorns* on his head."

Nate looked down at his thorn-pricked thumb. "Wow. I never thought of that before."

"Well, I guess if your thumb is going to be OK, we'd better get back to our 'painful toil,'" Dad told him.

Nate smiled and looked at the weeds. "Maybe in heaven where there's no curse, I'll actually *enjoy* gardening."

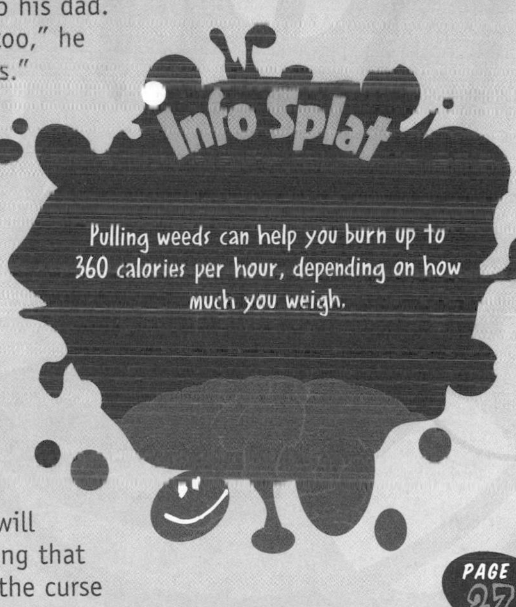

Info Splat
Pulling weeds can help you burn up to 360 calories per hour, depending on how much you weigh.

REACT NOW!

What other things will be different in a new earth where nothing is contaminated by sin? What blessings does God provide while we live with the curse?

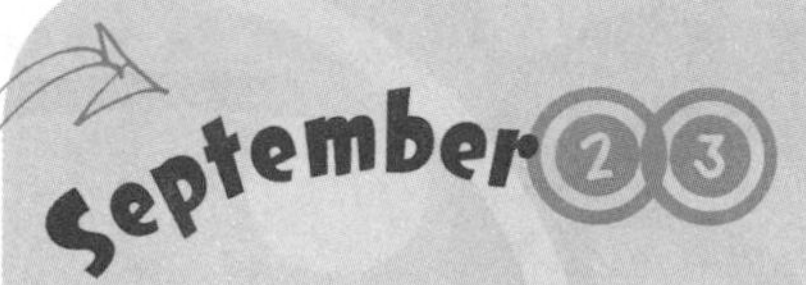

INCREDI-BIBLICAL

It is the Lord your God you must follow, and him you must revere. Keep his commands and obey him; . . . hold fast to him. Deuteronomy 13:4.

MISSIONARY AT HOME

Andrea stared at the pepperoni pizza in front of her and wanted to cry. She knew her dad's wife had prepared it on purpose to teach her a lesson. "Dad," Andrea began, "remember? I've decided not to eat pork because the Bible says it's unclean meat."

Andrea's dad looked at his wife, then back at Andrea. "Andrea," he said firmly, "either eat what's placed in front of you or go without dinner."

Tears filled Andrea's eyes as she took her plate to the kitchen and went into the bedroom she shared with her new baby sister. Her stomach growled, and she sat on the bed feeling very alone. The same issues came up every other weekend during her visits. She had even asked respectfully if she could do her chores on Friday so she wouldn't be working on Sabbath, but her dad and his new wife always seemed to plan yard work or housecleaning for Saturdays.

"God, what am I supposed to do?" Andrea prayed. "My dad doesn't respect either one of us."

When being obedient to God means being disobedient to your parents, remember to:

Obey your parents in every aspect that doesn't conflict with what God says, so you are taking a stand for what is right, not just being rebellious.

Be loving and respectful at *all* times. Lead your family *to* God, not away from Him, by your example.

Info Splat
Approximately 37 percent of all American kids live with a divorced parent.

REACT NOW!

Is your home a mission field? Are there people in your family who don't know God? What can you do to be an example for them?

~ INCREDI-BIBLICAL ~

Not to us, O Lord, not to us but to your name be the glory, because of your love and faithfulness. Psalm 115:1.

WHEN COACH LOST HIS COOL

The crowd's expectation weighed heavy on Eric and his team members. With seconds to go in the game, the home team and the guest team were only one point apart. Shoes squeaked on the shiny gym floor as the sweat-drenched boys maneuvered the basketball up and down the court while the coaches shouted encoded instructions from the sidelines.

Eric dribbled the ball, swiftly dodging and turning, until he was underneath the basket. When he took the shot, he felt a hand on his arm, and the ref's whistle shrieked.

"Foul!" came the call as the ref pointed at number 3 of the opposing team. "Two points!" he said to Eric.

The home crowd began to cheer, when suddenly a tirade came from the opposing team's coach. "You idiot!" he shouted at number 3. "I *told* you to watch your hands! How many times do I have to tell you? Get your shorts on the bench!"

The crowd fell silent as number 3 hung his head. The fun energy drained out of Eric as he stood there with the ball under his right arm. Both teams represented Christian schools, and regardless of the intense competition, a sense of disappointment came over him as he realized that God had been dishonored on the court.

Eric resolved that he would never let a game be more important than good sportsmanship. Both on and off the basketball court, he would represent God.

Info Splat

The most free throws made in one basketball game happened on March 21, 1953. Bob Cousey made 30 free throws during the Boston-Syracuse game. The game went into overtime four times.

How can you honor God in your everyday activities?

Incredi-Biblical

Be faithful . . . and I will give you the crown of life. Revelation 2:10.

BIGGER THAN THE YANKEES

Dan loved baseball. He loved to play it, watch it, talk about it, and dream about it. His favorite baseball cap had the Yankees symbol on the front, and he wore it everywhere. That is, everywhere except church.

"Why can't I wear it to church?" he complained. "Don't tell me that God hates hats or something."

"It's a sign of respect to remove your baseball cap for church," Mom told him. "Besides, it doesn't hurt for your scalp to get some fresh air."

Dan scowled and pulled his cap off his head. "What a stupid rule," he muttered as he got into the car.

As they were walking to the church door, Dad took Dan aside. "Remember when we went to the Yankees game last summer?" he asked.

"Of course," Dan said.

"Remember when we stood for the national anthem?"

"Yeah." Where was Dad going with this?

"What did you do with your hat?"

Dan paused. "I took it off," he admitted.

"Why?"

Now Dan knew where the conversation was going. "To show respect," he said.

"Well, we're here to salute a power that's a lot higher than a government," Dad said. "Don't you think the least you can do is show the same respect for God that you show for your flag?"

Dan nodded.

"By the way," Dad added. "I don't think God hates hats. One of the first things He's going to do when we get to heaven is put crowns on our heads."

Dan grinned. Dad had a point there.

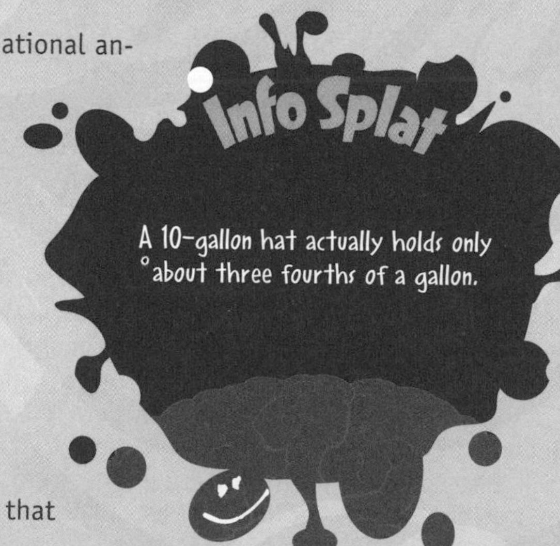

Info Splat
A 10-gallon hat actually holds only about three fourths of a gallon.

REACT NOW!

What are other ways we show respect when we go to church?

INCREDI-BIBLICAL

In that day, the deaf will hear the words of the scroll. Isaiah 29:18.

THOMAS HEARS GOD'S CALL

Thomas was small for his age. Ever since he could remember, he had struggled with being sick. Sickness had kept him from playing with the other kids the way he would've liked, and as he got older, it forced him to drop out of school and decline good job offers. Thomas often wondered what God's plan was for his life.

One day while watching his younger brothers and sisters play, he noticed a little girl sitting to the side. She looked very lonely. The kids told him that her name was Alice and that she was deaf. Thomas couldn't stand to see her sitting there all alone, so he decided to try to find a way to help.

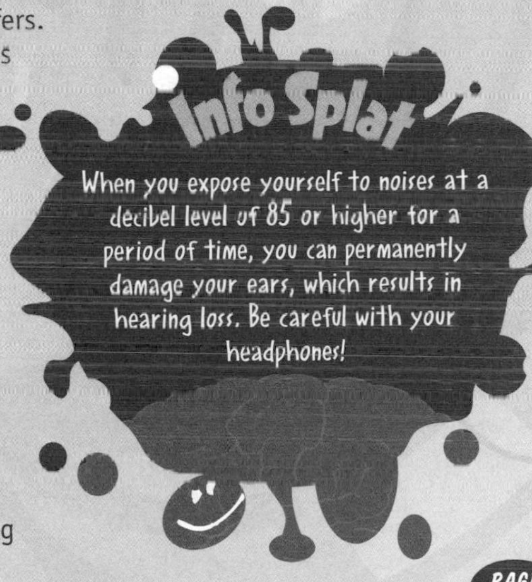

Info Splat
When you expose yourself to noises at a decibel level of 85 or higher for a period of time, you can permanently damage your ears, which results in hearing loss. Be careful with your headphones!

He called her over, and showed her his hat. Then he wrote the word "hat" in the dirt. Very quickly Alice caught on to the game. Her father was so excited that he asked Thomas if he would continue teaching her.

When Thomas found that there were no schools in America for deaf children, he was shocked. *God, how can they learn about Your plan of salvation if they don't have a place to learn at all?*

Thomas felt God inspiring him with a mission. From that time on, Thomas Gallaudet devoted himself to opening doors to a new life for deaf people.

That was the year 1815. Today Gallaudet University is the world leader in providing education for deaf people.

REACT NOW!

Do you feel called by God toward something you're passionate about?

INCREDI-BIBLICAL

There is a friend who sticks closer than a brother. Proverbs 18:24.

"STAY ON YOUR SIDE!"

"Mom! He's doing it again," Serena complained.

Mom craned her neck from the front seat. "Willie, stay on your side of the car."

Willie narrowed his eyes and scrunched his nose. He looked like a pig with a facelift.

"Mom!" Serena screeched.

"Willie!" Mom said sternly.

"What?" Willie said. "I was on my side!"

"Time for a rest stop," Dad said, letting the car slow down. "If only for my own sanity."

They pulled into the rest area. While Dad and Willie took the dog for a walk, Serena and her mom headed for the restroom. "Mom, how do you and your brother get along so well?" she asked.

"Well, he hasn't mutilated any of my dolls or set me on fire in more than 25 years," she joked. "That probably helps."

"You guys used to fight too?"

"Of course," Mom said. "But we still loved each other. And you know what? Willie is a gift for you from God so you can practice things like patience and forgiveness and tolerance. Sometimes when we're around people who are difficult, our own sharp edges get softened. I think my brother and I softened each other. Now we're a lot closer—to each other, and to God."

Serena thought for a moment. "I guess I could look at it that way," she said. "But you're not having any more kids, are you?"

"No," Mom said. "Why?"

"Because I think I have all the edge-softening I can handle," Serena laughed.

Info Splat

In the United States twins are born in 12 out of 1,000 births. Two thirds of these twins are fraternal (nonidentical).

How is God using the people around you to soften your sharp edges?

Incredi-Biblical

"Come, follow me," Jesus said, "and I will make you fishers of men." Mark 1:17.

TAKE THE DISCIPLE QUIZ!

Which of Jesus' disciples are you most like? After reading each of the descriptions, select the one that best fits you, and then look below to see which disciple you've chosen.

1. I am a strong leader. Sometimes I lose my temper and say things without thinking, but I don't mean to hurt anyone. I'm quick to defend at any cost what I believe is right.
2. I'm the kind of person that everyone likes, because people are comfortable being around me. I have a soft heart, and get the most satisfaction out of helping other people.
3. I know what I want, and I am very self-motivated. When I see an opportunity to get ahead, I take it. Sometimes other people feel threatened by me, but I don't mind arguing my rights.
4. I don't believe everything I'm told. I ask a lot of questions, and I'm cautious. I'm a real hands-on kind of person. When I am convinced that something is true, I hold on to it.
5. I want more than anything else to bring people to Jesus. I especially want my family to be close to Jesus.
6. I am an honest person, and I say what I'm thinking. I enjoy taking time to pray. When others describe me, they usually say I'm a good person who lives what he believes.

Now, which of these disciples are you most like?

__1. Peter __2. John

__3. James __4. Thomas

__5. Andrew __6. Nathaniel

Info Splat

If you compared yourself with any stranger on the planet, you'd find that you share 99.9 percent of the same genes. Only a tiny fraction of your set of genes makes you unique from every other human on earth.

REACT NOW!

Jesus chose people with different personalities and different talents to be His disciples. Do you accept people who are different from you, or is that something you need to work on?

Incredi-Biblical

The blood of Jesus, his son,
purifies us from all sin.
1 John 1:7.

POWER IN HIS BLOOD

Blood plays a very important role in our bodies, and it's no accident that God designed it to be a living example of how the plan of salvation works.

Did you know these facts?

1. Blood fights infection and helps to heal wounds.
2. Red blood cells carry oxygen to the body's organs and tissue.
3. Granulocytes, a type of white blood cell, "eat" bacteria in your blood vessels.
4. Blood carries important nutrients and hormones to your body's cells.
5. Blood carries carbon dioxide (a waste product) to your lungs to be exhaled from your body.
6. There is no substitute for blood.

Romans 1:20 tells us that we can understand more about God and His invisible qualities by looking at the things He has made. Look at the six facts about blood listed above. Do you see the special parallels between how our blood heals, cleanses, and protects us, and how God designed for us to be healed, cleansed, and protected by Jesus' blood? And, just as there is no substitute for human blood, there is also no substitute, and no other way to heaven, except through the blood of Jesus. There is definitely power in the blood.

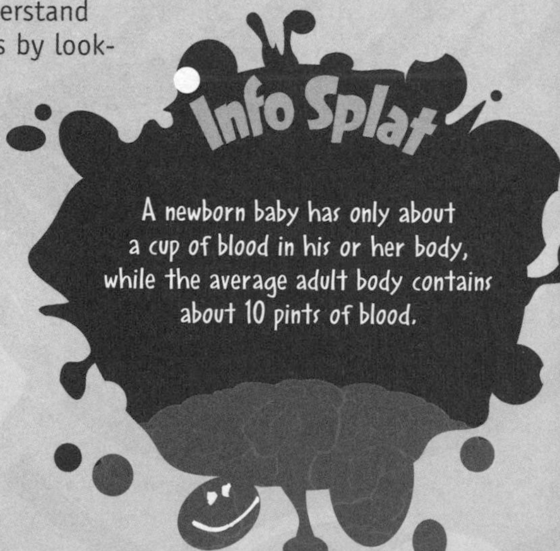

Info Splat
A newborn baby has only about a cup of blood in his or her body, while the average adult body contains about 10 pints of blood.

REACT NOW!

Jesus made the ultimate blood donation to save us. Do you think that donating blood to help people who need it could be a way to follow His example?

~ INCREDI-BIBLICAL ~

Those who are wise will shine like the brightness of the heavens, and those who lead many to righteousness, like the stars forever and ever. Daniel 12:3.

IT'S NOT YOUR JOB

Celeste's grandmother often said that the people who accepted Jesus because of her witness would be like stars in her crown when she got to heaven. For Celeste, that was a problem.

"My crown is going to be empty," she said sadly.

"Why do you say that?" Grandmother asked.

"Well, I've never been a missionary, helped anyone with a life-changing prayer, or been the reason a person was baptized," Celeste answered. "I'm just going to get a plain crown."

Her grandmother laughed. "Oh, Celeste," she said. "First of all, none of us *deserves* a crown at all, much less stars. We can't take credit for what we've done for God, because we are only instruments for what *God* is doing."

"Well, then, why hasn't God done anything through me yet?"

"He has, Celeste. Your whole life you've been in contact with many, many people who have seen Jesus in you. You've had influence on other people just because you've let God influence you. Besides, maybe you were only part of a person's journey. You may not even know how God has used you until you get to heaven."

Celeste felt hopeful.

"Don't forget that it's not your job to convict someone—that's the Holy Spirit's job. It's your job to keep being open to God, and let Him lead you." Grandmother gave her a hug. "You might be surprised when you get to heaven."

Info Splat

Around 1,210 U.S. Protestant churches have weekly attendance numbered at more than 2,000 people—nearly double the number five years ago.

REACT NOW!

Are you in tune with how God might want to use you? Today, watch and see if the Holy Spirit puts you in a position to touch someone with God's love.

~ Incredi-Biblical ~

If God is for us,
who can be against us?
Romans 8:31.

THE DISAPPEARING DOLPHIN

Get anything?" the scientist called from the deck of the expedition boat.

"Not yet," came the reply.

For six long weeks in December 2006, using underwater microphones and high-performance optical instruments, scientists from six nations hunted for the baiji. Their search turned up nothing. Even if a few baijis had managed to hide from them, the possibility that their species would survive was gone. The baiji, a freshwater dolphin that once lived in China's Yangtze River, is now considered functionally extinct.

Harvard biologist E. O. Wilson has predicted that half of all existing species will go extinct within the next 100 years. The reason: destruction of natural habitats, population growth, and pollution are threatening thousands of species.

After Jesus ascended to heaven, many people predicted that His handful of disciples would also disappear or become extinct. But even though Satan did his best to persecute and kill these believers, he was no match for God's power. Jesus' friends valued their relationship with God more than they did their own lives. The good news of God's plan of salvation and love for our world kept spreading, and the number of believers actually increased.

Still today, believers all over the world are forced to choose between giving up their faith in Jesus Christ and death. Those who choose death die trusting in Jesus, knowing that because of Him, their "extinction" is only temporary.

Info Splat

For decades dolphins have been known to have incredible healing powers. Now, dolphin therapy is a new step toward helping people with certain diseases. The diseases that have been treated successfully so far are autism, cancer, Down's syndromes and other neurological and movement diseases. It is believed that the dolphins relax the patient, thus stimulating the patient's immune systems. Doctors measure the result by monitoring the person's brain waves.

If we choose to follow Jesus Christ, are we alone? Why or why not?

October 2

~ INCREDI-BIBLICAL ~

Be merciful, just as your Father is merciful. Luke 6:36.

TEDDY NAMED THE BEAR

Jimmy, could you please take Steph to bed? I'm swamped," Mom called from the study. She sat surrounded by papers, trying to look over her notes for the last time before her exam the next morning.

Jimmy groaned. "OK," he said, and scooped up his little sister in his arms.

As Jimmy pulled Steph's blankets around her, she whined, "I need Teddy." She pointed at a tattered brown bear propped up against the wall of her room. Grunting, Jimmy reached over, grabbed the stuffed animal, and handed it to the little girl.

"I love you," she told the bear, covering it with kisses. Then she begged, "Tell me the teddy story."

Jimmy sighed. He was hoping for a fast getaway so he could instant-message a couple of his buddies. But then he looked into his sister's brown eyes. He thought a moment. "OK," he said, sitting down on the edge of her bed. "Many years ago there was a man named Theodore. He was the president of the United States, and his nickname was Teddy."

Info Splat

On a hunting trip in 1902, out of a sense of fair play, President Theodore "Teddy" Roosevelt refused to shoot a captured bear. After reading a newspaper cartoon that captured the event, a pair of Brooklyn candy store owners received permission to make bears using the president's name.

Just as the story was told to him when he was a little boy, Jimmy began the teddy bear story for his sister.

Later, leaving Steph asleep, Jimmy went back to his own stuff. "Thanks for being kind to your sister," Mom told him, reaching over with a hug. "I know you had things you wanted to do, but you chose to be patient with Steph. I'm proud of you. I'm sure God is proud of your loving heart too."

REACT NOW!

How did Jesus react to the children He knew here on earth? In what ways can we show mercy to others?

~ Incredi-Biblical ~

**Trust in the Lord with all your heart and lean not on your own understanding; in all your ways acknowledge him, and he will make your paths straight.
Proverbs 3:5, 6.**

BLESSED AMBITION

Norman joyfully anticipated his first day at the New York School of Art. At last he was enrolled in art classes. He was 14 years old and had left high school for art school. Becoming an artist had been his heart's desire for many years.

His instructors helped him get his first paid work, but soon he was hired as art director for the Boy Scouts of America. Norman's career had begun, and few people could have guessed where it would take him.

After two years studying at the New York School for Art, he enrolled at the National Academy of Design. From there he transferred to the Art Students League, where he studied with Thomas Fogarty and George Bridgman. Fogarty's instruction in illustration art led Norman to his first commercial work, while the technical skills he learned from Bridgman were useful for the rest of his life.

When his family moved to New Rochelle, New York, Norman began to freelance for magazines. At only age 22, Rockwell painted a cover for *Saturday Evening Post*—his first of 321 covers for the magazine.

Norman's personal life had sorrows, such as the death of his wife, but God continued to bless him. When asked about his remarkable success, he said, "I am only using the tools that God gave me."

In 1977 Rockwell received the Presidential Medal, the highest possible civilian medal. His works have been put in trust, and a museum has been made of his work area and home.

Info Splat

L&M Creative Foods lets you "taste" the good old days with Norman Rockwell Ice Cream. Sold in containers printed with Rockwell paintings, ice-cream flavors include home-style vanilla or chocolate, cookies and cream, butter pecan, and mint with chocolate chips.

Was Norman Rockwell's age a limiting factor in using his gifts? What does it take to succeed for God?

October 4

~ Incredi-Biblical ~

He performs wonders that cannot be fathomed, miracles that cannot be counted. Job 5:9.

ALONE AGAIN

"That dragon is huge!" Doug gasped as Cari joined him in front of the monster's habitat. Together they read the caption mounted below the glass wall.

"In December 2006, staff at the London Zoo discovered something unusual. Sungai, a female Komodo dragon that lives at the zoo, laid a clutch of eggs without having ever mated. Four of the eggs hatched, and after DNA tests revealed that Sungai was indeed the babies' only parent, scientists reported the first birth by parthenogenesis, or "virgin birth," for this species. Now Flora, a Komodo dragon at the Chester Zoo, is waiting for her fatherless eggs to hatch. Reptile genetics indicate that all the fatherless baby Komodos will be male.

"Other animals capable of virgin birth include such invertebrates as aphids and wasps, a handful of reptiles and fish, and turkeys. In some aphid species, a developing female inside the mother has another developing female inside her."

Info Splat

Take a look inside a Komodo dragon's mouth, and you'll see a long yellow tongue, razor-sharp teeth, and saliva so toxic that one bite of this bacteria laden spit can be fatal to a human.

"Wow, that's cool," Doug said. "I wonder how that can be."

"Well, I guess God can do anything," Cari said with a smile.

The two glanced around and realized that their class had gone on ahead of them. "Hey, we better hurry," Cari said, "or we'll get in trouble."

"Yeah, this'll be the last school field trip they'll let us go on," Doug laughed.

The two started running as they spied the last of their group heading toward the monkey house.

What does nature tell us about our Creator and His power? Do you believe in miracles? Why?

Incredi-Biblical

Do not be quickly provoked in your spirit, for anger resides in the lap of fools. Ecclesiastes 7:9.

RED FUR

"Aw, you're just losing it because you're a redhead," Luke teased Carol. She felt her face grow warm again, and she took a deep breath. Their lunchtime discussion about their favorite football teams had been pretty heated, but she knew her hair color had nothing to do with it.

"You know, Luke, you've got a pretty hot temper yourself," Maryanne told him as she handed Carol a steaming burrito.

The three teens were a few of several kids helping out as tutors at an elementary school. They'd become good friends and usually enjoyed comparing opinions. Just then a small group of younger kids came up to them. One of them had been crying. It was Alice. She was clenching her fists, and her face was twisted in anger.

Carol's green eyes softened as she bent to listen to the girl.

"Brent said that all girls are stupid," Alice said, the tears starting again. "I hate him! If he won't take it back, I'm going to pop him!"

Carol glanced at Maryanne, then said to Alice, "Come on, let's talk to Brent. God doesn't want us to hate anyone. He loves us, and He wants us to love each other."

Luke and Maryanne watched as Carol left with the young kids. "OK, so maybe I got a little carried away," he admitted. "It's just not worth it to hurt a friendship over football."

Info Splat

The color of a dog's coat relates to its assertiveness. Cocker spaniels with golden fur are more assertive than those with dark fur, and spaniels with a mixture of colors (particolor) are the mellowest. But environment, more than coat color, determines personality.

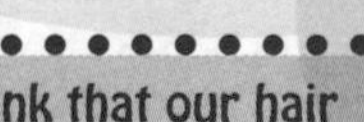

REACT NOW!

Do you think that our hair color affects our personality? Can anger be a good thing? What are some appropriate ways to deal with anger?

October 6

~ INCREDI-BIBLICAL ~

God saw all that he had made, and it was very good. And there was evening, and there was morning—the sixth day. Genesis 1:31.

AUTUMN LEAF COLOR

The leaf is nature's food factory. Thirsty plants gulp water from the ground through their roots and draw carbon dioxide from the air. Using sunlight, they turn water and carbon dioxide into glucose—making their own food.

This process, turning H_2O and carbon dioxide into sugar, is called photosynthesis. A special pigment called chlorophyll helps by capturing the sunlight and changing its unusable light energy into usable chemical energy. Chlorophyll does something else, too. High amounts of it give plants their green color.

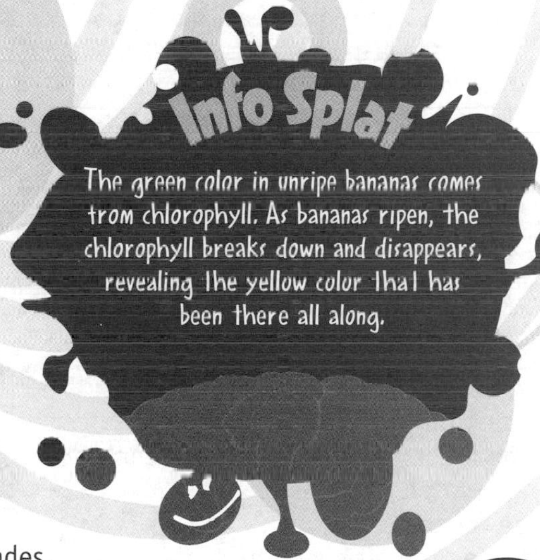

Info Splat
The green color in unripe bananas comes from chlorophyll. As bananas ripen, the chlorophyll breaks down and disappears, revealing the yellow color that has been there all along.

As summer leaves (ha, pun intended), and autumn sneaks around the corner, sunlight becomes less intense, and the trees know it's time to get ready for winter. The chlorophyll breaks down and photosynthesis slowly creeps . . . to . . . a . . . stop.

With the chlorophyll gone, the green fades, leaving other leaf pigments such as carotenoids. Those are the ones that show yellow, orange, and brown. Glucose, a leftover product of photosynthesis, is trapped inside each leaf. So the bright sunlight and cool autumn nights combine with it to produce the pigment that gives the red and purple color to other leaves.

Look outside during autumn, and you'll see golden bronze hickories, purplish-red dogwood, scarlet red maples, and russet oaks. What's more, you'll see evidence of our intelligent, artistic, loving Creator.

REACT NOW!

What do the colors around us and the many changes in seasons and nature tell us about God? Can we know how to be saved through nature around us?

∘~ Incredi-Biblical ~∘

And God is able to make all grace abound to you, so that in all things at all times, having all that you need, you will abound in every good work.
2 Corinthians 9:8.

TYRONE FINDS A GIFT

I can't do anything right here, Tyrone thought. His youth group had just finished day three of a five-day commitment at the gospel mission, and everyone but Tyrone seemed to have a job. Bobby, who served the soup, loved getting to know everyone. Claire had gotten busy gathering good used clothing and was passing it out to the residents when she saw a need. And Maureen had jumped at the chance to paint the kitchen.

Tyrone felt lost. He wanted to help, but he couldn't figure out where he fit in. That morning he'd just stood back and watched the bustling activity.

"What's wrong, son?" Mr. Melchik asked, coming by with a bucket and mop.

"I don't know what to do," Tyrone replied.

The manager put his hand on Tyrone's shoulder. "Ty, everyone has at least one gift that God has given them. Think about what yours may be, because this is a good opportunity to put it to use." He paused and looked around the room. "Remember, these people are grateful for whatever you may do for them."

As the afternoon passed, Tyrone prayed for guidance. "Lord, show me what to do," he pleaded. The next day, Tyrone watched as everyone worked on individual projects, with no apparent plan or goal. Suddenly he felt a strong urge to organize.

"We might be able to achieve more if we do it like this, Mr. Melchik," Tyrone suggested.

Mr. Melchik smiled. "Good for you, Ty," he said. "I think you have found your gift!"

Info Splat

Virginia has been named the Birthplace of U.S. Presidents for producing the most presidents of any state—a total of eight. The Mother of Presidents is Ohio, coming in close behind with seven. While you might not become a governor, a prime minister, or a president, God has entrusted you with special abilities of your own.

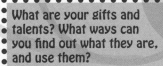

What are your gifts and talents? What ways can you find out what they are, and use them?

October 8

~ INCREDI-BIBLICAL ~

Happy are those who keep the law.
Proverbs 29:18, NRSV.

PIZZA, CAESAR?

"What's this?" the Roman soldiers muttered as they bit into the flat, soft bread. Their tour of duty had brought them to Palestine, and this was their first taste of the Jewish *matzo*, or unleavened bread. They liked it. Upon returning to Rome, they added a few spices and developed a dish that today we call—pizza.

Actually, no one is really certain of pizza's origins, but the kind of pizza we eat today is attributed to Raffael Esposito of Naples. In 1889 he baked a special pizza for Queen Margherita of Savoy, made to resemble the Italian flag. He used green basil, red tomatoes, and white mozzarella cheese. The dish was a hit.

Later, when Italians immigrated to other countries in the nineteenth and twentieth centuries, pizza became a favorite food all over the world. Many places have unique styles of pizza. The city of Chicago, Illinois, for example, is known for its deep-dish pizzas.

Info Splat

October is National Pizza Month in the United States, and you can celebrate at any of its 61,269 pizzerias. Americans eat approximately 3 billion pizzas each year. That adds up to about 100 acres of pizza every day, or about 350 slices per second.

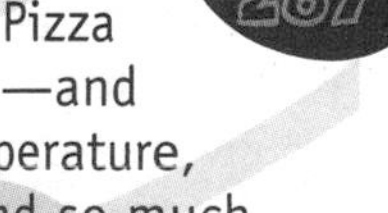

However, the Associazone Verzce Pizza Napoletana (True Neapolitan Pizza Association) recognizes only two types—the Marinara and the Margherita—and they have very specific baking rules. The Association regulates time, temperature, kneading, and baking procedures, and even the thickness of the crust! And so much for ordering an extra-large (20 inches) from Gordo's. Their pizzas can't exceed 14 inches in diameter.

Lots of rules, but the end results are worth it!

REACT NOW!

Do you think anyone should be able to tell certain pizza places how to make pizza? Why or why not? What are some rules in your own life that you've found helpful?

INCREDI-BIBLICAL

Just as each of us has one body with many members, and these members do not all have the same function, so in Christ we who are many form one body, and each member belongs to all the others. Romans 12:4, 5.

MORE PIZZA FUN

Here's another slice of life: See if you can swallow one more day of pizza devotional wisdom. (Hopefully it's not too cheesy for you.)

Whether it's cheesy or veggie, round or square, hot or cold—for many people, pizza hits the spot. And for Karl, there's nothing better than a great-tasting piece of pizza pie.

"Sam, let's order a large pizza," Karl said. School was out for the day, and the two boys had ridden their bikes to Gino's pizzeria. All around them kids were eating pizza, talking, and having a good time.

Sam grinned across the table at his friend and took a long drink from his glass of ice water. "Yeah, I'm starved," he agreed.

After a crusty old server had taken their order, Sam asked, "So, you going to the game on Sunday?"

"Sure, as long as I get the garage cleaned this weekend. My dad said, 'No clean garage, no game.'" Karl shrugged. "It won't take me too long if I start on it tonight."

Soon the pizza arrived. It surely smelled good! Pineapple and green olive—a little sweet and a little salty—was their favorite. But Karl looked at the circle of eight slices and said, "They didn't cut this right. It's all uneven. It's a mess."

"Who cares?" Sam replied, scooping out a slice from the round pie. "It all gets mixed up once it hits my mouth!"

"Yeah, I guess you're right. I'll do my part right now to check out your theory!" With that, the two guys dug into the messy but delightfully tasty pizza pie.

Info Splat

According to a recent Gallup poll, kids between the ages of 10 and 14 prefer pizza over all other food groups for lunch and dinner. Ninety-four percent of the U.S. population eats pizza.

REACT NOW!

How is the body of Christ like a pizza? Is it sometimes a little bit "messy"? Think of yourself as a slice of pizza. Each of us is a little different, but together we make a whole "pie."

October 10

INCREDI-BIBLICAL

Laziness brings on deep sleep, and the shiftless man goes hungry. Proverbs 19:15.

THE HARVEST

Mr. Van Brock had one last field to plant. He urged the mare forward, dragging the plow behind him. Micah dropped seeds as he followed the path of the plow.

"Don't forget to be generous with those seeds, son," his father reminded him.

"Yes, sir." Micah wiped the sweat from his forehead and moved on. It was only midmorning, and there was still much to be done on the farm. The only food that he and his family—Dad, Mom, and three sisters—would put on their table that year would be the harvest from these and the other seeds they planted.

The elevated soil of mounded plants warms quicker than the surrounding soil. This means you can start your planting season earlier. Also, excess moisture will drain off, flowing away from the seeds and plants.

They'd traveled from the Netherlands to America in the late 1830s, filled with hopes of a better life as they cleared fields and pristine woods. These pioneers brought seeds and farming methods with them, and learned new methods along the way.

One of Micah's friends was Good Feather, the son of a Native American chief. Good Feather's family taught Micah's family how to farm using a mounding method. "See, the water runs off the hill, so the seeds are not washed away," Good Feather had said as he patted the mound of dirt and nodded to his friend.

As the oldest child, Micah bore much of the responsibility on the farm. He didn't mind except when his friend Peter showed up, tempting him with a good time. "Take a break, and let's go swimming," Peter would beg, but Micah would shake his head.

"Maybe later," he'd say with a grin. "After I've got the seeds in."

At nighttime Mr. Van Brock read from the family Bible. "God says to us, in 2 Thessalonians 3:10, 'If a man will not work, he shall not eat.'"

That October harvest was good to the Van Brock family. Micah and his father were able to rest and enjoy the fruit of their labors.

REACT NOW!

Are you ever tempted to skip your chores or not to study for exams in school? Have you ever had a job that was so tough that you were tempted to quit? How does God say we should treat work in our lives?

~ INCREDI-BIBLICAL ~

O Lord, you are my God; I will exalt you and praise your name, for in perfect faithfulness you have done marvelous things, things planned long ago. Isaiah 25:1.

THE FAVORED CITY

"It was the moment to vote for the city to host the 2012 Summer Olympics,'" Allie read. "'There were bids from nine cities. The International Olympic Committee shaved the choices down to five cities: London, Madrid, Moscow, New York City, and Paris. Finally the committee picked London, a city that had already hosted the Olympics three times.

"'The bidding process was hotly debated and scrutinized. At first Paris took the lead, but London supporters campaigned for their city. With only a margin of four votes, London won the final round.'"

Allie put the school newsletter down on the lunch table.

"It sounds just like our school elections," she told her friend Mary. "Who's the most popular, what can the candidate do for you, etc. I get sick of it sometimes."

"I know," agreed Mary. "I mean, look at Clark. He's cute and popular, but you know what? He's not a nice person. He's not honest, either. I know that the things he's promising as class president are just to get him elected. I wish we could find somebody that would actually live up to what they're telling us. You know, some kid that is true to his word."

"I hear you," said Allie.

"I guess there just aren't many people you can count on." Mary shook her head sadly.

"You're right." Allie's eyes brightened. "But there's Someone I know who will always live up to His promises!"

Info Splat

Sochi, Russia, was chosen to host the 2014 Winter Olympics. Russian president Vladimir Putin helped win the bid by addressing delegates in three languages—English, Spanish, and French. This may have been the first time people heard Putin speaking English at a public ceremony.

Do you have trouble believing in what people say or do? How do you know Jesus will always come through for you? What do your friends believe?

October 12

Incredi-Biblical

A friend loves at all times. Proverbs 17:17.

A FRIEND IN NEED

Janna had known Mara for four years. They went to school together and had joined the swim team last year. Mara was a real "torpedo" in the swim meets. Now Janna suspected her friend was in trouble.

It was when Mara introduced a new friend one day after practice. "This is Paul, Janna," she said.

Paul flicked his cigarette onto the ground and gave Janna a nod. "Hey," he said. He looked distracted. "We gotta go now, Mara."

"See ya later, Janna. I'll call you," Mara called over her shoulder as she left. But weeks went by, and Janna barely heard from her friend. Then one day before swim practice Janna saw Mara slumped in the corner of the locker room. Her head was down, and she seemed to be sleeping.

"Mara, you OK?" Janna called to her. She moved closer to the girl. Mara did not respond.

"Mara! Mara!" Janna cried in alarm. She touched her friend's shoulder, and slowly Mara looked up. Her eyes stared blankly into Janna's.

"I'm . . . OK." Mara stumbled over her words. She was not OK, and Janna knew it.

Later Mara begged Janna not to tell anyone. "Please, it was just some bad stuff Paulie gave me. I'll be more careful," she pleaded.

Janna contemplated what to do. She didn't want to rat on her friend, yet it was obvious Mara was in trouble. What should she do? Janna opened her Bible that night and began to read and pray. The next morning she made a call. Mara called her that afternoon.

"My parents are furious!" she yelled. "Why did you do that to me, Janna? I thought that we were friends!"

"Mara, you are my friend. I love you," Mara replied. "God loves you. You deserve better than you have right now."

Info Splat

Drugs aren't cool. And smoking is cool only if you think bad breath, smelly hair, yellow fingers, coughing, and death are cool. Advertisements make it look very different, but think about who make the ads and why.

REACT NOW!

Would you have told on your friend? What do you think was going on with Mara and Paul? And what does God say about how we should treat our bodies? Did Janna really love her friend?

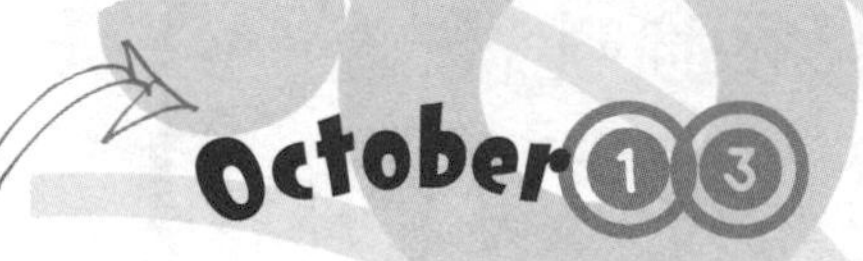

~ INCREDI-BIBLICAL ~

Keep alert, stand firm in your faith, be courageous, be strong.
1 Corinthians 16:13, NRSV.

MUSCLING IN

Gary's face grew hot as he looked at the sheet of paper Hal held out to him. Somehow Hal had lifted the answers to their next science test.

What should I do? Gary wavered. His grade could use the help, but he knew cheating wouldn't help him understand the material. Then Exodus 23:2 came to mind: "Do not follow the crowd in doing wrong."

Later that week Gary told his dad what had happened and showed him the graded test. "See?" he said. "I barely passed."

"Gary, let me share something with you that I read yesterday," his dad said. "There are two types of muscle fibers. We use the ones called fast-twitch for sprinting, and we use slow-twitch muscles in marathons."

Gary unconsciously made a fist and raised and lowered his arm as Dad continued. "Scientists recently discovered a third type of fiber they call IIX. This fiber has properties of both the slow- and fast-twitch muscles."

Gary nodded, listening. Trying to figure out what Dad was talking about. "When researchers inserted a gene in mice that changed some fast-twitch muscles into IIX fibers, they got some impressive endurance athletes that grow stronger every time they flex their little mice muscles." Dad laughed and then grew serious.

"Son, you were confronted with a choice—to cheat, or not. You flexed your spiritual muscle and said no to cheating. I'm proud of you for having the courage to stand strong for what's right."

Gary smiled. He remembered how hard it had been to turn down the chance to get a perfect score. But how great it felt to do the right thing!

Info Splat

Matt Nagle was the first paralyzed person to control his artificial hand by thoughts alone. A "Braingate" chip was implanted in Nagle's motor cortex that allows his hand to reach out for objects and grasp them just by thinking about it.

REACT NOW!

Do you know that you have a "spiritual muscle"? If you read God's Word, pray, have faith, and put your faith into practice, your "spiritual muscle" will grow strong. How do you plan to build up your muscles for God?

~ INCREDI-BIBLICAL ~

My message and my preaching were not with wise and persuasive words, but with a demonstration of the Spirit's power, so that your faith might not rest on men's wisdom, but on God's power.
1 Corinthians 2:4.

THE MENACE

"Hang on," Dr. Sumter called to his son. And Johnny did. He clung to his seat and breathed in the aromas of dust, sweat, and cooked food as the crowded African taxi sped through congested villages. In a nearby community, people struggling with a virus outbreak needed the missionary doctor.

Suddenly the taxi screeched to a halt. Looming on the path in front of them was a huge snake. Afraid, the driver froze.

"We've got to get to that next village," Dr. Sumter pleaded. "Run over it!" The driver violently shook his head no. "Run over it," Dr. Sumter repeated, but the sight of the nine-foot snake standing upright in the face of the taxi was overwhelming.

"Please, Lord, let the snake lie down," Johnny prayed.

Immediately the snake lay down across the road. The passengers began to murmur. "Look at that, look at that!"

"Go," shouted Dr. Sumter to the driver. Quickly the man revved the engine and passed over the prone snake. "Again!" Back and forth he ran the taxi, until he was certain the giant snake was dead.

Shouts of relief exploded from the taxi. Several riders jumped out, picked up the snake, and placed it on the hood of the car.

As they drove into the waiting village, the people cried out in relief that the menacing snake was dead. When they found out that it was truly God who had killed the snake, many believed, and soon a church building stood as a reminder of the all-powerful God of heaven.

Info Splat

The python holds the world's record for length of a snake, with the longest ever measured at 33 feet.

REACT NOW!

Have you ever prayed to God for power over something that seemed hopeless? What did God do?

October 15

INCREDI-BIBLICAL

Their destiny is destruction, their god is their stomach, and their glory is in their shame. Their mind is on earthly things. But our citizenship is in heaven. Philippians 3:19, 20.

SURPRISE IN THE WATER

Water flowing from your bathroom faucet—the same water you use to brush your teeth and wash your hands—is supposed to be clean. After all, it's been through sewage treatment plants where workers and machines purify it, right? Listen to some of the items found in "cleaned" water: caffeine, medications, and fragrances from various household products.

In the fall of 2006 researchers at the University of Washington discovered high levels of cinnamon and vanilla in Puget Sound. They estimated, based on the levels of these chemicals, that during the last three-day holiday weekend, local people had eaten 160,000 butter cookies or chocolate-chip cookies and 80,000 cinnamon cookies.

Dirty water is pretty disgusting, but dirty people can be even nastier. If we let unclean and unwholesome things sneak into our thoughts or lives, these unholy things will muddy up our thinking and make us unable to see clearly what God would have us do. We must have pure, clean hearts to receive His word and to keep a tight relationship with Him. This can mean passing up that movie or TV program you've thought about watching, choosing not to read a certain book, or making careful choices about your friends.

And if you're feeling as though you need a good cleaning today, don't worry. God's purification system is way more effective than any sewage treatment plant.

Info Splat

Drinking too much water too quickly can lead to water intoxication. Water intoxication occurs when water dilutes the sodium level in the bloodstream, causing an imbalance of water in the brain. However, you've got to drink way, way too much water to reach this state.

As Christians, what should our minds be focused on?

REACT NOW!

Incredi-Biblical

Therefore I tell you, whatever you ask for in prayer, believe that you have received it, and it will be yours. Mark 11:24.

THE BIKE RIDE

Craig and Marcy donned their helmets and mounted their bikes, listening as Mr. Adams prepped the group one last time. "Always stay together. Make sure that your bike is in good condition. And remember, your bike helmet will protect you. Wear it!"

The riders assembled into a line and sped off down the trail, their mountain bikes crunching through brittle leaves. Craig and Marcy stayed at the end of the long line of colorful riders as they passed through villages, homes, and businesses, and then a beautiful long stretch of "nothing." After a couple hours the group stopped to rest a few minutes and get refreshments. It was then that Craig turned to talk with Marcy. She wasn't there.

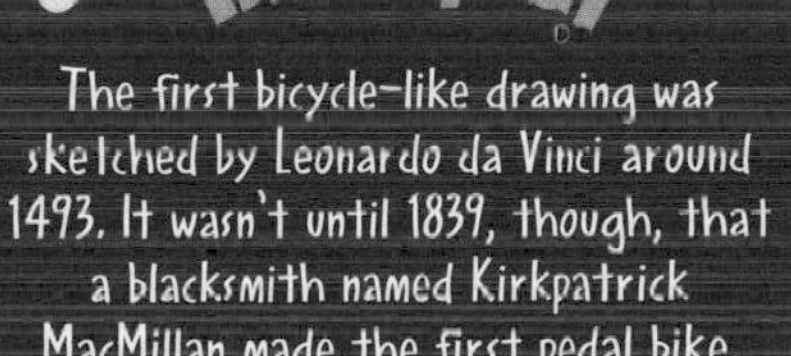

Info Splat
The first bicycle-like drawing was sketched by Leonardo da Vinci around 1493. It wasn't until 1839, though, that a blacksmith named Kirkpatrick MacMillan made the first pedal bike. In their early history, bikes were known as velocipedes.

Suddenly he realized that he'd been riding ahead of her for quite some time. He looked back. There was no sign of her, and behind them lay miles of forest.

"Mr. Adams, what should we do?" Craig asked.

"First, we pray," he said.

The group gathered together for prayer, then retraced their ride, looking from side to side, searching for Marcy. Dusk was falling. "Please, Lord, lead us to her," Craig prayed.

Eventually Mr. Adams stopped the group. "I have to call the police," he told them. "We need help." Everyone stood around, frightened for their friend. It was dark and cold. Craig rubbed his hands together.

Just then a car pulled up. Out popped Marcy.

"My bike blew a tire!" she explained. "I called as loud as I could to you guys, but you were long gone. So I sat down and prayed, and then this family pulled up and offered to give me a ride. God surely took care of me," Marcy said.

REACT NOW!

What did Mr. Adams, Craig, and Marcy do when they realized they were in trouble? Is God always there for us?

INCREDI-BIBLICAL

So God created man in his own image, in the image of God he created him; male and female he created them. Genesis 1:27.

AN UNUSUAL FRIENDSHIP

Harper and Truman knew each other in Monroeville, Alabama, where Harper's daddy was a lawyer and Truman visited his aunt every summer. Somehow neither of them fit in with the other kids, so they hung around together. Like her father, who used to be a newspaper editor, Harper was fascinated by words. She often told Truman of her dream to become a writer.

"Why don't we try to write a story ourselves?" the spunky Harper replied one afternoon. Truman fidgeted. He didn't want to get into any trouble with his aunts.

"You think it's OK?" he asked.

"Just watch!" Harper pulled a black Underwood typewriter out from beneath her daddy's study desk. "Let's do it. I can type." Little did Harper know that the story they would write that afternoon would be just the beginning. Later they both would become famous writers.

Harper Lee is best known for her book *To Kill a Mockingbird*. As a child she had observed how the people in her small Southern town treated others. Monroeville had its share of problems, and one of them was prejudice. When Harper grew older, she felt strongly that God had created all people equal. The bad attitudes and racial injustice she had seen growing up prompted her to write a book about it.

Info Splat

Harper Lee's first name was Nelle (her grandmother's name spelled backwards), but when she wrote her book she chose to go by her middle name, Harper.

How does God see all of His people? How should we see others when they appear different from us?

INCREDI-BIBLICAL

Guide me in your truth and teach me, for you are God my Savior, and my hope is in you all day long. Psalm 25:5.

FOOD MYTHS

Check out the facts!

1. Chewing gum takes seven years to digest. True___ False___
2. Greasy foods and chocolate cause acne. True___ False___
3. Coffee stunts your growth. True___ False___
4. Carrots are good for your eyesight. True___ False___
5. Eating bread crusts gives you curly hair. True___ False___

Answers:

1. *False.* Gum passes through your digestive system more quickly than food because your stomach doesn't digest it. Its gum base makes it last for many hours.
2. *False.* Stress, hormones, and genes that you inherit from your parents cause or aggravate acne. But a healthy diet and plenty of water help combat the breakouts.
3. *False.* There's no evidence behind this tall tale. However, caffeine is a stimulant. It increases heart rate, blood pressure, and blood flow to muscles, but decreases blood flow to your skin and inner organs. It can also cause headaches and nausea.
4. *True.* Carrots contain beta-carotene, which is found in yellow and orange food. This substance is converted into vitamin A, which helps you see in the dark. However, eating carrots will not cure nearsightedness, farsightedness, or astigmatism.
5. *False.* Even after eating crusts for many years, you won't have curlier hair. For that, you'll have to use a curling iron or get a perm. But don't cut those crusts. They contain eight times more antioxidants—substances in some foods that might help prevent cancer—than the rest of the loaf.

Info Splat

In 1901 a New York sports cartoonist named Tad Dorgan heard vendors yelling, "Get your dachshund sausages while they're red-hot!" As he sketched the scene Tad realized he wasn't sure how to spell dachshund, so he just called them hot dogs. The rest is history.

REACT NOW!

Have you heard other stories that aren't accurate? Think of a place you can go to find absolute truth.

Incredi-Biblical

The law of the Lord is perfect, reviving the soul. The statutes of the Lord are trustworthy, making wise the simple. The precepts of the Lord are right, giving joy to the heart. Psalm 19:7, 8.

DECISION

Andrea was about ready to go.

The concert was to begin in two hours. Afterward she and her friends planned to go out for ice cream to celebrate. They'd practiced for three months, and it was an honor to be included in the music festival. It was open to the public, and even the local newspaper was going to be represented there.

"Make sure you read tomorrow's newspaper," Mr. Singer had told his students.

Andrea had spent many hours practicing her flute part. She remembered all the times she had sacrificed other things to play in this concert. "Andrea, why don't you come with us to the mall?" "Andrea, come bowling with us tonight!" "Andrea, we're going swimming at the Y. Want to come?"

"Can't this time. I've got to practice," Andrea had responded again and again.

Now Mom called out, "Are you dressed, Andrea? It's time to leave."

"I'm ready." Andrea took a final look in the mirror. She loved her new dress, and even her hair looked good today.

Just then the telephone rang. "Oh, no," she heard Mom cry a moment later.

"Grandma was in an accident," Mom told her. "She's in the hospital." Eyes awash with tears, she looked at her daughter. "I'm sorry, honey, but this is an emergency. I have to go right now."

Andrea stared at her flute. *How unfair*, she thought. *First, Grandma's been hurt, and Mom won't be there to hear me*.

Then the doorbell rang. It was her friend Monica. "That's awful," she said when Andrea told her the news. "I'm sorry. But do you want to ride with us?"

An hour later Andrea stood poised to play, the flute lifted to her lips. As the sweet notes filled the room, the old woman looked up from her hospital bed and smiled.

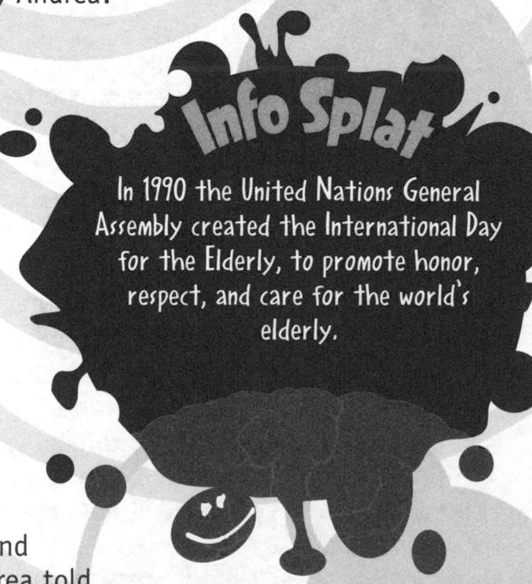

Info Splat
In 1990 the United Nations General Assembly created the International Day for the Elderly, to promote honor, respect, and care for the world's elderly.

REACT NOW!

Would it have been wrong for Andrea to go on to the concert? What would you have done? What guidelines can we use to make the right decision?

Incredi-Biblical

How can you say to your brother, "Let me take the speck out of your eye," when all the time there is a plank in your own eye? You hypocrite, first take the plank out of your own eye, and then you will see clearly to remove the speck from your brother's eye.
Matthew 7:4, 5.

THE EYES OF A CAT

Marla leafed through the magazine on the kitchen table. "A team of scientists has found that the complex compounds in pepper affect cells in the retina, making them more sensitive to infrared or heat wavelengths," she read. The article went to say that night vision was only slightly improved but that a com pound had been developed for soldiers to take that enabled them to see in the dark as well as cats do.

Then Marla put down the magazine as she heard Brittany's knock.

Soon Marla felt upset. Brittany went on and on about their friend Laurie. The news was very concerning, filled with unusual details and drama. *Can this be true?* Marla thought.

"And after that they went to . . ." Brittany continued with detail after detail. She seemed more excited with each word.

She's enjoying this, Marla thought. *And I am too*, she realized with a shock. She knew she could have stopped the story earlier, but hadn't. Remembering what she'd just read, she wished for super vision. *Jesus, please help me be more sensitive and see things clearly the first time around.*

Finished, Brittany took a deep breath. "Now, don't tell anyone else," she said.

Immediately Marla thought, *I need to call Barb about this*. A little jolt of excitement ran through her as she thought about spreading the news. Then she stopped herself. She looked at Brittany and remembered how God hated gossip.

"Let's stop this right now, Brittany," Marla told her friend.

Info Splat

The ancient tale of thieves using pepper to see in the dark was always thought to be just a myth, but the scientists at Bangalore University have proved differently. One problem with this discovery, however, is that the soldiers can't stop sneezing.

Are we ever "blind" spiritually? What can we do about it? How can we truly see?

Incredi-Biblical

Bear with each other and forgive whatever grievances you may have against one another. Forgive as the Lord forgave you. Colossians 3:13.

ON DUTY

Harvey grimaced as the elderly woman approached him at the nursing home desk. Every day Mrs. McDermott complained about something.

"Young man, I want you to tell someone in authority that my breakfast tea was cold today and my oatmeal was lumpy," she told Harvey smartly.

"What does she want me to do?" he asked Kathy and Nick at lunch. He was beginning to think he had made a mistake volunteering at the nursing home.

"Well, you could just not like her. Who could blame you?" Kathy said. "On the other hand, this is a chance to practice God's love for people like her. You could pray that God will show you how to love Mrs. McDermott."

"There must be a way of understanding her better," Nick added.

I don't want to understand her, Harvey almost said.

The next day Mrs. McDermott approached the desk again. "Young man," she began, "my son is coming to visit me today at 2:00 p.m. Make sure you give him the right room number. It's Room 103."

Two o'clock came and went, but no one showed up.

"Poor Mrs. McDermott," one of the nurses said to Harvey. "Every week she expects her son to visit her. Of course, he won't come. He died in the war you know, long ago. But he was all the family she had."

Harvey felt a rush of compassion. He swallowed hard and headed down the hall toward Room 103.

Info Splat

Harvey Ball was paid to make people smile. An insurance company hired him to create a logo that would improve its employees' morale. In 1963 he designed a yellow and black smiley face, which grew in popularity until it became known around the world.

How should we treat those who are difficult to love? Did Christ come for the lovable or the unlovable? Does God love us no matter what we do?

~ INCREDI-BIBLICAL ~

They found the stone rolled away from the tomb, but when they entered, they did not find the body of the Lord Jesus. He is not here; he has risen! Luke 24:2, 6.

TRUTH OR FICTION?

Beginning in October 2007, Britain's University of Nottingham offered the world's first master's degree in Robin Hood studies. The university is located near the forest where the legendary Robin Hood lived with his merry men. Today mangy woods are all that remain of Robin Hood's famous digs, and many people doubt he ever existed.

Some people have similar doubts about Jesus Christ, even though evidence and hundreds of witnesses support the belief that He lived on this earth, died, and rose again the third day after His death. John and Mary had been discussing this issue over lunch. John was a new Christian and had just finished reading Josh McDowell's book *More Than a Carpenter*. He was eager to share what he'd learned.

Info Splat

Several people set out to prove that Christianity is based on a myth, but in the end became Christians themselves. These include lawyer Frank Morrison who wrote the book ***Who Moved the Stone?*** and former journalist Lee Strobel, author of ***The Case for Christ.***

"I don't believe it," Mary stated with conviction. "I mean, come on, John, do you really believe that nonsense that someone died, rose from the grave, went to heaven, *and is God*?" She glanced at her friend, shaking her head. "So many pitiful, misled people do," she told him.

John looked Mary in the eye and with a broad smile asked, "Mary, who's in Gandhi's grave?"

"Gandhi, of course," she told him, with a puzzled look on her face.

"OK, and in Muhammad's grave?"

"Muhammad," she replied.

"So, who is in Jesus' grave?" John asked her.

Mary was silent. She struggled to reply.

"It's empty," she whispered.

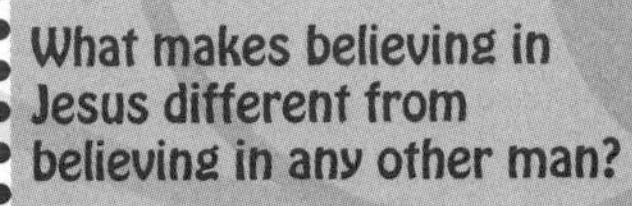
What makes believing in Jesus different from believing in any other man?

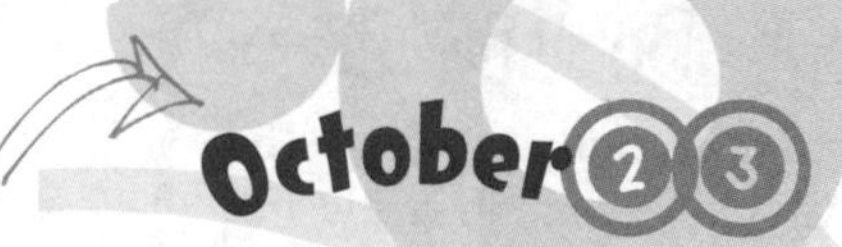

INCREDI-BIBLICAL

For we are all God's workmanship, created in Christ Jesus to do good works, which God prepared in advance for us to do. Ephesians 2:10.

SHAKING THINGS UP

"Anyone have any other ideas for VBS?" Mrs. Shoemaker asked her youth group. They'd met to finalize plans for the five-day "school" to begin in just a few weeks. It would run from 9:00 a.m. to noon, just as in previous years.

"While you're thinking, take a look at the program we're using," she told them. "And be creative—as I was the other day. I looked at the slice of pizza in my hand and thought, *This is way too boring.* So I added M & Ms." The class groaned as she licked her lips and remembered. "Yum!" she said. "It was the best pizza I've had in a long time!"

Darlene shook her head as she read the material, remembering that her church had used the same curriculum last year. She thought about the surrounding neighborhood. It was a poor community. Kids spent most of their summer days hidden inside hot homes, trying to avoid the trouble on the streets.

"How about we plan something different this year," she heard herself say. "Maybe schedule it at night to reach the most kids? We might get some parents, too. We could offer ice cream and popcorn, and the kids could play games on the church lawn. Maybe one evening they could even play in the church sprinklers. We could still teach them the Bible lessons, but this would be different, and fun, too.

Mrs. Shoemaker looked at Darlene with a big smile. "Sounds good!" she told the girl. "Let's talk about this. Maybe we need to shake things up around here."

Info Splat

Patti (who wrote this day's devotional reading) thinks the ultimate food combination is Jell-O and popcorn. "Nothing like a bowl of popcorn topped with green slime," she says. Try to stay open-minded about food. There are many great combinations of food—and people—out there!

REACT NOW!

How does it make you feel to meet someone who's life circumstances are different from yours? Does it make a difference if they are better off than you or worse off than you? Do you tend to act in a certain way?

October 24

~ Incredi-Biblical ~

For the Lord will not reject his people; he will never forsake his inheritance. Psalm 94:14.

HOW MANY STATES?

If you had lived in the United States between 1784 and 1788, you could have visited the state of Franklin. Yes, it's true. Franklin was a state made up of four western counties in North Carolina.

At that time the federal government was in debt and needed money to pay for the costs of the Revolutionary War. They asked the states to help, but there wasn't much cash lying around, and taxing the people was difficult. Instead of sending money, North Carolina gave four of its western counties to the government.

Immediately the state regretted its decision. It wanted the land back, but the residents of the area decided they didn't want to go. Since North Carolina hadn't given them very much help in the past, they ceded to the federal government.

Electing John Sevier as their first governor, the state of Franklin existed for four years. When North Carolina regained control of the area in 1788 and in 1789 gave up the section of land again, the area joined the new state of Tennessee. Sevier finished his term as the first and only governor of Franklin, served as a senator in North Carolina, and became the first governor of Tennessee. He had demonstrated his commitment to the area and its people.

Info Splat

John Sevier, or "Nolichucky Jack," was a fighter. He met his wife, Bonny Kate, during a Cherokee siege on Fort Watauga when he saved her by pulling her over the fort wall.

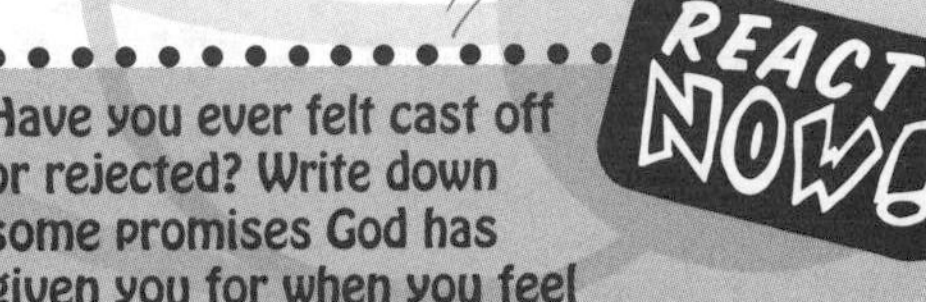

REACT NOW!

Have you ever felt cast off or rejected? Write down some promises God has given you for when you feel abandoned. Is there someone you can talk to about this feeling?

~ Incredi-Biblical ~

Do not turn to mediums or seek out spiritists, for you will be defiled by them. I am the Lord your God. Leviticus 19:31.

JACK-O'-LANTERN JACK

An Irish myth tells about a man nicknamed Stingy Jack," Andrew's teacher told the class. "According to the legend, God would not allow such an unsavory figure into heaven. But because Jack had made a deal with the devil, he could not go to hell. The devil sent Jack off into the dark night with only a burning coal to light his way. Jack put the coal into a carved-out turnip and has been roaming the earth with it ever since. The Irish refer to this figure as 'Jack of the Lantern.' "

After class Andrew thought about the story. His teacher had said you could find it by using an Internet search engine. Jack sort of wished he hadn't carved a jack-o'-lantern. Of course, he hadn't known its symbolism then.

Tonight was Halloween, and his friends were going trick-or-treating, but suddenly Andrew wasn't sure how he felt about going. He wondered what his best friend, Jesus, thought about the holiday. Sighing, Andrew listened to his friends talk about the great time they were going to have that night.

"Yeah, we're going to the old Hasbruck house," Greg said. "You know, the one where those people died in a fire. Shauna is bringing her Ouija board so maybe we can talk with them." He made a silly face. "Cool, huh?"

Everyone laughed. Everyone but Andrew. "See ya later! Can't wait!" they said to each other as they took off down the hallway.

"You coming tonight, Andy?" asked Greg.

Andy hesitated. He didn't want to sound uncool, but he didn't know what to say.

Info Splat

The Irish carved scary faces into turnips, beets, or potatoes and placed them in windows to frighten away wandering evil spirits. When Irish immigrants came to the United States, they found that the pumpkin, a fruit native to America, was larger and easier to carve.

What would you do if you were Andrew? Is it easy for you to rethink your standards? What does it take for a person to change their outlook and/or their actions?

October 26

~ Incredi-Biblical ~

The Lord is with me; I will not be afraid.
What can man do to me?
Psalm 118:6.

BIG TROUBLE

Lori scrambled atop her kitchen chair. "Look at that!" she screamed.

Luke followed her pointing finger and laughed. "It's just a mouse," he chided her. "Relax, I'll get something to shoo it out the door." He rummaged the kitchen closet and pulled out a broom, then went to the garage and got a box.

After some mad scrambling across the room, Luke managed to push the mouse out the glass doorway and back into nature. At that, Lori stepped down from the chair. "Thanks," she said. "I'm glad that the house is mouse-free!"

"I bet the mouse is happy too," Luke said.

Later he laughed about it with his buddies at football practice. "That mouse was so small, but Lori was so scared," he told Larry.

"Well, that's what big brothers are for," Larry reminded him.

Out on the field, Coach Ryan talked to the boys about the upcoming game. "Now, this team is tough," he told them, "but I know you can take them on."

The day of the game Luke's chest tightened as he watched the other team stride onto the field. They seemed huge. Suddenly he thought he knew how the mouse felt. "Gather round, guys," Coach Ryan told them. "We're going to pray before we begin."

Luke gulped hard and thought about how God had used David to defeat Goliath. *I may be small, like that mouse,* he thought, *but I have a Big Brother who will help me do my best.*

As he ran onto the field, Luke no longer felt afraid.

Info Splat
Cheese-eating mice (and humans) may not realize what they're tasting. Did you know that mold is part of what gives some cheeses their flavors? In fact, the blue in blue cheese is mold.

REACT NOW!

Do you ever feel that there is a problem that is too big for you to handle? Do you believe that God is powerful enough to take care of you?

Incredi-Biblical

[God's] perfect love drives out fear. 1 John 4:18.

THUNDERSTORM

Caroline woke to sounds of banging. Pulling her quilt up around her neck, she listened to the strange noises that seemed to come from upstairs.

BANG! CRASH! Now Caroline was fully awake. "What should we do, Cali?" she asked her cat. The orange-and-white calico lay next to her, purring, and peered at her from beneath sleepy, half-closed eyes.

From the next bedroom Caroline heard her dad's steady snoring. He was hard to wake from a deep sleep. She'd investigate this by herself.

Sliding out of bed, Caroline grabbed a pointy shoe and headed for the stairway. There she flipped the light switch, but nothing happened. She stood in complete darkness.

Gripping the shoe tightly in front of her, Caroline felt her way up the stairs. She jumped as Cali's tail brushed her leg. Finally Caroline reached the top of the stairway. In front of her, through the glass door that opened to the balcony, she saw flashes of light. Caroline stared at the door and then glanced around the room, listening carefully.

Nothing. No sound of movement. No shadowy figure waiting for her in the darkened room or hiding behind the sofa. No burglar.

It was just . . . lightning and thunder.

Caroline sighed with relief. She chuckled to herself and stumbled back down the stairs to her bedroom. Cali was waiting for her there.

Info Splat

Lightning heats air to more than 43,000° F. This hot air expands, then cools and contracts, causing air molecules to move and make sound waves that we call thunder. We hear rumbling noises because thunder from the top of the lightning stroke takes longer to reach us than thunder created near the ground.

What do you do when you are afraid? What does God say about fear?

October 28

INCREDI-BIBLICAL

But whoever listens to me will live in safety and be at ease, without fear of harm. Proverbs 1:33.

A POWERFUL PRAYER

Myrna, can I catch a ride with you to Bible school?" Adairys asked her friend.

"Of course," Myrna said.

Myrna, a missionary in Venezuela, uses her car to carry girls from their Christian school to neighborhoods where they teach Bible classes to children. She also takes students to churches, conventions, and youth rallies where they can encourage other young people to give their lives to God. She calls her car the Speed of Light vehicle.

Adairys, Elianny, and Sarai piled into the car, and soon they sped along the road to a program that was teaching children to pray. Suddenly the right front wheel dropped into a dip and pulled the car onto the shoulder. Yanking the wheel, Myrna veered back onto the road—into a lane of oncoming traffic.

"No!" Myrna cried, stomping on the brakes. The car flew to the right, turned upside down, and flipped before hitting the ground, bouncing up, and doing another half flip into the air. Finally the bumper hit a clump of trees, and the car dropped to the ground, flattening its left tires.

Amazingly, no one was hurt.

"I prayed to God and asked Him to protect us," Sarai told the others. "I knew that we had to rely on Him."

Myrna sold the banged-up car and used the money to buy another vehicle for ministry. Not only had God protected the group—He also provided a new car for His work to continue.

Info Splat

The speed of light, 186,282 miles per second, equals 671 million miles per hour.

REACT NOW!

What should we do first in an emergency? Does God always hear our prayers? Does He always answer the way we wish? Why, or why not?

INCREDI-BIBLICAL

Then Nebuchadnezzar said, "Praise be to the God of Shadrach, Meshach and Abednego, who has sent his angel and rescued his servants!" Daniel 3:28.

SOCCER MAYHEM

Chris and his dad sat on the edge of their stadium seats and watched the Mosi Cup finals, the championship game for the Zambian professional soccer league. At half-time an announcer told all the people in the stands to look under their seats for a piece of paper. Five papers invited fans onto the field to take a penalty shot against one of the goalkeepers. Out of the 30,000 people at the game, Chris was one of the chosen five. The prize was 50,000 Zambian kwacha.

A few tense moments later Chris won the kwacha. He and his dad left the field and went outside the gate to collect his prize. But when they tried to get in again, the gate was locked. The entrance guards would not let them back inside. Resigned, Chris and his dad watched the remainder of the game from outside the stands.

When the game finished, one of the men at the gate told them, "You better leave in your car now," and then walked away.

"Let's go," Mr. Ness told Chris. So they got back into their car and slowly wound their way through the crowded parking lot.

"Look, Dad," Chris cried out, pointing toward the stadium. A tumult had broken out inside. The teams had rushed toward each other, fighting, and people in the stands had joined in. Many of the soccer fans were injured, and, tragically, some were killed.

"Boy, God sure watched out for us, didn't He?" Chris said later.

Besides sports, another entertaining activity is celebrating Frugal Fun Day. Its inventors say, "Do one really fun thing that costs $5 or less. Free is even better." You could ride your bike, hike, picnic in the park, windsurf, or even knit. The possibilities are endless.

REACT NOW!

How has God watched over you and protected you from harm in the past?

When bad things do happen, how can you know God is still watching over you?

~ INCREDI-BIBLICAL ~

Ask and you will receive,
and your joy will be complete.
John 16:24.

THE POND

James Jacobson loved summer. No school, lots of free time, and swimming down at the town watering hole. He stuffed his towel in his bike basket and joined Jerry on the way to the pond.

"I can't wait to get into the water," James groaned as sweat trickled down his neck.

At home Mrs. Jacobson was cleaning the house. She frowned, suddenly feeling uneasy. "Lord, watch over the boys. Keep them safe," she prayed.

By now the two boys had reached the pond. It was quiet and deserted.

Jerry dropped his bike and ran to the water's edge. "Hey, James, let's see if we can throw a rock across the whole pond!" he exclaimed.

"OK," James replied, and began to hunt for just the right rock. "Found it," he called.

Jerry didn't reply.

James turned to discover Jerry lying on the ground, convulsing and grunting. His eyes were half closed, and he was biting his tongue. Rushing over, James turned Jerry on his side to protect his airway, then grabbed a towel and put it under his head.

"Dear God," James prayed, "please send help!" He looked frantically around him, not knowing whether to stay or run for help.

Next to James, Jerry rolled around noisily. He seemed to be having trouble breathing. James quickly cleared the area around his friend.

"It's OK, Jerry. You'll be all right. God will send someone. I know He will."

Just then a car pulled up.

"Thank You, God. Thank You," James whispered.

Info Splat

Epilepsy, a controllable condition caused by abnormal electrical activity in the brain, results in seizures like Jerry's. The condition is fairly common. If you or someone you know has epilepsy, it's good to know how to help in case of a seizure.

What did James do to help his friend? What do you do when things get scary?

~ INCREDI-BIBLICAL ~

Every good and perfect gift is from above, coming down from the Father of the heavenly lights, who does not change like shifting shadows. James 1:17.

THE RIGHT MEDICINE

Joseph stretched out his hand toward the small brown dog, hoping to pet it. He loved animals. But this dog had been acting oddly, walking in circles and yelping for no reason. Joseph knew that something was wrong with it, and thought that if he could pick it up and examine it, perhaps he could help.

At the moment his right hand touched the curly brown hair, the dog leaped at him and sunk his teeth into his skin. Joseph tried to pry the dog off, but before a passerby wrenched the dog from his arm he'd been bitten 14 times.

"My son!" cried Joseph's mother. She knelt beside her boy, watching helplessly as he moaned in pain.

"The dog has rabies," a man nearby said. Mrs. Meister's heart grew cold with fear. To be bitten by a rabid dog meant certain death.

"Bring the boy to Monsieur Pasteur's laboratory," someone told her. With help she scooped up Joseph and brought him to the French scientist's door, begging for assistance.

Louis Pasteur had a dilemma. He had the new vaccine for rabies, but it had been tried only on dogs. If the vaccine did not work, the boy would die, and Pasteur could be arrested for murder. If he did not try to save Joseph, the boy would die an agonizing death from rabies.

After much prayer, Louis decided to give the poor farm boy the vaccine. Joseph lived, and Louis Pasteur became famous.

Info Splat

The treatment for rabies used to be almost as scary to people as rabies' deadly symptoms, because it required a series of painful injections in the belly. Modern medicine has improved the method. It's not as painful, and injections no longer are done there.

REACT NOW!

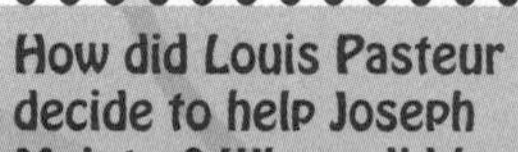

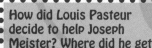

How did Louis Pasteur decide to help Joseph Meister? Where did he get his intelligence and gifts? What gifts have you been given that can be used to glorify God?

Incredi-Biblical

May God . . . give you a spirit of unity among yourselves as you follow Christ Jesus, so that with one heart and mouth you may glorify the God and Father of our Lord Jesus Christ. Romans 15:5, 6.

EARTHQUAKE!

Aaaaiiiieeee!" The woman screamed, running frantically into the street as her house shook, shuddered, then collapsed to the ground in a heap. Under her feet the ground bucked and heaved. With tears running down her cheeks the woman turned to a neighbor for comfort. But the other woman stood frozen in shock, staring at the space where her own house had stood minutes before. Two small children clung to her hands, wailing for their daddy.

In August 2007 reports from Peruvian Civil Defense authorities indicated the 7.9 earthquake had killed at least 510 people, injured more than 1,500, and destroyed nearly 17,000 homes, leaving 85,000 people throughout the coastal region homeless. But the massive quake had rocked more than the country's coastline. People from all over the world moved together to help the quake's victims.

Info Splat

Scientists estimate that there are 500,000 detectable earthquakes in the world each year. Of these, 100,000 can be felt, and 100 of them cause damage.

"There are families that are sleeping on the street . . . there are no water and electrical services. We have coordinated with the local authorities to bring timely assistance to the displaced," reported Victor Huamán, emergency response coordinator for ADRA/Peru.

In a statement from the Colombian Red Cross, David Pulido said, "We came here to carry out search and rescue, but sadly, we didn't find people alive under the rubble. Now we are working to provide basic health care and relief to families in Paracas and elsewhere," he added. "We are working as one big Red Cross team, no matter where we come from."

REACT NOW!

When have you felt the most united, or agreed, with someone else? Can you find unity with people when you disagree? Why does God value unity?

Incredi-Biblical

My covenant was with him, a covenant of life and peace, and I gave them to him; this called for reverence and he revered me and stood in awe of my name.
Malachi 2:5.

HEROES

"Yesss!" Amy squealed, jumping through the classroom door. "Guess what! Guess where I'm going for my birthday!"

Naomi gasped. "No way!" she hollered. "No way!"

"Yeah," Amy laughed. "I've got tickets for Jump In Boy!"

When the bell rang, they slid into their seats, still chattering about the upcoming concert. "My aunt sent me tickets," Amy whispered. "I haven't shown my parents yet."

Naomi frowned. "They'll let you go, won't they?"

"Sure!" Amy replied confidently. "I mean, I hope so. Sandy and Keet are my inspiration."

"Good morning!" Mrs. Hunt greeted the class. "Last night I asked myself this question: Who is your hero?" She paused. "You know, whether we admire someone who has some great moves on the court, a beautiful smile, or the power to make us feel good about ourselves, I believe God made us with the desire for a hero."

Amy grinned at Naomi. "I think I've found mine," she whispered.

"But when we find someone that inspires us," continued Mrs. Hunt, "it's up to us to take a closer look. Do our heroes deserve our adoration? Do they promote something that's good, true, and lasting? Do they care—I mean really care—about others? If the answer's yes, then great! They're pointing us upward. Now, you're going to write a short paragraph about the ultimate hero in your life."

As the class got to work, Naomi poked Amy with her pencil. "So?" she asked with a grin.

Amy wasn't sure how to answer.

Info Splat

Every year, Animal Planet accepts nominations and votes for Hero of the Year. The 2006 winner was Mona Rutger. She owns a center that rescues and cares for abandoned or injured animals. More than 60 percent of them return to the wild.

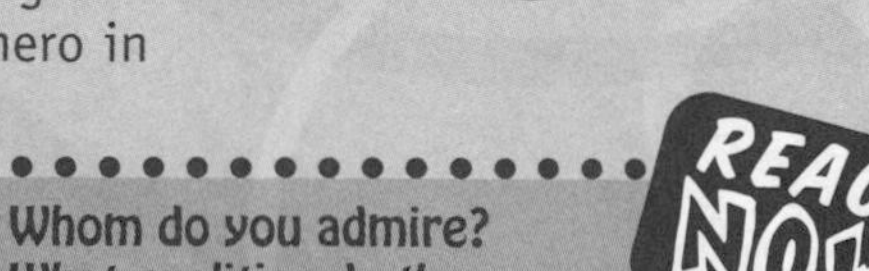

Whom do you admire? What qualities do they have that are worth imitating? Who is the ultimate hero? Why?

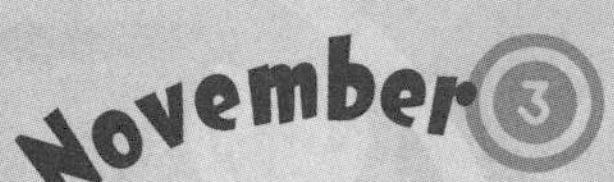

INCREDI-BIBLICAL

All kinds of animals, birds, reptiles and creatures of the sea are being tamed and have been tamed by man, but no man can tame the tongue. It is a restless evil, full of deadly poison.
James 3:7, 8.

SPEAKING OF HYDRAS

Go snorkeling in some fresh water, and you just might find the fastest draw in the West. The hydra, a small, jellyfish-like animal, can fire its stinging cells with surges as short as 700 nanoseconds that create accelerations of up to 5,410,000 g's.

If you're wondering how we can know this, it's thanks to the University of Heidelberg's new framing-streak cameras that run at 1.4 million frames per second. Scientists used these cameras in 2006 to capture for the first time the activity in the hydra's stinging tentacles, and discovered just how the jellyfish was able to penetrate crustaceans' shells.

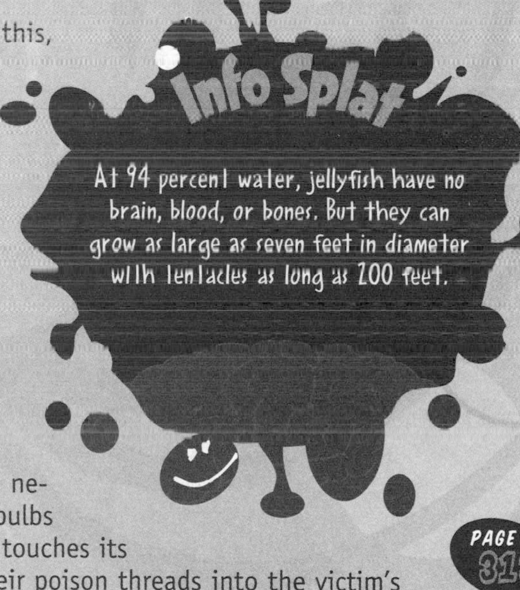

Info Splat
At 94 percent water, jellyfish have no brain, blood, or bones. But they can grow as large as seven feet in diameter with tentacles as long as 200 feet.

The hydra, at only one centimeter long, attaches itself to surfaces using a simple adhesive foot. At its other end is a mouth with tentacles covered with stinging cells. These cells hold structures called nematocysts, which look like miniature lightbulbs with coiled thread inside. When the hydra touches its prey, these nematocysts explode, firing their poison threads into the victim's body. The tiny hydra can take out its larger, crusty prey with energy that matches the velocity of a speeding bullet.

God has given us a power similar to the hydra's draw. Our tongues, or the words we say, can pierce even the crustiest shell. If we don't give our thoughts and words to God each day, our tongues can be as deadly as stinging cells.

REACT NOW!

If no one can tame the tongue, who can? How will you use your words today? Think of some ways you can use your words to help, not hurt, others.

INCREDI-BIBLICAL

**For the Lord takes delight in His people;
He crowns the humble with salvation.
Psalm 149:4.**

SEEING PAST PRIDE

Hannah rummaged through the boxes of eyeglasses and held up another pair. "Don't you like these?" she smiled half-pleadingly. The man shook his head. "Another," he insisted, looking at the glasses with distaste.

Hannah sighed. She wasn't sure she could find another pair to match the man's prescription. But she reached back into the nearest box to search again. Finally she gave up. She had picked through every box, and there were no more glasses that fit. "I'm sorry," she apologized. "You may choose one of these pairs." Disgruntled, the man finally decided on a pair of glasses and left the mission clinic.

That night Hannah told the group about her experience. "I thought people here would be grateful," she reflected. "They have so little. Instead, they're not much different from people back home. They're picky, and, I don't know, some of them are kind of rude." She felt frustrated and a little sad. "We came to help, but no one seems to want what we have to offer."

"Yeah," agreed Jeremy, "I don't get why someone who can't see wouldn't just be happy with clear vision. So what if the glasses look a little weird to them? Someone, once, wore them and must have thought they looked OK."

"Maybe it's deeper than that," Pastor Joe commented. "It's a hard thing to accept someone's help. Sometimes we refuse the assistance we require because we're too proud to see our great need."

"Or maybe just too vain," Hannah grinned. "Can we pray for that man?"

"Sure," agreed Pastor Joe. "And let's ask the Lord to give us glasses of love and understanding for these people, too."

Info Splat

When an eyeglasses lens breaks, the cracks in the glass move faster than 3,000 miles per hour. To capture this on film, a camera must shoot at a millionth of a second.

When have you let your pride get in the way of accepting someone's help? What's the worst that can happen?

November 5

~ Incredi-Biblical ~

You will seek me and find me when you seek me with all your heart. Jeremiah 29:13.

WHO DID YOU SAY YOU ARE?

The bell rings, and a flood of students rushes down the front steps. "Over there!" Tad points to the left. "Do you see him?"

You scan the faces, looking for your friend who is meeting you for soccer practice, but every face looks the same. "Help!" you scream, covering your eyes, your noodle legs collapsing underneath you. "I have prosopagnosia!"

Kids look nervously at each other and back away as they try to process the ginormous long word. You start to sweat, realizing you have the single defective gene that causes face blindness.

Imagine. Sufferers of face blindness, whether caused by a brain injury or heredity, deal with this symptom every day. They experience doubt and indecision in social situations, and find it hard to follow story lines on television since they can't distinguish between the actors. While they cope with prosopagnosia in different ways—finding other ways to identify people, making excuses, or staying away from large crowds—people with face blindness are left feeling unsure of who's who.

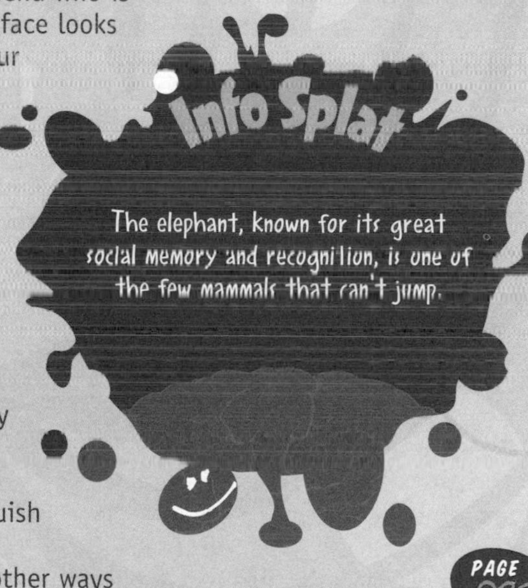

Info Splat
The elephant, known for its great social memory and recognition, is one of the few mammals that can't jump.

Aren't you thankful that God doesn't suffer from face blindness? Even with the billions of people living on earth, God could pick you out of a crowd in a heartbeat. He knows your face. More than that, He knows *you*. Every part of you is known by your Creator, and more than anything He longs for you to know Him, too.

REACT NOW!

Reflect for a few minutes about the hours Jesus spent on the cross. Did you know He would have came to earth and died only for you? How well do you know your Savior?

INCREDI-BIBLICAL

Do not seek revenge or bear a grudge against one of your people, but love your neighbor as yourself. Leviticus 19:18.

THE TROUBLE WITH NICK

Jared slumped low in his desk and glared at the back of Nick's head. *He just doesn't know when to stop!* he fumed. All morning Nick had been making jokes at Jared's expense, and Jared was sick of it. *The next time he tries something, I'm done.*

A pencil poked him in the shoulder. "Hey," his friend Heidi smiled. "Pencil sharpening fest. You in?"

"Sure," Jared said, handing Heidi his pencil.

Nick tipped his chair back and turned to Jared. "Thank you, Heidi," he smirked. "Did you say thank you to your girlfriend, Jared?"

Jared's jaw tightened. "You know, Nick, you're being a real jerk today." Nick looked surprised and started to say something, then turned back around and bent his head over his worksheet. A little ashamed, Jared remembered his teacher's words about respect.

"You have every right to talk with someone about his or her behavior," she'd said, "but name-calling is a low blow, the easy way out. Show some respect and speak in love."

After school Jared overheard Nick's mom talking with his teacher. "I hope Nick hasn't been too much trouble," she said. "Since his dad left last month he's been having a hard time with things."

A sick feeling settled in Jared's stomach. He wished he had dealt with the conflict in a different way. *Tomorrow,* he vowed, *I'll apologize. Nick is responsible for his own behavior, and so am I.*

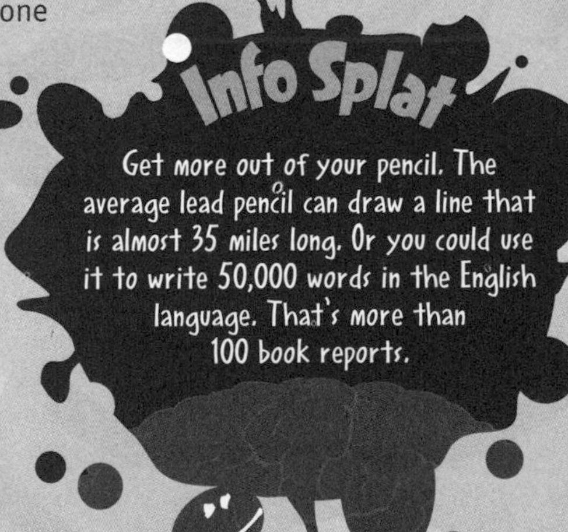

Info Splat
Get more out of your pencil. The average lead pencil can draw a line that is almost 35 miles long. Or you could use it to write 50,000 words in the English language. That's more than 100 book reports.

REACT NOW!

Make a poster with an acrostic of the word R-E-S-P-E-C-T. In what ways can you show respect for others today?

November 7

~ INCREDI-BIBLICAL ~

**The Mighty One, God, the Lord!
The Mighty One, God, the Lord! He knows!
Joshua 22:22.**

THE OTHER ALTAR

The Reubenites, the Gadites, and the half tribe of Manasseh packed up and headed for the land that God had given them on the other side of the Jordan River.

Soon word spread like wildfire through the Israelite camp. "They've built another altar of burnt offerings. And after all God has done for us!" they hissed. "That's it! We're preparing the army."

The next morning, the Reubenites, the Gadites, and the half tribe of Manasseh were surprised to see Israelite military delegates. "The entire congregation of God wants to know why you're breaking faith by turning your back on God and rebelling?" the delegates demanded. "Don't rebel against Him or against us by building your own altar apart from the altar of our God."

The men gaped at the Israelites, then cried, "Our Mighty God knows our hearts! He'll let Israel know if this is a rebellious betrayal. But that's not it. We built this altar as an altar of unity. This way, your children won't be able to say to our children in the future, 'The Lord made the Jordan a boundary between us and you have no part in Him.'

"There's no way we want to rebel against or turn our backs on God by building an altar other than the altar of our God that stands before His tabernacle," they told the Israelites.

What an about-face for the Israelites' attitudes! Happily, and probably a little sheepishly, they returned back to their camp.

Info Splat

The Israelites were understandably upset. Rebellion against God is a serious thing. But some other laws just don't make sense. In Singapore it's illegal to chew gum. In San Francisco you can't pick up and throw used confetti. And a law in Missouri states that a man must have a permit to shave.

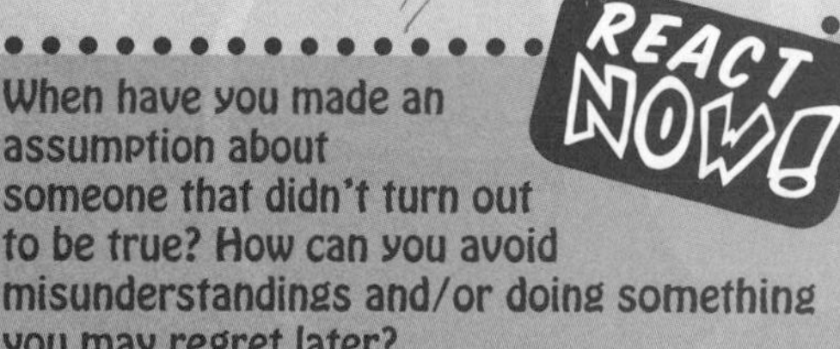

When have you made an assumption about someone that didn't turn out to be true? How can you avoid misunderstandings and/or doing something you may regret later?

INCREDI-BIBLICAL

Whoever welcomes one of these little children in my name welcomes me; and whoever welcomes me does not welcome me but the one who sent me.
Mark 9:37.

INVISIBLE CHILDREN

In the street behind her stretched a long line of students. She saw dreadlocks and freckles and backpacks and water bottles. She saw wide eyes and felt the excitement of action rippling through the crowd.

One night. One several-mile hike. She and many others had walked from all over to sleep at this spot—the green across from the city's capitol building.

An ocean away, children in Uganda lived in fear that a rebel army would kidnap them while they were sleeping and force them to be soldiers. Each day they hiked miles into towns and slept on porches, on cement floors, crammed together in small spaces where they would be safe. She wanted people to know, to notice, and to do something to keep the Uganda children safe.

"Look at all the people!" she heard someone whistle. *Yeah,* she thought, *just a fraction of the thousands of Ugandan kids that must do this every day.*

Her group shuffled toward a booth where volunteers handed them T-shirts that read "Invisible Children." Then she posed for a Polaroid shot in front of the grass, where more people were spreading out tarps and sleeping bags.

"Here's some paper for your letters to the president and senators," a girl with a bandanna told her. "Thanks for coming out."

I'm just one person, she thought. But she knew one thing. If each person she saw writing letters for the Ugandan kids had thought that, the lawn would be empty.

Info Splat
Although most nongovernment organizations say that 200,000 to 400,000 people have been killed in Darfur, the Sudanese government claims that only about 9,000 have died.

REACT NOW!

Find out more about the invisible children by visiting www.invisiblechildren.com.

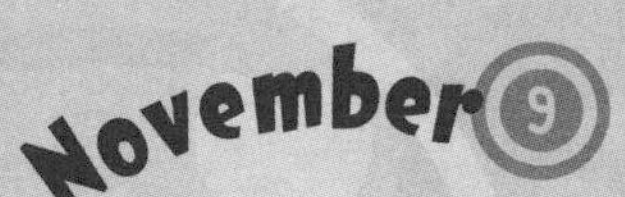

INCREDI-BIBLICAL

He went on: "What comes out of a man is what makes him 'unclean.'"
Mark 7:20.

UNCLEAN!

"My favorite thing to grill is pork," Paul grinned. "Pork ribs in my aunt's sweet and sour sauce . . . yum!"

"Eww, gross!" Marcia exclaimed. She wrinkled her nose as Paul told the class about his family's summer barbecues in Maine. Marcia's family was vegetarian, and she didn't understand why anyone would want to eat anything that had lived and breathed. *Plus,* she thought, *the Bible tells us not to eat pork. It's unclean.*

The class applauded as Paul sat down, and soon it was Marcia's turn to tell about one of her family traditions. "Every July," shared Marcia, "our family finds another family who needs food or clothing or something like that, and then we give them a Christmas in July." She glanced over at her teacher, who smiled and nodded. As Marcia finished and sat down to her friends' applause, she noticed her classmates looking at her, impressed. She felt a warm glow of pride.

At lunch Marcia and Jessie talked about Paul's barbecues. "I would never eat pork," Marcia declared. "It is so disgusting. How can people eat that kind of stuff?"

Jessie shrugged. "There are worse things than eating pork," she said.

"Yeah?" Marcia said. "Yuck. I can't think of much." Finishing her cheese sandwich, she threw her trash away. The warm glow of pride she'd felt earlier was starting to burn.

Info Splat

Pigs are rated the world's fourth most intelligent animal. Many years ago sea captains kept pigs on board because they believed, if shipwrecked, pigs would always swim toward the nearest shore. Today in Denmark there are twice as many pigs as people.

What does God say about pride? Grab a concordance and look up ***PRIDE, PROUD,*** and ***HUMBLE*** to find out.

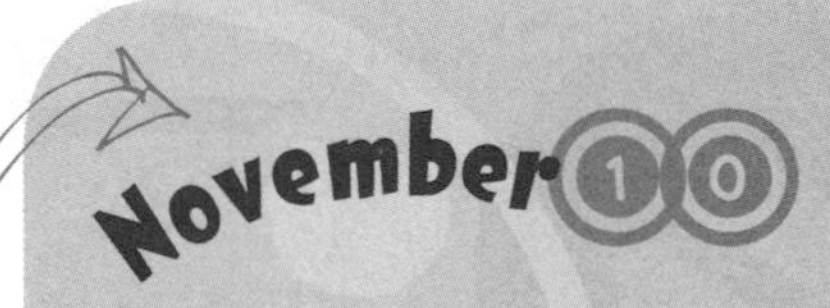

~ INCREDI-BIBLICAL ~

Who, being in very nature God, did not consider equality with God something to be grasped, but made himself nothing, taking the very nature of a servant.
Philippians 2:6, 7.

ANTS ON THE MARCH

If you crouch to peer at a jungle floor, you'll see thousands of tiny ants busily scurrying along the ground. Ants are some of the strongest and most hardworking creatures God created. Each day ants join their colony neighbors in collecting food, moving dirt, and scouting out new territory. In a day's work they often lift 50 times their own weight! But ants demonstrate more than industriousness and muscle power. Inside the South American army ant, God places a servant's heart.

When the colony of army ants goes to work each morning, their commute is anything but smooth. Imagine driving down a highway with car-size potholes, and you'll know something of what ants find when they travel—gigantic cracks and holes.

If every ant in the long line fell into these holes and climbed back out, it would slow down the entire colony. Instead, when an army ant spots a pothole, it immediately tries the hole on for size. If the hole is bigger or smaller than its body, it pops back out and scurries on. If the hole's a match, the ant spreads out its legs and waits, plugging the hole. Sometimes army ants will even cooperate to plug a large hole. And there they remain, patiently enduring the hundreds of ant feet tramping over their backs. When the ants sense the end of the line, they climb out to catch up with the rest of the group.

These plugger ants may not be hoisting food, but researchers have found that when these creatures stop to serve, the colony's overall food intake shows a clear gain.

Info Splat

Myrmecology, the study of ants, has found that for every human in the world, there are 1 million ants. A leaf-cutter queen ant mates only once, but is able to produce as many as 300 million offspring.

When have you stepped aside for someone else? How did it make you feel?

November 11

~ Incredi-Biblical ~

For our struggle is not against flesh and blood, but against the rulers, against the authorities, against the powers of this dark world and against the spiritual forces of evil in the heavenly realms. Ephesians 6:12.

DEMON TROUBLE

They'd just dropped off to sleep when the pounding on their hut door jerked them awake.

"Teacher! Come quick!"

Tana and her husband, Jon, hustled out of bed and opened the door. A pinched face peered up at them, eyes wide and fearful. "We're with you," Tana reassured the girl in Spanish. "Let's go." Clasping hands, they hurried away from the hut toward the girls' dormitory. Light from the windows made yellow squares on the ground in front of them, but the small group felt a strange darkness pressing in, slowing their pace.

Finally they reached the dormitory. Inside they found Anna, one of Tana's students who'd recently decided to be baptized. Her face was pale; her hair clung to her forehead in wet ringlets.

"Anna," Tana said, kneeling down beside the girl. "What is wrong?"

Anna simply mumbled and groaned. Jon, feeling an evil, otherworldly presence in the room, dropped to his knees and began praying for Anna. "Lord Jesus," he pleaded, "please keep Anna in Your arms. Fight for her."

As Jon prayed, Anna began to shake. Tana held the girl in her arms and joined Jon in prayer. "Help us, Jesus!" Tana cried. "Dear God, You have all power over Satan and his angels. In Jesus' name we tell these demons to leave! Anna is Your child, bought with Your Son's blood. Thank You for Your great love and mercy. Don't let Satan touch her."

Slowly Anna's shaking subsided and her groans quieted. She opened her eyes. "Jesus, You saved me!" she whispered.

Info Splat

"Those who follow Christ are ever safe under His watchcare. Angels that excel in strength are sent from heaven to protect them. The wicked one cannot break through the guard which God has stationed about His people." Ellen White, ***Maranatha***, p. 130.

REACT NOW!

Even though you can't see your heart beating, it's there keeping you alive. Compare this with the forces of good and evil.

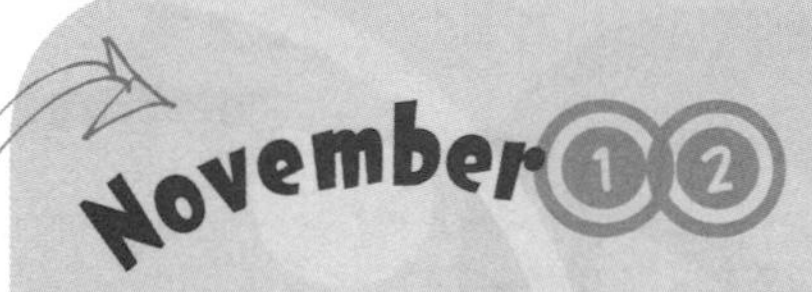

~ INCREDI-BIBLICAL ~

How good and pleasant it is when brothers live together in unity! Psalm 33:1.

THE LIGA HISPANA

Falta!" the referee shouts. "Foul!"

The action on the court freezes, leaving one player bouncing the basketball, hard, on the concrete. He looks for an open teammate who will grab his pass from the sidelines and take the ball down the court.

Swoosh! The ball is back in play, and the two teams grapple again for the next point. Basketball is about winning, but here in Seattle, in the *Liga Hispana,* it's also about community and support.

The 24-member Latino basketball league brings together Seattle's Mexican community. It links people who are new to the United States with those who have been here for a while. The court is a place where wives gather to talk about the best places in town to buy tortillas and where kids play together and snack on such favorite Mexican foods as *elotes,* ears of corn smothered in mayonnaise. The league is a place for Mexican immigrants to learn a new language and to find leads on jobs. A few years ago at least 200 *émigrés* came to the courts to hang out every Sunday.

If you think about it, that Seattle basketball league isn't that far off from our church. When the disciples started meeting together after Jesus went back to heaven, they hung out for many of the same reasons. They came together to support each other, to find the best places in town to share the good news, and to learn the new language of love that Jesus had been trying to teach.

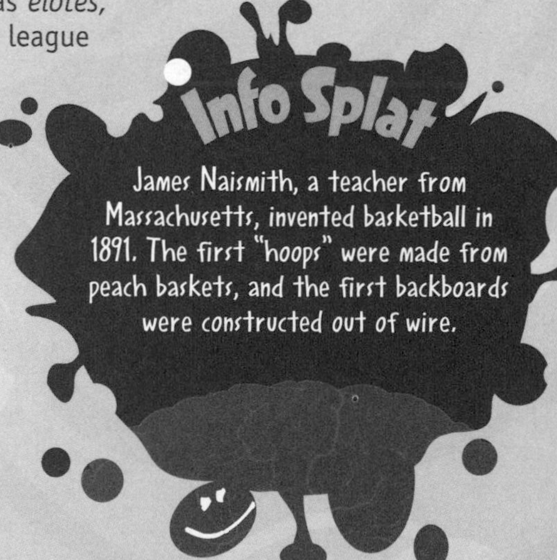

Info Splat
James Naismith, a teacher from Massachusetts, invented basketball in 1891. The first "hoops" were made from peach baskets, and the first backboards were constructed out of wire.

REACT NOW!

Read about the church in the book of Acts. How are things different today? What specifically can you do to help make your church a place of support?

November 13

~ INCREDI-BIBLICAL ~

David thought, "I will show kindness to Hanun son of Nahash, just as his father showed kindness to me."
2 Samuel 10:2.

THE BOOK THAT KEPT ON GOING

Wow," Lynne exclaimed, sliding a book to Tori. "You have to read this!"

"Really," Tori said. She picked up the library book and frowned. "What are you going to do to me if I don't?"

Lynne grinned. "OK, you don't *have* to read it. But it's really good."

So Tori did, and the next week she passed it on to Eric, who recommended it to Ulrich, who praised it so highly to Mark that Mark's dad was the last to hear about it. He was the last, at least for a while, because the book disappeared into his study and didn't come out for a few weeks.

Finally one Sabbath morning Mark saw the book again. It was sitting beside his dad's Bible. "Dad!" Mark cried. "I've been looking for that for weeks! It's way overdue!"

"I'm afraid it's my fault," admitted Dad. "I've been reading it off and on ever since you gave it to me. What a powerful story! I was so encouraged by it. Then God impressed me to write it into my sermon this week."

Info Splat
If you do something good for three people, and they each help three more people, and those three each help three more people, five good deeds later 2,187 people will have been touched.

After church Mark stood beside his dad in the church foyer. "That story touched my heart," said elderly Mrs. Patterson so softly that Mark could barely hear her. "I'm going to share it with my children."

Mark looked up at Dad. "It just keeps going, doesn't it?" he asked.

Dad smiled. "Sure does, son, as long as we're willing to share it."

REACT NOW!

What if, like Lynne, you don't see the results of your sharing? Think of a time in your own life when you've experienced gifts that keep on giving.

INCREDI-BIBLICAL

The wind blows wherever it pleases. You hear its sound, but you cannot tell where it comes from or where it is going. So it is with everyone born of the Spirit. John 3:8.

WIND POWER!

"Catch that wind!" the ship's captain screamed to his crew. Muscles bulging, the Egyptian sailors strained to pull the sails into place. But when the wind finally snapped open the sails and pushed the vessel along the river, it wasn't because the sails had caught the wind. They'd simply hung from their masts and waited for the wind to fill them up.

Like the ancient Egyptians, people have used the wind's energy from the beginning of time. In Persia the world's first windmills were built and used to grind wheat and other grains. Later Hollanders improved the windmill's design. Today wind energy is huge in such places as California and Montana, where windmills generate electricity. As other energy suppliers—like oil—run low, people look to alternative sources.

It's a little tricky to harness the wind, though. Like a wild horse or a hungry gorilla, the wind is unpredictable. And like the facial expressions you sometimes see on your teacher's face, wind can be hard to understand. Where is it coming from? And what is it going to do? After all, the wind is a powerful force. It can whip up water, uproot trees, and topple buildings. Yet it also evaporates floodwaters. And on a boiling-hot summer day, wind dries the sweat dripping from your upper lip and cools you off.

Jesus said the wind reminded Him of a life led by the Holy Spirit (John 3:8). You'll be amazed at what can happen when you follow history's example and harness the power of the Holy Spirit in your own life.

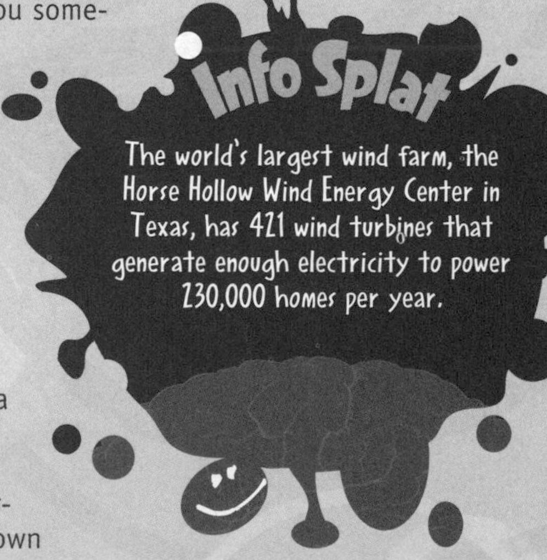

Info Splat
The world's largest wind farm, the Horse Hollow Wind Energy Center in Texas, has 421 wind turbines that generate enough electricity to power 230,000 homes per year.

REACT NOW!

What other things does Jesus compare the Holy Spirit to? Use your Bible concordance to find some answers.

November 15

~ INCREDI-BIBLICAL ~

These words you hear are not my own; they belong to the Father who sent me. John 14:24.

VERONICA'S NEW BUSINESS

Never give up hope; never give up your dreams. It doesn't matter if you don't have a dime or a cent to your name; never ever, ever, give up. And always remember where you come from."

Veronica listened as her father spoke. She sat, watching him take alabaster and turquoise stones and sculpt them into "beautiful swirls of design." Often her father, a firefighter and tribal policeman in the Zuni Pueblo, collected stones so he could make a little extra money by selling the carvings. Veronica knew he sculpted stones to help his family survive.

Then, when Veronica was just 10 years old, her father died fighting a fire in a nearby town. Her family was devastated. In addition to losing *him*, they struggled, without Father's income, to put food on the table. Veronica had to do something. With the help of some neighbors who taught her more advanced techniques, the girl began sculpting stones the way her father had.

Info Splat

Natural diamonds are formed deep underground, at least 93 miles under the earth's surface. There, the heat and pressure are great enough to squeeze carbon atoms together to make the diamond's crystal structure.

Eventually people noticed her designs. Veronica, now grown, moved to California and kept carving. Living in a new place gave her new ideas, and she found her sculptures improving. After several years Veronica moved back to Zuni Pueblo and opened her own gallery. She uses it for others as well, giving local artists a chance to showcase their work.

Now a stone sculptor whose work the New York *Times* calls "outstanding," Veronica Poblano uses her father's words to inspire others.

REACT NOW!

How can you, today, go about your Father's business? Look for a way that you can share His words with others.

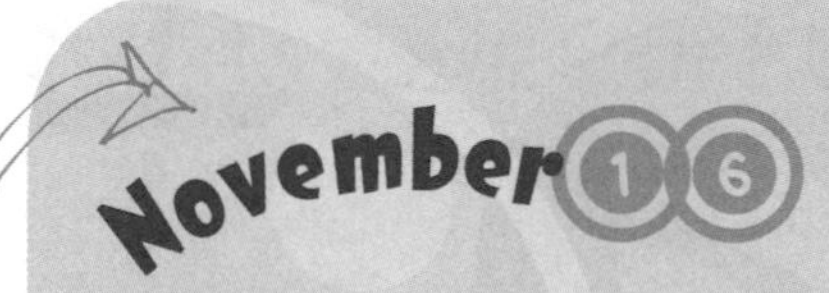

INCREDI-BIBLICAL

Therefore, my brothers, I want you to know that through Jesus the forgiveness of sins is proclaimed to you. Acts 13:38.

FILL UP ON FORGIVENESS

"Mom!" Hollie screeched. "Cassie got into my stuff *again*!" Her face brewing thunderclouds, Hollie stomped out to the kitchen where her mom was making dinner. Rounding the corner, she stopped. There stood Cassie, clinging to Mom's jeans, lip quivering.

"I'm sorry," Cassie cried. "Forgive me?"

Hollie just glared. "I've had enough! Mom, she won't quit, and I don't care if she's sorry. My forgiveness tank is empty on this one."

Mom picked up Cassie and looked thoughtfully at Hollie. "I think you're right," she said.

Surprised, Hollie asked, "What?"

"You're right. Your tank is on empty. And you're not the only one. I feel that way too sometimes, and so did a guy named Peter."

"Oh," said Hollie. "I know what you mean. He thought forgiving seven times was enough, right? Then Jesus told him to forgive seven times seven."

Mom nodded. "Peter thought seven times was plenty, because back in Moses' day, that was a number associated with cleansing. But God's ways are far greater than our own. Jesus may have remembered the verse in Daniel that talks about God giving the people "seventy-sevens," or 490 years, to stop their evil ways. He let Peter know that for us to be like Him, He's willing to refill our mercy and forgiveness tanks over and over."

After thinking for a minute, Hollie smiled. "Since Jesus can forgive me, I know He'll help me forgive you, too, sissy. Here, let's find something to play."

Info Splat

In the Old Testament, if someone damaged your eye, you could be compensated by damaging theirs (Exodus 21). At the time that was a lesser punishment than other laws gave. But Jesus said, "Do not resist an evil person. If someone strikes you on the right cheek, turn to him the other also" (Matthew 5:39).

REACT NOW!

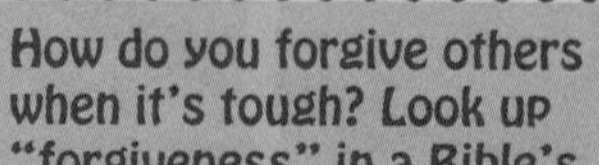

How do you forgive others when it's tough? Look up "forgiveness" in a Bible's concordance and share what you find.

November 17

~ Incredi-Biblical ~

This is how we know what love is: Jesus Christ laid down his life for us. And we ought to lay down our lives for our brothers. 1 John 3:16.

PLANTS THAT PLAY FAVORITES

It's true that plants don't have brain functions such as memory, but scientists have recently discovered evidence of selfless concern in plants, at least when it comes to members of their own family. Although animals (including humans) often recognize and prefer family, this is the first time plants have been known to favor kin!

Researchers from McMaster University in Canada have found that plants get aggressively competitive when potted with "strangers" of the same species, but actually assist "family member" growth.

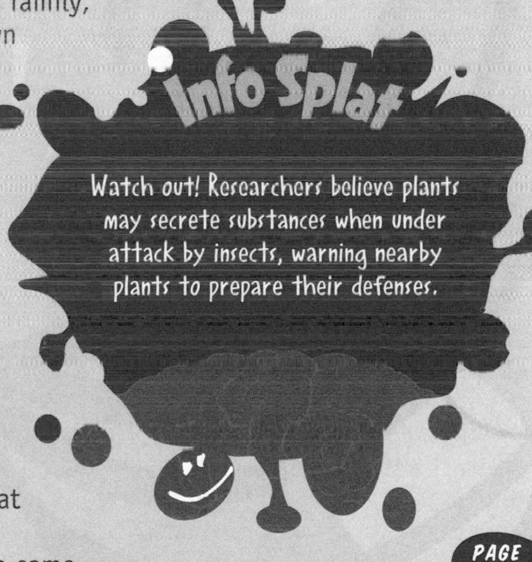

Info Splat
Watch out! Researchers believe plants may secrete substances when under attack by insects, warning nearby plants to prepare their defenses.

After experimenting with sea rocket, a member of the mustard family, here's what the researchers discovered. If you put two "stranger" plants in the same pot, the plants increase their root growth. It's as if they're saying, "Hey! Grow, grow, grow! Get the extra nutrients and water before that other guy knows what hit him!"

However, if you put two plants with the same "mother plant" in the same pot, the family members are content. They don't grow extra roots. Instead, they take the nutrients and water they need, leaving the rest for their sibling. Sweet, isn't it?

It doesn't always work out that way among family members. Often those we're closest to get treated the worst. But in these sea rocket plants, you can see God's ultimate plan for His family: all His children working together and looking out for each other.

REACT NOW!

What does the phrase "the family of God" mean to you? What about people who aren't Christians? Is God their heavenly parent too?

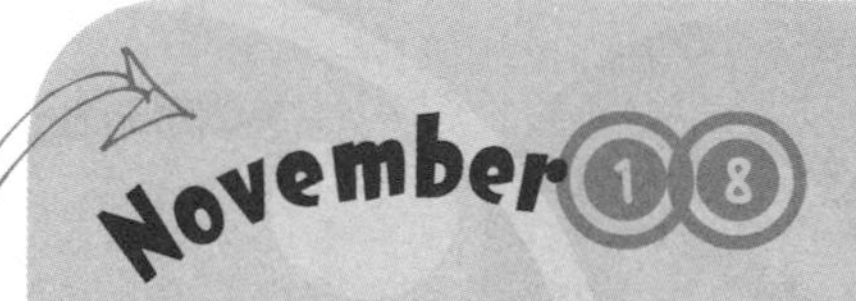

∘~ INCREDI-BIBLICAL ~∘

Praise be to God, who has not rejected my prayer or withheld his love from me! Psalm 66:20.

PRAYER FOR A GENERATOR

Chris yanked with all his might, but the generator didn't even sputter. What was the deal with this thing? He felt himself growing frustrated. Wiping sweat from his forehead, he stepped back to let the pastor have another try.

The rest of the group stood in twos and threes, worriedly talking and praying. The generator was their only power source for the church's lights, and they had another meeting there tonight. Surely God hadn't led them this far to let the darkness stop them.

Still nothing. Pastor Abi swiped his hands on his pants. "Chris," he said, "you give it another try." The sturdy boy took the whipcord in one hand, placing the other on the machine. *Come on, you dumb thing,* he thought. *Work with me*. With a forceful tug, he tried to make the motor turn over. Silence.

Then Pastor Abi laid his hand on Chris's shoulder. "You know, I have a feeling God has planned this moment just for you." Chris wondered what he could mean. He wasn't even sure if he believed in God. But Pastor Abi continued, "I'm going to pray now, Chris, that God will fix this generator. But not for me, and not for the meetings tonight. I'm going to pray that He will do this so you can see His power and care for *you*."

After a few simple words, the pastor said "Amen," and motioned for Chris to try again. The loud rumble of the generator was the sweetest sound he'd ever heard.

Info Splat

Running a generator outside is no problem, but inside it can lead to deadly carbon monoxide poisoning. Carbon monoxide, an odorless, colorless, tasteless gas, kills more than 500 Americans each year.

REACT NOW!

When have you seen God working in your life in a powerful way? What can you do to hear His voice more clearly in your life?

November 19

~ Incredi-Biblical ~

The Lord had said to Abram, "Leave your country, your people and your father's household and go to the land I will show you." Genesis 12:1.

HOPE IN BOSTON

God called Abraham to leave the city of Ur. He asked Ruth to leave the country of Moab. And He told Pastor Gerald Bell, a corporate banker, to leave his suburban home and become a minister.

Pastor Bell's story makes us wonder if thankfulness is more than saying thank you. Gerald Bell, a banker, enjoyed golf and many of the other "finer" things in life. Then, as he tells it, several years ago God spoke to him, calling him into the ministry of saving souls. Bell talked to his wife, Cynthia, and after hearing him out agreed that this was a call from God. So Cynthia and Gerald moved with their two children to one of Boston's toughest neighborhoods.

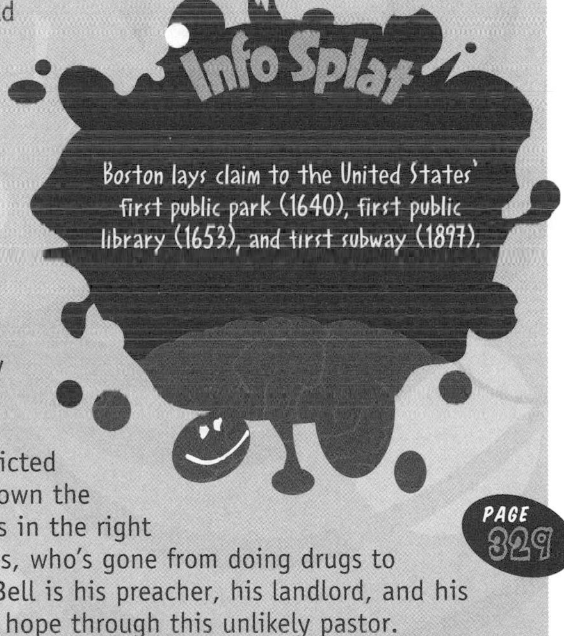

Info Splat
Boston lays claim to the United States' first public park (1640), first public library (1653), and first subway (1897).

There in the inner city, Bell's ministry grew. He's still a banker during the day, but nights his heart and the doors of his church are open to drug dealers and convicted criminals. He's been shot at. He's faced down the barrel of a gun. Yet Pastor Bell knows he's in the right place. He helps men like Carmen Christmas, who's gone from doing drugs to owning a barbershop. To Carmen, Pastor Bell is his preacher, his landlord, and his friend. Carmen thanks God for giving him hope through this unlikely pastor.

"This is where I'm from, and this is where God has placed me," Pastor Bell says.

REACT NOW!

Who in your life has given you hope? Why don't you thank them for it today?

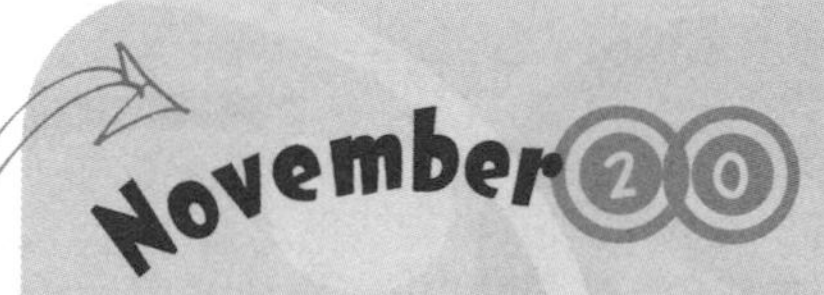

Incredi-Biblical

For I am the Lord, your God, who takes hold of your right hand and says to you, Do not fear; I will help you. Isaiah 41:13.

A BULLY NAMED WILL

David?" Mom called down the hallway. "Weren't you going to go for a run tonight? It's almost dark."

David glanced up from his book and craned his neck to look out the window. Sure enough, the sun was already sliding behind the trees. "I'll go tomorrow," he called back, wanting to finish the chapter.

But when morning came, all David wanted to do was grab a few extra minutes of sleep before his shower. The run would have to wait, and so would breakfast, since he'd slept in so long. School wasn't much better. David had forgotten his lunch, and mooching off his friends' unwanted food left him with a gurgling stomach. Then, as he hurried to class, he realized he hadn't finished his English assignment. "Oh, no," he groaned.

Later, when he complained about his awful day to his teacher, Mr. Braykneee gave him a long, serious look. "H'mmm," he said. "It sounds as though you're suffering from a weak will."

"I am?"

"I believe so. You know what needs to be done, but your will is like a flabby muscle. The part of you that chooses to do something that's best for you in the long run gives in too easily to the bully who says, 'Wait till later.'"

"The bully, huh?" David grimaced at the thought.

"Yep. That mean dude's name is Mr. Flesh. He's tough, and he fights to kill, but once you use your will as God directs, he's a goner."

"Thanks," David laughed as suddenly he got it. "I can't live like this much longer."

Info Splat

"The real greatness and nobility of the man is measured by the power of the feelings that he subdues, not by the power of the feelings that subdue him" (Ellen White, *Testimonies*, vol. 4, p. 656).

REACT NOW!

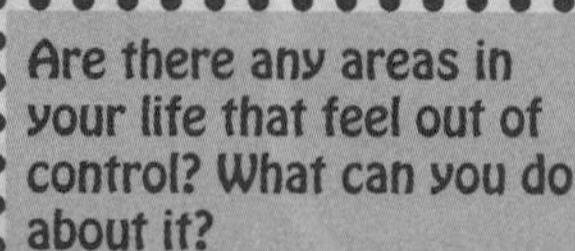

Are there any areas in your life that feel out of control? What can you do about it?

November 21

~ INCREDI-BIBLICAL ~

So when the Samaritans came to him, they urged him to stay with them, and he stayed two days. John 4:40.

A DEADLY WART

Prejudice is like an ugly wart. If you've ever had a wart, you know what I mean. Warts are painful, reoccurring bits of dead blood vessels, and they can spread like crazy. The best way to get rid of a wart is to understand it and to take action. Sometimes medicated Band-Aids work well. Other times, you can kill the wart only with a doctor's help.

During the Civil War many soldiers fought to kill the dreaded wart of prejudice, and thousands of Americans lost their lives in the fight for free skin. The worst losses came on Antietam battlefield in Maryland. If you go there today and stand by Burnside's Bridge, you can still see the foxholes where determined Georgians held off the Union army. It's hard to imagine that on September 17, 1862, the now-peaceful river and hills swarmed with men in uniform.

Info Splat

You want to kill off a wart? Try bananas! Cut a piece of banana skin and rub the wart with the inside of the peel. Then tape the banana skin in place. Do this every day (or night) for as long as it takes. The wart should get mushy, and you can slowly scrub or pick it off. This doesn't always work, but it has for many people, so it's worth a try.

The most monumental wart-fight ever fought, though, took place more than 2,000 years ago. Look! Do you see Him? It's Jesus, going right to the root of our prejudices against God and each other.

Ever look down on someone poorer than you? Read about the widow in Mark 12:41-44. Do you struggle with skin color or ethnicity? Remember how Jesus praised the good Samaritan and hung out with an outcast woman at Jacob's well.

Jesus wants to help you fight this battle, too. Can't kill the wart? Call on the Master Healer.

In what other places in the Bible does God teach us about prejudice?

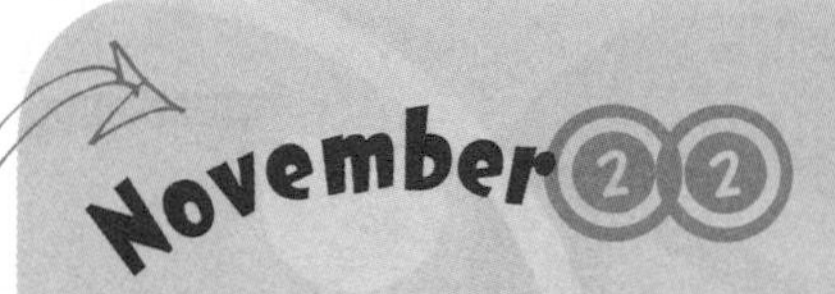

~ INCREDI-BIBLICAL ~

"For my thoughts are not your thoughts, neither are your ways my ways," declares the Lord. Isaiah 55:8.

WEIRD AND UNEXPECTED!

There is a lot of weird news out there.

Take, for instance, the story of the man who was in a coma for much of 19 years. He awoke slightly sometime during those years and vaguely remembers some of the family celebrations he was taken to during that time. Imagine how you'd feel if you fell asleep tonight and didn't wake up until 2028! When a train hit Polish citizen Jan Grzebski in 1988, doctors gave him only two years to live. But almost two decades later Jan woke up to a non-Communist country, nonrationed food, and cell phones. The first face he saw? His wife's, who cared for him all through his coma.

Then there's the pod of dolphins that protected swimmers from a great white shark. At first the swimmers thought the dolphins were attacking them. Then they spotted the shark cutting toward them. For 40 minutes the dolphins formed a protective barrier around the swimmers until the shark decided to take off.

Did you hear about the 25-year-old shipping clerk from New York? Charles McKinley decided to visit his parents in Texas by shipping himself the 1,500 miles—in a big box. He traveled by truck, plane, and delivery van before being deposited in his parents' driveway. What did Charles get for his trouble? He was arrested, and detained for a while at the sheriff's department. You see, it's not legal to ship yourself.

God specializes in the unexpected too. After all, His Son was born from a virgin, one of His missionaries was swallowed (and spit up) by a huge fish, and in a short time from now, He'll be coming back in the clouds of heaven. With His help, we can be ready for that awesome surprise.

Info Splat

The loudest noise ever heard was made by a volcanic eruption at Krakatoa, near Indonesia, in 1883. The sound was heard in Australia, approximately 3,000 miles (5,000 kilometers) away.

REACT NOW!

How have you seen God work in unexpected ways in your own life? What are some things you can do to be ready for His return?

November 23

~ Incredi-Biblical ~

O Lord God, you are God, and your words are true, and you have promised this good thing to your servant.
2 Samuel 7:28, NRSV.

CAN'T TRUST THAT GRANDMA!

"Noooo, Grandma!" shrieked Emma as the older woman pushed on the back of the recliner, pulling it toward the floor. Emma clutched the arms of the chair, feeling herself tip backward. She knew her grandma wouldn't drop her on purpose, but she'd seen her thin arms and wasn't sure how much weight they could hold.

"I'm not going to drop you," Grandma insisted, but Emma jumped out of the recliner before Grandma could pull it back any farther.

"I'm sorry, Grandma," she said sheepishly. "I know you wouldn't mean to, but . . ." Her voice trailed off and she grinned, trying to make her grandmother feel better.

Info Splat

Does that guy smell a little fishy to you? Researchers have discovered that smelling the hormone oxytocin makes people more likely to trust others to look after their money.

If you've ever participated in a "trust fall," in which you stand up above a group of people and fall backwards into their arms, you've experienced a little taste of faith. You can't see behind you, but you let go and trust that your friends will catch you.

It can be tough. Of course, it's a lot easier when you know the people behind you. When you know their strength and are sure of their care for you, it's not so bad to free-fall.

Faith and trust are built through relationships. The more you get to know God, the more you'll see that He will never let you down. His arms are strong. His love for you is everlasting.

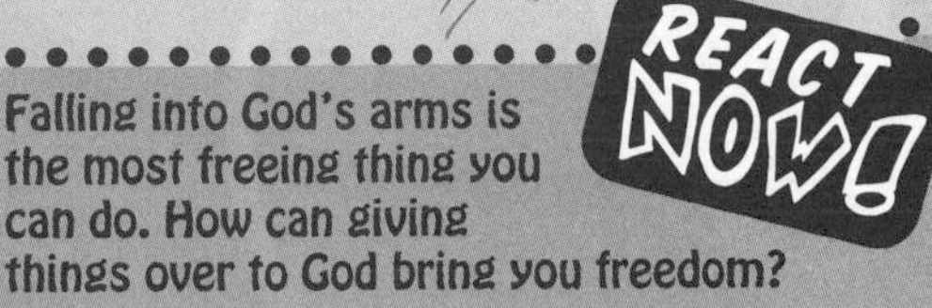

Falling into God's arms is the most freeing thing you can do. How can giving things over to God bring you freedom?

~ Incredi-Biblical ~

Then he gives the command and it all melts; he breathes on winter—suddenly it's spring! Psalm 147:12, Message.

HALO EFFECT

A study in 2007 revealed that there might be more to icebergs than previously thought. (Yep, our knowledge of earth really is just the tip of the iceberg.) Scientists have discovered that free-floating icebergs are ocean oases for a surprising number of creatures.

The researchers found that animals such as seabirds, phytoplankton, krill, and fish find their dinner around the icebergs. And then, as the ice melts, trapped terrestrial material inside the bergs is slowly released into the ocean. If you're a fish, it's like finding a snack shop in the middle of the sea.

The icebergs cause a halo effect, as the creatures spread out around them in a radius of more than two miles. This area can be quite large, especially with bergs as big as a dozen miles long and 120 feet high, stretching down to 10,000 feet underwater. These floating islands of ice have a major impact on the ecology of the ocean around them.

It's amazing that something so cold and hard becomes a center of life in the middle of the ocean. But it is not too different from the change that takes place in your heart when you open up to Jesus. In Ezekiel 36:26 God says, "I will remove from you your heart of stone and give you a heart of flesh."

That's one miracle melt you can share—in a halo effect—with others.

Info Splat

One large Antarctic iceberg, if melted, could supply the whole city of Los Angeles with water for five years! Icebergs may not seem too huge from the surface, but remember, 90 percent of an iceberg is underwater. Ships beware!

REACT NOW!

How can you tell if your heart is flesh or stone? This is a good topic for discussion. Have you ever, seriously, known someone with a "heart of stone"?

November 25

~ Incredi-Biblical ~

From the fullness of his grace we have all received one blessing after another. John 1:16.

A NEW LIMBER FOR LORI

Lori gripped the broom handle and attacked the mess of leaves on the courtyard floor. What a mess! She briefly looked around the school, trying to assess the damage from the tropical storm. A few trees down, a flooded classroom, and lots and lots of leaves. Not too bad.

She knew the other teachers were grateful that the storm hadn't been worse. Several years before, Hurricane George had hit the island of Puerto Rico hard. Tropical Storm Jeanne was mild in comparison.

Pulling her hair up into a ponytail, Lori realized she was thirsty. *I should get some water,* she thought. *Or one of those icy* limbers*!* The school's snack shop carried slushies, and soon all Lori could think about was the taste of one.

Then one of the cooks came around the corner, smiling at the student missionary sweeping the leaves into piles. Looking up, Lori saw a *limber* in her hand. "Here," the cook said. "Would you like one?"

"Gracias," Lori said with a big grin. She licked the sweet cherry ice, then squeezed the paper cone for a bite. The ice wouldn't budge. *Urg,* thought Lori, squeezing harder. Slowly, the ice shifted, then—*splat!* The entire slushie flew out of the cone and landed on the ground.

"Oh, no," groaned Lori. *That would have been so good. Oh, well. I guess I'll have to wait for another day to eat a* limber.

"Sorry," she heard the cook say a few moments later. In her hand, the cook held a brand-new *limber*!

Info Splat

When a tropical storm's winds hit at least 74 miles per hour, it becomes a hurricane, and hurricanes are powerful. In one day they make enough energy to power the United States electrically for six months.

What way has God shown you grace this past week? Think of a situation in which you can show mercy to someone else.

INCREDI-BIBLICAL

Jesus answered: "Don't you know me, Philip, even after I have been among you such a long time? Anyone who has seen me has seen the Father. How can you say, 'Show us the Father'?" John 14:9.

MICHAEL'S BRIGHT IDEA

The Hispanic family in the emergency room didn't speak English, but they needed help badly. How could they explain their son's condition to a nurse or doctor who knew only a couple of words in Spanish?

Just then a nurse rushed over, carrying a large picture board. Icons covered both sides of the board, and as the mother looked, she excitedly found the ones she needed to describe what was wrong with her son.

You may have heard mission stories about teachers and preachers who carried picture boards with them into faraway lands. Through these pictures the people, who didn't understand their language, learned about the God who loved them.

Or perhaps you've met someone who may not speak the same language as you, but with whom you can communicate using pictures and gestures. And if you have deaf friends, or if you are deaf, you may use sign language to share ideas.

The medical picture boards, developed by Michael Weston, make communication in emergency situations easier. Michael came up with the idea after Hurricane Andrew when he saw the large number of people who didn't get help because of communication problems. As of 2007 the boards were in almost every state in the United States.

God, too, sent a picture board of sorts to this world. In Jesus you have a clear picture, in your language, of the God who longs to spend eternity with you.

Info Splat

Spanish, the official language in 21 countries, is the first language of about 330 million people worldwide. Around 100 million others speak Spanish as a second language.

REACT NOW!

In what ways does Jesus speak your language? Bonus read: See God's picture gift by reading ***THE DESIRE OF AGES,*** by Ellen White.

November 27

INCREDI-BIBLICAL

Jesus said, "Father, forgive them, for they do not know what they are doing." Luke 23:34.

GOOD ANGER

Fist so tight
Knuckles white
Mind on fire
Down to the wire

Andy's anger spilled onto the page as his pencil made bold marks in the spiral notebook. His knee jiggled underneath the desktop; his mind flashed away from English class and back to the ball field.

He could hear his little brother crying long before he rounded the corner of the school building and he ran out, heart pounding, onto the field. He saw no one but Noah, heard nothing but his buddy's sobs. Noah's shirt was torn and his nose was bloody.

"Who did this to you?" Andy grilled him. Noah wouldn't answer.

Info Splat

Uncontrolled anger can give you high heart rate and blood pressure, difficulty breathing, back and head pain, and sweating. You may find it hard to concentrate, or feel depressed or worried. However, anger can be positive when controlled and directed in a healthy way.

That night Andy tossed and turned. *God, are You listening? Noah is the sweetest, most innocent person I know. How could you let this happen to him?* he shouted silently. *What kind of God are You? Couldn't You do anything? So why didn't You?*

Now, in class, Andy's jaw tightened. *I know You can handle my anger, God,* he prayed again. *I get that You've given us the freedom to choose, and I know You give it to everyone, even the ones who hurt Noah. Please help me deal with these feelings.*

A few weeks later a teacher on yard duty caught the kids harassing Noah. As Andy saw the group sitting in the principal's office, he realized he felt only sadness for their choices. *Thank You, Lord,* he thought, grateful that God had changed his attitude.

REACT NOW!

Why do you think God chose to give us freedom of choice? What would you have done if you were in Andy's place?

~ INCREDI-BIBLICAL ~

They went out at the head of the army, saying: "Give thanks to the Lord, for his love endures forever." 2 Chronicles 20:21.

THE BATTLE CHOIR

Begin!"

The armored soldiers circled each other, jabbing and thrusting, ducking and dodging, trying to find the other's weak spot.

"Huuuh!" A sword pierced through armor, and the victor raised his arms in triumph.

"Done!" An instructor strode over to the men. "Take a break," he ordered. "Fresh soldiers fight better than worn ones."

The men strode toward a crowd clustered around a crudely drawn map in the sand. One man mumbled something and pointed.

"Reviewing our plan?" their general asked, joining the group.

Just then a messenger burst into the practice arena. Perspiring, he stopped and rested his hands on his knees, trying to catch his breath.

"Water," called the general. Turning to the messenger, he asked anxiously, "What news?"

"Change of plans," the man gasped, gulping down the skin of water he'd been offered. "Won't be needing these men in front."

"What?" The general stopped short. "Why not?"

"King's putting the choir in front," responded the messenger. "The singers will lead."

"Singers?" the general echoed. He laughed. "Joke's over. What else do you have for me?"

"It's true, my lord. While your company of men was off sharpening their swords, the rest of Judah was at court, listening to the king. We're going to win! God sent a prophet to tell us that the battle is in His hands. Then King Jehoshaphat ordered a choir for the front ranks. We'll march out praising God, sir."

As the men of Judah marched to battle, God set up ambushes for their enemies and confused them so that they fought with each other. When Judah's army reached their enemies, they found only dead bodies. No one had escaped.

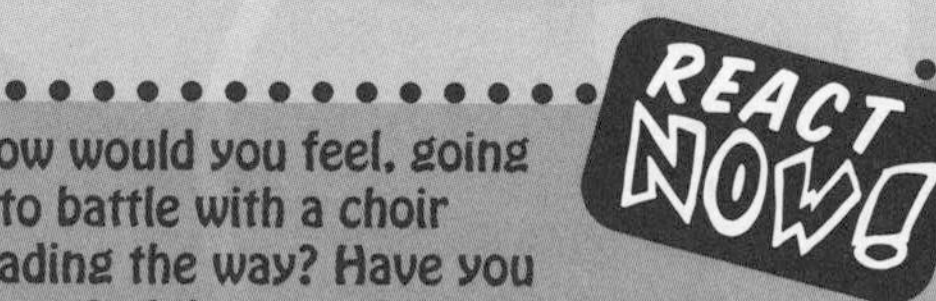

How would you feel, going into battle with a choir leading the way? Have you seen God do something like this in your life? Why would He?

November 29

~ INCREDI-BIBLICAL ~

They will be my people, and I will be their God. I will give them singleness of heart and action. Jeremiah 32:38, 39.

JUST DO SOMETHING

"Class, please line up for recess," the teacher called. Jodie lifted her head but continued to straighten her desk. Matt did a cartwheel across the room. Chris was still typing.

"Atrocious," mumbled the teacher. "Boys and girls," she called again, "This is not acceptable. Please line up now."

Nicholas crumpled a piece of paper and threw it at the trash can. "Score!" he shouted. Over in the corner of the room Heather and Liz played with matches.

"That's enough," the teacher said again. "If you're not in line in 10 seconds, we'll skip recess today."

Five minutes later she was still waiting, hands on her hips, by the door. "Hurry, class!" she said again.

Maybe you've known someone like that: much talk and little or no action. You may find it easy to let things slide because, well, they do too.

In 2007 world leaders met to discuss an urgent situation in Darfur, an area in Sudan, Africa. While trying to defeat rebel movements, the government of Sudan had wiped out entire villages. Direct violence, disease, and starvation claimed approximately 400,000 lives. In all, about 2.5 million Darfurians fled their homes to seek refuge in camps and other countries. Another 1 million still lived in fear of bombings, torture, and other horrible crimes. Appalled, the United States labeled Darfur a genocide.

But for all the promises and threats to Sudan's President al-Bashir, no consistent behavior had taken place. A news report put it this way: Silence was not killing Darfurians. Inaction was.

Info Splat

Ask a friend to copy you. They must listen closely and watch your actions. If you tell them to wave, touch their chin, and touch their forehead, but you wave, touch your chin, and touch your ***NOSE***, odds are that they will touch their own nose.

Have you found yourself "talking the talk" but not "walking the walk"? What can you do about it?

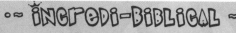

~ INCREDI-BIBLICAL ~

I can do everything through Him who gives me strength. Philippians 4:13.

A FUNERAL FOR "I CAN'T"

The first and second graders at the school where I teach recently attended a funeral service for one of their classmates. He'd been a very popular member of their class, but one morning they learned of his passing. Solemn and silent, they trooped outside to an open field and gathered around the gravesite as their teacher read the eulogy. It went something like this.

"Friends, we are gathered here this morning to bury the memory of I Can't. I Can't was with us for a long time, and he was especially present when things were difficult. He affected the way we did things, the way we lived, and the way we worked. It is not easy to let go of I Can't, but it is time for us to move on. I Can't is survived by his brothers, I Can and I Will, and by his sister, I'm Doing It Right Now. Although his siblings are not as well known, we hope they will become more important as time goes on. Today we lay I Can't to rest. By the grace of God, let us all try to get on with our lives without him. Amen."

The students gravely lowered I Can't into the ground, whispering their good-byes. Then they marched back inside just in time for handwriting class, to which one said, "I can do it!"

Info Splat

True tombstone epitaphs for your funny bone:
*Here lies a man named Zeke.
Second-fastest draw in Cripple Creek.

*Looked up the elevator to see if the car was on the way down. It was.

*See, I told you I was sick!

REACT NOW!

What can't you do? Make a list of your "I Can'ts" and give them a proper burial. Then write down some goals and the steps you'll use to reach them. Ask Jesus to help you reach them, and go for it!

~ Incredi-Biblical ~

The blood of Jesus . . . purifies us from all sin. 1 John 1:7.

A PROVEN CURE

"I hate being sick!" Eric wailed. "Why is it with all those brilliant scientists out there, they can't find a cure for the common cold?"

There's an answer to Eric's question. Scientists and doctors know that hundreds of different viruses cause colds. When you have a cold, your body produces antibodies to fight the infection. Once you recover, your body still remembers how to fight that particular infection and you'll be protected against it. The next time you get a cold, it's probably a completely different virus.

Info Splat
If you have a cold, you probably have as many as 100 million individual cold viruses mutating in your throat and lungs.

That's why there's no vaccination to prevent a cold. You can get a flu shot that protects you from the three most common flu viruses—and with only three to five flu viruses floating around every year, you're pretty safe. But there's no one vaccine that can protect you from all the hundreds of different types of cold viruses circulating all the time.

Sin is a little like the common cold. It comes in many different forms, and it's everywhere you look. As long as we're born on this sinful earth, there's no vaccine that will prevent us from getting contaminated with it. But unlike the common cold, there *is* a treatment to cure all the symptoms of sin—including its most severe symptom: eternal death. The treatment is Jesus. Apply Him to your system today!

REACT NOW!

Does sin ever feel like a sickness to you? Do you really want to be "cured" from it?

INCREDI-BIBLICAL

For we are God's fellow workers.
1 Corinthians 3:9.

TONY'S WILD RIDE

Tony was selling Christian books in Naples, Italy, shortly after World War II. One day his supervisor said, "Tony, I'd like you to attend the annual meeting of Christian booksellers in Florence this year. You'll need to take the train."

Soon Tony found himself standing at the train station in Rome. The young man's heart dropped when he realized that even the third-class seating area was full.

"I must get to that meeting!" he told himself. I guess I'll just have to ride on the outside of one of these train cars. With that, Tony swung up onto a narrow area on the outside of a nearby passenger car. Moments later the train whistle blew, and Tony embarked on the ride of his life.

At one stop along the170-mile (275-kilometer) route, another man climbed up and hung on next to Tony. "How far are you going?" he asked.

"All the way to Florence," Tony replied.

"What do you do?"

"I sell books," Tony explained.

"What kind of books?"

Tony thought, then said, "I'll show you." Silently he asked God to give him strength to hold on with one hand while he retrieved his samples and told the man about each book.

"I like these books!" the other hanger-on said. "I want to buy this one!" So Tony, still desperately hanging on to the outside of the train, sold the man the book. He wasn't sure if anyone in Florence would believe his story, but that wouldn't stop him from telling it!

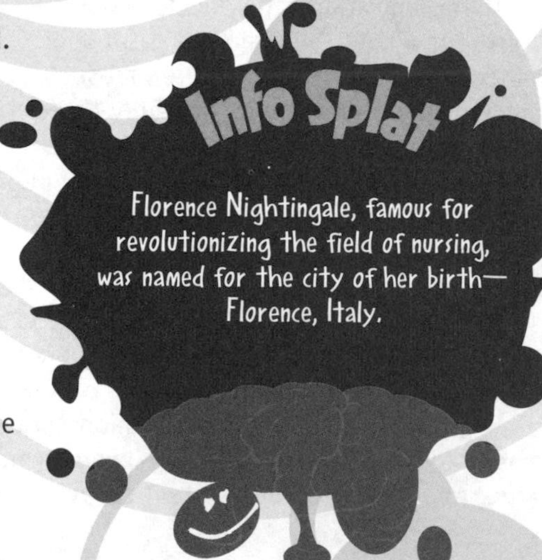

Info Splat
Florence Nightingale, famous for revolutionizing the field of nursing, was named for the city of her birth—Florence, Italy.

REACT NOW!

If you could sell or give a Christian book to someone right now, who would that person be? What book would you want them to have? How can you make that happen?

December 3

~ INCREDI-BIBLICAL ~

I have chosen the way of truth;
I have set my heart on your laws.
Psalm 119:30.

CASH IN THE TRASH

Nine hundred dollars in the garbage! For one person it was a tragedy; for another it was the discovery of a lifetime.

Kim Bogue, who worked as a janitor in the civic buildings in Santa Ana, California, accidentally threw away her wallet with her lunch. The wallet contained $900 in cash as well as Kim's credit cards, and she was devastated. She looked and looked for the missing wallet, even praying that God would help her find it. She was saving up for a trip back to her home in Thailand, and the loss of several hundred dollars made a big difference to her.

Meanwhile, a homeless man searching through the trash for recyclable cans and bottles came across the remains of Kim's lunch—and her wallet. It's pretty much guaranteed that a homeless man could find a good use for $900. But he didn't keep it for himself, even though he needed the money. Instead he brought the wallet to someone who worked in a nearby building and asked if she could find the owner.

The wallet found its way back to Kim Bogue, who gave the homeless man a $100 reward. Her prayer was answered. But what about the homeless man?

His story was covered in the newspapers, but the man didn't want anyone to know his name. He preferred to stay anonymous. He just did what he believed was the right thing to do.

Info Splat

Up to 842,000 adults and children are homeless in North America in any given week. As many as 3.5 million people may be homeless over the course of a year.

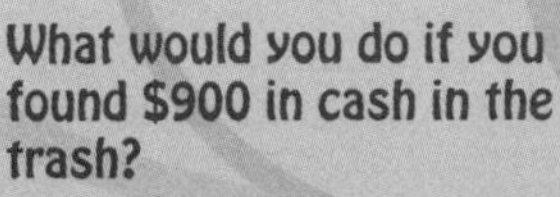

What would you do if you found $900 in cash in the trash?

December 4

~ INCREDI-BIBLICAL ~

Today, if you hear his voice, do not harden your hearts. Hebrews 4:7.

WHEN TIME RUNS OUT

"Ryan! Come down and get ready for school, please."

"Just a minute, Mom!"

Five minutes later the same voice drifted up over the stairs. "Ryan! It's time to come down and get your shoes and jacket on for school!"

"I'll be right there!" Ryan called. He was building a Lego model, and he had just a few more pieces to add.

"RYAN! We have to leave *right now* if we want to get you to school on time!" This time Mom sounded really angry. "Get down here *right this minute!*"

Ryan left his model and grabbed his sweatshirt from the bed. "You don't have to yell, you know. I was *coming,*" he grumbled as he hurried over the steps. "Why are you always so mad at me, Mom?"

In the Bible we read that God will judge the wicked when Jesus returns to the earth. Some people say, "Why is God so angry? Why does God destroy the wicked? I thought God was a God of love."

The fact is that God gives everyone many, many chances to know His love and to follow Him. But sooner or later time will run out. It's not that God has stopped loving, but that people have made their choice to follow Him or not. Someday this world will run out of chances.

Will you choose to love and follow Jesus while He's still calling you?

Info Splat

The largest Lego ship ever built was a model of the U.S.S. *Harry S. Truman*, built by German Malle Hawking and displayed in Denmark in 2006. It weighed 352 pounds and used 300,000 Lego bricks.

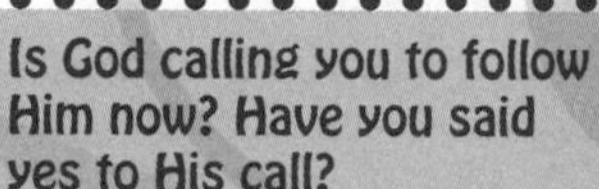
Is God calling you to follow Him now? Have you said yes to His call?

REACT NOW!

PAGE 344

~ Incredi-Biblical ~

I counsel you to buy from me gold refined in the fire, so you can become rich. Revelation 3:18.

GOLD STRIKE!

"Gold!" The miner gasped. He bent over, catching his breath. "Gold!" he shouted. "I found gold!"

In March 1848 workers discovered gold at a California mill owned by John Sutter. At first the news didn't stir up much interest. But within weeks people from all over California were rushing to the gold fields, hoping to get rich.

On December 5 of the same year, U.S. president James Polk confirmed its discovery. In his State of the Union address he told the whole country that there was gold in California.

Over the following months, waves of immigrants from all over America and the rest of the world flooded to California. The "Forty-Niners" were all looking for gold and expecting to make their fortune. Some did; many didn't. There was no easy way to get to California in 1849. Whether traveling by ship below and around South America or overland across the U.S., the journey was long and dangerous. Many people died on the way.

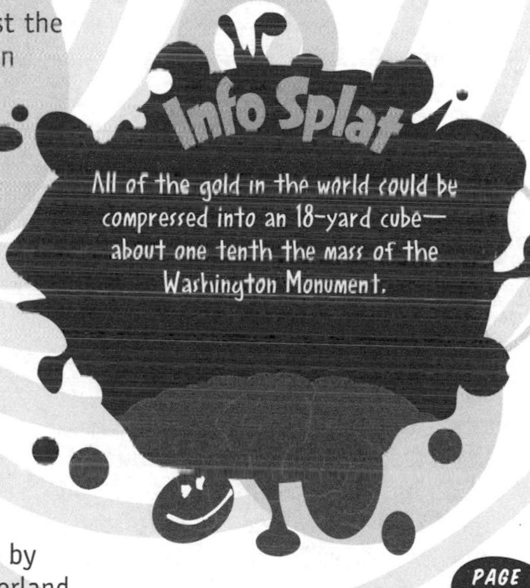

Info Splat
All of the gold in the world could be compressed into an 18-yard cube—about one tenth the mass of the Washington Monument.

Gold has always been considered one of the most valuable and precious metals. In the Bible gold is sometimes used to represent a person's character that has been made pure and holy by God's Spirit.

If every Christian was eagerly hurrying to develop a character just like that of Jesus, that would be a gold rush worth joining!

REACT NOW!

Do you believe God can make gold out of your life? Are you willing to give Him control and let Him do it?

Incredi-Biblical

Therefore, as God's chosen people, holy and dearly loved, clothe yourselves with compassion, kindness, humility, gentleness and patience. Colossians 3:12.

A NEW EXTREME SPORT

"Extreme sports" are popular with all kinds of people. Whether it's mountain climbing, bungee jumping, or snowboarding, some people are always ready to take on a challenge that will get their heart pumping a little faster.

But what about . . . extreme *kindness*?

Could being kind to people be an extreme sport?

Brad Stokes, Val Litwin, Erik Hanson, and Chris Bratseth think so. The four young men from British Columbia got together a few years ago to begin doing "random acts of kindness" for strangers. They were partly inspired by Brad's mom, who died of cancer. The terrorist attacks of September 11, 2001, also encouraged them to take kindness to extreme levels. "We wanted to be the change we wanted in the world," Chris Bratseth says.

In 2002 the group took "extreme kindness" on the road, with a cross-Canada tour in which they talked to people about the power of kindness. They also worked at a soup kitchen, spent nights on the streets with homeless people, took senior citizens shopping, and went swimming in the cold to help a swim team raise money for a trip out of the country.

The Extreme Kindness crew encourages young people to find things they are passionate about, and then use those passions to help others. They believe kindness really can change the world.

Info Splat

The term ***EXTREME SPORTS*** was first used in the late 1980s and early 1990s to refer to sports such as hang gliding, scuba diving, rock climbing, and bungee jumping. The term was made more popular because of the X Games, a series of made-for-TV extreme events.

Think of one act of "extreme kindness" you could do for someone today—and do it!

December 7

~ INCREDI-BIBLICAL ~

As for God, his way is perfect; the word of the Lord is flawless. 2 Samuel 22:31.

OFF-KEY KARLA

Karla and her three friends were going to sing in church for the first time. They'd been practicing their song for weeks. Mrs. Bradley, the school music teacher, had helped them pick a song and learn it, and she had run through it with them again and again.

The four girls gathered in the earliteen Sabbath school room for a last practice between Sabbath school and church. They had worked so hard on the song. It just had to be perfect.

At last they stood behind the pulpit, and Mrs. Bradley played the opening chords. All four girls started to sing. Almost immediately Karla knew something was wrong, but she didn't know what until she noticed Jenni shooting a sideways glance at her. Then it hit her. She was singing in a different key from all the others!

Info Splat
About 1 in 10,000 people has perfect pitch.

Karla stopped singing, waited a minute, and joined in again—this time on-key. But when the high note came in the chorus, her voice cracked and went off-key again. Looking down into the congregation, she was sure she saw a couple of the guys covering their mouths to hide a laugh.

"That's it! I'm *never* singing in public again!" she announced as soon as church was over.

Her mom offered a hug. "You know, making mistakes can be embarrassing, but it's not the worst thing in the world," she said. "Nobody's perfect. Mistakes happen to everyone. What really matters is what you do next."

REACT NOW!

What do you think Kara's mom meant? What do you "do next" after you make a mistake? What's a good way to respond when you feel embarrassed?

December 8

INCREDI-BIBLICAL

Have you entered the storehouses of the snow or seen the storehouses of the hail? Job 38:22.

ARE YOU A SNOWFLAKE?

If you see snow this winter—or even if you just imagine it—think about the often-mentioned fact that no two snowflakes are exactly alike. Of course, it's impossible to check every snowflake that's ever fallen to be sure that no two are alike, but because their structure is so complex, it's highly unlikely that any two complex snow crystals could ever be identical.

The life of a snowflake begins high above the ground, in a cloud. Water vapor starts to condense on the surface of an ice crystal, and it turns into a six-sided prism—a hexagon.

As the crystal grows, branches sprout from each of the six corners of the hexagon. As the temperature changes within the cloud, the shape of the branches, or arms, changes over time. But all six arms grow at the same rate and in the same way, so the snowflake remains perfectly symmetrical. Since each snow crystal follows a different path through the clouds, each one ends up looking different.

You and I are like snowflakes. Each one of us is created unique by our Creator. We each follow a different life path and are shaped by our experiences. We are all different, yet all beautiful and valuable in God's eyes.

Info Splat

Each individual snow crystal is clear. But in a group they look white, because so many surfaces are reflecting back the light that the light has scattered, and appears white.

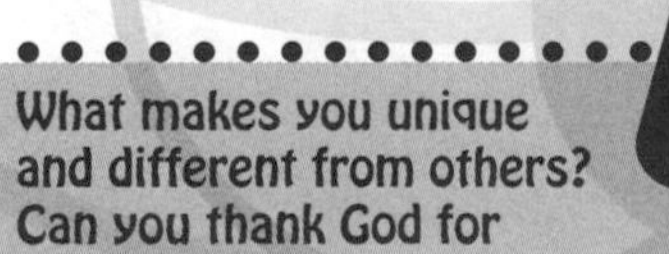

What makes you unique
and different from others?
Can you thank God for
making you that way?

REACT NOW!

~ Incredi-Biblical ~

If any man builds on this foundation using gold, silver, costly stones, wood, hay or straw, his work will be shown for what it is, because the Day will bring it to light. It will be revealed with fire, and the fire will test the quality of each man's work.
1 Corinthians 3:12, 13.

AMY GOES TO INDIA

Amy stared in the mirror and sighed. "Mother, I wish I had blue eyes!" she said for the hundredth time.

"The good Lord gave you brown eyes," Mother said simply. "He knew what He was doing."

Amy was the oldest of seven children. Her family lived in a small village in Northern Ireland in the late 1800s. Her family were dedicated Christians, and Amy wanted to serve God in some way.

At age 20, when Amy heard the great missionary to China, Hudson Taylor, speak, she became convinced that God had called her to be a missionary. Sadly, she was often sick and bedridden for weeks at a time—an unlikely candidate for overseas service—but she held on to her dream. She went to Japan for 15 months, then to India where she found her life's work.

Info Splat
Many people believe that Christianity was originally brought to India by Thomas, one of Jesus' apostles. Ancient traditions describe "Doubting Thomas" as the first missionary to India.

Amy Carmichael founded an orphanage and a mission in Dohnavur, India. As she worked among the dark-haired, brown-eyed people of India she was often thankful that her childhood prayer for blue eyes hadn't been answered. If she'd been blue-eyed, it would have been even harder for the people of India to accept her. Her brown eyes, she decided, were all part of God's plan.

Amy lived in India until her death at the age of 83. At her request, instead of a headstone on her grave, the orphanage children put up a birdbath with the word "Amma," which means Mother.

REACT NOW!

Today's Bible verse is one that inspired Amy Carmichael when she was young. What do you think God is building in your life?

INCREDI-BIBLICAL

For if you forgive men when they sin against you, your heavenly Father will also forgive you. Matthew 6:14.

TURKEY TRAGEDY

Throwing a 20-pound frozen turkey out of the rear window of a speeding car . . . Is that *your* idea of a good time?

To 18-year-old Ryan Cushing, it sounded like a cool practical joke. To 44-year-old Victoria Ruvolo, it was a tragedy. Victoria was driving on the freeway when the turkey hit her windshield, shattering the glass, and breaking every bone in her face.

Although surgeons had to rebuild her face using metal plates and screws, things could have been even worse. The impact was so serious that doctors said it could have caused lasting brain damage for Victoria. Even so, she had a long recovery.

Ryan Cushing, who was horrified at the result of his careless act, faced a charge of first-degree assault. He could have served up to 25 years in prison. But one person argued for a lighter sentence—Victoria Ruvolo.

In court Ryan Cushing wept, repeating again and again to Victoria, "I'm sorry."

"It's OK," she said as they hugged. "I just want you to make your life the best it can be."

Ryan was sentenced to six months in jail, with probation and psychological counseling.

A careless act can have consequences we could never imagine. It might even destroy someone's life. But an act of kindness and forgiveness can change a life.

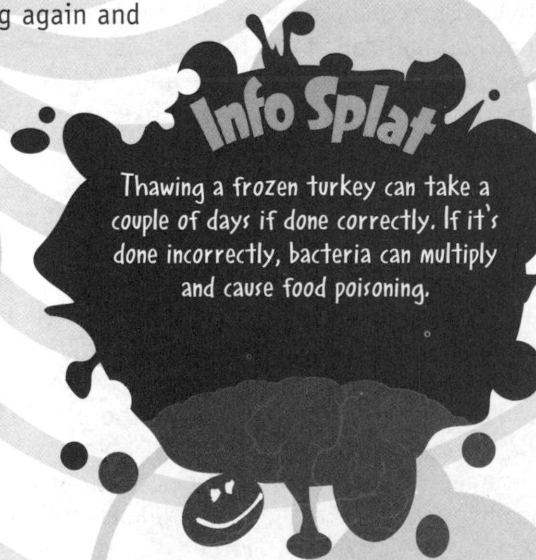

Info Splat
Thawing a frozen turkey can take a couple of days if done correctly. If it's done incorrectly, bacteria can multiply and cause food poisoning.

REACT NOW!

Have you ever done something that had far more serious consequences than you ever expected? Were you forgiven?

INCREDI-BIBLICAL

The acts of the sinful nature are obvious . . . jealousy. . . . I warn you, as I did before, that those who live like this will not inherit the kingdom of God.
Galatians 5:19-21.

NO SMALL ACTORS

Chandelle's dad pulled the car up in front of the church. "See you in an hour," he said. When Chandelle didn't move, he added, "Is something wrong? Don't you want to go in?"

Chandelle shrugged. "Kinda hard to get excited about practicing for the Christmas musical when I've got such a stupid part."

"What do you mean, a stupid part? There aren't any—"

"I know." Chandelle rolled her eyes. "There are no small parts, only small actors, right? Seriously, Dad. You know I should have had the part of Mary. I can sing better, *and* I'm a better actor than most of the girls. Tiffany got the part because she *looked* better. All kinds of good things happen to her just because she's *pretty*."

Dad was silent for a few minutes. "I hope that's not true," he said. "I wouldn't like to think the choir director would make a choice for that reason."

In 2007, staff at a German aquarium built a Nativity scene at the bottom of a shark tank. At first, staff said they'd wanted to act out scenes from the Nativity, but said it would disturb the animals, which included stingrays, sharks, and flying gurnards.

"It *is* true, Dad. Everyone knows it. Everything goes right for Tiffany, and everything goes wrong for me!"

Dad put a hand on Chandelle's shoulder. "Sometimes things *do* seem a little unfair," he admitted. "But envying someone else is never a solution. You can't make things better for yourself by being angry at Tiffany and putting her down. The only person whose destiny you have any control over is you."

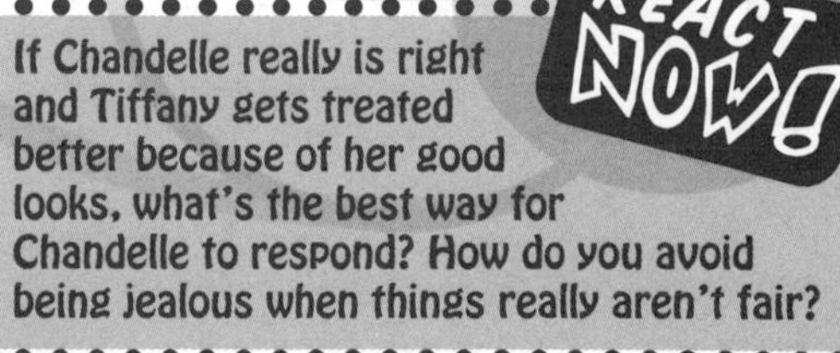

If Chandelle really is right and Tiffany gets treated better because of her good looks, what's the best way for Chandelle to respond? How do you avoid being jealous when things really aren't fair?

∘~ INCREDI-BIBLICAL ~∘

[Your beauty] should be that of your inner self, the unfading beauty of a gentle and quiet spirit, which is of great worth in God's sight. 1 Peter 3:3, 4.

BEAUTIFUL LUCIA

Lucia, or Lucy, was a Christian who lived in the Roman Empire early in the fourth century, and that was not a great time to be a Christian. Legends say that when her parents tried to marry her to a pagan, Lucy refused the offer of marriage and asked that the money they'd set aside for her dowry be given to the poor instead.

Since Lucy's family was rich, her future husband wasn't too thrilled. (Think of the money he'd never get.) He fought back by informing the authorities that Lucy was a Christian. And like so many other Christians of that time, she died for her faith.

On December 13, people in Sweden, Denmark, and other countries celebrate St. Lucia Day. It's considered the beginning of the Christmas season. Swedish girls dress up as Lucia, wearing white dresses and carrying a crown of candles. In many families daughters get up long before daylight to fix sweet rolls, then dress as Lucia and bring breakfast in bed to their parents.

Lucia contests are held throughout Sweden as each community crowns its own "Lucia," with one girl becoming the national Lucia. Being pretty isn't the only thing that matters, but it does help if you want to win.

The original Lucia wasn't famous for her good looks. She was famous for being faithful to God, even at the cost of death. That kind of commitment is a lot more important than winning a beauty pageant!

Info Splat

In some parts of Italy, children believe that Saint Lucia brings gifts, carried on a donkey, so they leave food out for Lucia and her donkey. But the children are told that if they see Lucia delivering the gifts, she'll throw ashes in their eyes and blind them!

Would you rather be remembered for your good looks or for doing the right thing? Which is easier?

INCREDI-BIBLICAL

When you give a banquet, invite the poor, the crippled, the lame, the blind, and you will be blessed. Although they cannot repay you, you will be repaid at the resurrection of the righteous.
Luke 14:13, 14.

FILTHY-RICH FOOD

The world's most famous chefs met in Bangkok, Thailand, to prepare a 10-course gourmet meal that cost $25,000 *per person*. Menu items included beef tartare with caviar and oysters, crayfish with mushrooms, and $350 worth of shaved truffles on each plate. Forty wealthy guests—from the United States, Europe, the Middle East, and Asia—came to the sixty-fifth floor of a Bangkok luxury hotel for the experience.

Even the chefs were amazed at how expensive it was. All were top chefs from restaurants in France, Italy, and Germany, and a meal in any of their own restaurants would probably have cost about $250. But for this special event, every diner paid $25,000.

It's mind-boggling that people could spend that kind of money on a luxury meal in a country in which, according to a 2000 United Nations report, 30 percent of the population lives in poverty.

God has invited us to an amazing feast that will be held after He returns to this earth. The menu will be even more incredible than the world's top chefs would provide—and the entertainment will be out of this world! But it's not just a dinner for those who can "afford" it. It's not for the rich and famous. It's for the poor, the sick, the lonely, and any and all who accept Jesus' invitation to celebrate with Him in heaven.

Info Splat

During his or her lifetime the average person eats about 50 tons of food.

PAGE 353

REACT NOW!

What's the fanciest meal you've ever eaten? What was the most fun meal you've ever eaten? Which would you rather experience again?

INCREDI-BIBLICAL

Do not be afraid. I bring you good news of great joy that will be for all the people. Today in the town of David a Savior has been born to you; he is Christ the Lord. Luke 2:10, 11.

TAKE THE CHRISTMAS QUIZ!

As every store plays Christmas music, schools prepare Christmas parties and programs, and holiday decorations are everywhere, take a minute to think about what this time of year means to *you*. Check all the statements that apply to you.

___ I look forward to Christmas; it's my favorite time of year.
___ Christmas was more fun when I was little and got more toys.
___ I find Christmas stressful and can't wait for it to be over.
___ I like spending time with my family over the holidays.
___ I don't like spending too much time with my family.
___ At Christmas I think a lot about Jesus' birth and what it means.
___ Christmas for me is mostly about presents and having fun.
___ I worry about getting presents for everyone.
___ I worry about what presents I'm going to get.
___ Christmas really doesn't mean a lot to me.
___ I think Christmas is a pagan celebration and doesn't have much to do with Christianity.
___ Christmas is a time for me to get closer to God.

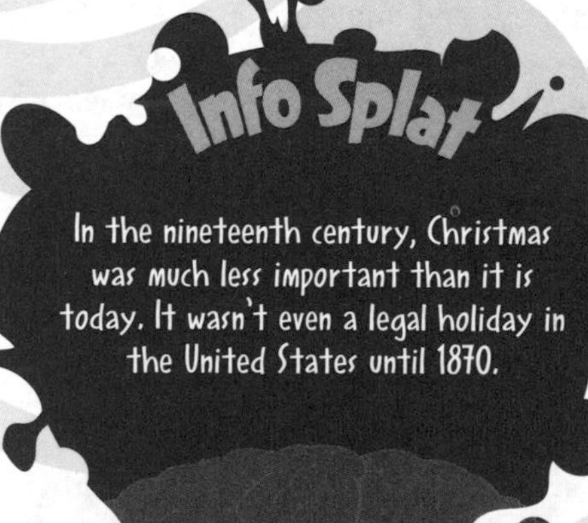

Info Splat
In the nineteenth century, Christmas was much less important than it is today. It wasn't even a legal holiday in the United States until 1870.

This time of year means different things to different people. It's busy and sometimes crazy. Between the tinsel and the time off school, it's hard to focus on what's *really* important.

REACT NOW!

Use the next 10 days to think about what Christmas means for you and how you can use it as a time to strengthen your relationship with God. What can you add to your Christmas celebration to make it more meaningful? What can you take away?

INCREDI-BIBLICAL

Before I formed you in the womb I knew you, before you were born I set you apart. Jeremiah 1:5.

DO YOU REMEMBER WHEN . . .

What's your earliest memory? Most people can't remember much before they were preschool age—about 3 or 4. At one time, scientists thought that babies' brains couldn't form memories.

Now researchers are discovering that babies can remember things from as young as 6 months. A 6-month-old may be able to remember something that happened the day before, while a 2-year-old might remember something from a year ago.

But while baby brains are able to create memories, they're not able to hold on to those memories. Both children and adults forget things, but younger children forget more information. That's why most of us don't have a lot of memories from early childhood.

If your family has photo albums from when you were a baby, you have a record of a time that you can't remember. Though your own memories don't reach back that far, other people have saved those memories for you.

God's memory of us reaches very far back, even way back before we were born. He knew us long before we knew ourselves, and He has always had a plan for each of our lives. Though our human knowledge is limited, God's knowledge of us, and what's best for us, knows no limits.

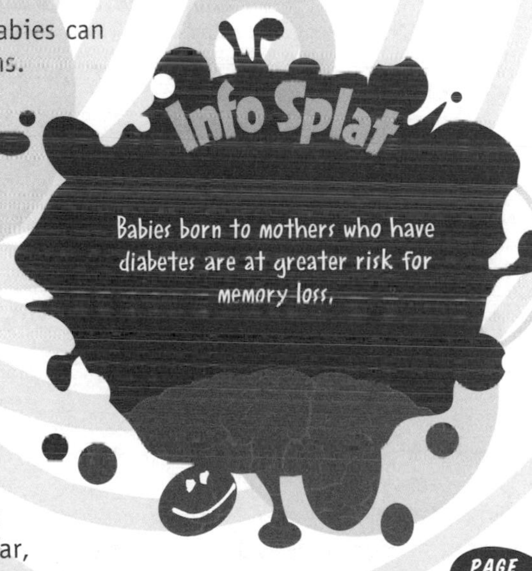

Info Splat
Babies born to mothers who have diabetes are at greater risk for memory loss.

REACT NOW!

Think about your earliest memory. Is it a good one or a bad one? Why do you think that event stood out in your mind?

INCREDI-BIBLICAL

Blessed are you when people insult you, persecute you and falsely say all kinds of evil against you because of me. Rejoice and be glad, because great is your reward in heaven, for in the same way they persecuted the prophets who were before you. Matthew 5:11, 12.

MOVING INTO CHURCH

You may enjoy going to church, but have you ever considered *living* in your church? Why would anyone move into a church building?

Ten Christian young people in the Ethiopian village of Begge moved into a local church after they had to leave their homes. Their families threatened to execute them for converting to Christianity. The young people fled to the church for safety and lived there for several months.

Their situation isn't as strange as you might think. Young people in Ethiopia who choose to become Christians often have to leave their homes.

Also in Begge, three Christian families had to move into a church when others in the village burned down their homes. Although no one was injured, all three families lost their belongings.

It's hard for those of us who live in safety to imagine how it would feel to be driven from your home and have your life threatened—just for being a Christian. We might experience friends who don't understand our beliefs; we may have to put up with peer pressure. But very few of us will ever know what it feels like to be rejected by our families and driven from home because of our faith in God.

Jesus left His home in heaven to come to earth for us. Would you be willing to leave home for Him?

Info Splat

Ethiopia in unique among African countries because—except for an invasion by Italy that lasted for a short time during World War II—it was never a European colony.

Take some time to pray for Christians who are persecuted around the world.

INCREDI-BIBLICAL

We have different gifts, according to the grace given us. Romans 12:6.

THE SURPRISE COIN

You've probably heard the bells ringing and seen the Salvation Army kettles outside stores and in shopping centers near Christmastime. At this time of year lots of people stop to put in a handful of coins or a couple of dollars. It's a small way we can do something to help those who don't have much at Christmas.

One Christmas a shopper in Vermont did a lot more. The volunteer who was working with the kettle that day didn't notice anything unusual at the time, but when other volunteers counted the money at the end of the day, someone noticed a single coin in a protective plastic case.

The coin was a 1908 Indian head coin. The face value was $2.50, but the coin was worth at least $250 and possibly as much as $14,000. Somebody, in a quiet way, had used their valuable coin as an extremely generous gift.

The gifts we have to offer may not seem like much on the surface, but if you look more closely, each of us has something of value to give. Jesus has given all His children gifts through His Holy Spirit. Like the gold coin in the Salvation Army kettle, the purpose of our gifts is to share His love and bless others.

Info Splat

The anonymous donor in Vermont wasn't alone. Since 1982 more than 300 gold coins have been dropped into Salvation Army kettles around the United States. In Fort Lauderdale, Florida, someone once dropped a diamond engagement ring into a kettle.

What gifts do you have? How can you use them to glorify God and help other people?

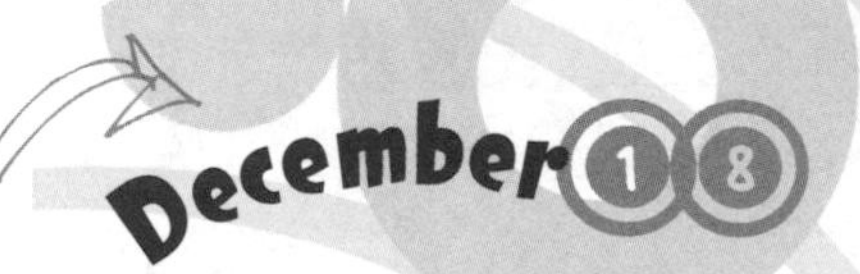

INCREDI-BIBLICAL

Command them to . . . be generous and willing to share. In this way they will lay up treasure for themselves as a firm foundation for the coming age.
1 Timothy 6:18, 19.

A BOXFUL OF LOVE

What did you bring?" Devon asked as he dumped the contents of a shopping bag out on the table in the church basement.

"Some hairbrushes, toothbrushes, a bunch of toy cars, and stuff. What'd you get?" Sheena asked him.

"Crayons, pens, pencils, coloring books—stuff like that," Devon said. "We picked up some Bible bookmarks at the Christian bookstore too."

Other kids arrived with shopping bags of small gifts they had brought too. Brightly colored green and red shoeboxes were piled high on the table. The Pathfinder director showed them how to pick out a variety of items to fill a shoebox full of gifts for a needy child in another country.

As Devon put toys, soap, a hairbrush, and a package of crayons into the shoebox he thought about the child who might open the box on Christmas Day. The gift boxes were for kids who lived in war-torn countries and places where there was terrible poverty. There wasn't much for those kids to celebrate at Christmas—except God's love, and the love of some people in another country who cared enough to send a few presents.

Devon prayed that the gifts in his shoebox would help a child somewhere in the world to have a happier Christmas.

Info Splat

Samaritan's Purse, a U.S. Christian organization, sends more than 7 million boxes of Christmas presents to children in 95 different countries.

What have you done this Christmas to share God's love with others? What can you do?

INCREDI-BIBLICAL

Jesus answered, "If you want to be perfect, go, sell your possessions and give to the poor, and you will have treasure in heaven. Then come, follow me." Matthew 19:21.

GOOD SAINT NICK

Our modern-day Santa Claus has his roots in a third-century Turkish Christian named Nicholas. When his wealthy parents died and left him with a large amount of money, young Nicholas took personally Jesus' advice to the rich young ruler and decided to give everything he had to the poor.

He used his whole inheritance to help the sick, the needy, and the suffering. While still a young man, he became a bishop in the church and was known and loved throughout the whole area for his care and concern for the poor—especially for children.

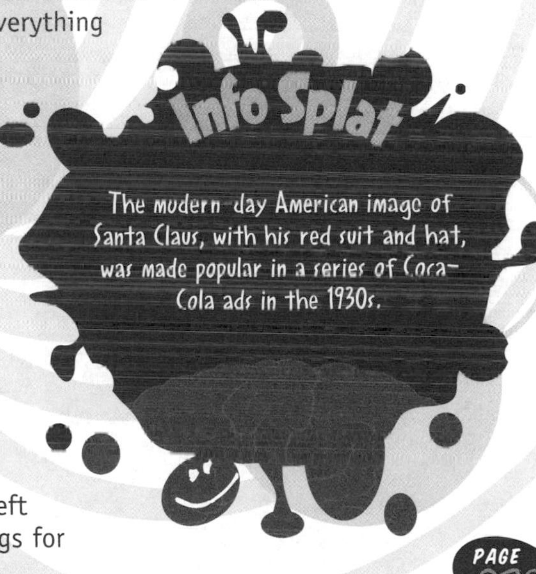

Info Splat
The modern-day American image of Santa Claus, with his red suit and hat, was made popular in a series of Coca-Cola ads in the 1930s.

Like many Christians, Nicholas suffered for his faith under the Roman emperor Diocletian. He was exiled and imprisoned. Later released, he died in the year 343. After Nicholas's death, many stories and legends sprang up about him. Tales were told about how he generously left gifts of gold or silver in shoes and stockings for those in need.

Known as Saint Nicholas, his feast day was celebrated in December, so the stories of Nicholas's generosity became associated with Christmas gift giving. Saint Nicholas eventually became Santa Claus.

As you look at the pictures of Santa that decorate stores and homes at this time of year, remember that it all started with a young man who obeyed Jesus' command to give to the poor.

REACT NOW!

What can you do this Christmas to follow in the true spirit of Saint Nicholas and help those who are poor?

INCREDI-BIBLICAL

Now about brotherly love we do not need to write to you, for you yourselves have been taught by God to love each other.
1 Thessalonians 4:9.

THE 75,000-MILE CHRISTMAS CARD

For Christmas 1953 Roy Stern and his wife, Betty, sent Dick and Hedy Rewalt a Christmas card with a picture of four snowmen on the front.

Dick kept the card. As a joke, the next Christmas he decided to send the same card back to the Sterns, signing his own name.

A tradition was born. For Christmas 1955 the Sterns sent the card back. And ever since, for more than 50 years, the same card has gone back and forth between Roy and Betty Stern, and Dick and Hedy Rewalt. Signatures and greetings added over the years show when kids were born, grew up, and left home.

"If I'd known it was going to last this long, I'd have bought a nicer card," Betty said in 2006. But the original card, which is held together with clear tape and has traveled about 75,000 miles, is a priceless record of a lifelong friendship.

Some of the friends that you go to school and church with today may still be your friends 50 years from now—and even longer. What can you do now to lay the foundations for strong lifelong friendships? What can you do to help your friendships last into eternity?

That first card the Sterns sent for Christmas 1953 carried a three-cent stamp.

REACT NOW!

Can you start a tradition this year that you will continue with friends or family members in future years?

INCREDI-BIBLICAL

With words of hatred they surround me; they attack me without cause. [The Lord] stands at the right hand of the needy one, to save his life from those who condemn him. Psalm 109:3, 31.

TEXT MESSAGE MEANIES

I can't wait for the holidays to start," Ciara said one morning as she shoved her books into her backpack. "I hate school!"

Her sister Leah looked up in surprise. "Why do you hate school?" she asked. "You get A's in everything."

Ciara sighed. Leah just figured that because schoolwork came easily to her, she must enjoy school. But the fact was that every single day Ciara dreaded getting up and going there.

She dreaded walking into the classroom where several girls giggled and whispered about her. She hated going into the washroom at recess where there'd be remarks about her weight, her clothes, and her hair. She knew she'd never be good enough to fit in with those girls.

But just fitting in wasn't the problem. Ciara didn't mind being alone—if only they'd leave her alone. She was tired of the rude comments, the anonymous notes. The latest thing was that several classmates with cell phones sent text messages to one another about her during class. She'd heard them laughing and seen them looking at her, though so far no teacher had caught them.

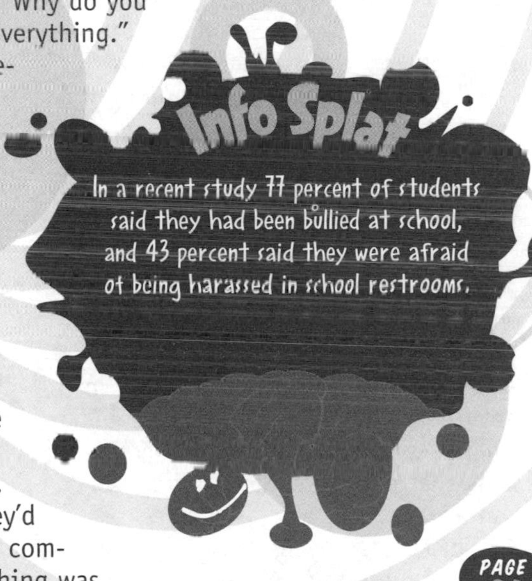

Info Splat
In a recent study 77 percent of students said they had been bullied at school, and 43 percent said they were afraid of being harassed in school restrooms.

Being the victim of bullying can make school a nightmare and holidays a welcome break. Treating others with love and respect, as Jesus commands us to do, can make school—or church, or your neighborhood—a better place for everyone.

REACT NOW!

Is there anyone like Ciara in your class or in your church group? Is there something you can do to make this person's life a little easier?

~ INCREDI-BIBLICAL ~

The land produced vegetation: plants bearing seed according to their kinds and trees bearing fruit with seed in it according to their kinds. And God saw that it was good. Genesis 1:12.

LAYER UP

Layers, layers, layers. Go outside during wintertime in some parts of the world, and you won't want to be without a thick jacket, scarf, gloves, and thermal underwear. But you're not the only one layering up for the season.

Trees use light to produce their own food in a process called photosynthesis. But it doesn't work when the ground is frozen, because the tree can't absorb water from the frozen soil. Some trees drop their leaves in winter—they're called deciduous trees. Others hang on to their leaves and protect them.

Evergreens, trees that hang on to their leaves, are coniferous. Their "leaves" are actually needles, and the tree puts a lot of extra energy into making these needles. But the effort pays off.

A conifer's needles are designed to survive in snow and cold. They are tough and strong, and covered with a layer of wax that keeps moisture inside. But they don't just layer up. The needles also contain chemicals that act as an antifreeze. Their prickly surface and distinctive smell protect them from animals that might eat them during the winter.

Just as the evergreen tree is specially adapted to survive cold northern winters, God has made us with the skills we need to survive life's difficulties. Like trees, people come in many different varieties, but we all have what it takes to make it through trials—with God's help.

Info Splat

Not all coniferous trees are evergreens. Some, like the larch, drop their needles in winter.

What abilities has God given you that help you make it through tough times?

~ INCREDI-BIBLICAL ~

Calling his disciples to him, Jesus said, "I tell you the truth, this poor widow has put more into the treasury than all the others. They all gave out of their wealth; but she, out of her poverty, put in everything." Mark 12:43, 44.

A WONDERFUL MEAL IN MEXICO

A mission worker arrived in a Mexican village on the night of December 23. Hungry and tired, she stopped for just a few minutes at the home of a local family, planning to go on afterward and find a restaurant that was still open where she could get something to eat.

The mission worker visited briefly with the family, whom she had met on other visits to the village, and held and admired their new baby. Then, in her limited Spanish, she explained that she needed to leave. She was anxious to find food and a place to stay for the night.

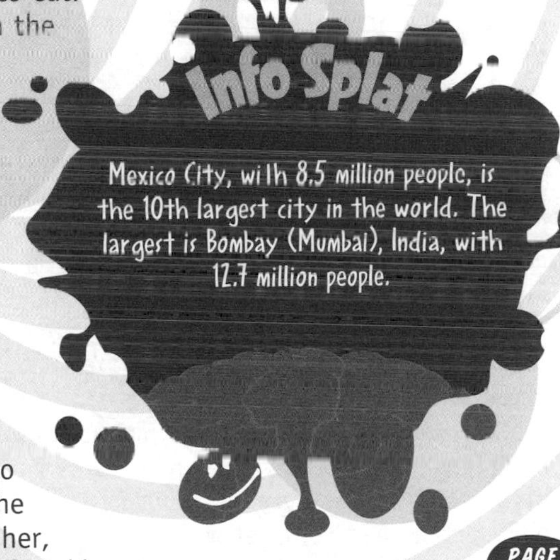

Info Splat
Mexico City, with 8.5 million people, is the 10th largest city in the world. The largest is Bombay (Mumbai), India, with 12.7 million people.

"Have you eaten?" they asked.

"I am going to find a restaurant now," she replied.

"Please, stay and eat with us," the father of the family begged.

The missionary thought about the offer. The family was poor and had little to offer. She knew from other visits that if she offered to take them to a restaurant with her, they would say no. They wouldn't feel comfortable there. But they were so eager to share the food they had.

"Sí," she said, gratefully accepting their simple meal. As she ate, she reflected, *This is a home where people share what they have, no matter how little it is. This is a place where Mary and Joseph would be welcome if they came looking for a bed for the night.*

REACT NOW!

Are you willing to share what you have with others, even if it isn't very much? When was the last time you willingly shared something you didn't have enough of?

December 24

Incredi-Biblical

But when you give to the needy, do not let your left hand know what your right hand is doing, so that your giving may be in secret. Then your Father, who sees what is done in secret, will reward you. Matthew 6:3, 4.

THE CASE OF THE SECRET SANTA

People who lived in Kansas City between 1979 and 2006 never knew when their Christmas might turn out to be a little extra-special.

For 27 years a Secret Santa roamed the streets of Kansas City in the weeks before Christmas, handing out $20, $50, and even $100 bills to anyone who looked like they could use a little extra money. Over the years the man dressed as Santa, who traveled the streets without letting anyone know his true identity, gave away about $1.4 million.

Christmas 2006 was Larry Dean Stewart's last chance to play Santa. For the first time the wealthy man dropped his disguise and let people know who he really was–an ordinary Christian who'd grown up poor and wanted to share with others the blessings God had given him. Mr. Stewart had cancer, and knew it might be his last chance to share his form of Christmas kindness. He also wanted to make it clear that although he wore a red suit, his true loyalty was to Jesus Christ, who'd inspired him to give to others.

Larry Dean Stewart died in January 2007, just a few weeks after giving out his final Christmas gifts. "Part of my daily prayer was 'Lord, let me be a better servant,' " he said before he died. "I had no idea this is what He had in mind, but I'm happy. I'm so thrilled that He is able to use me in this way."

Info Splat

Bronner's Christmas Wonderland in Frankenmuth, Michigan, is the world's largest Christmas store. Movie star John Wayne ordered a Santa suit by phone from Bronner's in 1976.

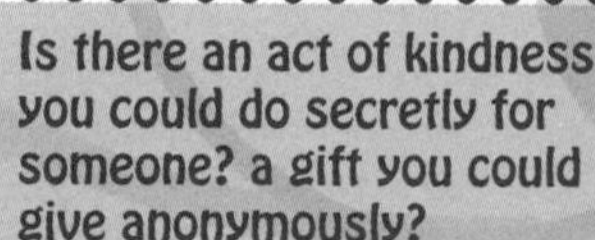
Is there an act of kindness you could do secretly for someone? a gift you could give anonymously?

REACT NOW!

December 25

~ INCREDI-BIBLICAL ~

You are to give him the name Jesus, because he will save his people from their sins. Matthew 1:21.

WHAT'S YOUR BEST PRESENT?

The presents are opened. The wrapping paper has been thrown away. Christmas dinner is over, and you've already looked at, tried on, and played with all your presents.

Is Christmas over?

Sometimes Christmas falls on Friday. That means that as the celebration and excitement of the holiday winds down, the special hours of Sabbath begin. Christmas is a once-a-year celebration of God's gift of love to this earth. Sabbath is a weekly celebration of God's love in our lives.

Maybe this year one of your parents, or grandparents, or an aunt or uncle will ask, "What was your favorite present?"

What will you say? The new jeans? The electronic game system? The digital camera? The book you know you'll enjoy reading? The money you can save up to buy what you *really* want?

Info Splat
It's estimated that 8,000 tons of wrapping paper are used in Britain at Christmastime—the equivalent of 50,000 trees.

It's great to get presents. It's even better to give presents. But the best gift of all is knowing that God loved you enough to send Jesus. Not just as a baby in a manger, but as the Son of God, who would live, die, and rise again to give us eternal life.

That's the gift that lasts long after the wrapping paper has been cleared away, the tree has been taken down, and the Christmas music is off the radio.

REACT NOW!

This Christmas, have you thanked God for His greatest gift of all?

INCREDI-BIBLICAL

So you are no longer a slave, but a son; and since you are a son, God has made you also an heir. Galatians 4:7.

MERRY BOXING DAY

In many countries the day after Christmas Day is known as Boxing Day. Nobody is quite sure where the name comes from, but it may come from times rich people traditionally gave their servants a box of gifts, including leftovers from the Christmas Day feast, to enjoy the day after.

Back in those days the rich would probably keep the best of everything for themselves, and give their servants the things that weren't quite so good—the leftovers, the secondhand clothes, the gifts that weren't as nice. After all, the family gets the best of everything. Servants have to be content with what's left.

The Bible often calls us God's servants, but it also points out that we are not just servants. God treats His people not like servants, who get second-best, but like members of the family, who get the best of everything. Jesus told His disciples that they were to consider themselves, not His servants, but His friends.

In God's kingdom we don't get second-best. We don't get Boxing Day presents. We get the original and best Christmas present of all. We get the gift of salvation from God's only Son, who came to earth just for us.

Info Splat

In Ireland Boxing Day is sometimes known as Wren's Day. Traditionally, children would kill a wren and take its body from door to door, begging for money that they would (supposedly) use for the bird's funeral. Kind of like trick-or-treating, but with a dead bird.

REACT NOW!

As you're enjoying your Christmas presents, have you thanked God for His gifts to you? Take some time to say that important "Thank You."

Incredi-Biblical

Do not store up for yourselves treasures on earth, where moth and rust destroy, and where thieves break in and steal. But store up for yourselves treasures in heaven, where moth and rust do not destroy, and where thieves do not break in and steal. Matthew 6:19, 20.

ANGELS OF RECORD

In 2007 the people of Bismarck, North Dakota, held the world record for the largest number of snow angels ever made when 8,910 people gathered on the state capitol grounds to lie down and wave their arms in 10 inches of snow.

The snow-angel makers included people of all ages, such as the 5-month-old baby who made her "angel" by being spun around in her car seat, and the woman celebrating her ninety-ninth birthday who said she was making her first snow angel ever. "I feel just like a kid!" she reported happily.

The snow angel category in the *Guinness Book of Records* was created in that very same spot in North Dakota in 2001, when 1,791 people made snow angels. The record stood for five years, until 3,784 snowy Michigan college students snatched it away.

Info Splat

The record for most snow angels made at the same time in different locations was set by the London District Catholic schools in London, Ontario, Canada, on February 2, 2004, when 15,851 students, parents, and teachers made snow angels at 60 different schools.

Even before the citizens of Bismarck had their record officially confirmed by the *Guinness Book of Records*, Michigan was making plans to win back the title. By the time you read this book, a new world record in snow-angel making may have been set.

World records are made to be broken. Like every human accomplishment, they may be fun to do, but they don't last forever. You may get the chance to break a world record someday, but it's far more important to win the prize that will last for all eternity—eternal life with Jesus. That's something that can never be taken away from you.

React Now!

If you could break a world record, what would it be in? What would you most want others to remember you for?

Incredi-Biblical

All the days ordained for me were written in your book before one of them came to be. Psalm 139:16.

LOOKING BEHIND

Andrea and her mom sat going through their photo album. "What are your best memories from this year?" Mom asked.

Andrea flipped over to the pages that showed their summer vacation. "Definitely the camping trip," she said. "Sleeping in the tent and having family worship by the campfire was the best thing ever."

"What about you, Kevin?" Mom looked over at Andrea's younger brother, who was building a spaceship model on the floor in front of the fireplace. "What was your best memory of this year?"

Kevin thought for a minute. "Probably my birthday," he said. "I had a great party, and I got so much good stuff."

Andrea was still looking through the album. "I liked when Uncle Pete and Aunt Angela came to visit, too," she said. "We really had a lot of great memories this year."

It's fun to look back at the past and enjoy good memories. God gives us family and friends to enjoy and to share good times together. Best of all is when we keep Him at the center of our good times, so we can look back and remember that He's been with us through it all.

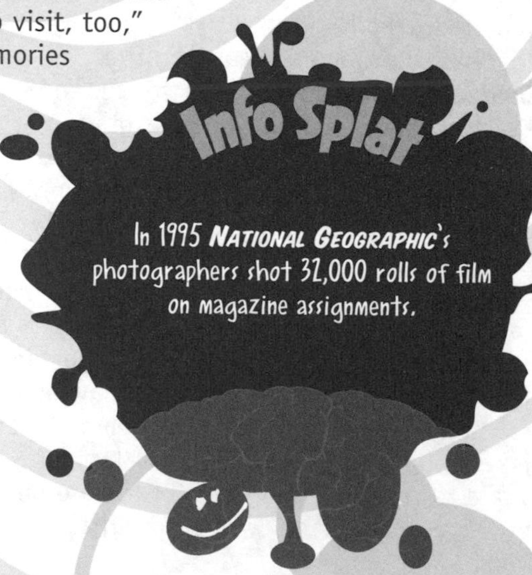

Info Splat
In 1995 NATIONAL GEOGRAPHIC's photographers shot 32,000 rolls of film on magazine assignments.

What's ***YOUR*** best memory of this year? What do you think is God's best memory of time spent with you?

INCREDI-BIBLICAL

With the Lord a day is like a thousand years, and a thousand years are like a day.
2 Peter 3:8.

WHAT'S WITH THE LEAP?

As we come to the end of another year, you may be wondering, Why does every year have 365 days, except for leap years, which have 366?

In ancient times many societies had lunar calendars with 12 or 13 months following the cycles of the moon. The thirteenth month was inserted as an "extra" month every two to three years to keep the calendar in line with the seasons.

However, people figured out pretty quickly that it took a little more than 365 days for the earth to make a full rotation around the sun. In fact, this was figured out even before people realized that the earth *was* rotating around the sun. A 365-day calendar, with a leap year every fourth year, was introduced by King Ptolemy III of Egypt in 238 B.C.

Why the leap year? Because a year is actually 365.2422 days long. 0.2422 of a day is about six hours, which doesn't seem like much, but without some adjustment that missed time would keep adding up, until spring was no longer happening in springtime! Adding an extra day every four years keeps the seasons where they're supposed to be.

Little things—such as six hours out of a whole year—may not seem like much. The little bits of time we spend doing the things we enjoy may not seem like much either, but they can add up to lifelong habits. Choose to use every minute wisely.

The last leap year was 2008. The next one will be 2012. Years divisible by 100 are not leap years, unless they are also divisible by 400. So 1800 and 1900 weren't leap years, but 2000 was.

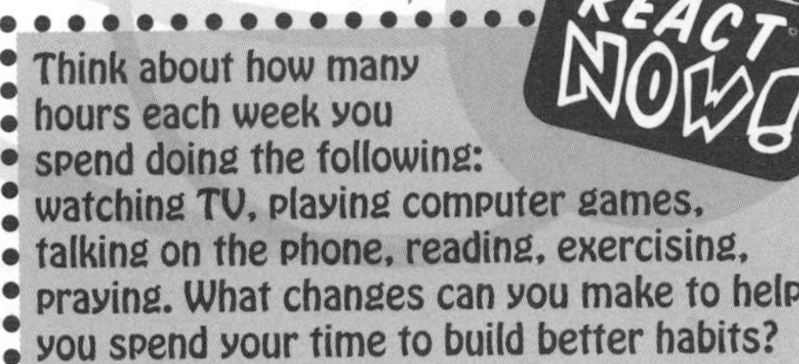

Think about how many hours each week you spend doing the following: watching TV, playing computer games, talking on the phone, reading, exercising, praying. What changes can you make to help you spend your time to build better habits?

Incredi-Biblical

Greater love has no one than this, that he lay down his life for his friends. John 15:13.

FROM KAMIKAZE TRAINEE TO PASTOR

During World War II the Japanese military used *kamikaze* pilots—soldiers sent on suicide missions to crash their planes into enemy targets. Young men were taught that the greatest honor they could hope for was to give their lives for their country, so they should be proud to be chosen for a suicide mission.

Shigehara Suzuki, whose mother was a Seventh-day Adventist, was training to be a kamikaze pilot. He was a hard worker who believed in doing his best in everything. One night, while some of his fellow servicemen were in town, he sat in the barracks, polishing his shoes. Noticing that his friends' shoes weren't polished and thinking that they might get into trouble at inspection the next day, Shigehara polished their shoes too.

Shigehara survived the war and was never sent on a suicide mission. Later he learned the reason. His commanding officer, who had noticed Shigehara shining his friends' shoes and admired his kind and helpful spirit, had always moved Shigehara's name to the bottom of the list so he would never be sent on such a mission.

After the war Shigehara accepted his mother's Seventh-day Adventist faith and served the rest of his life as an Adventist pastor. He had been taught that the greatest honor was to die for his country, but he learned that the greatest honor in God's eyes is to live for others.

Info Splat

In the last years of World War II nearly 4,000 kamikaze pilots died as a result of crashing their planes into enemy targets. About 4,900 U.S. sailors were killed by kamikaze attacks on their ships.

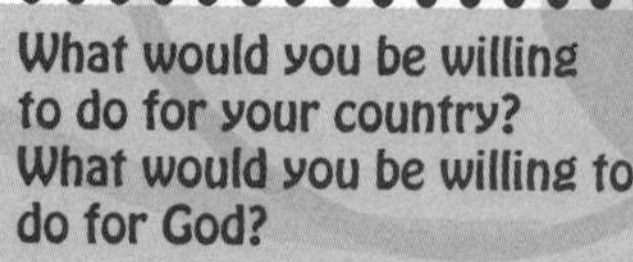

What would you be willing to do for your country? What would you be willing to do for God?

INCREDI-BIBLICAL

**With man this is impossible,
but with God all things are possible.
Matthew 19:26.**

HAVE A STRONG NEW YEAR!

According to one American Web site, these are the 10 most popular resolutions people make at New Year's.

1. Spend more time with family and friends.
2. Get more exercise.
3. Lose weight.
4. Quit smoking.
5. Enjoy life more.
6. Quit drinking.
7. Get out of debt.
8. Learn something new.
9. Help others.
10. Get organized.

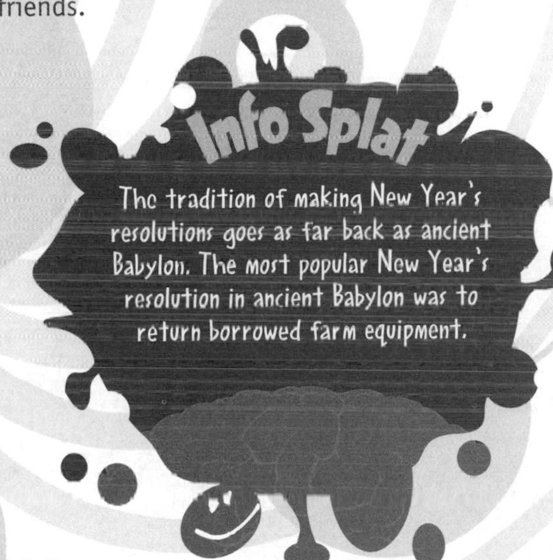

Info Splat
The tradition of making New Year's resolutions goes as far back as ancient Babylon. The most popular New Year's resolution in ancient Babylon was to return borrowed farm equipment.

Do any of those fit with *your* plans for the new year? If a list were made of the most popular resolutions for teens, what do you think they would be? What about Christian teens? Should Christians have different goals?

Some people make resolutions; some don't. Some keep them; some break them. A New Year's resolution is just one more way of setting a goal for yourself—saying what you'd like to accomplish. If you try to do it on your own, you probably won't succeed. But if you rely on God's strength as He promised through His Holy Spirit, you'll be amazed what you can accomplish in the coming year.

Make your most important resolution: staying close to Jesus. With Him by your side, it'll be a wonderful year.

REACT NOW!

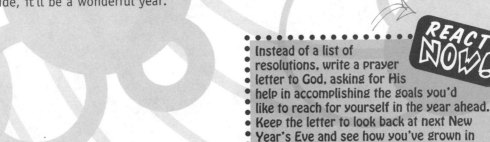

Instead of a list of resolutions, write a prayer letter to God, asking for His help in accomplishing the goals you'd like to reach for yourself in the year ahead. Keep the letter to look back at next New Year's Eve and see how you've grown in your relationship with Him.

More Info Splat

Original moon machines

America's Saturn 5 rockets were used to launch the Apollo space missions to the moon. Each rocket was 364 feet tall and weighed 2,903 tons on the launch pad. It burned 15 tons of fuel per second.—*Amazing Questions and Answers*

Making themselves at home

Northern cardinals often spend all four seasons in the same backyard.—*Birds and Blooms*

New Year's menu

To celebrate New Year's, Scottish people traditionally eat haggis: sheep lungs, heart, and liver chopped and mixed with oatmeal and spices, cooked in a sheep's stomach.—*Kids Around the World Celebrate*

A long weekend

In Israel today Muslim shops are closed on Friday, Jewish shops are closed on Saturday, and most Christian shops are closed on Sunday.—*The Complete Idiot's Guide to the World of the Bible*

Low-impact bearobics

When bears hibernate, they lower their body temperature only slightly and continue to burn 4,000 calories a day.—*The New York Times Second Book of Science Questions and Answers*

Subway style

The underground railway in Russia, called the Moscow Metro, is decorated with marble halls, crystal chandeliers, and elaborate murals. Its design was intended to show the people the power of Communism.—*The World of Caves, Mines, and Tunnels*

More Info Splat

Black lungs
When a smoker inhales and then blows out tobacco smoke, about 30 percent of the burned particles are exhaled. The rest—70 percent—collect as black soot in the lungs.—*How Come? Planet Earth*

Animal in armor
A turtle's shell, or carapace, is made up of about 50 bony plates formed in the skin. The backbone and ribs are fused to the carapace.—*Visual Encyclopedia of Animals*

Lighting up the city
The most common type of lightning—cloud to ground—is nearly twice as common over large cities as over surrounding areas. —*Discover*

Peppermint power
When people are exposed to peppermint before an exam, they tend to make fewer mistakes and have a quicker reaction time. This is because peppermint opens the bronchial tubes in the lungs and increases oxygen uptake.—*Outsmarting Female Fatigue*

Spoon compass
The ancient Chinese used a compass called a sinan. It was a magnetic piece of iron in the shape of a spoon. When placed on a polished slab of stone, the bowl of the spoon swung around to point north, and the handle pointed south.—*Ancient Transportation*

Pet killer
While about one fourth of humans die of cancer, it is worse for our pets. About half of dogs and a third of cats die of cancer.—*The Healing Power of Pets*

Beaten by a bug

The human brain responds to a stimulus in about 200 milliseconds (about one fifth of a second). A cockroach can respond to a stimulus and take off running in 15 to 20 milliseconds.—*National Geographic*

Sleep debt

Losing even 90 minutes of sleep for just one night can reduce your daytime alertness by as much as 32 percent.—*Prevention*

Allergy attack

Allergies prevent 68 percent of Americans from having a good night's sleep. They also interrupt outdoor activities for 53 percent, and keep 50 percent of people from being able to concentrate.—*The 100 Simple Secrets of Healthy People*

Name in code

The scientific name for the eastern hog-nosed skunk is Conepatus leuconotus. This comes from four words: konis, which means "dust," pateo, which means "I walk," leukes, which means "white," and notos, which means "back." Put them together and you get "white-back that roams the open or desertlike country."—*This Is Not a Weasel*

The seeing brain

The human brain has 100 billion neurons. Every time a person sees an image, between 30 million and 400 million neurons fire in the visual cortex.—*Natural History*

Been standing in the cuisine?

Cuisine is the French word for "kitchen," but it has come to mean "fine food" in English.—*World Geography and Cultures*

More Info Splat

Gobbling up energy

Some people require the benefits of driving an SUV. But consider this: driving a big SUV instead of a car for one year wastes more energy than if you left your refrigerator door open for six years, left a television on for 28 years, or left the bathroom light on for 30 years.—*Ranger Rick*

Hold on to your hat

Neptune is the windiest place in the solar system. Wind speeds reach 900 miles per hour. The fastest recorded wind on Earth was in an Oklahoma tornado, where the wind blew 318 miles per hour. —*Outside*

Leather castles

Before the year A.D. 1100 most castles were built of wood and caught fire easily. The walls were often covered with wet leather to keep them from burning down.—*100 Things You Should Know About Knights and Castles*

Mixed-up pooches

Cockerpoos are dogs bred from cocker spaniels and poodles. Labradoodles are a cross between Labrador retrievers and poodles. —*Working Like a Dog*

Don't eat the kids

The males of small fish called sand gobies take care of their eggs when female gobies are nearby. But when the females leave and are no longer watching, the males eat a few of the offspring.—*Yes Mag*

That's a big hug!

A big male orangutan stands only about four feet tall, but his outstretched arms can span nearly eight feet.—*Last of the Wild*

MY Prayer Journal

Keep track of your prayer requests and praises throughout the year. Then you'll be able to look back and see how God has been involved in your life!

Date	Prayer Request	Answered Prayer

Date	Things I'm Thankful 4

Keep Praying!

Date	Prayer Request	Answered Prayer

Date | Powerful Scriptures & Quotes

BIBLE

Sabbath Action Blast #7: Guess This Tune

Play a game of Guess This Tune with family or friends. You will need either a piano or CDs of familiar or not-so-familiar Christian music. Divide your group into two teams. Play a note or two of a song on the piano or a second or two on the CD. Have each team guess. If neither side gets it right, add a note or play the CD a little farther.

When a side actually guesses it, you can continue by singing along with the song!

—Heather Down

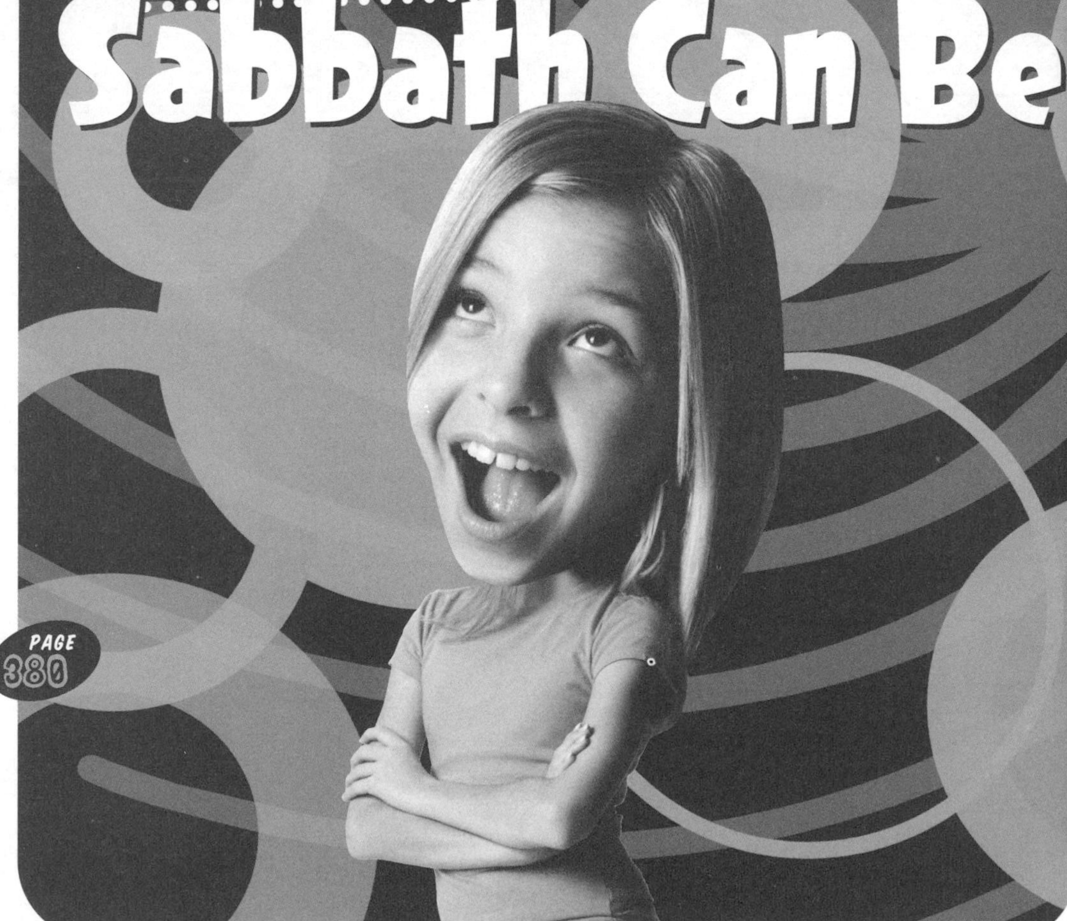

Find more Sabbath fun at www.guidemagazine.org. Videos, games, stories, discussion forums, advice, and more!

Find 99 more fun ways to celebrate God's special day in *Sabbath Action Blast*, a new Guide book. Get it at www.adventistbookcenter.com.

a Blast!

Need something fun to do on Sabbath? Try out these games!

Sabbath Action Blast #62: Bible Spelling Bee

Before playing this game, you will need to write out a list of words from the Bible and put them in columns of easy, medium, and hard. Now you can play!

Divide into two teams, plus a moderator to read the words. The moderator reads a word to a player on the first team. If that person doesn't spell the word correctly, then the other side gets a chance to spell it. Work from easy to hard on the word list. Have the moderator keep track of points.

—Stephanie Hubbard

TRUE STORIES POINTING TO JESUS
Guide
08/09/08
www.guidemagazine.org
Meet new friends at www.guidemagazine.org
COVER STORY 2
Freedom's Song
FREEDOM
EQUALITY

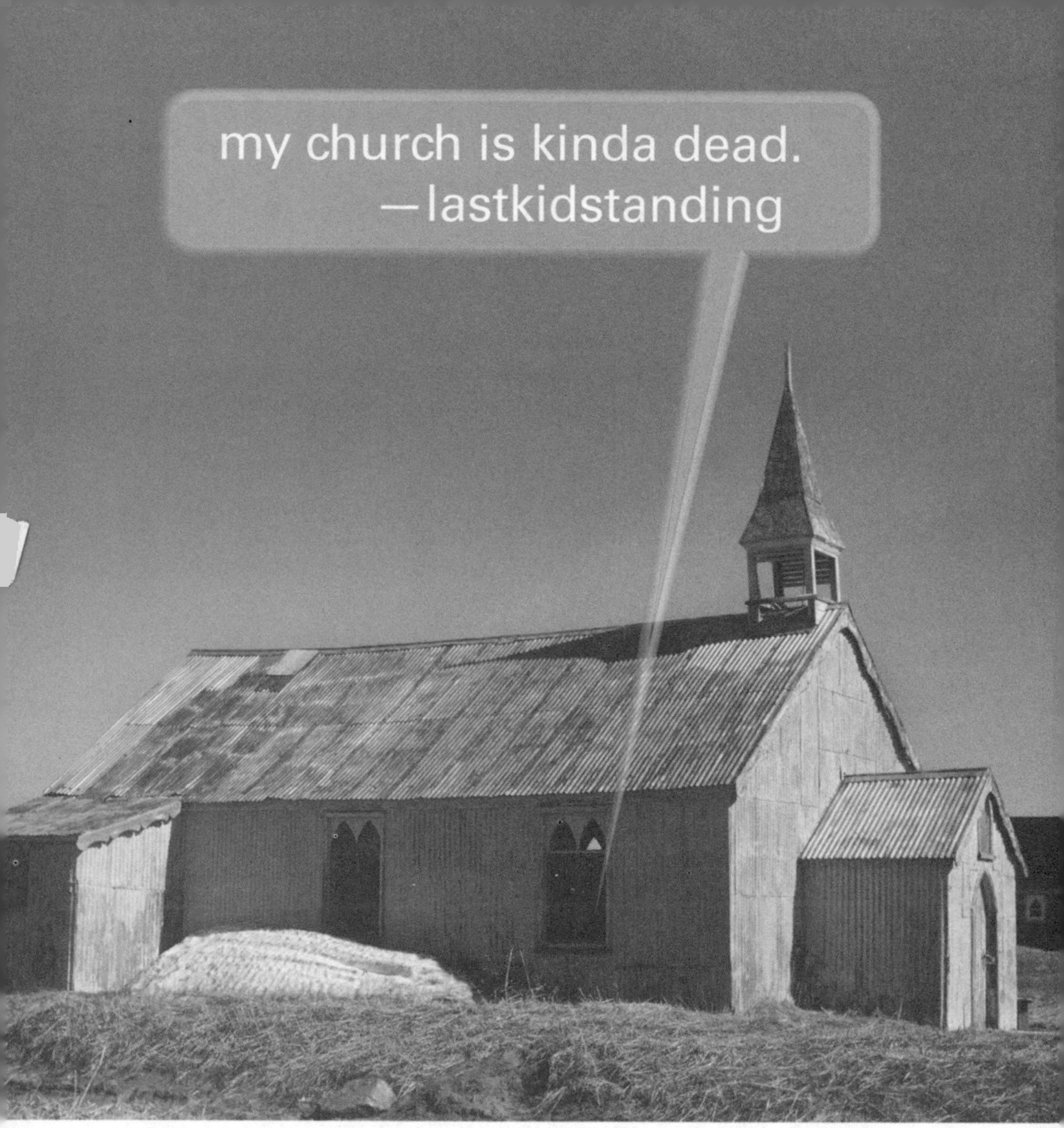
my church is kinda dead.
—lastkidstanding